KT-420-096

Global Perspectives on Investment Management

LEARNING FROM THE LEADERS

Continuing a tradition of lifelong learning

A CFA INSTITUTE PUBLICATION

Book Editor

Rodney N. Sullivan, CFA

Editorial

Maryann Dupes

Daniel J. Larocco, CFA

David L. Hess

Mary A. Whalen

Production and Marketing

Eric M. Franzen

A. Elizabeth Morris

Trish Downey Phipps

Katherine M. Valentine

Rosellen O. Fry

Kara H. Morris

Elizabeth K. Turrisi

Special Thanks

We would like to thank Katrina F. Sherrerd, CFA, for her support for this book and her commitment to education during her long tenure with the organization.

©2006 CFA Institute

All rights reserved. No part of this publication may be reproduced or transmitted in any form or by any means, electronic or mechanical, including photocopy, recording, or any information storage and retrieval system, without permission of the copyright holder. Requests for permission to make copies of any part of the work should be mailed to: CFA Institute, Permissions Department, P.O. Box 3668, Charlottesville, VA 22903.

CFA®, Chartered Financial Analyst®, AIMR-PPS®, GIPS®, and Financial Analysts Journal® are just a few of the trademarks owned by CFA Institute. To view a list of the CFA Institute trademarks and a Guide for the Use of the CFA Institute Marks, please visit our website at www.cfainstitute.org. CFA Institute is a nonprofit corporation devoted to the advancement of investment management and security analysis. Neither CFA Institute nor its publication's editorial staff is responsible for facts and opinions contained in articles in this publication.

ISBN 978-1-932495-52-2

Printed in the United States of America

2006

This book is published in the spirit of furthering the mission of CFA Institute...

To lead the investment profession globally by setting the highest standards of ethics, education, and professional excellence.

Table of Contents

This book qualifies for credit under the guidelines of the CFA Institute Professional Development Program. Each article qualifies for 0.5 PD credits. To record your PD credit, you may either enter it manually in your PD Diary or take a self-test, available at www.cfainstitute.org/ memresources/pdprogram/self_tests_list.html, and have the credits automatically posted to your PD Diary.

Foreword

One of the requirements of any field worthy of carrying the appellation "profession" is a commitment by its members to continue developing their knowledge as new concepts and thoughts emerge. Physicians must keep on top of new medical developments, lawyers have to stay abreast of changes to laws and interpretations, and investment professionals need to be versed in the field's new tools, methods, interpretations, and applications. For investment professionals carrying the CFA credential and membership in CFA Institute, staying current is second nature given the intense pressure arising from free and open capital markets. But for most investment professionals, if my own experience and observation as a long-term practitioner is any guide, the organization of their continuing education efforts is haphazard at best.

In the world of post-CFA learning, members may not want too much structure to the learning process but, rather, would like a framework for following where their interests lead. Learning after receiving the CFA charter can involve a myriad of approaches, from a tight specialist tack, to exploration about prized conundrums, to an investigation into valuation-based trading strategies. But regardless of topic, it only makes sense that precious time devoted to the study of markets be with high-quality material from a trusted source.

Time is the investment professional's most valued asset. Thus, one of the key roles of CFA Institute is to aid our time-constrained members with their lifelong learning by providing or identifying high-quality content. By "aid," we must mean bringing efficiency to the process of sifting through all the many research papers, periodicals, and other means of disseminating investment concepts that can be put into action. By definition, the work must be practitioner oriented. We can, through our staff but most importantly through our many member volunteers and other contributors, vet and ferret out the best of the best for our members to take advantage of. This book, which draws heavily from our longest running conference program, the Financial Analysts Seminar, is one example of this effort.

Fifty years ago, the predecessors to CFA Institute had the wisdom to create a seminar—the Financial Analysts Seminar—where students of markets could get away for a week to discuss and debate the issues and concepts of the day to further their understanding of how markets work. Early instructors included the likes of Benjamin Graham and Sid Cottle, and early students included such notable disciples as a young Warren Buffett.

A 50th anniversary has a way of motivating all to bring out their best, to make it special. And the 50th anniversary of the Financial Analysts Seminar was no exception. At Northwestern University this past summer, a truly luminary set of instructors raised the bar regarding the quality and relevance of their presentations. The result was an extraordinary learning experience spanning the field from how ethical principles finally collapsed the practice of (mutual fund) market timing, to behavioral finance at work, to groundbreaking ideas on portfolio construction.

Given our mission of aiding our members in their continuing education, we were confronted with the challenge of having had great content presented to 250 participants but a membership of more than 85,000. In the past, we have addressed this issue in two ways: through webcasts of the sessions (found at www.cfawebcasts.org) and through our print and online conference proceedings series (found at www.cfapubs.org), which our team has smartly decided to convert to a quarterly format of the best of the best. Despite the tremendous use of the internet for work applications, our research, as well as that of others, demonstrates that for any thought-provoking piece that runs more than a page or two, investment professionals prefer a paper copy to review where and when they choose. We often think of the desire for a free market of monetary securities; it is obvious that there is at least as strong a desire for a free market for time and place.

Thus, to commemorate the 50th anniversary of the Financial Analysts Seminar in a way that leverages our conference programs as well as our conference proceedings series, we have packaged here some of the best presentations in the form of a book for your reading and reference. Although we have emphasized the presentations from the 50th anniversary of the Financial Analysts Seminar, we have also included a few notable presentations from other conferences that we believe will have a lasting impact. And we have taken it upon ourselves to provide this book to you at no added cost beyond what is already embedded in your member dues. I think of this as a small dividend back to you, our owners. I hope you do as well.

Because the lifeblood of a great professional association is feedback, Rodney Sullivan, CFA, and I would be delighted to hear any thoughts on this commemorative book or on any aspect of your lifelong learning endeavors where we can be of assistance. Feel free to address us at rodney.sullivan@cfainstitute.org or jeff.diermeier@cfainstitute.org, and happy reading.

Jeffrey J. Diermeier, CFA
CFA Institute President and CEO

Preface

The genesis of the idea for this book can be traced quite simply to the CFA Institute mission. Manifest in this mission is the call "to lead the investment profession globally by setting the highest standards of ethics, education, and professional excellence." This wonderful collection of presentations made by today's top thinkers and practitioners in our industry moves us nicely along the path to accomplishing that ambitious yet worthy goal.

Although this book is organized along the traditional topic areas or specializations, one theme in portfolio management today is clear: The point of demarcation between the traditionally independent roles in the investment management arena is now blurred. With the blurring of these roles, I encourage readers to reach out and expand their knowledge into less familiar territory. The presenters here offer ideas to shape and even sway one's thinking on investment management. Within these pages are viewpoints that are as varied as the topics covered. The result is a panorama of the current investment landscape, a portfolio of penetrating global ideas that transcends borders.

One common bind that ties these authors is their unflappable intellectual curiosity. This curiosity aims to separate relevance from noise in the markets, to reduce the whole complex world to a more rational scheme with insight and clarity. The lessons learned from this common denominator are far too many for this brief preface, but I cannot resist calling attention to a few of the key insights.

A healthy functioning global market requires trust and a supporting regulatory structure. Because we have seen the consequences of unethical response in our industry, Noreen Harrington urges us to keep the benefits of the ethical response—placing client interests first and foremost—top of mind. In so doing, she guides the serious minded reader with a strong moral compass. I encourage readers to then take a coveted seat at the table with Swiss central banker Philipp Hildebrand, who shares how a remarkable new generation of risk sharing across financial markets has enabled the healthy functioning of global markets. He describes how new participants in new markets with access to new products allow investors to save, invest, transfer risk, and finance trade to a much greater extent than ever before. As chair of the International Accounting Standards Board, the efforts of Sir David Tweedie, FSIP, to preserve the virtues of financial markets are also commendable. Tweedie offers a holistic approach to building higher standards into the fabric of global markets that increase transparency and foster cross-border investment.

Extending this effort, Jack Gray clarifies the advantages of long-term thinking. A distinctly narrow focus on the near term, what he calls "short-termism," too often leads to poor decisions that result in the destruction of wealth. Such short-termism often stems from our fascination with managing risks, but in so doing, do we lose sight of what is ultimately important? Gray proffers that long-term investing is much more complex than buy and hold. Continuing this line of thought, Peter Bernstein suggests that because the future is always uncertain, perhaps the challenge of managing risk is really about the quality of the decisions we make in the face of uncertainty. A myopic focus on measuring and quantifying risk can undeniably lead to low-quality decisions.

This year's Financial Analysts Seminar hosted a unique event—two interview sessions with legendary stock pickers John Neff, CFA, and Bill Miller, CFA. These two industry giants give an insider's perspective on seeking value opportunities in equity markets with unconventional insights built on a solid framework of a lifetime of experience.

The asset allocation decision is arguably the most important decision an investment manager makes. A plethora of ideas specifically related to asset allocation and portfolio structuring are revealed by the industry's top practitioners. Abby Joseph Cohen, CFA, paints a picture of a global environment in flux with economic energy shifting predictably with comparative advantages altered by the dominant demographics of Asia and Europe. Although arriving at a somewhat different set of conclusions, Marc Faber also keeps the rise of Asian economies in mind. He sees the global macro environment embroiled in stagflation brought about by a slowing global economy accompanied by rising commodity prices. Also, the latest developments in constructing a dynamic long-term asset allocation framework are discussed by Luis Viceira, and Dan diBartolomeo brings the portfolio management focus squarely to the needs of the private wealth investor.

Robert Shiller, author of *Irrational Exuberance*—a phrase made famous by Alan Greenspan—notes that the recent equity bubble demonstrates the extraordinary power of emotions. To his way of thinking, the next speculative bubble worthy of attention is the overvalued real estate market.

Turning to another important area of the investment arena, fixed income, Ed Altman offers pearls of wisdom that can only come from many years of groundbreaking credit research experience. Of paramount importance to investors in the rapidly growing corporate debt market is gaining insight into credit risk and the corollaries of default and recovery rates.

We live in a dynamic global economy that is becoming more integrated and synchronous. This collection, a portfolio of new practical insights from industry experts, carries readers along a global journey that explores the many dimensions of our interlocking international economy. I hope the journey is a fruitful one, but above all, I hope this book embodies the mission of CFA

Institute by encouraging a tradition of lifelong learning. If we are successful in our mission, our members will not be the only ones to benefit; the profession at large and capital markets in general will benefit.

As a final note, because the presentations contained in this collection parallel the *CFA Institute Conference Proceedings Quarterly* series, we hope this book entices readers to seek out this related publication either via our website (www.cfapubs.org) or in print. I also would like to encourage readers to nominate topics and ideas for future publication efforts by contacting me at rodney.sullivan@cfainstitute.org.

Rodney N. Sullivan, CFA
Editor

ETHICS AND PROFESSIONAL STANDARDS

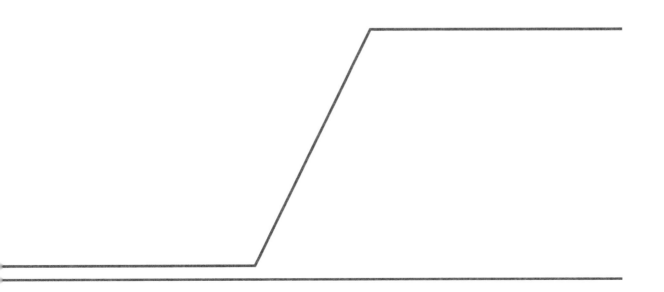

Transparent, Translucent, or Transient: Where Have IFRS Left Us?

SIR DAVID TWEEDIE, FSIP

The business of finance and investment is international, and accounting standards should be too. Many people believe that a common set of principle-based standards will increase transparency and foster cross-border investment, thereby reducing the cost of capital. To this end, the International Accounting Standards Board is adopting best standards from around the world in consultation with national standard-setters. In many countries and industries, convergence to these common standards is already taking place.

Like CFA Institute, the International Accounting Standards Board (IASB) is an international organization because that is the direction the markets are headed. Our job at the IASB is to provide the tools needed to make sound investment decisions and to make the markets more transparent. In theory, we are setting out to do something very simple: Come up with a single set of high-quality global accounting standards. Once we have done that, it will not matter whether a transaction takes place in Boston or Brisbane or Beijing or Brussels; the accounting will be the same.

> The [international reporting] roadmap...is going to change accounting in the United States and throughout the rest of the world in quite a major way over the next six years.

Implications of Different Accounting Standards

Accounting differences matter, which is why we are developing the international standards. Originally, reconciling differences between countries was the province of multinational corporations, who would convert foreign statements of their subsidiaries back to U.S. GAAP or whatever the accounting of the parent company was—a very expensive task. What put international standards firmly in the picture was the Asian financial crisis of 1997. At that time, some Asian

Sir David Tweedie, FSIP, is chair of the International Accounting Standards Board, London.

companies looked fine by the local standards, but suddenly, they went bankrupt. Short-term financing became unavailable, interest rates shot up, investment stopped, growth stopped, and unemployment rose. There was a massive crisis of confidence. As a result, those countries realized that they had to do something quickly to change their accounting because investors simply did not trust it. There were only two choices: U.S. GAAP or IAS (International Accounting Standards). The United States itself said U.S. GAAP was the by-product of dealing with U.S. domestic pressures and that it was not written for international markets. Thus, the focus turned to IAS.

The International Accounting Standards Committee (IASC) was the organization first responsible for IAS. Initially, IAS basically allowed companies to handle accounting the U.S. way, the U.K. way, and a couple of other ways. Then, IASC started closing off these options. Suddenly, things that had been done in the United States or the United Kingdom for 20–30 years did not appear in IAS anymore. This change forced us at the U.K. Accounting Standards Board to start looking at the U.K. standards. In addition, in 1995, IASC and the International Organization of Securities Commissions (IOSCO) made an agreement that if IASC could produce some 30 standards of appropriate quality on agreed subjects, any company using those standards could go to any stock exchange worldwide without having to reconcile its statements to local standards. The 30 standards were completed in 1999. Several of them did not meet IOSCO's quality criterion; nevertheless, the exercise meant that people were starting to pay attention to IASC.

Soon afterwards, the IASB replaced IASC, and at about the same time, the European Union (EU) started a chain reaction when it decided that, beginning in 2005, listed companies in the EU should use IFRS (International Financial Reporting Standards—the new international standards). In 2006, 100 countries will be using these standards. Progress toward adoption of IFRS has been steady. Japan now has an agreement to achieve the convergence of Japanese standards with IFRS. China signed an agreement in 2005 saying that, in 2007, Chinese listed companies will be using IFRS. Canada, surprisingly, is not moving to U.S. GAAP but to IFRS.

Approach to a Common Standard

At the IASB, our agenda was to start with the 34 standards (including the 30 required by IOSCO) that we inherited from the former IASC. We soon decided that we could not deal with certain industries immediately—for example, oil and gas as well as mining. A complete revamping of the standards applying to them was needed, but we knew that we could not do that by 2005. Thus, we had to recommend that companies in those industries continue to do what they had been doing. There were similar problems with insurance companies. In many countries, accounting for insurance companies is a black hole, but in a few years, we will have a completely new insurance standard.

One of the forces for convergence is countries' desire for strong, stable, and liquid capital markets to fuel economic growth. A common set of standards does just that. Research has shown that investors are much more comfortable investing in their home country than in foreign countries, which is not surprising because investors understand the accounting in their own countries. But once everybody has the same accounting, investors' investment horizons can expand, which is why countries are accepting IFRS. Unfamiliar standards create a risk premium, which increases the cost of capital. That, in turn, reduces investment.

The IASB started off with liaison relationships with eight major standard-setters. Those in Europe—France, Germany, and the United Kingdom—now use IFRS. Similarly, Australia and New Zealand use IFRS, and as I have said, Canada and Japan are moving to IFRS. That leaves only the United States. In 2002, the IASB established a formal relationship with the U.S. Financial Accounting Standards Board (FASB). We agreed to remove the differences between our two sets of standards and to stop creating new ones. Also, we agreed to align our standards and to interpret them in the same way. Once again, the idea was to get rid of the reconciliation that companies had to do when they went to the U.S. markets.

Ultimately, we are looking for the best standard. If the United States has it, then we should have it. If we have it, the United States should want to have it. If neither of us has the best standard, then we should look outside to see who has a better one, or we have to write another one.

For instance, in the United Kingdom, we have a business combination standard that is similar to the one in the United States. We test goodwill and brands for impairment; we do not mindlessly depreciate them. We have brought in changes in asset disposal provisions, moving to the higher standard held in the United States. The United States has also dealt with EPS calculations and changes in accounting policies, which are no longer embedded into this year's income but, rather, which lead to the previous financial statements being restated. For share options, we adopted the U.S. standard but made it compulsory to treat them as expenses. The United States has maintained its own standard but changed the disclosure requirements to the expenses option.

Roadmap to Reconciliation Elimination

Working together is powerful, but it takes too long. For this year, we are doing something else. The European Commission and the U.S. SEC have been talking about creating a roadmap for getting rid of reconciliations and bringing our standards together. The FASB and the IASB have been working together for several months to flesh out what this roadmap means in practice. First, we decided to have a similar conceptual basis to accounting, called the "conceptual framework." The conceptual framework is the basis of modern accounting. Our objective is to enable informed decision making. Reliability is a concern, but relevance is important too. Fair presentation matters so that investors can see what the information is.

Everybody in the industry knows the definitions of assets and liabilities, which is why companies continue to keep them off their balance sheets. An asset is the right to a stream of benefits in the future; a liability, an obligation that will lead to resources leaving the organization. When do you recognize them? When we can measure them reliably. How do we measure them? There is a big debate going on about that. How do you present the information in a sensible way?

There are huge arguments about the conceptual framework. In the accounting, it ought to be simple: Every debit has a credit. If you spend money, you either get an asset or an expense. Notice that I did not define expenses, just assets, because if it is not an asset, then it has to be an expense. Some companies, however, have invented another category—a "whatsit." This is an expense that they would rather not have go through the income statement, so they place it on the balance sheet. As an example, say a new hotel starts up and has a loss in the first year. Some companies treat that as a cost of starting a new hotel. So, they add it to the hotel costs and amortize it over 50 years. That is a policy ripe for abuse. One can imagine a former chief financial officer of Eurotunnel saying, "What a dreadful year we have had. We have cumulative losses of €2 billion, but look how strong the balance sheet is getting." A loss is a loss and has to be written off. That is how we protect the income statement—by defining assets very carefully. For there to be an asset, there must be a benefit for the future.

Areas for Major Change

The roadmap to which I previously referred is going to change accounting in the United States and throughout the rest of the world in quite a major way over the next six years. The idea is that when we get to the end of this reconciliation process, which we think we will do in two years, we will be well on the way to getting rid of a lot of the major differences between the standards. The next phase, the long-term agenda, will not be finished until 2011 or 2012. Following are some of the things that are liable to happen.

Borrowing costs

IFRS currently provide an option: The company can either recognize borrowing costs as an expense or capitalize them. So, for IFRS, we have decided to do it the U.S. way. We are going to get rid of the expenses option.

Government grants

We have a very outdated standard in this area. We need to be aligned with the U.S. standard.

Joint ventures

For joint ventures, we think that rather than proportionate consolidation, equity accounting as used in the United States is the answer. We are moving in that direction.

Segment reporting

The U.S./Canadian style of segment reports, which provide the management information, is recognized as being the most useful. We are changing IFRS to fall into line.

Business combinations

In this area, we still have differences between the U.S. standard and IFRS. We are working to have an identical standard on both sides of the Atlantic in a year or so.

Consolidation/SPV (special purpose vehicles)

This area is a huge issue. We have a difference with the U.S. standard. The United States tends to consolidate a subsidiary when a company holds greater than 50 percent of the equity of another entity. We think the answer is control, as does the rest of the world. We are trying to get together to find out how to implement this standard. The ability to direct the financing and operating decisions or the ability to control the directors, sometimes with no shares whatsoever, is the critical variable.

Fair value measurement

The United States is about to produce a standard specifying how to measure assets and liabilities at fair value. We are going to pick up the U.S. standard and ask for comments on it.

Revenue recognition

The United States has numerous rules on revenue recognition. We have quite a few as well. We are looking at this issue, again in an effort to develop a rational, principled approach.

Liabilities vs. equity

You would think that this issue is about as straightforward as it gets, but we have actually discovered all sorts of problems. For example, for many European companies, if shareholders have the right to demand their money back, then it may meet the definition of a liability.

Performance reporting

We need to overcome the obsession with a bottom-line number like EBITDA (earnings before interest, taxes, depreciation, and amortization). But what else is there? A single number on the income statement does not encapsulate everything that is important about a company. It is the components that matter. But how can we craft this? Again, we will need input from the investment community on this issue. What information is important for investors when they look at how the income is going to project into the future? What sort of categories do investors want to know, and how do we display them? Ideally, we need to get the relevant components on the income statements so they are apparent; we need to move the cash flow statement into line so that investors can differentiate the accruals from the cash flow, or life blood of the company.

Research Agenda

We also have a research agenda that includes items that are about to hit our agenda and that of the FASB in the United States.

Leases

One of my goals before I die is to fly in an aircraft that is actually on an airline's balance sheet. The fact is that on leasing, we have international standards that are harmonized perfectly, but they are all absolutely useless. They do not work. The U.S. literature on leases is substantial, and aircraft still do not appear on balance sheets. Why not? Because we have a rule that says a company has to lease an asset for most of a life before it can be put on the lessee's balance sheet. What does "most of a life" mean? It apparently means that if a company takes the present value of the future lease payments and it comes to at least 90 percent of the value of the asset when it is first put into service, then the leasing liability and the asset go on the balance sheet. Not surprisingly, this relationship is typically roughly 88 percent. If we dropped the rule to 80 percent, then leases would come in at 79 percent. Leases are structured to achieve the desired result. For the airlines, this is a binding contract. It thus constitutes an obligation that we can measure. It is a liability. Where the accounting has to go is clear, but the leasing industry thinks that this change would be the end of western civilization as we know it. But the bottom line is that leasing an asset is the same as borrowing from a bank, and it should (and will) be on the balance sheet.

Financial Instruments

In the United Kingdom, we have IAS 39, which is similar to U.S. SFAS (Statement of Financial Accounting Standards) No. 133. It is incomprehensible. We have major disagreements with the banking industry in Europe. But this is one standard that needs to be rewritten for the United States, as well. It does not have to be so complicated and is another area where we are going to consult with the financial community as we discuss exactly how to show the effects of financial instruments.

Derecognition/Securitization

What if a company sells something? When should it leave the balance sheet? This is another major area we have to look at.

Pensions

Big pension deficits are a problem for various companies. Pension deficits are caused by a variety of factors: bear markets, falling interest rates, and the fact that people have developed the dreadful habit of living longer. On the surface, falling interest rates should be a good thing. But if a company has promised someone a pension of $10,000 a year and annuity rates are 10 percent, the company must have a capital sum of $100,000. If annuity rates fall to 5 percent, the company must have $200,000.

Assets have fallen, and liabilities have risen, but this has been hidden by bad accounting. For example, if a company has a fund with $40 million in assets and $40 million in liabilities and the market declines $10 million, the fund has a deficit of $10 million. But does the company show it? It does if it is located in the United Kingdom but nowhere else. Outside the United Kingdom, companies typically reduce the effect of changes in pension schemes. For a start, companies will reduce the ensuing deficit by 10 percent of whatever is higher—assets or liabilities. In the example of $40 million in liabilities and $30 million in assets, a company would take $4 million off the deficit, leaving a total deficit of $6 million. Then, the remaining amount is spread over the working lives of the employees—say, 10 years. So, instead of a deficit of $10 million, the company shows a deficit of $600,000. Try to explain that number to anybody who is inexperienced in pension accounting.

This illogical accounting must change. The $10 million deficit must be shown because that is what really happens. But that is not all. Against the pension charge taken in the income statement, the company is allowed to offset what it expects to get from its pension assets over the long term. Some of these assumptions have been heroic. Companies in the S&P 500 Index reported in their income statements from 2000 to 2004 estimated gains from the assets on their pension funds of $498 billion, but the actual number was $197 billion, so there is $301 billion of flow through income that did not exist. We have to change all that. This is going to be a fight, but it is a fight that we have to win.

Rocks in the Road Ahead

International accounting standards are only one leg of a four-legged stool. The other, equally critical, legs are corporate governance, enforcement by the regulatory authorities, and auditing. Some countries are now using IFRS, removing a little bit, and then insisting that the auditors report a fair presentation on IFRS. Eventually, this tinkering will render the standards meaningless unless we put in a statement saying that companies cannot use the term "IFRS" unless they are in full compliance.

We want to write principle-based standards rather than rules. For leases, for example, the main objective is to show the liability incurred by signing a lease contract and the right to the asset obtained through the lease. That is the standard. If a company has not met that objective, it has failed—no exceptions, no 90 percent rules. For principle-based standards on financial instruments, the accounting is simple: Show all financial instruments at market value and take the gains and losses to the performance statements. That is it. These will not be soft standards, but that is where we think we have to go.

Our goal is to "tell it like it is." Doing so will lead to volatility because companies will not have things to smooth. That will be the analysts' job. Analysts can assess the long-term trends for a company, but we want to show the facts. The management discussion and analysis, or management commentary, will become one of the most important parts of financial reporting. It will present the raw numbers and explain what they mean, which will be critical for everybody.

In five years' time, any country that has still not adopted IFRS or is not using converged U.S. GAAP will have a problem. Investors will want to know why it is different from the rest of the world. The aim is to reduce costs, to increase transparency, and to facilitate cross-border investment, thus leading to a lower cost of capital and higher growth.

The danger still exists that the effort to come up with a unified set of standards will fall apart and break into regional standards, such as European standards, U.S. standards, and Asian standards. We have to fight that tendency. The United States is firmly on board, but this is truly a global exercise.

What we need to do is join forces at this early stage with global organizations, such as CFA Institute. We want analysts' views—both positive and negative. We need to hear from the investment community.

This presentation comes from the 2006 CFA Institute Annual Conference held in Zurich on 21–24 May 2006.

More from Sir David Tweedie, FSIP

This section presents the speaker's lively question and answer session with the conference audience.

Question: What standards have given European companies the most difficulty, and what has been the IASB's response?

Tweedie: The one that's been complained about the most is the one on financial instruments. That's one we're rewriting with the United States. It is very complicated. I think companies are feeling they're getting answers that don't quite reflect what is happening. We're looking at all that, and we have to try to simplify it. It is certainly better than having nothing, which is what we had before, but it is one that we inherited, and we have to change it.

Question: What is the likelihood of the United States moving to mark-to-market accounting of pension funds for the year-end?

Tweedie: The United States is moving toward showing the actual deficits on the balance sheet. We're discussing joining this project soon, which I hope will have the effect of getting rid of all pension fund smoothing devices.

Question: Will applying international standards to emerging markets cause these markets to become more efficient and, therefore, potentially less profitable for investors?

Tweedie: I think that the emerging markets will recognize that it is to their advantage to use IFRS. The problem for most investors is that if they don't understand the accounting, then they don't invest. That is one of the reasons that China has decided to come into line. The emerging markets are some of the most fervent supporters of what we're doing. A few companies may suffer, but the good ones won't, and they will attract investment.

Question: What's been the approach of the American Institute of Certified Public Accountants (AICPA) to global performance standards?

Tweedie: The AICPA has supported it. Of course, our main contact in the United States is the FASB, which sets the standards, but certainly the U.S. accountancy institutes have been very supportive. There has been no opposition from them at all.

Question: Can a better presentation of cash flow accounting help to counter the abuses that can occur with accrual accounting?

Tweedie: Yes. Recently, we were discussing with representatives of the FASB a whole new income statement and aligning that with the cash flow statement. That is one of our major projects, and again, it is something we'd like to discuss with analysts to see what they want from both of these statements.

Question: How can people provide input during public comment periods or give feedback in general?

Tweedie: Our due diligence process is similar to that of the FASB, but we've discovered that being international forces us to be even more transparent. As the United States does, we start off with a discussion paper that lays out the issues and follow that with an exposure draft before finally moving to a standard. These discussion papers and exposure drafts can be found at http://www.iasb.org/current/index.asp.

The comment period on discussion papers and exposure drafts is normally four months, and sometimes, we have a roundtable meeting at the end of that period. We will ask people to come in and explain their views and discuss the issue with others, which is extremely helpful because it is not confrontational with the board on one side and a respondent on the other. In fact, many respondents with differing views may be around the table.

The draft proposals are debated to see if a consensus exists. We welcome the comments of CFA Institute because we also get letters from industry, which may have a different perspective. For example, in the United Kingdom, the national standard-setter—the Accounting Standards Board (ASB)—had a position on acquisition accounting that industry started to argue against. Nobody seemed to want it. Then the investment houses in the United Kingdom came in with 30–40 letters in support of the ASB's proposals. The debate was over. That's why we need input at an early stage. The more we can align with analysts' views, the better it is because ultimately our objective is to make sure investors get the information they need.

Question: How do IFRS relate to private equity funds?

Tweedie: Private equity funds are customers in the sense that they are trying to analyze what's going on in various companies. What we need to do is make sure that the price in the markets is the fair price. With more transparency, people will be less likely to sell at a price below fair value.

Question: When you see an annual report for the first time, what's the first thing you look at?

Tweedie: I look at the notes and the cash flow statement. We had a classic case several years ago with a company in the United Kingdom that showed large profits. But if you looked at its cash flow statement, the operating income was hugely negative. The profits were phony, so you look at the cash flow statements and the accounting policy notes to see what happened. That's where I start analyzing a company.

Question: Do you think market participants behave rationally?

Tweedie: Sometimes. I must say that I think the educational programs that are going on now are much better than they were when we started. I think that the higher the level of professionalism in the investment industry, the better the markets are going to operate.

Avoiding Short-Termism in Investment Decision Making

Long-termism (or long-term thinking) is no panacea for investment decision making, but it does offer advantages over short-termism. Unfortunately, both the investment environment and human characteristics predispose people and institutions to short-termism. Therefore, individuals and institutions need to take several specific steps to resist the instinctive but flawed logic of short-term decision making.

Imagine you are the chief investment officer of a large fund that prides itself on being a long-term investor. Knowing this reputation, the owner of a business approaches you about making a significant direct investment in his business. The owner wants a patient investor who will stay with the company through bad times, a degree of commitment he has yet to see from most institutional investors, whose dominant focus is on short-term performance. He believes your fund to be the type of long-term investor he needs. After appropriate due diligence, you invest in the business.

Excessive short-termism results in permanent destruction of wealth, or at least a permanent transfer of wealth.

After two years, the business has generated an annualized return of 50 percent, and you receive an offer to buy out your share. Calculations indicate that the best long-term option for the fund is to sell and reinvest the proceeds elsewhere, an option that is rationally the most beneficial for your investors and thus is the one that best discharges your fiduciary obligations. You accept the offer. And when you do, angry phone calls pour in from the owner and from the press, who pillory your fund for being a mere chaser of short-term performance. Yet, making a short-term decision does not necessarily indicate an abandonment of your commitment to long-term investing. Long-term investors must monitor the short term and occasionally take action based on shorter term signals and opportunities. Long-term investing is more subtle than a naïve strategy of buying and holding.

Jack Gray is a strategist at Grantham, Mayo, Van Otterloo and Company, LLC, Sydney, Australia.

In what follows, I will elaborate on this often subtle distinction in the context of assessing the

- excesses of short-term investing,

- ways in which short-termism develops,

- broad burden of guilt all participants bear for short-termism, and

- benefits of long-termism.

I will conclude with three steps to getting to the long term.

Excessive Short-Termism Is a Sin

A growing number of reports argue that short-termism has become rampant in both the private and the public sectors and that this behavior is damaging the real economy (see, for example, BCA 2004; CFA Centre 2006; Marathon Club 2006). The structure of the U.S. equity mutual fund industry highlights the emphasis on short-termism. Of the roughly 7,000 such funds, a mere handful are closed-end. Were there many long-term investors, they would demand many more funds that could ignore the business terror of short-term redemptions.

Naturally, there are contrary views that long-termism too can be costly. In "What's Wrong with Short-Termism Anyway?" Cole (2005) argues that during such periods as the present when companies are awash with capital, it is easy to waste that capital without the short-term discipline of the market. Hedge funds, typically seen as short-term villains, argue that they provide that beneficial discipline. Occasionally, they may be right. Before the recent Swedish election, a hedge fund was clamoring to take a board seat at Volvo in order to release the huge cash pile the company had accumulated. The company screamed "short-termism," and the prime minister threatened to make "such actions" illegal. Yet, given the tendency of companies to waste excess cash and even to generate suboptimal returns on retained earnings, the hedge fund's actions may have been in the best long-term interests of Volvo's investors.

But merely screaming long-termism does not make it so. Managers are adept at justifying almost all short-term underperformance by chanting the mantra of long-termism.

Problems Caused by Short-Termism

Excessive short-termism results in permanent destruction of wealth, or at least a permanent transfer of wealth. In a recent issue of the *Financial Analysts*

Figure 1   Turnover in U.S. Equity Mutual Funds, 1945–2005

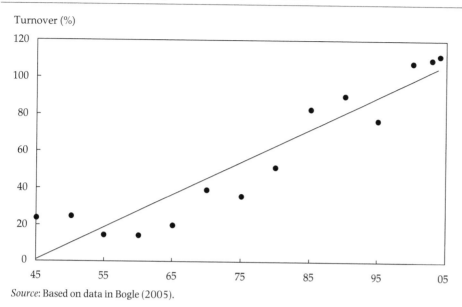

Source: Based on data in Bogle (2005).

Journal, Bogle (2005) presented data on turnover trends among U.S. equity mutual funds from 1945 to 2005, shown in **Figure 1**. The evidence is clear that after a brief period of stability from 1945 to 1965, turnover in equity funds has steadily increased to the point where funds are now holding stocks for an average of nine months, less than the one-year earnings forecasts on which they claim to base their decisions. Some people argue that technology-driven greater access to and speed of information flows, augmented by the competitive pressures of hedge funds, demand greater turnover to stay ahead of the market. Bogle's evidence is firmly against them. Excessive short-termism is profoundly damaging to investors' wealth.

As Bogle (2005) showed, from 1983 to 2003, the S&P 500 Index's annual return averaged about 13 percent. Net of fees, market impact, and transaction costs, the average U.S. equity mutual fund earned about 10 percent, around 77 percent of the market. Shockingly, the average investor earned just over 6 percent a year, around 48 percent of the market. Not only were mutual funds churning through their stocks, holding them for about nine months, but also the average investor was churning through his or her mutual funds, holding them for about two years. The mutual fund industry encourages investors to churn by emphasizing excitement and by appealing to investors' desire to buy today what they should have bought yesterday. The resulting wealth transfer is not in the direction of the end investor. Mutual funds properly encouraged people to evolve from savers to investors, but now they improperly encourage them to become consumers. Once investors see themselves as consumers, they will become short-term thinkers and chase yesterday's winners—piling into nanotechnology funds this year because these funds outperformed last year when investors were in underperforming biotech funds.

Like life, the essence of investing lies in its variability, not in its averages. Unfortunately, Bogle's data do not reveal the cohort of funds that both outperformed and had high turnover, those that did add longer-term value through consistent shorter-term action. Doubtless, that cohort is modest in number.

Individual investors are not alone in the short-term game. Institutional investors too are driven by excitement, herding, and keeping-up-with-the-Joneses, as evident by the current rush into hedge funds, private equity, and other alternative investments precisely at a time when risk is not being rewarded—when all these strategies are expensive. As a single dramatic illustration, consider the Vodafone debacle of just a few years ago. In March 2000, Vodafone's market capitalization was £214 billion, but relative to assets, sales, dividends, and profits, it was massively overpriced. A belief in new paradigms was needed to justify a market cap to sales ratio of 32 and a dividend yield close to zero, a distortion caused by Vodafone being the hot stock. To highlight the absurdity of the situation, Grantham, Mayo, Van Otterloo & Co. LLC gathered data from 15 U.K. industry sectors with a combined market equal to Vodafone's £214 billion. For the same price as Vodafone, investors could have bought 15 diversified sectors with a profitability 10 times and assets 100 times that of Vodafone. They did not, and Vodafone's subsequent fall cost them dearly. The problem was exacerbated by Vodafone acquiring companies outside the U.K. equity index, which meant that to maintain a benchmark weight in the stock, investors had to allocate capital to it and away from companies whose longer-term prospects might not have been evident in shorter-term performance.

This momentum investing, essentially buying and holding for a fixed period those stocks that have gone up the most, is the quintessential form of short-term investing, one that pays no attention to fundamentals. The efficient market hypothesis notwithstanding, momentum outperforms through a short-term self-fulfilling process. This private gain comes at a public cost of lower overall economic growth as capital is diverted from stocks with greater long-term prospects. The players in the game are caught in a "reverse prisoner's dilemma" in which co-operating is optimal for each player in the short term but suboptimal in the long term and the cost of defecting and being "wrong and alone," in Keynes' pithy phrase, is excessive. Breaking that cycle demands external (government) and/or collective action. In France, investors get extra voting rights for holding a stock for longer. As long ago as 1986, Warren Buffett called for a 100 percent tax on short-term turnover, and recently, Bogle argued for an extra dividend for longer-term holders of a stock.

The Burden of Guilt for Short-Termism

I once took a totally scurrilous straw poll at a conference where I asked the participants to vote on who was most responsible for the evident excessive short-termism. The media won, with 89 percent shooting the blame to them. But all were held responsible: governments, regulators, fiduciaries, fund members, asset consultants, managers, trustees, fund executives, and so forth. Everyone in the investment chain was declared culpable to varying degrees. And everyone blames everyone else. Managers blame the demands for full disclosure and the frequent reports to regulators. Managers also blame consultants who also demand monthly reports, which absurdly forces investment horizons to converge to reporting horizons. Consultants say they ask for monthly reports because trustees demand them. Trustees blame the members of their fund for short-termism, who in turn, blame the media for emphasizing short-term performance. The media claims it is merely reporting the news, doubtless in a fair and balanced way. Breaking this "reverse prisoner's dilemma" also demands collective action.

Principal–agency frictions are a major driver of short-termism. Although young investors saving for retirement *should* have investment horizons of, say, 30 years, none of their agents—fiduciaries, managers, consultants, regulators—have horizons even 20 percent that long. Managers responsible for nuclear decommissioning do seem to have 30–40 year horizons. No one else does.

Perhaps some investors' *intentions* are genuinely long term, but generally, investors, fiduciaries, regulators, and governments have one-year to three-year horizons; investment managers, corporations, and consultants have anywhere from monthly to one-year and occasionally three-year horizons, depending on the pressures they are under; the media has weekly to hourly horizons; and some traders have the shortest horizons of all. With almost no players in the investment game having long-term investment horizons, and none with a franchise for the long term, the system is biased toward the short term through a substantial principal–agency horizon misfit.

Benefits of Long-Termism

Long-termism offers three distinct advantages over short-termism: slightly better predictability, lower risk, and lower costs as a result of lower turnover.

Improved predictability derives from slightly stronger signal-to-noise ratios caused by the mean reversion of valuations, profit margins, and real rates. But the more important advantage of long-termism is that it lowers risk. **Figure 2**

Figure 2   Real Value of $1 Invested at Start of Period with Reinvested Dividends

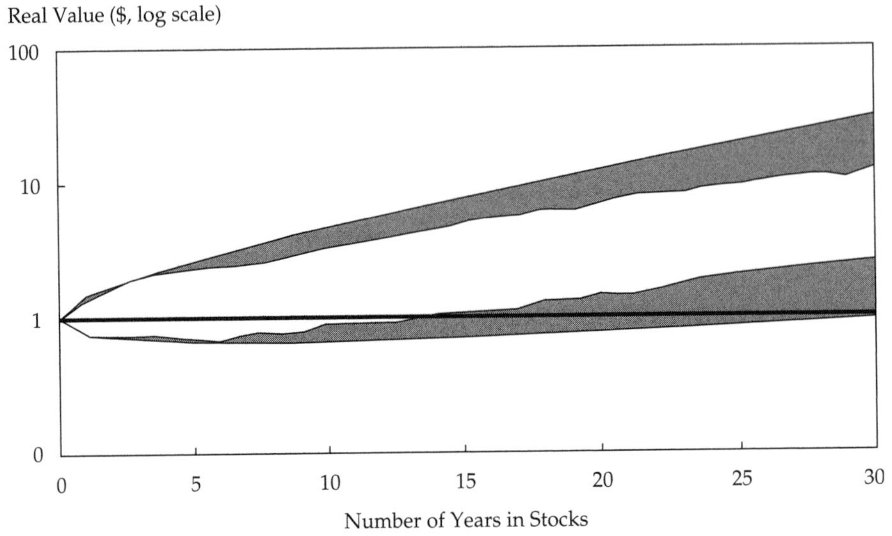

Source: Based on data from Smithers & Co. Ltd.

represents total-period wealth in real terms using U.S. equity data over periods up to 30 years. If returns were random, 90 percent of the time they would lie within the wider range shown on the graph (gray and white areas combined). Although under this assumption the *probability* of loss does decrease with time, the expected *impact* of that loss increases. Following Samuelson, Kritzman (2000) showed that with the same U.S. equity data as above, a 0.1 percent chance exists that after 30 years, an investor will have lost nearly three quarters of his or her real wealth. Because, in fact, markets do mean revert over the longer term, this risk is reduced. In Figure 2, 100 percent of the *actual* data lie within the narrower, white range. Over long horizons, holding-period dispersion is far lower than the efficient market hypothesis suggests. After 5 years, the difference is minimal, but by about 13 years, the difference in dispersion between random and mean-reverting returns is sufficient to justify long-termism. With a few assumptions about risk aversion, mean reversion justifies the holding of riskier assets over the long term.

Because markets are only slightly predictable, long-term investors will occasionally generate poor *relative* returns for long periods. Because very few managers are willing to accept that level of business and career risk, there are few competitors to arbitrage away long-term advantages. For instance, Tobin's *q*, the ratio of the market value of the U.S. equity market to the replacement cost of its tangible assets, should and does mean revert around 1, after some adjustments for depreciation. A high *q* encourages overinvestment and hence poor long-term real returns, and a low *q* leads to underinvestment and strong

Figure 3   Price to Replacement Cost (Tobin's q), 1 January 1926 to 31 December 2004

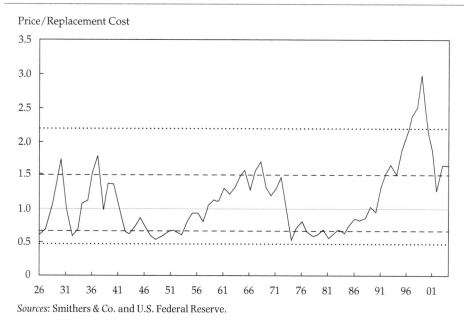

Price/Replacement Cost

Sources: Smithers & Co. and U.S. Federal Reserve.

long-term returns. But q has long cycles, as evident in **Figure 3**. Based on that valuation, long-term investors can find themselves in the psychologically and career-damaging position of not surviving in spite of eventually being right. That is the pain long-term investors must be prepared for.

Limits of Long-Termism

Although long-termism is generally beneficial, it is neither a panacea nor a paragon of investment virtue. For instance, some very high-frequency hedge funds can make money over the long term by consistently adding value over the very short term. Rational long-term investors will not ignore that opportunity simply because managers have a short-term focus. In a different context, not all investors should have a long-term focus. Most 75 year olds probably should not. Moreover, some justifications for long-termism are *in*appropriate and potentially wealth destroying. For instance, those who suffer from the disposition effect, whereby investors hold losing stocks for too long and institutional investors hold losing managers for too long, can rightly claim to have a long horizon, but for the wrong reasons.

Sometimes, institutions are focused too much on the long term. For decades, defined-benefit asset allocations were set by actuaries who foresaw stability in the long term because that is what they were trained to see. They saw equities outperforming over very long periods, so they invested preponderantly in equities. But equities do not always outperform, even in the long run. Equities have to be priced to outperform, and when they are priced at a high level, they will underperform for long periods of time.

John Maynard Keynes, an early, eloquent, and forceful advocate of long-term investing, also saw its limitations: "It is not wise to look too far ahead; our powers of prediction are slight, our command over results, infinitesimal"—a valuable warning against a naïve belief in the power of long-termism. Imagine you are an investor in 1951 doing asset allocation largely on the basis of yield. The dividend yield of the S&P 500 has exceeded the 10-year bond yield every year for the past 80 years, and for a strong theoretical reason: Being riskier than bonds, equities should offer higher yields. Based on that very long-term view, you make asset allocation decisions, and for the next 40 years, you are wrong as the relationship between bond and dividend yields reverses—slight predictive powers indeed.

Human Predisposition to Short-Termism

Behavioral economics provides strong arguments and evidence of the market rationalists' model of *homo economicus*. Humans are not rational calculating machines. We do not have fixed preferences. We do not and probably cannot calculate the expected utility of most of our decisions, and we do not attempt to maximize expected utility. At best, we are, in Herbert Simon's terms, "satisficers" not optimizers. According to Kahneman, affect is an integral part of our economic behavior: "An exclusive concern with the long term may be prescriptively sterile because the long term is not where life is lived. Utility cannot be divorced from emotion. . . ." Moreover, "a theory of choice that completely ignores feelings such as the pain of losses and the regret of mistakes is not only descriptively unrealistic, it leads to prescriptions that do not maximize the utility of outcomes as they are actually experienced." We struggle to behave rationally, but emotion intervenes. Surprisingly, being completely devoid of emotion is also a hindrance. People who lack normal emotional responses as a result of massive brain trauma become, in effect, rational calculating machines. But they seem incapable of making any decisions. Decision making requires imagining possible futures for which affect is crucial.

The neuroscientist Antonio Damasio has done some fascinating work on the way emotion affects decision making. In one study (Damasio 1994), Damasio gave people $20 to play a 20-round coin-toss game, each round costing $1 to play. The decision is whether to play a given round. If your call is correct, you receive $2.50; if incorrect, you receive nothing. The rational and optimal decision is to play every round because the expected return per round is $1.50.

But participants tend not to play every round. After losing a few rounds, they pull out because they fear further loss. Fear overcomes rationality. The same experiment was conducted with a group of people who had suffered mild damage to the portion of the brain that controls emotion (Shiv, Loewenstein, Bechara, Damasio, and Damasio 2005). These people experience slightly less fear than normal, a clear evolutionary disadvantage. They also do not play every round, but they play significantly more rounds than the control group, and their winnings are, on average, 13 percent higher. For good or ill, emotion is inextricably tied to human decision making and predisposes us to short-termism. Long-term thinking and action pose decided challenges for us humans.

One barrier we can overcome is highlighted in a study of bookmakers who establish the odds on horse races. John Mauldin (2006) described a study done by Paul Slovic. The bookmakers were given five pieces of information and asked to set the odds on a horse race. The odds were then compared with actual results. After that, the bookmakers were given 10 pieces of information and asked to set the odds. Next, they were given 20 pieces of information, then 30, and then 40. The more information they had, the more their confidence rose. But their accuracy did not improve. The same is true for economists and investment professionals. The more information we have, the more confident we become. And with that confidence, we tend to make more decisions, and those decisions become increasingly short term and more likely to be wrong.

During World War II, British Bomber Command determined that too many planes were crashing, not because of enemy fire but because of accidents. The obvious solution was to increase maintenance. In essence, it was decided that more information and more frequent action would alleviate the problem. Paradoxically, increased maintenance resulted in *more* planes falling out of the sky. The more often maintenance crews worked on the airplanes, the more they saw, the more confident they became, and the more mistakes they made. Resisting the temptation to fiddle, to do something, is critical to being a successful long-term investor, but our evolutionary heritage acts against us. Survival decisions are triggered in the limbic system, a primitive part of the brain that provokes instinctive responses. That limbic system helped us survive in an unpredictable world of hunters and hunted. But behavior that provided a survival advantage a quarter of a million years ago on the African veldt puts survival at risk in the jungles of Wall Street.

Three Steps for Getting to the Long Term

The following guidelines should help investors become more longer term in their thinking and action.

1. Recognize and Overcome Barriers to Long-Termism

Barriers come in a variety of forms: cognitive, psychological, and institutional. The first step is to recognize the limits to our ability to think long term—one being the inadequacy of data, another, the limitations of causality. Andrew Lo has quaintly and correctly chastised the profession for suffering from physics envy because the bounds to rationality are intrinsically deeper and broader in investing than they are in physics.

Overcoming barriers demands a clear vision of investment purposes and beliefs, followed by the choice of a manageable, but flexible, portfolio of important types of information, themes, ideas, and data relevant to those purposes and beliefs. This portfolio should be enhanced by reading the masters. Read and reread Keynes' Chapter 12 of *The General Theory of Employment, Interest, and Money*; it is filled with wisdom and insight. Read Fischer Black. There is more insight in one of his footnotes than in entire volumes.

The psychological barriers to long-termism are so demanding it is likely that some people are temperamentally unsuited to long-term thinking. If so, institutions need to identify such people and exclude them from long-term investment management because financial and other incentives may be insufficient to moderate their temperament.

Long-term thinkers need to be especially cognizant of the new insights into group decision making. Some committees make good decisions; some do not. Creating an open market for ideas within the committee seems to foster improved group decision making. Committees should sign up for a behavioral audit that attempts to record and systematically review the deeper psychological reasons behind decisions, not the rationally reconstructed published version. With the committee's permission, to discourage short-termism, management should present and discuss only long-term trend performance and the rare short-term exigencies that are relevant to the long term, with shorter-term data posted on an intranet. Committees should also have the option to do nothing. Such an option stands directly opposed to the innate psychology of committees. Why meet without an expectation of doing something?

2. Be Sensitive to the Short Term but Avoid Gresham's Law

Gresham's law (bad money drives out good) has an informational parallel: Comforting short-term, urgent drivel drives out discomforting long-term, important information. Focusing on the latter hedges the risk implied in the metaphor of drinking from a fire hose. Almost every minute, TV "news" reports on the rise and fall of markets: The NASDAQ is up 1.3 points; the Nikkei is down 3.7 points; gold is up $1.50. Perhaps no one actually makes decisions based on such random, meaningless noise, but the barrage of constant drivel inclines us toward knee-jerk short-term action. The challenge is to recognize and filter those few short-term signals that do have longer-term significance. That requires contemplation, but as Pascal observed 400 years ago, "All [our] miseries derive from not being able to sit quietly in a room alone." Clients should feel a warm inner glow when they enter their manager's office and see people with their phones and PCs off, their eyes closed, their feet up, thinking. I'm told that Northwest Mutual requires its senior executives to have a day every two weeks when they turn off all their electronics, close their doors, and just think. Uncluttered focused minds are more likely to discern short-term information relevant to long-term strategies.

A small number of strategic partnerships with managers, consultants, and/or like-minded funds helps maintain that clarity and the concomitant discipline. Appropriate partnerships with managers should include well-structured performance-based fees, sufficiently transparent to allow for informed questioning of turnover and agency effects.

3. Develop and Use a Statement of Investment Beliefs

A fund should spend substantial time developing and writing down what it believes about investments and markets, and why. For instance, does it believe markets are inefficient? If so, why? What is the evidence? Is inefficiency secular or cyclical? Is it more evident in some markets than in others? What are the consequences for the fund? Critically, investment beliefs must be referred to and used in decision making; else, they become objects of derision like so many sterile mission statements.

Investment beliefs should include a long-term investment statement (or LoTIS) that articulates the fund's beliefs about the relevance and benefits of long-termism and how those views will be reflected in decision making. In particular, the LoTIS should address the anchors of long-term value added. There are rhythms in economic history. Almost identical events do not necessarily have almost identical consequences, but reading history helps investors recognize the rhythms. For instance, there are rhythms to stock market bubbles. A generation hence will be a watchful time. By that time, the pain of the TMT (technology, media, and telecommunications) bubble will have faded from memory, and those with the scars will be dismissed as old and thus irrelevant. All that is then needed is a strong economy that makes us feel secure because at a macro level, we find succor in stability. Paradoxically, we simultaneously crave excitement, but more at an individual stock or sector level. The next new, new thing, be it a dot-com or a tulip bulb, will provide that excitement. Finally, stir this brew with excessive liquidity and watch the bubble form. Effective long-term thinkers are sensitive to such rhythms.

The LoTIS should also include a charter of decision making, estimates of risk tolerance (including the fund's tolerance for *explicable* underperformance), and justification for the fund's strategic exposure to long-duration alternative assets.

Conclusion

Excessive short-termism is a sin for which we all bear some guilt, so overcoming short-term thinking requires collective leadership. The benefits of long-termism should not be overstated as it too has risks. Funds, investors, managers, and consultants require wisdom and courage to embrace it, especially the wisdom to know when to have courage.

This presentation comes from the 2006 CFA Institute Annual Conference held in Zurich on 21–24 May 2006.

References

BCA. 2004. "Beyond the Horizon: Short-Termism in Australia: A Call to Think into the Future." In *2004 Annual Review*. Business Council of Australia:36–55 (http://www.bca.com.au/upload/BCA_Annual_Review_2004.pdf).

Bogle, John. 2005. "The Mutual Fund Industry 60 Years Later: For Better or Worse?" *Financial Analysts Journal*, vol. 61, no. 1 (January/February):15–24.

CFA Centre for Financial Market Integrity and Business Roundtable Institute for Corporate Ethics. 2006. "Breaking the Short-Term Cycle." CFA Institute (http://www.cfapubs.org/doi/pdf/10.2469/ccb.v2006.n1.4194).

Cole, Robert. 2005. "What's Wrong with Short-Termism Anyway?" *Times Online* (http://business.timesonline.co.uk/article/0,16849-1673145,00.html).

Damasio, A.R. 1994. *Descartes' Error: Emotion, Reason, and the Human Brain*. New York: Grosset/Putnam.

Kritzman, M. 2000. *Puzzles of Finance: Six Practical Problems and Their Remarkable Solutions*. New York: John Wiley & Sons.

Marathon Club. 2006. "Investing for the Long Term," (http://www.marathonclub.co.uk/docs).

Mauldin, John. *ed.* 2006. *Just One Thing: Twelve of the World's Best Investors Reveal the One Strategy You Can't Overlook*. John Wiley & Sons: Hoboken, NJ.

Shiv, Baba, George Loewenstein, Antoine Bechara, Hanna Damasio, and Antonio R. Damasio. 2005. "Investment Behavior and the Negative Side of Emotion." *Psychological Science*, vol. 16, no. 6 (June):435–439.

More from Jack Gray

This section presents the speaker's lively question and answer session with the conference audience.

Question: If some people are better at thinking long term, should we consider this attribute when selecting trustees?

Gray: I do not think the answer is known yet. Certainly, I think that some people have the courage to stand alone for a longer time than others. But that can be a plus or a minus because some people run the risk of being contrarian simply for the sake of being contrarian. When selecting a committee, you should probably put some hypothetical situations before prospective members. But I do not know if any definitive evidence is available to indicate which people are long-term thinkers and which are not.

Question: Are such long-term investors as endowments better at managing the tendency toward short-termism?

Gray: Endowments stand out as having done a very good job of investing. One reason for their success is that they are institutionally inclined toward the long term. But another reason is that they have far fewer agents than most fund managers. It does not matter what sort of agents are involved; it is number that counts. Agents can be brokers, investors, or consultants, and they can be the best intentioned agents imaginable. Intentions are far less important than number. More agents—of any kind—mean more agency friction, and more agency friction means more short-term thinking. Certainly, endowments tend to take a long-term view of their investments, but I think having fewer agents has a significant effect on their behavior.

Question: Can we rely on the market to modify our short-termism?

Gray: The market tends to reward short-termism. Consider momentum. In a perfectly efficient market, momentum should not work. In fact, it works. That is classic short-termism, and investors are rewarded for that. So, the market rewards investors for short-term thinking, but it rewards them even more for long-term thinking—if investors are willing to be patient.

Question: Is increasing turnover correlated with bubble markets or the emphasis on telecommunications and technology?

Gray: I have not seen any data on that specifically, but certainly the market can go through periods when it is carried away with excitement, and such periods lend themselves to momentum behavior that tends to gravitate toward new technology.

As I said earlier, humans crave the comfort of certainty. On the macro level, we crave stability, such as low inflation and steady (but not dramatic) growth. But on the micro level, such as specific stocks, we love excitement, and new technology stocks offer excitement.

Question: How much of the financial services industry do you think would have to be dismantled to reduce turnover and agency issues?

Gray: That's a terrific question for which I have no numbers. In Australia, however, I have been trying to get numbers on the supposed value added by each agent that comes between an individual investor and the investor's money. At this point, I calculate that six agents typically come between investors and their money, and I suspect that most of those agents add no value and perhaps even detract value. I would be thrilled if someone would take the time to look seriously at frictional costs and added value generated by agents. I suspect that a lot of the system could be dismantled with little or no loss to the investor, but I have no data.

Question: Could you name some more masters to read?

Gray: Certainly. In addition to those I've already mentioned, I recommend Robert Merton and Paul Samuelson, especially for his paper that, 40 years ago, debunked the myth that long-term investors should necessarily hold riskier assets. His ideas in the paper are much more subtle than he is sometimes given credit for. Also, read the economist John Hicks, a contemporary of Keynes, who had many useful insights into the markets.

The Role of the Whistle-Blower: Ethical Dilemmas in Investment Management

NOREEN HARRINGTON

If a company is well run and if an industry has sound leadership, then whistle-blowing will never happen because the conditions that encourage unethical behavior will not emerge. In light of the widespread mutual funds trading abuse scandal that emerged in 2003, the mutual fund industry needs leadership from regulators and shareholders. But most of all, the industry needs ethical leaders from within its own ranks to step forward and set the necessary examples, especially by focusing on genuine long-term performance rather than short-term gains. And despite personal hardships and potential career-ending risks, blowing the whistle is ethically the right thing to do.

No one wants to be a whistle-blower. No one dreams as a little child, "I hope one day I grow up to be a whistle-blower." Certainly, I did not. I was an industry insider. I worked at prestigious firms, including Goldman, Sachs & Co. and Barclays Capital. I was successful in my career. Why would I want to jeopardize everything that I had worked so hard to accomplish? And believe me, whistle-blowing can jeopardize everything. Certainly, it can turn a person's life upside down, as it did to mine. So, why did I blow the whistle in 2003 on the mutual fund market-timing scandal?

I realized that I could no longer be proud of myself, my work, or the industry in which I had built my career unless I took a stand.

Some people have referred to my actions as courageous, but I do not consider myself to be a particularly brave person. No, I think my motivations had less to do with courage than with pride. I am proud of what I do for a living. Managing people's money is a matter of tremendous responsibility. People trust me and my industry with the assets they have accrued through a lifetime of work, assets that their families are counting on. They count on us to do the right thing with their financial legacy. And I am proud of all of my colleagues who work every day to meet their responsibilities and fulfill the trust of their clients. So, I became

Noreen Harrington is managing partner at Alternative Institutional Partners, New York City.

a whistle-blower because I realized that I could no longer be proud of myself, my work, or the industry in which I had built my career unless I took a stand.

Becoming a Whistle-Blower

In 2001, I was working for the Stern family, one of the most prestigious names in finance, only to discover that one of their sons, Eddie Stern, was stealing from 95 million unsuspecting Americans. I did not work directly with Eddie. I ran a fund of funds for the family's wealth, so I did not normally focus on the work that he was doing. But bits of information began filtering through to me. The returns on his fund, Canary Capital Management, were not adding up, and I began wondering why. But nothing spurred me to action until one night when I happened to be working late at Canary's New Jersey office—a place where I did not ordinarily work—and I noticed two young men putting through a large number of tickets. So, I asked, "Who are you trading with?" One of the men crowed, "We just picked off this guy for $10 million." "But the market is closed," I said. (I must have had m-o-r-o-n written across my forehead.) "Oh," he answered, "we put these tickets in late." I stood there completely dumbfounded. They were bragging, and I knew they were bragging about something that was not right.

I went home that night, and I asked myself why such a prestigious family would bother doing such a thing. They are worth $3 billion. They do not need the money, and they know they cannot take it with them. So, why would they be doing this?

My next thought was that I must be wrong. I must have misunderstood. That young trader must have misspoken. But I could not get the doubts out of my head. So, I began doing my own research, and what I found was that Canary was engaged in market timing and, as that young trader had so braggingly declared, after-hours trading. Armed with this information, I confronted Eddie Stern. I asked him what he was doing. And by the answer he gave, I understood instantly that he knew he was breaking the law because his response included the exit strategy he had apparently planned long before. If the regulators came looking for him, he told me, he was going to turn in the mutual funds because the regulators would want the mutual funds more than they would want him. And he was right. But even at this point, I did not know how right he was because I did not know how extensive the market-timing scandal was.

After I resigned from Stern at the end of August 2002, I told myself that the problem was isolated to one fund, one family. And I asked myself, "Do you want to turn your life upside down for one family?" I certainly did not want to, but my conscience would not let me drop the issue, so I continued digging for information, and I found that the problem was industrywide. The stealing in the industry was absolutely staggering. It had been going on for more than a dozen years, and the sums were running $10 billion to $15 billion a year. Granted, no single investor felt an enormous pinch, but the collective effect on the wealth of millions of investors, people who were entrusting the industry with their 401(k) money, their retirement savings, their nest eggs, was devastating.

I realized at last that I was dealing with an industry that had taken the wrong turn because what I was perceiving was not just a matter of hedge funds doing something illegal on their own. Mutual fund executives had to be complicit. Certainly, not every leader in every company knew what was going on. But within any one company, a lot of people had to sign off for certain things to happen. For example, Bank of America had actually installed a terminal at the offices of Canary so that Canary could connect with Bank of America's back-office systems and conduct after-hours trading. No fund gives access to its back-office systems unless a lot of department heads have signed off on the deal. Perhaps not every person connected the dots, but the dots were right there for all of them to see.

As for me, I was still hoping someone else would blow the whistle. After all, I was convinced that plenty of other people knew what was going on. But no one stepped forward, and I realized at last that I would have to because one aspect of being a senior person in an industry is accepting responsibility for the behavior of that industry. So, after much anguish and deliberation, I reported my findings and concerns in March 2003 to New York State Attorney General Eliot Spitzer. Fortunately for me, his office had just hired a former colleague of mine from Goldman, Sachs & Co.—David Brown—and Brown was to head the investigation. Therefore, I had instant credibility with the attorney general, and the attorney general's office had credibility with me. Brown was smart and knowledgeable and spoke the same financial language that I spoke, and when the two of us sat down together to discuss the issue, one of the first questions we asked ourselves was, Why would mutual funds do this? The answer was simple: to boost assets under management and the value of the mutual fund company. No matter how much damage was being done to their clients, the funds were making money from the fees generated by the illegal activity.

After offering my information, I left the attorney general's office feeling relieved. A tremendous weight had been lifted from my shoulders. The trouble was over for me. I could now sleep soundly. I had done my duty, my conscience was clear, and the burden now lay in the hands of the attorney general.

Within three months of receiving my information, Eliot Spitzer announced indictments and investigations. People were being brought to justice just as they should have been. Then, a reporter asked Spitzer whether his office had ferreted out the problems on its own. He said, "No, someone helped us, but I am taking that name to my grave." Well, instead of putting a lid on it, that statement just spurred the media into investigative mode. They started digging and digging and digging—until one night a reporter from the *Wall Street Journal* called my home and said, "We are running a story that names you as the whistle-blower." My reaction to the call was priceless: I could not speak. Nothing gives the truth away quite like absolute, frozen panic. It was like a neon finger pointing at me. And so I learned that the trauma was not yet over for me. My quiet life was now the center of a media circus. And let me emphasize that my life was indeed quiet and that I liked it that way. I am not a public speaker. Even when I had a senior position at Goldman, Sachs & Co., I did not like to speak at conferences. And now, suddenly, I was being interviewed on "60 Minutes" and other news shows. I was not at all prepared for such a dramatic change, and I certainly did not want it. It was all quite frightening. I honestly feared for my safety at times, and so did my mother. I found myself, at my age, having to call my mother every night to reassure her that I was safe.

The Kindness of Good People

When I look back on all that has happened, I find that I have learned less about myself than I have about other people. Good people, people who have sound ethics and who understand the crime that occurred, come up to me and thank me. Some even hug me. They thank me for looking out for them, for looking out for their money. They thank me for my public service. And I am thankful to them for reminding me that each of us has a responsibility to do the right thing for our industry.

Of the numerous people in the industry who have supported me, one early supporter stands out. Shortly after the scandal became public, Mark Anson, CFA, former chief financial officer of the California Public Employees' Retirement System (CalPERS), telephoned me and said, "What can we at CalPERS do for you?" I almost dropped the phone. Then, I replied, "You just did it. You restored my faith that this industry has good people in it and that with their help I will survive this crisis." To me this was a sign of the leadership that people like Anson and organizations like CalPERS provide. CalPERS has led this industry in diversifying its workforce, and because of Anson, it has led the industry in choosing environmentally sustainable investments. Organizations like CalPERS understand that their money is power, and they can use that power to make a difference for the better. I received many other calls after that one from Anson, but it has always represented a turning point for me.

My courage was also bolstered by the awareness that other women have also stepped forward in equally uncertain situations: former Enron Corporation Vice President Sherron Watkins, former WorldCom Internal Auditor Cynthia Cooper, and former U.S. Federal Bureau of Investigation attorney Coleen Rowley—three whistle-blowers named "People of the Year" by *Time* magazine in 2002. Believe it or not, research conducted by Sheila Wellington, management professor at New York University, indicates a gender bias among whistle-blowers: Women are more likely to blow the whistle than men. And at least one study indicates that this bias arises from the fact that women tend to be the moral leaders of our children. They have a tremendous influence on our children's ethics, and one of their motivations in their careers is that they need their work to be important. Therefore, if a woman sees the value of her important work threatened, then—at least according to this scenario—she is more likely to blow the whistle. Other research by the consulting firm Caliper points out that women tend not to be in the inner circle of top management; therefore, they perceive the choice of becoming a whistle-blower less threatening to their own status than do men.

The coincidence of so many women stepping forward as they have does seem remarkable, but I remain skeptical of such research. I would like to think that any ethical person, male or female, would respond if presented with such a challenge.

Occasionally, as I reflect on the results of my actions, I do feel a sense of pride. My old boss of 11 years at Goldman, Sachs & Co., (former U.S. senator and current governor of New Jersey) Jon Corzine, said to me when the scandal broke, "Noreen, I went to Washington, DC, to make a difference, to do public service. But you helped 95 million people. That will always be your legacy."

Leadership Means Whistle-Blowing Never Happens

I cannot say that I intentionally went looking for such a legacy, but I can say that my life is different now. I am forever Noreen Harrington Whistle-Blower. That is my new surname. But I stand here today to say that whistle-blowing should never happen. Whistle-blowing happens only when an industry is in crisis.

If the doors of an organization are open, if its executives are willing to listen, if people feel safe within that organization, then that organization has provided a path for correcting flaws in the system. The first step for leaders in this industry is to make sure that doors are open and that people are heard. We often say that our greatest assets are our people. If that is so, if we indeed believe the words that we speak, then we need to listen to our people and respect their judgment. We need to assure them that it is safe to raise concerns and issues. When the leaders of our industry do that, then our industry will no longer need a whistle-blower. Now that I am once again an insider, I would like to be part of the solution, part of the leadership that brings this wonderful industry back to the place of respect that it deserves.

Laws are in place to protect whistle-blowers, but the laws could be stronger. This is an issue that I have frequently raised with people in Washington, DC.

If employees are willing to stand up and do the right thing, then a safety net needs to be provided for them. They need to be protected financially so that their families are not put at risk for the ethical stand they take. Legislation needs to do more than make sure that people survive a trauma like mine. It should, in fact, reward whistle-blowers. It should see that whistle-blowers prosper for having done the right thing. And such policies should not simply be legislated; they should be initiated by companies in the industry. If a person raises an issue and stands up and says, "We cannot do that. It hurts our shareholders," then that person should be rewarded. If by speaking up an employee prevents a fraud from being committed and saves a fund and its investors from paying $200 million in fines, that person should be rewarded just as well as some whiz kid whose trading has earned the fund $100 million. If we do not reward those people who practice true and thorough due diligence, then we do not value them as an asset. After all, employees like that do not just save the firm from paying a $200 million fine; they save the reputation of the entire firm. They protect the brand. That is something that should be praised, rewarded, and encouraged. In contrast, if an employee becomes aware of an ethical issue and does not bring it to the company's attention, that employee should receive a negative mark.

In a sense, it all comes down to protecting reputation—not only the institution's reputation but the person's reputation as well. For example, I may now walk the earth as Noreen Harrington Whistle-Blower, but I would much rather have that name than the names Eddie Stern now has attached to himself and his family. When I leave this world, the Harrington name will be as untarnished as it was the day I came into this world, and that is more valuable than any amount of money.

What We Have Learned

Looking back at the mutual fund scandal, we should have learned at least the following things:

- The board of directors system failed to serve the shareholders it was meant to serve.
- The compensation system had misdirected incentives.
- The culture encouraged arrogance. It encouraged employees to think that rules were for other people and that anything they did was okay as long as they did not get caught.
- The culture encouraged short-term thinking. With so much emphasis placed on quarterly numbers, people were motivated to cut corners and to make

immoral and unethical choices that were rationalized as excusable because the numbers were being met.

Such problems are not limited to any single industry. Look at Enron, WorldCom, Tyco International, and HealthSouth Corporation as but a few examples. The same flaws afflicted those industries. But this is our house, and we have to clean it up. We have to be sure that no such debacle happens again, and to do that we have to create a climate that discourages unethical behavior. Several players can help the industry achieve this goal—among them are regulators, leaders in the mutual fund business, leaders in nonfund organizations, and the media.

Role of Regulators

I am a fan of regulators. I appreciate especially their role as guarantors of fair and open markets for all investors. But regulators tend to be reactive, and they tend to act after damage has already been done. Fortunately, Stephen Cutler, former director of enforcement for the U.S. SEC, tried to change that reactive stance before he left his position. After the fund scandal broke, he met with me and asked me how I thought the SEC could do a better job. I told him that I perceived the SEC much as I perceived a company's compliance department, and I have strong views about compliance departments. If a company runs compliance as if it is the police, then it will get the same sort of voluntary cooperation that police tend to get, which is not much. But if a compliance department is viewed not as the police but as a resource intended to help employees do a better job and avoid the kind of mistakes that can do serious damage not only to the company and its clients but also to their own careers, then employees will cooperate. It works the same way with the SEC. If people in the industry view the SEC as the top cop, they will avoid interaction with the SEC. So, I told Cutler to open the place up. Educate people about the role and value of the SEC. Create a toll-free hotline that people can call without fear of repercussion. Help them understand which behaviors are unacceptable and which are okay.

To Cutler's credit, he made a lot of valuable changes. He himself became a bigger media figure, so people knew who he was and what he was trying to accomplish. The SEC has created that toll-free number as I suggested, and it has reached out to educate its constituencies. It has tried to embrace the industry by offering more conferences, and it has an online center for complaints and enforcement tips, located at http://www.sec.gov/complaint.shtml.

Role of Mutual Fund Leaders

The industry, however, cannot sit back and wait for regulators to set things straight. In fact, most firms in the industry would not want that to happen. Most firms would rather have as little to do with regulators as possible. My own section of the industry, the hedge fund business, often acts as if it would rather not give regulators the time of day. When regulators tell hedge funds that they intend to regulate them, the classic response from hedge funds is, "We are smarter than the regulators. We can find loopholes." This is a short-sighted point of view. Hedge funds hold no cards. They might be able to delay regulation for a brief time, but they cannot avoid it in the long term. So, they ought to embrace the idea of regulation. Fortunately, hedge funds are starting to reassess their initial poor reaction, and a very prominent person in the business, Jim Chanos, a man who is outspoken, ethical, honest, and thoughtful, has decided that hedge funds must become proactive in their relationships with regulators. He is going to lead a lobby for hedge funds. He intends to embrace the regulators, and rather than avoid regulation, he intends to help the regulators tailor regulation to the realities of the business. That is the kind of leadership we need. Otherwise, we will have regulations that are wasteful and time consuming and that, in the end, do not accomplish their most important goals: stopping fraud and protecting the investor.

Therefore, well-managed mutual fund companies must take a leadership role. After all, it is their own reputation, their own brand, that is tarnished by unethical behavior. They should thus reach out to regulators, and they should set their own powerful example for ethical standards. When an employee walks into a meeting and says, "We can do such and such, and no one will be the wiser," that employee is putting the company's reputation on the line, and everyone in that meeting should stand up and set that employee straight. The old adage—"once lost, hard to reclaim"—has never been truer. Goldman, Sachs & Co., my former employer, was asked to participate in market timing and turned the offer down. And it did so because it could see no long-term benefit in harming its investors and jeopardizing its brand just so some short-term timers could make profits. The ethical response is obvious, especially because we have seen the consequences of the unethical response. Our task now is to keep the benefits of the ethical response that obvious.

Industry leaders also need to address extra-financial issues (EFIs), such as corporate governance and commitment to sound environmental and social practices. Numerous reports indicate that EFIs affect a firm's risk management capabilities. The results of failed corporate governance are dramatized by companies like Enron, WorldCom, and Adelphia Communications Corporation. Weak capital management undermines corporate profits. Weak environmental management can lead to problems, such as those faced by Monsanto Company. Weak management of licenses and inappropriate treatment of staff and customers can result in such problems as those experienced by McDonald's Corporation. All such failures put shareholders at risk. Conversely, good risk management is a competitive advantage and highlights a company, such as Johnson & Johnson, as a leader that sets an example to follow. Finally, business development and strategy innovation need to be emphasized. Companies that are adaptable and innovative, companies that embrace change and anticipate regulatory developments, are leadership companies. New research by the Enhanced Analytics Initiative (EAI) indicates the value of ranking companies according to three areas of risk management: brand, strength, and innovation. In my own business of hedge fund management, I have found that evaluating companies according to not only finances but also these areas of risk leads to consistent outperformance and alpha generation.

Role of Nonfund Leaders

One effect of the mutual fund scandal is that shareholders and other interested parties have taken on a leadership role. Many state benefit authorities—those for New York and California in particular—are becoming more aggressive as shareholders. They are raising issues with boards of directors, and they are demanding answers. The Teamsters dealt recently with the Coca-Cola Company on a compensation package. Hedge funds have taken on the role of activists, in many cases a very good role, by raising questions and using the power of their own stock to make sure they are heard. Independent directors are also helping to create change within their funds. Several new groups of interested parties have been formed, and one such new group, EAI, is focusing on long-term EFIs that could affect a company's long-term financial performance and reputation. These EFIs tend to be qualitative rather than quantitative and also relate to economic externalities, such as pollution, that are generally excluded from mainstream research analysis. EAI is working with sell-side research providers to incorporate EFIs alongside their mainstream research to improve the quality of research by helping investors identify undervalued companies over long time horizons.

Several other organizations have also stepped forward. Certainly, CFA Institute has taken a leadership role in ethics and education. CalPERS has demonstrated the value of being a vocal shareholder. And the Council of Institutional Investors (CII), which represents a lot of state money, is trying to raise the bar and make it expensive to be involved in any new fund scandals. CII is encouraging states to establish rules by which an entire firm accepts responsibility for anything that any part of that firm does. Such rules prevent a firm's executives from saying, "Well, the fixed-income guys were in the scandal, but equities were not. So, on the whole, we are clean." Under the proposed corporate governance guidelines, if part of a firm is involved in fraud, then the entire firm is punished.

Role of the Media

Today's media is as prone to short-term thinking as portions of our own industry. Too many people in our business want to see a quarterly number, make a bet, turn a quick profit, and get out. The media is similar. It is looking for a quick headline, and in some cases, it goes about getting that headline in an irresponsible manner. Good journalists are capable of doing thoughtful, determined work. They research the issues, and they do not write about those issues until they understand them. We need more journalists like that because such journalists act as watchdogs not only for our industry but also for society in general. They cannot replace regulators or ethical leaders in the industry, but they can complement them. What we do not need are journalists who are concerned only with shocking headlines and superficial reporting. Journalists like that are not fulfilling their proper role.

Conclusion

For generations now, the United States has been a leader in the financial world, but recent scandals have damaged our credibility. To reestablish our leadership position, we need the best and the brightest in this industry to help us demonstrate not only to U.S. investors but also to the rest of the world that we are trustworthy and that we deserve to return to our former pinnacle of trust and leadership. We need executives in the industry, as well as in institutions such as CFA Institute, to show us the way forward. And in this effort, I recommend that we follow the advice of the great moral leader Mahatma Gandhi, who said, "If you want change, you must be the change you want to see."

This presentation comes from the 2006 Financial Analysts Seminar held in Evanston, Illinois, on 16–21 July 2006.

More from Noreen Harrington

This section presents the speaker's lively question and answer session with the conference audience.

Question: Why did you blow the whistle to Eliot Spitzer rather than to the SEC?

Harrington: I'm a Wall Street insider and had been under the rules of the SEC at the time for more than 20 years. Still, in my opinion, I was reporting a crime, and crimes are reported to the attorney general.

Question: After you resigned and dealt with the aftermath of your whistle-blowing, how did you survive financially?

Harrington: I was in the fortunate position of having been very successful prior to it. So, I had a tremendous career, and if the aftermath of blowing the whistle had been career ending, it would have still been fine. I couldn't work for a while—it was too overwhelming—but a lot of laws and legislation now exist that protect whistle-blowers. In the United States, the Department of Labor's Occupational Safety and Health Administration protects whistle-blowing employees of publicly listed companies.

So, I think the bottom line is that a lot of laws have been passed to protect whistle-blowers financially if they have been discriminated against for reporting a potential shareholder fraud to a supervisor, federal regulator, or member of Congress. But a lot more needs to be done to ensure the financial well-being of whistle-blowers who may not be in a position as favorable as mine.

Question: Was your perception of the market abuse an easy call, like somebody stealing money from the cookie jar, or was this something that required you to put one, two, three, or four bits or pieces of information together?

Harrington: At first, bits and pieces of information went into my brain that didn't make sense. The dots weren't connecting. The numbers for Stern's returns on his fund didn't make sense, and in this industry, when things don't make sense, you ask more questions.

But the crowning moment didn't come until that one fateful night in the New Jersey office when I stumbled upon the guys from the fund putting all those tickets through. That was like catching somebody with his or her hand in the cookie jar, but it was only by luck that I did.

Best Practices in Corporate Governance

JAMES S. RIEPE

Investment professionals have a fiduciary responsibility to use their proxy votes to promote sound corporate governance. In applying that responsibility, however, they should consider the competing interests of all corporate stakeholders while giving primary consideration to their clients—the shareowners. Institutional investors should establish principles and processes that portfolio managers can follow as they evaluate the unique requirements of each proxy vote.

Investment professionals sometimes wonder whether corporate governance is just one more item on a politically correct agenda and, therefore, one of little concern to the real work of their profession. But corporate governance reflects the way that a company is managed, and the way a company is managed has much to do with determining the value of its stock. Thus, investment professionals who do not take a keen interest in corporate governance are missing not only an opportunity but also an obligation to manage more effectively the funds for which they have a fiduciary responsibility. In fact, investment professionals often bear a fiduciary obligation to vote on proxy issues, and some of those proxy issues can have a material impact on the future finances of the corporation that generated them. Our fiduciary function, therefore, is not simply a technical one, limited to voting proxies. Our responsibility with respect to proxy issues is to separate the wheat from the chaff, to protect the value of a company for our clients and ourselves.

No longer are corporations given a free pass on issues that affect society and the environment. Corporate actions that affect these areas are under growing scrutiny.

My discussion of corporate governance begins with a description of the environment in which corporations are currently operating. Next, I describe the various ways of defining corporate governance and point out the definition that I believe works best. After that, I highlight the stakeholders to whom corporations must be responsive, paying particular attention to share*owners*

James S. Riepe is senior adviser and a retired vice chairman of the board of directors of T. Rowe Price Group, Inc., Baltimore.

and share*holders* and the differences between the two. The role of investment managers in the governance process is then reviewed, and I offer, as an example, the approach that T. Rowe Price Group applies to its governance responsibilities. Finally, I review some of the lessons to be learned from the corporate scandals of the past several years.

Current Corporate Environment

We operate in a highly charged environment in which several "triggers" have served to elevate the prominence of corporate governance discussions. By identifying those triggers, we can better understand the atmosphere in which we are operating.

Triggers of Current Conditions

First, corporate stock ownership has broadened significantly. Rather than resting in the hands of just a few wealthy individuals or corporations, equities are now widely held through public and private pension plans, defined-contribution retirement plans, mutual funds, and direct individual ownership. Because of this broadening, public interest in common stocks and in the corporations that issue them is far more widespread today than it was several decades ago, and the debate about corporate behavior is more obviously relevant to the general public than ever before. Proxy voting, therefore, is no longer an insider's game.

Second, the transparency of corporate behavior has improved enormously. Corporate critics continue to complain about the opacity of corporate operations, but the fact remains that not only investors but all interested parties have far greater access to corporate data and decision-making processes than they did in the past, even the very recent past.

Third, as the public has grown more aware of social responsibilities, so too have corporations. No longer are corporations given a free pass on issues that affect society and the environment. Corporate actions that affect these areas are under growing scrutiny.

Fourth, management compensation has moved directly into the cross-hairs of public scrutiny. With expanded disclosure, executive compensation has become a target of criticism—by both serious and superficial observers. Inappropriate management compensation has provided rich fodder for those who want to point to what is wrong with corporate oversight in our country. The dramatic acceleration of cash compensation, the expansion of equity incentives, the growing concentration of high compensation among the top managers of many corporations, and the too frequent absence of any relationship between compensation and corporate performance have all served to attract the critical attention of investors, journalists, and now politicians and regulators. The latest revelation that top executives of numerous high-tech companies backdated their stock options to increase the return on those options has only added more fuel to the fire.

Finally, the greatest bull market in stocks in 70 years reached a euphoric bubble that brought with it some very visible—and inevitable—excesses. By 2000, those excesses had reached extraordinary heights, and now, six years after the bubble's bursting, we are continuing to clean up the mess.

Postbubble Environment

Several incidents of corporate misbehavior and the prosecution of the executives involved awakened us to certain business practices and management activities that were well beyond the pale of appropriate behavior. Investors and board members alike were forced to reexamine the corporate oversight process. Unfortunately, as the media focused its attention on what was perceived as oversight failures, politicians and regulators took notice, and the corporate community became the subject of a virtual feeding frenzy that often exaggerated the extent of governance failures.

The result was a political response that culminated in the U.S. Sarbanes–Oxley Act of 2002—along with public hearings designed to embarrass corporate executives. And the regulatory response occurred at both the federal and state levels. In addition, media coverage ensured that one of the major challenges during this period was how corporate managers could convince the public, and in some cases their investors, that not every single manager had succumbed to hubris, greed, or outright fraud. Although some were sensational, instances of fraud were actually limited in number, especially when compared with the enormous size of our economy and capital markets; but those frauds were highly visible, and they were terribly costly to investors. Of greater concern, they were accompanied by far too many examples of corporate behavior that, although not always illegal, were surely excessive or improper.

The reality is that most instances of fraud, improper practices, and ethical lapses are far more attributable to *failures of management* than to poor corporate oversight. Confusing the two, I think, leads to unwarranted and counterproductive actions that may not improve the substantive oversight of a board and may actually reduce a board's effectiveness as it allocates precious time to ineffective legal and regulatory exercises.

In addition to directors, institutional investors—the intermediaries who act on behalf of shareowners—have also come under scrutiny. Institutional investors are being blamed for passively accepting executive compensation that some believe has grown wildly out of control. As one result, shareowners have begun voicing their expectations for a higher degree of integrity, ethical standards, and organizational oversight from the managements of the companies they own. When investors turn their money over to investment managers, they expect those investment managers to hold managements to high standards and ensure that the corporations in which they invest are acting in the shareowners' interests. Thus, the bar has been raised not only for corporate management but also for those of us who invest on behalf of others.

Given this environment, we should not be surprised at the renewed and vigorous scrutiny of corporate managements, boards of directors, and financial intermediaries. Nor should we be surprised that corporate governance seems to be the vehicle of choice for effecting the way managements and boards are conducting the affairs of our corporations. But what exactly is meant by the phrase "corporate governance"?

Defining Corporate Governance

The term "corporate governance" has many definitions, most of which are colored by the agenda of the person or group creating the definition. Among the definitions that seem most cogent to me are the following:

- a system by which companies are directed and controlled,
- a framework designed to encourage the efficient use of resources and accountability in the use of those resources (I find this definition appealing because it implies oversight and the stewardship of property in the corporate setting),
- a process by which corporations are made responsive to the rights and wishes of stakeholders, and
- an approach for governing a corporation (this definition is the one I prefer because it is simple and it provides a large enough umbrella under which we can discuss the responsibility that we, as investors, have with respect to some of the functions of corporate governance).

Stakeholders

Governance, in its most basic form, involves three key players: management, the board of directors, and shareowners. Management reports to the board, and the board reports to the shareowners. Each key player has the authority and responsibility to influence a corporation's actions. But to some, governance does not encompass all the constituents who believe they hold a stake in a corporation's activities. Among the most frequently named stakeholders whose interests deserve to be represented are equity owners, debtholders, employees, customers, and managers.

Some will argue that equity owners are the only stakeholders that matter. But the ability of most companies to raise debt financing is critical to their future, and the buyers and holders of that debt are clearly stakeholders in a company's future. Employees are another important stakeholder group. Their jobs depend on the corporation enduring and prospering. The corporation's future depends on the work of its employees, and equity owners would hold an empty bag if there were no employees.

Peter Drucker best articulated the idea that, above all else, a corporation must define and pursue its mission. He also asserted that the customer is central to that mission. Just as equity owners can anticipate no return without employees, they can also anticipate no revenue without customers.

Finally, the managers who are charged with directing and leading a company must certainly be considered stakeholders. Both directors and shareowners rely on a company's managers to lead the company toward success.

Most observers will agree that the aforementioned groups—shareowners, debtholders, employees, customers, and managers—are all stakeholders in a corporation's life. But the importance assigned to each group varies with each observer's perspective—and agenda. Each company values its stakeholders within the context of its business, its corporate history, and its culture.

Shareowners

We all learned in Finance 101 that owners of common stock clearly and legally own a corporation's equity. But owners of equity, especially today, come in many different forms, and their varied interests must be served. Shareowners include the following:

- individuals, some of whom are day traders and others, long-term investors, and some of whom hold many shares and others, only a few;
- mutual funds, some of which are looking for long-term growth and low turnover whereas others are looking for a catalyst for change;
- pension funds, which have long-term liabilities to meet but short-term pressures on their performance;
- hedge funds, which typically look to generate quick gains;
- arbitrageurs, who buy a stock after an initial merger announcement and who need the merger to occur in order to gain, regardless of whether the merger is good or bad for the corporations involved; and
- special interest groups, who buy shares just so they can submit proxy questions that pursue their agendas.

Each of these groups owns shares and is a legitimate owner, but each has a different goal in mind and different time horizons for its investment.

Each wants the company to pay attention to its particular agenda, which the corporation must balance against its business goals and the expectations of other stakeholders.

Shareholders

In addition to the owners of the shares are others who hold the shares. Some shareholders also own shares, but other shareholders are intermediaries who hold shares for the owners. Each shareholder has different goals and time horizons. Determining which group to be most responsive to is a challenge for managers and directors. When all is going well for a corporation, little conflict exists. But when a company is struggling or considering a major decision, specific groups can become more vocal, and determining whose interests to serve can be difficult when those interests conflict.

Because of the relationship between shareholders and shareowners, the responsibility for influencing corporate governance often falls not on shareowners and their beneficiaries but on those who are delegated the responsibility for investment decisions—that is, investment managers.

Role of Investment Managers

In a narrow sense, investment managers have a fiduciary obligation to represent the interests of the shareowners who are their clients. They also have an investment responsibility that includes making decisions that are designed to bring about desirable financial outcomes for their clients. In executing those responsibilities, investment managers—like corporate managers—have to recognize the effort needed to balance the interests of the various stakeholders.

Responsible investment managers should consider the impact of corporate decisions, not only on shareowners but also on other key constituencies that may influence the future of a company. This may seem to be an unusual assertion because it appears to place other interests above those of the shareowners, but I would argue that these other interests need to be evaluated in the context of their impacts on shareowners. For example, dramatically reducing the size of a stock option program in order to reduce potential dilution and option expense may have a positive effect on a company's financial statements, but it may also have a negative effect on the company's ability to attract and retain key employees. These opposing interests must be balanced.

Consider another, more specific, example. Several years ago, when Oracle Corporation was trying to acquire PeopleSoft, Oracle indicated that much of PeopleSoft's software would be redundant with Oracle's and it would be eliminated from the product line. The reaction among PeopleSoft customers was fierce, and that reaction forced Oracle to change its strategy. Customers as stakeholders in PeopleSoft (and potential stakeholders in Oracle) demonstrated themselves to be critically important in Oracle's strategy and thereby caused a change in corporate behavior. Just as managements and boards have to recognize the interests of their various stakeholders, investment managers must too. Investment managers are not sacrificing the interests of their clients when they consider the impact of corporate decisions on others and on the long-term future of a company.

By recognizing the real but frequently divergent interests of a corporation's stakeholders, we gain some insights into the social responsibility issues that are increasingly being put in front of corporate managements and boards. For example, suppose I have clients who own stock in a company that is a major source of pollution. If I support proposals urging that company to accelerate its pollution control investments, I may sacrifice short- and/or long-term financial returns for my clients. If I do not support those proposals, I protect my clients' financial returns but endanger the physical safety of a wide range of stakeholders that could even include my clients. These are very thorny problems with no simple solutions.

Institutional investors are generally viewed by critics as passive or unwilling to oppose the decisions of managers and directors. They are also accused of having conflicts of interest that influence them to be supportive of management. And when institutional investors do disagree with management, they are too often accused of voting with their feet instead of using their shareholding power to influence management decisions. Of course, one reason that institutional investors can appear supportive of management is that corporate managements often talk to their institutional investors before they take certain actions. Thus, management has already had the benefit of investor input before an action is presented in a proxy statement.

Although activism may not be a typical behavior among institutional investors, many exceptions to their perceived passivity can be found. In fact, some managers buy a stock with the intention of prodding for some kind of change. But in most cases, institutional investors support the managers of the corporations in which they buy stock. After all, one of the reasons that they buy the stock is that they like the way the company is being managed and have concluded that the company's management typically acts in the best interests of the investor.

That inclination notwithstanding, investors still have a responsibility to scrutinize the actions of managers and directors, and this scrutiny is formalized through the annual proxy voting process. Investment managers should not delegate to a third party the responsibility for deciding proxy issues. They can solicit third-party input, but the responsibility of the decision should rest with investment managers. The proxy voting process should not be put on ''automatic pilot,'' and this principle applies to index fund managers as well as active managers.

Therefore, managers need to establish a proxy response system that ensures proxies are properly considered and voted. To illustrate the elements that should be included in such a system and the manner in which it should function, I think it is best to consider an actual functioning system.

T. Rowe Price Proxy Voting System

The proxy voting system at T. Rowe Price is hardly perfect, but it is well grounded in its principles (which are consistent with the firm's principles) and thorough in its processes, and it contains elements that should appear in the proxy voting system of any responsible investment firm.

Proxy Principles

The culture and governance structures at T. Rowe Price have always encouraged us to take seriously matters being considered by proxy vote. Proxy voting is a privilege and responsibility of owning stock, but because our clients nearly always delegate voting responsibility to us, the responsibility for exercising that privilege becomes ours. Nevertheless, we consider our votes in the context of our clients' interests. In fact, the most important fiduciary responsibility T. Rowe Price has during the proxy process is to vote in a manner that will enhance the investment merit of the company in question. We are unapologetically in the business of making money for our clients, so our intent is always to act in their best financial interests when we vote their shares.

We also respect and listen to management and the recommendations of a company's board of directors, but we are not afraid to oppose management if we believe our clients' interests are not being served. The difficulty is in deciding what exactly are our clients' interests because, as I have mentioned earlier, a client's interests are not determined by financial returns alone. The challenge is to make an informed judgment and then act on that judgment. Finally, we try to make our decisions in context, taking careful note of the circumstances of each company. Thus, on a common issue, we may vote one way for one company and the opposite way for another company.

Proxy Process

We have a proxy committee that oversees the proxy voting process and establishes voting guidelines for our portfolio managers. The committee consists of senior investment, operations, and legal professionals and sets guidelines independently of our firm's management. The committee solicits information from T. Rowe Price investment staff and uses third-party advisers, such as

Institutional Shareholder Services (ISS), but final judgments on guidelines are made by the committee.

Although the committee adopts voting policies on a number of corporate governance topics, it is the responsibility of each portfolio manager to make decisions on proxy issues and cast the proxy votes for each portfolio company. This is a critical element in our process, and not all firms follow this approach. Nevertheless, we believe the manager who made the decision to own a corporation's stock is the proper manager to evaluate an action planned by that corporation. As a result, T. Rowe Price will occasionally find itself voting on both sides of an issue with the same company because one portfolio manager has judged in favor of it while another portfolio manager has judged against it.

If a manager votes on an issue that differs from the committee's guidelines, he or she must provide a written rationale for that vote. After the managers submit their voting recommendations, any recommendations that are inconsistent with the committee's guidelines must be reviewed by the proxy committee. If the committee finds that the departure from the guidelines has a defensible rationale, then the recommendation is cleared.

The committee pays particular attention to conflicts of interest, whether they exist within a particular fund or asset pool or whether they affect a particular manager. Although it does not occur frequently, the most typical potential conflict occurs when T. Rowe Price owns the stock of a company that is also a client of the firm. Certainly, this is the most frequent source of criticism from outside sources, and it is one of the primary reasons that our proxy committee is entirely independent of management.

Statistical Highlights

From 2001 to 2005, T. Rowe Price voted at approximately 18,000 shareholder meetings on about 50,000 proposals. On the one hand, 86 percent of our votes were in favor of management, which can be interpreted as being strongly supportive of management. On the other hand, that same statistic indicates that we voted against management 7,000 times, which indicates a willingness to oppose management recommendations when necessary. The sheer number of proxy votes required of investment managers is one of the reasons that some investment managers turn the process into an automatic, rather than a deliberative, effort.

Voting patterns on typical issues
During 2001–2005, T. Rowe Price voted against individual directors 17 percent of the time, in favor of shareholder proposals affecting compensation 30 percent of the time, and against restraints on governance (such as staggered terms for directors, poison pills, and various antitakeover provisions) almost uniformly.

We tend to cast votes against directors when we think that they do not meet the criteria for the appropriate degree of independence (criteria that have been formalized by the U.S. SEC, NASDAQ, and the NYSE for listed companies). We will also vote against a director if we believe that director sits on too many boards because we question whether he or she can allot the time needed to do the work required. Furthermore, if directors miss more than a quarter of their board meetings, we are inclined to oppose renomination.

We vote against inside directors who are nominated for the audit, compensation, or nominating committees. Those three committees in particular ought to be populated solely with independent directors. We also tend to oppose independent directors who appear to have personal ties to a company's CEO or other top management. Finally, we oppose equity compensation proposals if the compensation is concentrated in the hands of a few executives. We are typically less concerned about the overall dilution issue that critics tend to focus on and more concerned about concentration, which leads to disproportionate compensation for a few executives.

Majority voting system preferred

We believe the majority voting system best serves the interests of all shareowners, although it is not perfect. Directors should be required to receive a majority of the shares of those that are voting. The traditional way of electing directors is not as effective as a majority vote, but we are not in favor of some of the other approaches that have been proposed, such as cumulative voting, which we believe can result in far too many special interest directors on a board.

Conclusion

I believe there are some particular lessons to be learned from recent corporate upheavals as applied to corporate governance.

1. Being a corporate director no longer means being a pal of the CEO and stopping by for lunch four or five times a year, nor does it mean that a director is now the guarantor of management behavior. We should expect professional stewardship from corporate directors, but we must also be realistic in our expectations.

2. Investors and directors should be alert to signs of management hubris. Most of the executives who violated laws or made egregious errors did not initially set out to do so. They fell victim to an arrogance that affected their judgment. Top managers who are unchecked by their boards of directors become prone

to such behavior. Directors are in the position to recognize such behavior and should act in investors' interests.

3. Longstanding business practices cannot be accepted as a defense for inept, inappropriate, or fraudulent leadership. "Our business has always operated this way" should never be an excuse. Business practices have to be examined constantly in light of a changing environment.

4. Managers, directors, and investors have to consider all stakeholders' interests when making decisions. Those interests can be prioritized, but they all have to be considered.

5. The culture and values of a corporation need to be understood. Not only does culture help explain past management behavior; it indicates the likelihood of future behavior. It particularly helps an investor to anticipate management responses under challenging circumstances, when behavior is most severely tested. This understanding entails more than just reading the chairman's annual shareholder letter. It means getting to know the managers, understanding their goals for the company, and observing what they do to achieve those goals.

6. The current scrutiny of corporate behavior is not a passing fancy. And investment managers are likely to find themselves under the same scrutiny as corporate managers.

Being an active participant in the corporate governance process is a privilege and responsibility of stock ownership. As investment professionals, we too have a duty—not to the media, not to the critics, but to our clients—to fulfill our role in this oversight process with all the diligence expected of a fiduciary.

This presentation comes from the 2006 Financial Analysts Seminar held in Evanston, Illinois, on 16–21 July 2006.

More from James S. Riepe

This section presents the speaker's lively question and answer session with the conference audience.

Question: How long does it take a portfolio manager to review a proxy?

Riepe: The time varies. A typical proxy has four questions on it. One or more of the questions may be covered by the guidelines developed by our proxy committee, so the portfolio manager can simply follow the guidelines for those questions. For the most part, managers focus on the questions that affect financial issues. That is where they put their time and effort.

Question: How many proxies, on average, does a portfolio manager address during the proxy season?

Riepe: Some of our portfolio managers have as many as 250 companies in their portfolios, so they often rely on the analysts for specific companies to help them decide how to vote. But the managers have to sign off on every proxy.

Question: Do we need legislation in the United States that requires CEOs to act in the best interests of shareowners while being mindful of the interests of other stakeholders?

Riepe: Sometimes, it takes political pressure to get things done, but regulations, particularly politically generated regulations, tend to be heavy-handed and broad and, therefore, not especially effective. I would argue that the most effective way to mold corporate behavior is for executives to see themselves and their peers on the front pages of national newspapers—and not for pleasant reasons. If that doesn't affect behavior, I don't know what will. It is probably a lot more effective than a visit from an SEC regulator.

Question: Do you follow up on the impact of your votes?

Riepe: Mutual funds have to disclose all of their proxy votes, which leads to a contradictory situation because one of the advantages of the traditional proxy process is that investors have confidentiality in their voting, thus safeguarding them from management pressure. But within 90 days of the end of the proxy season, mutual funds must now post all of their proxy votes. So, that information is available on fund websites. But based on access rates, the public seems largely unconcerned about our voting records.

Peers, however, look at our votes and can use them to gauge their own voting. Company managements also look at our votes and let us know their thinking on those votes. Typically, we do not announce how we will vote ahead of time, so we do not get lobbied to change an intended vote. Sometimes, however, if a portfolio manager feels strongly about an issue, he or she may go public in an attempt to influence the votes of other investors.

The last time such a public campaign occurred was during the run-up to the Disney vote in 2004, after which Michael Eisner was stripped of the chairmanship. At that time, a number of us institutional investors made public our intentions in order to influence other people to join us. By and large, however, portfolio managers would rather keep their votes below the radar. They don't mind management knowing, but they would rather that information not be broadcast through the media because it becomes a distraction.

Question: How do you respond to poorly performing companies?

Riepe: Any investor has a right to ask whether management is running the company effectively. If the situation is bad but investors are convinced that current management will make positive changes, they might remain an investor. But if bad management appears to be entrenched, investors can always vote with their feet. If investors feel that the company itself is sound but management needs changing, then they may stay in and use the proxy process to affect the board. They can be as aggressive in the proxy as necessary. They can use the media. They can make public statements. Some hedge funds seem more willing to take such aggressive courses than are most long-only managers. But the merit of the investment, aside from all emotion, is the primary factor in deciding whether to hold or unload a stock.

Question: Assuming that you are opposed to staggered boards, what structure do you prefer?

Riepe: I prefer annual election of all the directors. The staggering of elections, such as having different directors elected each year over a three-year period, was first used as an antitakeover strategy, and a weak strategy at that. Companies that continue to use staggered boards are just poking their fingers in their investors' eyes. It is not worth the damage they are doing to their own credibility.

Question: Do you have a view on separating the chairmanship from the CEO?

Riepe: I think that choice should be company specific. I know of no structural reason to separate or combine the two roles. The issue is currently getting a lot of media coverage on the mutual fund side because the previous head of the SEC for some reason deemed it important to mutual fund governance. But the role of the chairman can be weak or strong, depending on the company. The decision itself has cosmetic value for some but no structural value. For some companies, separating the chairmanship from the CEO is a wise thing to do; for others, it is unnecessary.

Question: Assuming that proxies have value but that some investors are indifferent to this, does a secondary market in proxies make sense? Investment managers could sell their proxies to the highest bidder and make money for their clients.

Riepe: I read of a hedge fund that took a big position in a stock, perhaps 15 percent, because it wanted to influence company management. But it really did not want a 15 percent interest in the stock, so it hedged out 10 percent, which left it with a 5 percent equity position but a 15 percent voting position. I understand that the SEC is looking into that particular incident.

In my view, separating voting power from actual ownership would be very dangerous for both corporations and their investors. So, I would oppose the idea of a secondary market for voting privileges.

Question: If T. Rowe Price manages the 401(k) and the pension fund of a company whose stock it also owns, how does it protect itself from pressure from that company?

Riepe: We never get pressure from large companies. We do, however, get occasional "friendly inquiries"—calling it pressure would be an overstatement—from smaller companies that are 401(k) clients. Every manager is put on high alert about how to handle such calls. What happens, I think, is that a CEO assumes that a mutual fund is like any other vendor, and there is no reason that he or she should not call us to try to influence our behavior. Sometimes, we will simply call the company's attorney and say, "Look, we are sure the CEO is simply uninformed, so you might just want to let him know what he can and cannot do." That usually ends the problem right away. As a side note, we have sometimes voted against the recommendations of company managements, and we have never had one leave us as a client.

Question: What percentage of a board of directors should consist of management?

Riepe: This issue is company specific. But in my experience, there is real value in having a couple of insiders at the table because independent directors are, by definition, part-time overseers. They are not immersed in company operations, so having a couple of people at the table who know the company inside and out is a positive thing. But I would say no more than two insiders are needed.

Another benefit of having two inside directors is that if one manager is speaking at a board meeting, the other manager can observe the presentation and gauge the attitudes of the other directors. So, from my perspective, two is probably the right number for most companies. I also believe that inside directors should constitute no more than 25 percent of the board.

Question: What do you look for when evaluating stock option compensation programs?

Riepe: I think current concerns about stock option compensation are leaving us with an unintended consequence. I was trained as an accountant, so I understand the expensing issues and believe that options have always been accounted for properly. Because they have been recognized on the balance sheet, aggressive option programs have been dilutive; that is their "cost." Putting a hypothetical value on them and moving them to the income statement occurred not because option programs were out of control but because of concern about executive compensation.

People were using options in an inappropriate way. I have seen proxies in which 30–40 percent of an annual program goes to only a few people in the program, and in many cases, those few people already owned large amounts of stock in the company. Yet, the option expensing proposal is presented as if it has been an accounting problem. But it is not. The problem started because of abuses in executive compensation, not because people thought such plans were too dilutive.

The other unintended consequence is that companies, as a response, are moving to restricted stock. Some investors are applauding this as a better solution. But in my view, using restricted stock makes matters worse. It deleverages management's and employees' equity interest in that company because restricted stock is going out at one share for every four or five option shares. Companies issue restricted shares with a three- or four-year vesting. It is just cash in the form of stock. It is very different from an equity option with a 10-year life for which recipients are receiving four or five times the number of options they would with restricted stock. And with options, poor stock performance can make them worthless; even if the stock price declines in value, restricted shares still have value.

So, I think it is a mistake for companies to shift everything to restricted stock as a way of getting under the "option radar." Furthermore, companies that have broad-based, egalitarian option programs are penalized because of those that had programs that enriched a few executives. The latter are the programs we oppose.

Question: What is your opinion on class-action lawsuits after stocks have had a significant decline?

Riepe: Class-action lawsuits have proven to be very good for class-action attorneys and have become a compensation strategy for the plaintiff's bar. Some of them are legitimate, but separating the legitimate from the illegitimate is a big challenge. I happen to like the English system in which the plaintiff has to put up money, and if the plaintiff loses, that money is paid out. I think that we need a mechanism to discourage frivolous class-action suits. We all have read about a law firm in New York, Milberg Weiss Bershad & Schulman LLP, with a plaintiff who has participated in more than 120 shareholder litigations. As far as I am concerned, the system is not working properly.

Question: Do you believe that the increasingly litigious nature of society as well as the growing amount of paperwork caused by well-intentioned legislation, such as Sarbanes–Oxley, have made the recruitment of directors more difficult?

Riepe: Yes. I think we are going to see a gradual deterioration in the quality of directors. One of our best directors recently resigned from three boards because his lawyer warned him that his entire net worth was at risk. The worse the excesses, the worse the corrections. The pendulum always moves symmetrically, too far in both directions.

Recently, we complained to U.S. Senator Paul S. Sarbanes (D, MD) that the requirements of Sarbanes–Oxley were costing hundreds of millions of dollars. Accountants, lawyers, and managers are spending far too much time and effort trying to guarantee that they do nothing to violate any aspect of Sarbanes–Oxley. It is like wearing a belt and suspenders and having someone hold up your pants all at the same time.

But nothing is going to happen to Sarbanes–Oxley until Senator Sarbanes leaves the Senate at the end of 2006. Perhaps after that, some rational heads will modify the legislation to make it more reasonable, keeping the good parts and removing the worthless, bureaucratic requirements. But anything that appears to weaken disclosure or controls will be attacked in the media, and that puts pressure on the politicians, so I am not optimistic that conditions will improve any time soon.

Question: If a group of unit holders, perhaps members of a not-for-profit organization or an activist religious denomination, wanted to vote their own proxies, would you transfer your proxy votes back to them even if they intended to take a position with which you did not agree?

Riepe: Yes. If they want to vote their own proxies, we give the proxies to them. That is why I made a point of differentiating between the share*owner* who actually owns the shares and the share*holder* who, like a mutual fund customer, invests in the fund and not directly in the stock. Occasionally, a social responsibility issue will catch our not-for-profit clients' attention, and they will ask us to vote a certain way. That is their call. If the item of concern is an investment issue, we will advise them about our preferences from a financial perspective, but if they own the shares, the proxy is theirs.

Question: Can you name a few research firms that specialize in providing investors and portfolio managers with a screening system to assess how a corporation is doing in regards to corporate governance? What do you think of their quality?

Riepe: We work closely with several such organizations, including ISS and Glass, Lewis & Co., but I often find their methods to be too formulaic. For example, ISS voted against my firm's option program because the "overhang" of unexercised options was too high a percentage. We told them they should be looking at the annual dilution, the burn rate, not the overhang. Our overhang is high because our employees stay with us a long time and usually do not exercise options until they get to the end of the 10-year term. That to me sounds like a good situation because it demonstrates that our key people want to own equity.

The response from ISS was that because they evaluate so many thousands of companies, they have to use formulas, and sometimes their formulas have unintended consequences. I am, therefore, skeptical of governance rating systems, although I should add that T. Rowe Price gets very high ratings.

Each company has its own characteristics, and formulas can miss important details. For example, a company might receive a high rating for its board of directors because its chairman is separate from the CEO and 90 percent of its directors are independent. But if the directors do a poor job, whether they are independent or not is of little importance. As I indicated earlier, structural solutions are not necessarily good solutions. Consider Enron Corporation as an especially egregious example. For a dozen years or so, the head of the audit committee was the head of a major accounting department in a big university. On paper, this seemed like a good thing, but as we all know, the results were not good at all. Each company must be examined according to its particular circumstances.

ECONOMICS

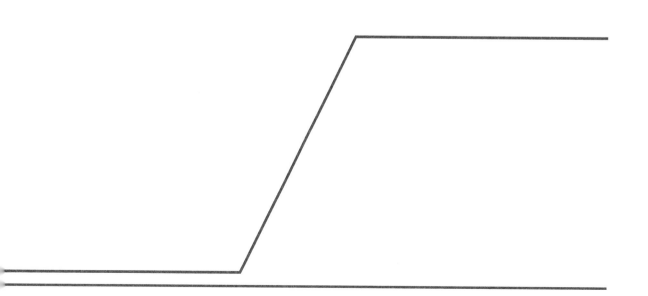

The Virtues of Flexible Financial Markets: A Central Banking Perspective

PHILIPP M. HILDEBRAND

In recent years, global financial markets have evolved (and grown) remarkably. But the recent evolution of financial markets has meant that *new* participants in *new* markets have access to *new* products that allow them to save, invest, share and transfer risk, and finance trade to a much greater extent than ever before in history. All this change, however, does not come without risk.

By virtue of implementing monetary policy, central banks are active financial market participants. In the case of the Swiss National Bank, market operations extend beyond the implementation of monetary policy. Our National Bank Act mandates that we manage our currency reserves in accordance with the principles of modern asset management. New developments in financial markets, therefore, directly affect us as an active market participant. Moreover, the Swiss National Bank is required by law to contribute to financial stability. It thus has a strong incentive to try to gain an understanding of the rapid evolution of financial markets to the extent that this evolution influences the outlook for financial stability.

In this presentation, I will first discuss the remarkable evolution of global financial markets in recent years. I will then focus on the virtues of flexible financial markets. In closing, I will make some tentative suggestions about some of the potential risks associated with modern financial markets.

> The potential Achilles' heel [in our financial system] is the risk management systems and processes of the 12 most important investment banks.

Evolution of Global Financial Markets

Global financial markets have grown dramatically over the past three decades. According to recently published data, the total value of the global financial

Philipp M. Hildebrand is a member of the governing board of the Swiss National Bank, Zurich.

Figure 1   Global Financial Stock as a Percentage of GDP

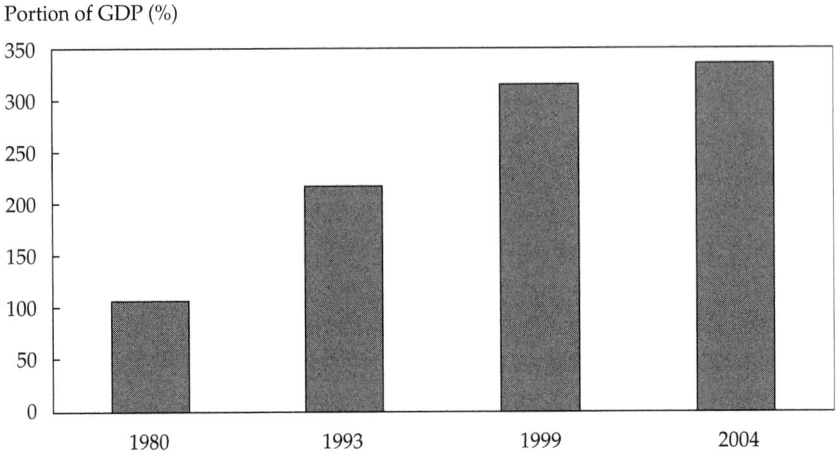

Portion of GDP (%)

Note: Financial stock includes equity, private and government debt, and bank deposits.
Source: Based on McKinsey & Company (2006).

stock—including bank deposits, government and private debt securities, and equities—has increased more than tenfold, from US$12 trillion in 1980 to US$136 trillion in 2004.[1] This represents more than three times the value of current global GDP. As illustrated in **Figure 1**, the ratio of the global financial stock to GDP has tripled since 1980. Rapid technological change and market liberalization are the two forces that have been instrumental in driving the remarkable evolution of global financial markets during the past quarter of a century.

Technological change has several facets. The use of new technologies has enhanced product innovation. It has also facilitated and lent support to breakthroughs in our understanding of the theoretical foundations of financial markets. Finally, technological change has vastly improved our ability to disseminate information, which, in turn, has revolutionized the way financial markets function.

In parallel, a series of political choices reshaped many of the fundamental organizing principles of global financial markets and the world economy. President Reagan in the United States, Prime Minister Thatcher in the United Kingdom, the push toward the Single European Act in the European Union, and of course, the collapse of the Soviet Union—all provided crucial political momentum for market liberalization and deregulation in the 1980s. Governments and legislative bodies throughout the developed world gradually but increasingly committed themselves to free and open financial markets. Finally, as a corollary of a growing commitment to market forces in the developed

---

[1] See also McKinsey & Company (2005, 2006). These data do not include real estate.

world, the so-called Washington Consensus on the benefits of capital account liberalization began to shape economic policy debates in favor of liberalization and deregulation in many of the key emerging economies.

The consequences of rapid technological change and increasing political momentum toward liberalization and deregulation of capital markets have been far reaching. They relate to geography, products, and market participants. Let me briefly touch upon each of these three dimensions.

Geography

We are likely still at the beginning of a geographical rearrangement of global capital markets. The four most important financial markets—the United States, the Euro zone, Japan, and the United Kingdom—currently account for more than 80 percent of the global financial stock. But the financial stock of regions with currently much smaller shares, such as China and Eastern Europe, is growing rapidly. Their average annual growth rates for the period from 1993 to 2003 amounted to 14.5 percent and 19.3 percent, respectively, compared with 8.4 percent for the global financial stock. Another indicator of the ongoing geographical shift in global financial markets is the evolution and distribution of countries' currency reserves. **Table 1** illustrates that in 1980, the 10 largest reserve holders were all developed nations. Today, 8 of the 10 largest holders are Asian emerging economies.[2]

The developed economies still account for the bulk of the world's financial stock. Equally, capital flows between developed economies account for the overwhelming majority of total flows. Nonetheless, as the currency reserve numbers indicate, change in the geographical makeup of the world's financial markets is under way and may have important repercussions in terms of how the global economy functions as well as what kind of financial architecture is required to manage it (see Summers 2006).

Products

Beyond geography, capital market liberalization and technological progress have deeply affected the evolution of financial products. New types of products, such as asset-backed and mortgage-backed securities and collateralized debt obligations, have been established and are used successfully. In addition, a variety of derivatives products are used in the management of a wide range of risks.

The striking evolution of derivatives products provides a sense of the extent to which product innovation has been a force in recent years. According to statistics from the Bank for International Settlements, the value of the assets underlying exchange-traded derivatives increased at an annual rate of more

---

[2] These figures on foreign exchange reserves do not include gold.

Table 1 Foreign Exchange Reserves

Rank	Country	Reserves (billions)
1980		
1	Germany	US$44.5
2	France	25.3
3	Italy	21.6
4	Japan	21.6
5	Saudi Arabia	20.8
6	United Kingdom	18.8
7	Switzerland	15.3
8	Libya	12.8
9	Spain	11.3
10	Netherlands	10.4
Total		US$202.4
2005		
1	Japan	US$829
2	China	819
3	Taiwan	253
4	South Korea	210
5	Russia	176
6	India	131
7	Hong Kong	124
8	Singapore	115
9	Mexico	73
10	Malaysia	70
Total		US$2,800

Sources: National sources and IMF.

than 25 percent over the past two decades to reach about US$58 trillion in 2005 (BIS 2006). The value of the assets underlying OTC derivatives attained approximately US$270 trillion, more than six times the amount of global GDP.

Even more impressive is the outright explosion currently occurring in the market for structured credit derivatives. The value of outstanding credit derivatives contracts has more than quadrupled over the past two years to reach an estimated US$17 trillion at the end of 2005 (IMF 2006). It now exceeds the stock of corporate bonds and loans. The market for credit derivatives has overtaken the market for commodity derivatives and has reached approximately the size of the market for equity derivatives. Most of the recent growth has occurred in the area of the most complex products, such as credit default swaps. Collateralized debt obligations, which synthetically package derivatives to adjust credit exposure, have also grown rapidly in recent years.

Market Participants

Global capital market liberalization has also had a profound effect on the nature and composition of financial market participants. The forces of increasingly liberalized and global financial markets have blurred many of the distinctions between traditional categories of financial firms. In many countries, notably in the Anglo-Saxon world, capital needs are increasingly financed through capital market operations, at the expense of traditional lending from the banking sector. Moreover, in many industrialized countries, savings and investments are increasingly made via "new" intermediaries, such as insurance companies, pension funds, and other investment vehicles (e.g., mutual funds, private equity partnerships, and hedge funds). Let me illustrate these developments with a few statistics.

During the past decade, the hedge fund industry grew in size at an annual pace of 20 percent. Currently, an estimated 10,000 hedge funds manage assets in excess of US$1.2 trillion. The global private equity market is estimated to be around US$2.5 trillion and made up of roughly 8,000 funds. Institutional investors, including insurance companies, pension funds, and investment companies, have also recorded significant increases in their assets. Assets under management by global institutional investors nearly doubled between 1995 and 2003 to reach US$47 trillion (IMF 2005). Investment companies grew more than three times as fast as insurance companies. Pension funds have also grown dramatically in recent years. They now constitute the largest institutional investor category in the Organization for Economic Cooperation and Development (OECD) and manage assets amounting to more than 40 percent of world GDP. Indeed, in such countries as Switzerland and the Netherlands, total assets managed by pension funds exceed 100 percent of GDP, as can be seen in **Figure 2**. Pension funds in the Euro zone hold nearly 40 percent of the long-term government bonds outstanding. In light of these numbers, it is not surprising that a title in the Geneva Report on the World Economy series refers to pension funds as the "new giants" (Boeri, Bovenberg, Coeuré, and Roberts 2006).[3]

In summary, the effects of increasingly liberalized global financial markets have been far reaching, integrating new regions, driving financial product innovation, and deeply affecting the financial landscape in terms of market participants. As a result, the depth and flexibility of global financial markets have increased dramatically since the beginning of the liberalization process of financial markets.

---

[3] For the effects of pension funds on monetary policy, see the recent speech by Lorenzo Bini Smaghi, "The Growth of Pension Funds and Financial Markets: Implications for Central Banks," 4 May 2006 (available at http://www.ecb.int/press/key/date/2006/html/sp060508.en.html).

Figure 2   Pension Fund Assets as a Percentage of GDP, 2004

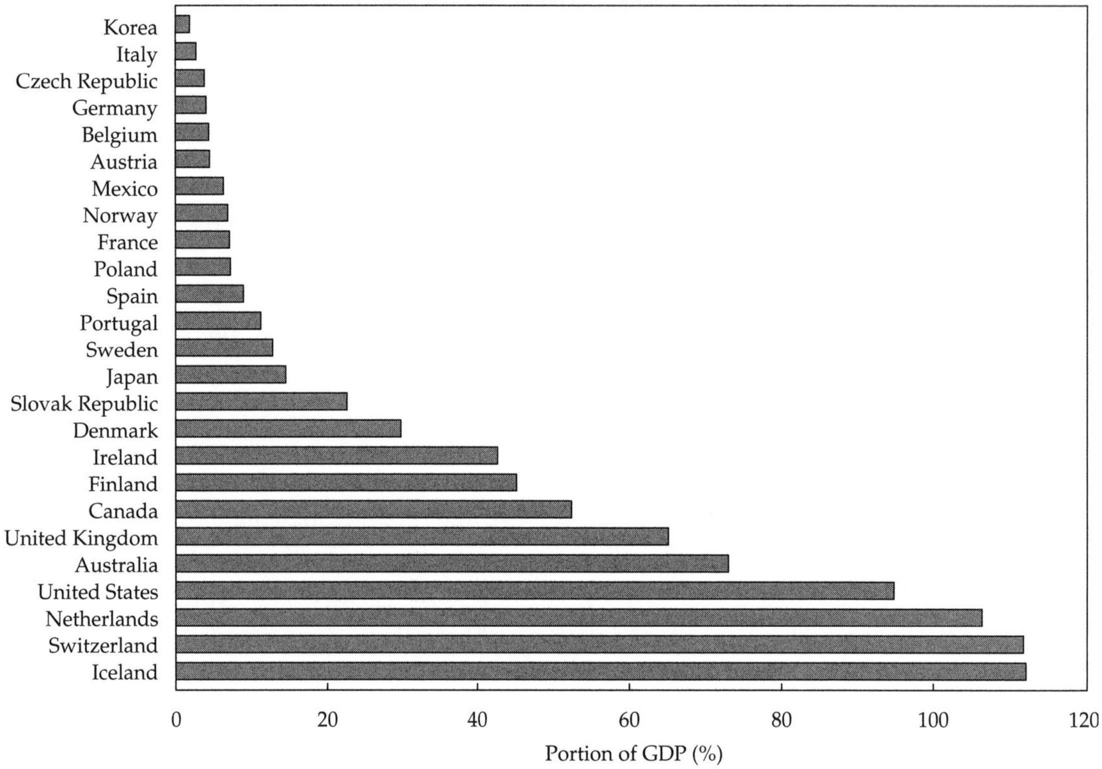

Bar chart showing Portion of GDP (%) for each country:

- Korea
- Italy
- Czech Republic
- Germany
- Belgium
- Austria
- Mexico
- Norway
- France
- Poland
- Spain
- Portugal
- Sweden
- Japan
- Slovak Republic
- Denmark
- Ireland
- Finland
- Canada
- United Kingdom
- Australia
- United States
- Netherlands
- Switzerland
- Iceland

X-axis: Portion of GDP (%), 0 to 120

Source: Based on OECD (2005).

Virtues of Flexible Financial Markets

Let me turn now to the benefits of flexible financial markets. Broadly speaking, financial markets have three functions. First, they facilitate the accumulation of capital by transforming short-term savings into long-term investment. Viewed from a saver's perspective, financial markets make it possible to decouple income from consumption and, therefore, to smooth consumption over the life cycle. Viewed from a producer's perspective, financial markets provide access to capital and allow for large-scale and efficient production of goods, which enhances prosperity.

The second function of financial markets is to facilitate the transfer of risk. Financial markets allow participants to diversify, insure, and hedge risk: Investors can diversify the risk they are able and willing to bear and thus decrease their overall risk. Individuals and corporations can insure themselves against a wide range of adversities and risks, from personal disability to natural disasters. Producers can hedge against future price changes in input factors and in their future production, thus reducing inherent business risk.

The third function of financial markets is to facilitate the financing of trade. Trade, and in particular international trade, is heavily dependent on well-functioning financial markets. Financial markets ensure mutual payment and allow for the bridging of temporary trade imbalances. In the absence of financial markets, exports would always have to equal imports because there would be no way of transferring a country's aggregate claims or obligations into the future. In effect, it would be impossible to run trade surpluses or deficits, which allow a country to smooth its aggregate consumption.

Financial markets have, of course, existed for centuries, if not millennia, and their functions are by no means new. But the recent evolution of financial markets has meant that the benefits associated with the traditional functions of financial markets have undergone a quantum leap. The point is this: *New* participants in *new* markets have access to *new* products that allow them to save, invest, share and transfer risk, and finance trade to a much greater extent than ever before in history. Let me now be more specific about the benefits associated with these remarkable, recent financial market developments.

Allocative Efficiency

Perhaps most importantly, financial markets have become much more efficient in allocating capital in the past 30 years. Standardization, high turnover, and diminishing marginal costs, together with new information technologies, have strongly reduced the cost of accessing financial markets. Nowadays, financial capital can easily be deployed to places where its return is highest (i.e., where it is most needed and, therefore, most efficient). Capital is hunting investment opportunities in distant corners of the world or is financing young entrepreneurs' ideas that would have been untapped only some decades ago.

Enhanced Risk Management

The emergence of new innovative products has meant that risk can now be intermediated to a much greater extent than ever before. Every imaginable kind of risk is now routinely deconstructed, reassembled, and then transferred to those who are willing to bear these risks at the lowest cost. In other words, virtually every type of need can be catered to in terms of product design. These innovative products ultimately make it possible to redistribute existing risks such that the risk borne by each individual is significantly reduced.

Liquefied Assets

New financial market instruments have liquefied previously illiquid assets. Think of mortgages and loans, which can now be pooled, securitized, and traded as asset-backed securities. There are several benefits of this evolution.

Banks' balance sheets are freed up so that they can assume other and more profitable risks. This allows banks to develop new products, which in turn, allow prospective home owners to get easier and cheaper access to mortgage loans. Current home owners profit by being able to extract equity from their houses in order to smooth consumption over their lifetimes. Furthermore, higher liquidity reduces the illiquidity risk and thus decreases the risk premium. Although the liquefaction of mortgages and other loans is already highly advanced in the United States, this trend is still in its infancy in continental Europe. In the years to come, I expect further innovation in this area in Europe. Augmented possibilities in the area of equity extraction in Europe's housing market presumably have the potential to boost domestic consumption and thereby contribute to global rebalancing.

Transparency and Market Efficiency

New financial instruments have increased market transparency by providing an efficient and timely price discovery process for many assets and risks that were, in the past, simply not priced by markets. Thus, financial markets now gather and process more information, better evaluate and monitor firms and managers, and should thus also exert more control on corporate governance. An increase in transparency reduces problems of asymmetric information, such as moral hazard and adverse selection inherent in most financial transactions, and may, therefore, have played a role in the reduction of risk and a corresponding compression of risk premiums in recent years. Along with heightened transparency, one would also expect a higher degree of market efficiency, to the extent that assets are now more accurately priced. New information technologies allow more diverse opinions to be expressed in the marketplace, which should, in turn, result in asset pricing that is more in line with fundamentals.

Higher Economic Growth

Improved allocation of capital, better risk sharing, more liquid assets, and more transparency are all possible channels through which economic growth is enhanced. The knowledge on the finance–growth nexus is admittedly still incomplete. Nonetheless, there is strong empirical evidence that greater activity in the financial sector enhances the performance of the economy as a whole (see, for example, King and Levine 1993; Levine 2005). The current rapid pace of innovation and strong economic growth in most parts of the world can, therefore, at least partly be attributed to rapidly growing financial markets. **Figure** 3 illustrates a strong relationship between income and financial depth. Clearly, this relationship is no proof of causality. Nonetheless, it is intriguing to observe how closely financial and economic evolution appear to be related.

Figure 3 Financial Stock as a Percentage of GDP vs. GDP per Capita, 2004

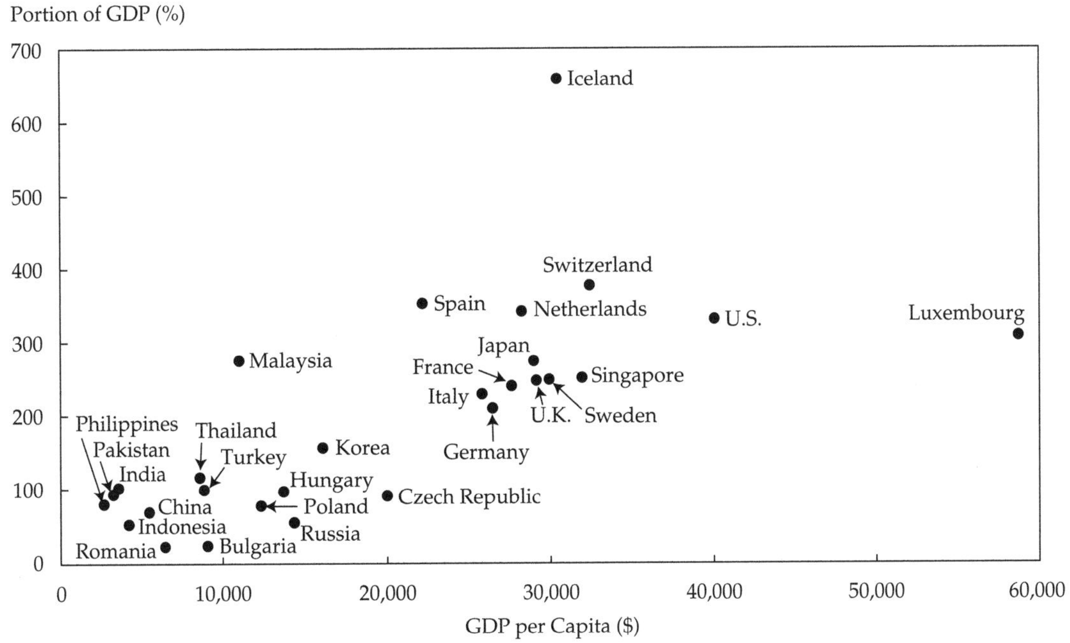

Portion of GDP (%)

Note: GDP per capita is based on purchasing power parity.
Source: Based on McKinsey & Company (2006).

Network Externalities

The actual benefits provided by financial markets are arguably growing even faster than the growth of financial markets would suggest. This is because financial markets exhibit network externalities. In other words, the access of new participants benefits not only new participants but also all participants because every new participant is a potential counterpart for all existing participants and thus increases market liquidity for all participants.

Higher Resilience to Shocks

Finally, more flexible financial markets have likely made economies more resilient to shocks. The more flexible that financial markets are, and the more that risks are diversified, the more our financial markets will be able to absorb these shocks and the less severe the impact of such shocks will be on the real side. In this context, let me ask a simple question: How many people would have predicted in the spring of 1997 that the U.S. economy would go through the Asian crisis, the Russian default, the Long-Term Capital Management (LTCM) crisis, the bursting of the internet bubble, the corporate governance scandals, the terrorist attacks of September 11, the wars in Afghanistan and Iraq, and a near quadrupling of the oil price without any discernable disruptive impact on the growth performance of the economy? Of course, we cannot know for sure, but the flexibility of financial markets likely played an important role in making the U.S. economy as resilient as it has proven to be during the past decade.

Conclusion

So far, the story is an excellent one. But central bankers are paid to worry even in good times. Let me, therefore, conclude these reflections on the virtues of flexible financial markets with some brief comments about the potential risks associated with modern financial markets. For central banks with responsibilities to promote or contribute to financial stability, these risks are particularly relevant.

Given the growing significance of global financial markets, the economic consequences of a major financial crisis could obviously be severe. Moreover, the dramatic efficiency gains in financial markets also mean that modern financial markets are potentially capable of transmitting a regional financial crisis rapidly throughout the global financial system. In other words, through contagion effects, modern financial markets could themselves become a potential source of systemic risk.

A second concern that preoccupies many central banks is the liquidity risk associated with the fact that market participants assume that financial instruments behave in particular ways with respect to their price and liquidity dynamics. In reality, we know that our genuine understanding of the price and liquidity dynamics of increasingly complex and sophisticated financial instruments can only become more accurate through the effects of time and experience and to the extent that we are able to monitor the behavior of these instruments under different economic and market conditions. As a result, we face the risk that fat-tail events not sufficiently captured by risk management models could cause an unexpected drying up of market liquidity. Such sudden shortages of liquidity could have serious repercussions in a heavily securitized market where credit risk is managed on the premise that liquidity is available and securities can be traded readily.

Other risks are associated with modern financial markets. They range from infrastructure and settlement risks associated with some of the new instruments to the potential links between new market participants and extreme levels of price fluctuation and market volatility. One thing many of these risks have in common is that they elicit calls for increasingly far-reaching regulation of financial markets. Although some regulation may indeed be required to guarantee the integrity of financial markets, the threshold for such regulation should be set high.

Let me finish with two simple criteria that might guide us in determining whether new regulation should be considered as a response to the rapid evolution of global financial markets. To my knowledge, former U.S. Federal Reserve Board Chairman Alan Greenspan first elaborated these criteria in 1997.[4] Arguably, they have lost nothing of their relevance nine years later. First, we should be clear about the objective of any new regulation. Are we trying to protect retail investors? Are we trying to minimize systemic risk, or are we trying to avoid fraudulent behavior on the part of market participants? Once we are able to agree on a clear objective for any new piece of regulation, we should consider actual regulation only if there is overwhelming evidence that market participants lack the incentives or the capability to adequately manage potential new risks associated with financial innovation.

By applying this yardstick, I suspect we will find that, in many cases, new regulation will not be an adequate response to innovation in financial markets. Indeed, additional regulation will often risk stifling the kind of innovation that has proven so beneficial in recent years. Rather than seeking regulation, market participants, central banks, and regulators should focus on strengthening an already active dialogue with the aim of furthering our understanding of new types of risk associated with modern financial markets. As I have argued elsewhere, a focal point should be the risk management systems and processes of the world's largest and most complex financial firms.[5] The better these firms understand and effectively manage and control their risks, the more we will be able to enjoy the benefits of modern financial markets while minimizing their potential adverse effects. The lessons of the recent past are encouraging. Global financial markets have proven to be remarkably resilient in their ability to absorb large shocks and thereby minimize their effects on the real economy. At the same time, the evidence of recent years is no guarantee for a benign future.

An important contribution central banks can make to help preserve the virtues of flexible financial markets is to remain firmly committed to maintaining price stability. Ultimately, financial markets are shaped by market participants. By setting high standards of professionalism for current and future generations of financial market participants, CFA Institute makes an important contribution to preserving the integrity and thus the flexibility of financial markets.

This presentation comes from the 2006 CFA Institute Annual Conference held in Zurich on 21–24 May 2006.
Author's note: I would like to thank Caesar Lack and Nicole Brändle for their valuable inputs.

---

[4] See Remarks by Chairman Alan Greenspan, "Government Regulation and Derivative Contracts," 21 February 1997 (available at http://www.federalreserve.gov/Boarddocs/speeches/1997/19970221.htm).

[5] See speech by Philipp M. Hildebrand, "Finanzmarktstabilität und Hedge Funds: wirksame und unwirksame Überwachungsansätze," 9 November 2005 (available at http://www.snb.ch/d/download/referate/ref_051109_pmh.pdf).

References

BIS. 2006. "BIS Quarterly Review." Basel, Switzerland: Bank for International Settlements (March).

Boeri, Tito, A. Lans Bovenberg, Benoît Coeuré, and Andrew W. Roberts. 2006. *Dealing with the New Giants: Rethinking the Role of Pension Funds.* London: Center for Economic Policy Research.

IMF. 2005. "Global Financial Stability Report." International Monetary Fund (September).

———. 2006. "Global Financial Stability Report." International Monetary Fund (April).

King, Robert G., and Ross Levine. 1993. "Finance and Growth: Schumpeter Might Be Right." *Quarterly Journal of Economics*, vol. 108, no. 3 (August):717–737.

Levine, Ross. 2005. "Finance and Growth: Theory and Evidence." In *Handbook of Economic Growth.* Edited by Phillipe Aghion and Steven Durlauf. Amsterdam: Elsevier.

McKinsey & Company. 2005. "$118 Trillion and Counting: Taking Stock of the World's Capital Markets" (February).

———. 2006. "Mapping the Global Capital Market 2006, Second Annual Report" (January).

OECD. 2005. "Pension Markets in Focus." Organization for Economic Cooperation and Development (June).

Summers, Lawrence H. 2006. "Reflections on Global Account Imbalances and Emerging Markets Reserve Accumulation." L.K. Jha Memorial Lecture, Reserve Bank of India, Mumbai (March).

More from Philipp M. Hildebrand

This section presents the speaker's lively question and answer session with the conference audience.

Question: A lot of risk management talk right now at the highest levels of academics is moving away from the typical statistical kind of analysis to the notion of a risk culture. Do the proper risk cultures exist within the financial organizations with whom the central banks of the world work?

Hildebrand: I tried to indicate in my comments some of the problems associated with model-based risk management. It always reminds me of a story. An old friend and former partner of LTCM once told me everything was fine until all correlations went to 1. That has stuck in my head as the best expression on the limitations of models.

Of course, that doesn't mean we should ignore models. On the contrary, I think we should continue to work hard to develop and improve our models. But beyond relying on models, we need to focus on risk culture. It is not easy for a central banker to talk about "soft" things like culture and ethics and so forth. And it may be hard to pin down exactly what we mean, but I think we intuitively know what it is all about.

One of the crucial elements for an effective risk culture, especially for the largest financial firms, is to make sure that risk is managed at the top level. That is, risk is something that not only the CEO or the executive board should be intensively involved with but also presumably the supervisory board. The notion that risk can be left to the chief risk officer and his or her staff is really one of the most flawed assumptions.

Some of the experiences around LTCM have caused firms to restructure the way they manage risk—not in terms of models but in terms of processes inside the management structure. That's why whenever I talk about risk, I emphasize that it is not just risk management; it is also risk management processes. The top level of management needs to focus on risk management because only then can you put risk in serious competition against the profit motive, which in good times will always tend to favor more risk. If the risk side is inferior in the management structure, you will always have an asymmetry problem between the profit motive and the risk motive. That needs to be addressed through the way a firm structures management, and if that's what is meant by a risk culture, then I think the answer is yes.

Of course, the people who look at risk need to be properly trained and educated. Otherwise, all the right processes will not help you. It is a combination of models, highly competent staff, and perhaps most importantly, the right processes inside these large organizations.

Question: How are central banks prepared to deal with another problem in the derivatives area?

Hildebrand: For one thing, we (and when I say "we," I mean the community of central banks that is coordinated through the Bank of International Settlements) have invested a lot of time and resources in trying to understand the implications of both the nature of the instruments and their size in the financial markets.

In addition, we have focused on understanding the way that the largest financial firms manage their own risks. The potential Achilles' heel is the risk management systems and processes of the 12 most important investment banks. The advantage we have in this domain is that we are dealing with a limited number of firms that really matter in this context. So, we can address in a focused way the concerns we have.

Furthermore, we've spent a lot of time, but probably are still in the early stages of, thinking about how to manage a liquidity crisis where several central banks are involved. The notion that a major liquidity crisis would be contained to one country, and thus to the domain of one central bank, is probably flawed.

Question: Aren't the regulators and central banks fostering a moral hazard by, in effect, declaring the largest financial institutions to be too big to fail?

Hildebrand: Central bankers, hopefully, are reasonably competent and ideally reasonably smart people. So, I would be highly skeptical about any set of individuals, let alone any small set of individuals, substituting themselves for market judgment. It is an issue that needs to be approached with great care.

To address some of the concerns with regard to lending of last resort, at the Swiss National Bank, we have moved from a system of creative ambiguity to constructive clarity to make it clear that lending of last resort will occur only under certain circumstances to try to minimize the potential problem of moral hazard.

Question: Is there a single greatest risk to global financial stability?

Hildebrand: The greatest risk is probably unknown because all big crises are seldom like the previous ones. For all of us who were active during the financial crisis in the late 1990s (the Asian crisis), one of the things we learned was that you don't get replays in this area. So, no matter what you think you've learned, the next crisis will likely be different from what you had anticipated. Therefore, it is quite hard to make a prediction here.

If what you're really asking me is what's my biggest concern, I would say that we need to fully understand what happens when liquidity disappears. For example, trying to trade Treasury bonds and finding that, although there are prices on the screens, you really can't trade them (the 1998 situation) is the kind of scenario that I worry most about. In particular, this scenario is worrisome given the fact that many of these modern instruments that have proven to be so beneficial are premised on the notion that liquidity is available and that these securitized instruments can be traded. So, my personal biggest concern is that we need to do a lot of work learning under what circumstances liquidity could dry up and what that would mean for the global financial system.

Question: Because of the Sarbanes–Oxley Act of 2002 (SOX), are U.S. companies better prepared to deal with risk relative to their global peers who are not subject to SOX?

Hildebrand: The United States encountered some exceptional events, and so did the financial markets as a whole. A lot of these problems had very little to do with systemic risk or liquidity but, rather, ultimately with fraud and criminal behavior. I'm not sure that any piece of regulation can really prevent criminal activity and behavior. So, the first thing we need to think about is whether regulation is even the right instrument to address these types of issues.

But given the magnitude of some of the events that occurred, it is not entirely surprising to see a fairly ferocious regulatory response. The U.S. system has always proven to be flexible, and to the extent that the "cure" does overshoot, perhaps being too all encompassing in terms of regulatory ambitions, there will be a counter movement in time to try to rectify this situation, partly premised on the recognition that no matter how hard you try, you cannot entirely cover all fraudulent and criminal behavior through extensive regulations that may then actually begin to undermine the overall efficiency of financial markets.

Question: What about the regulation of hedge funds?

Hildebrand: I think there's two dimensions. The first is to try to focus on understanding the instruments. Again, I think we've made some good progress here in recent years with various dialogues between the central banking community and the hedge funds.

Hedge funds have been an important source of innovation. And in this case, we're probably talking about a very small number of the largest investment banks that have a grasp of their risk management processes, mechanisms, models, and so forth with regard to their interactions with hedge funds. So, any focus by regulatory authorities or central banks should be on that element (in other words, on the link between large investment banks and hedge funds). Any additional efforts that may be appealing to the public or the media just draw away valuable and scarce regulatory resources from the key area.

The other dimension is the question of retail customer protection. There may be some need here for regulation to the extent that hedge funds are increasingly becoming a tool that's available to retail investors. Regulatory authorities may want to look at that area, but that has nothing to do with the issue of financial stability.

Question: Do you take gold into your views on inflation?

Hildebrand: You can't look at gold by itself. You need to look at the entire movement that we've seen in commodity markets. The question of whether it is an indication of inflation expectations can be answered for the moment with a no. If you look carefully at the relationship between some of the price movements in commodities and gold and inflation expectations, you realize that certainly for the time being, there is no clear link between any significant deterioration of inflation expectations and the price movements in gold.

How Central Bank Policies Affect Global Economies and Markets

The world is more interconnected now than ever before, and as a result, central bank policy affects not only the country's domestic economy but also the economies of other nations. To have an edge in this environment, investment professionals need to pay attention to global (not just U.S. or even European) central bank policies with an eye, in particular, on Japan, China, and India.

Investment professionals are always looking for ways to improve performance for their clients. To this end, they need to recognize that the policies of one central bank can have unintended and surprising consequences globally. A good example of such interconnections can be seen in the Japanese carry trade.

> In the emerging post-Greenspan world, low long-term rates in the United States also reflect to some degree currency manipulation by Japan and China.... The world is clearly interrelated as never before.

Japanese Carry Trade

From a central bank perspective, the most important thing in the world at this moment may not be what the U.S. Federal Reserve (Fed) and its new chairman do next; the most important thing may have already occurred. That is, after six years of a zero interest rate policy, the Bank of Japan just raised its rate by 0.25 percentage points, marking the beginning of the end of the Japanese carry trade.

The Japanese carry trade has had an enormous global impact. In my opinion, the increased correlation between global equity and bond markets has, to a major extent, been caused by the Japanese carry trade. Many hedge funds and other large institutional investors have been borrowing money at a zero short-term interest rate in Japan and moving it to other financial and

---

David M. Jones is president and CEO of DMJ Advisors, LLC, Denver.

commodity markets in the world in search of a higher return, and they have been perfectly willing to absorb the currency risk. Such behavior, I believe, has contributed importantly to our new, highly speculative world financial and commodity markets. In particular, the Japanese carry trade has affected the behavior of U.S. long-term interest rates and helped finance speculation in the oil market as well as in global markets for other commodities.

Conundrum Explained

Former Fed Chairman Alan Greenspan puzzled over the behavior of long-term interest rates. The conundrum, as he put it, was why, after 14 Fed rate hikes, were long-term interest rates as low as they were? Many explanations were advanced—low inflation expectations; a global savings glut; a lessening in home bias, meaning that instead of going mainly into domestic investment, savings in Europe and Asia came into the United States and thus helped to keep long-term interest rates low. But an additional significant factor in that conundrum of low U.S. long-term rates was the Japanese carry trade. One can now see that any central bank with a policy as easy as Japan's would motivate major investors to borrow at zero short-term interest rates and seek higher returns by investing in stocks, bonds, commodities, and other assets around the world.

In the emerging post-Greenspan world, low long-term rates in the United States also reflect to some degree currency manipulation by Japan and China. In an effort to keep their currencies from appreciating and hurting their exports, these countries are accumulating huge dollar reserves. Such moves, in turn, keep money flowing into U.S. dollar investments. The world is clearly interrelated as never before.

Oil and Speculation

Consider oil for a moment. In my view, a substantial amount of the recent increase in oil price is a result of the speculative behavior financed, in part, by the Japanese carry trade. I recognize that this is a controversial assertion, but I believe that if oil is trading at $78 a barrel, perhaps as much as $30 of that elevated oil price is caused by speculation as well as, of course, worries about the global supply effects of a Middle East crisis. An end to speculation and a lessening in global tensions (notwithstanding a slowdown in the world's economies) could thus lead to a decline in the crude oil price to as low as $48 a barrel by mid- to late 2007. For portfolio managers, two lessons should be learned from this situation. First, seemingly unrelated events (such as the Bank of Japan's monetary policy and the surging price of oil) can, in fact, be more closely related than one might think. Second, just because global, financial, and commodity markets are behaving a certain way now does not mean that relationships will not change.

Fed Monetary Policy Transmission

The starting point of the U.S. monetary policy process is the Federal Open Market Committee (FOMC)—see Appendix A for more detail. Based on the votes of the seven members of the Board of Governors of the Federal Reserve and five voting Federal Reserve Bank presidents, the FOMC sets a federal funds rate target. The first sector that has traditionally been affected by a Fed policy change is the banking system. In the past, policy changes would manifest themselves through their effects on bank reserves, which are either held at the Fed or held internally in vault cash accounts. Typically, a tightening in bank reserve pressures has reflected an increase in the ratio of borrowed reserves to total bank reserves. This ratio change is caused by a banking tradition against borrowing at the Fed discount window out of concern that it will be viewed as a symptom of the borrowing bank's financial weakness. Since January 2003, however, the discount rate has been linked directly to the federal funds rate, and this ratio effect is not quite as pronounced as it used to be.

In moving beyond the banking system, one has to ask, What percentage of total credit extended to businesses and consumers does the banking system account for today? The answer is only about 25 percent. Therefore, the capital markets, which extend the other 75 percent of total credit (in the form of, for example, mortgage-backed securities), are the next and more important part of the transmission process.

Another area affected by monetary policy is credit spreads. Like interest rates, credit spreads are behaving in a somewhat atypical manner, being narrower than many would expect at this point, following a prolonged series of Fed tightening moves. Moreover, I believe the primary explanation for the behavior of credit spreads is the same as that for abnormally low levels of long-term interest rates (i.e., carry trades). As hedge funds and other large institutional investors borrow at a zero interest rate in Japan and lend around the world, credit spreads are being kept narrower than would otherwise be the case. Finally, having drilled this far down into the monetary policy transmission mechanism, it is not hard to understand that these effects would be felt in the stock and currency markets.

The Fed also keeps a close eye on aggregate demand, which is the total of consumer spending, business fixed investment, residual fixed investment, government spending, and net exports. If the Fed has injected too much liquidity into the economy, it will manifest itself through the interest-rate-sensitive sectors of aggregate demand, such as housing, automobiles, and durable goods. As a rule, if these sectors are growing too fast, the Fed has pumped too much liquidity into the economy.

After aggregate demand, the monetary policy transmission mechanism affects the ultimate economic indicator, real GDP (the output of all goods and services produced domestically). The Fed is counting on the banking system and the capital markets to operate on aggregate demand to affect output growth. But one should consider not just output growth alone but output growth relative to something called "sustainable potential."

Sustainable potential is an economy's long-term "speed limit"—estimated to be the sum of trend productivity growth plus labor force growth. At present, I estimate that 3.4 percent is a reasonable number for the U.S. economy's sustainable potential, consisting of 2.5 percent trend productivity growth plus 0.9 percent labor force growth. With future growth in the labor force projected to slow as Baby Boomers retire, however, this estimate of sustainable potential could eventually be closer to 3.0 percent.

In sum, the monetary policy transmission mechanism starts with the FOMC decision and then moves to the banking system, which provides only 25 percent of total credit, and then through the capital markets, which provide 75 percent of total credit—thus affecting short-term rates, long-term rates, credit spreads, the stock market, and the dollar. All of these mechanisms affect aggregate demand—particularly, the interest-rate-sensitive sectors of housing, automobiles, and other consumer durables—and also business fixed investment. And the Fed has to balance all of this against its twin goals, which are, of course, to keep U.S. output growth in line with its sustainable potential and to maintain stable prices.

Factors Affecting Productivity Growth

Understanding the mechanism by which monetary policy is transmitted is important, but appreciating the dynamic nature of this modern economy is even more so. Specifically, investment professionals need to recognize that U.S. productivity growth is a critical factor in determining how fast the economy can grow without igniting inflation and how the United States can ultimately improve the standard of living for most of its citizens. Thus, a discussion of the factors involved with U.S. productivity (output per worker hour) growth is in order.

Productivity growth has seen a rare acceleration, reflecting the information technology (IT) revolution combined with heavy business capital spending. From 1970 to 1995, U.S. productivity growth was a paltry 1.5 percent. But in the period from 1995 to 2000, productivity growth accelerated to 2.5 percent, which is rare for an economic super power like the United States. A further acceleration to 3.1 percent was seen in the U.S. productivity growth during the 2000–2005 period. So far in 2006, productivity growth has slowed markedly.

Flexible labor and product markets

The United States benefits from flexible labor and product markets. As a result, workers can move from job to job and from region to region as businesses in such sectors as technology, construction, manufacturing, and medical care ebb and flow. Without flexible labor and product markets, the essential capitalistic process of "creative destruction" would be curtailed and the challenges of globalization would be difficult to meet.

Competition

A high level of competition in labor and product markets provides the consumer with the best possible deal. In contrast, many countries set up a regulatory structure that protects inefficient labor and product markets. Some countries that tightly regulated their labor and product markets in the past are being forced to change because of globalization. To the extent that these anticompetitive practices remain in effect, productivity growth is impeded.

World-class universities

Educational quality is important, but just as important is a willingness to work with the private sector. With a strong link between U.S. academia and the private sector, U.S. productivity can benefit from intensive research and development, improved supply chains and production procedures, and more educated and skilled workers.

Entrepreneurial spirit

At the heart of improving U.S. productivity is the individual entrepreneurial spirit. U.S entrepreneurs are unequaled in their creative and innovative skills in support of risk-taking, profit-making activities. U.S. entrepreneurs have built increasingly efficient global networks of research, design, production, assembly, distribution, and marketing, and they have disseminated new technology.

Capital markets

U.S. capital markets are deep, liquid, and sophisticated. Moreover, the United States has a vibrant private capital industry. Not all countries have such supportive, low-capital-cost financial market activities for business capital investment, which, in turn, have a strong impact on productivity growth. Strong capital markets thus go hand-in-hand with the entrepreneurial spirit, competitive labor and product markets, heavy business spending, and strong U.S. productivity growth.

China, India, and the United States

With a US$13.5 trillion economy that has been growing at or above its sustainable potential, the United States is the locomotive of the world's economies. Despite impressive growth rates, China's and India's economies are much smaller, with GDPs of US$2 trillion and US$670 billion, respectively.

At this point, I will consider what the future may hold for China and India by first comparing them with Japan and then by applying the previously mentioned sustainable growth approach to their economies. Finally, I will consider the dynamics of their interactions with the U.S. economy.

For two decades (the 1950s and 1960s), Japan grew at about 10 percent a year. In the 1970s, growth slowed to 4 percent as Japan suffered from the 1970s oil shock, among other factors. Although Japan remains the second biggest economy in the world, it endured (after the bursting of a huge asset price bubble) deflation and recurring periods of recession in the 1990s. In my opinion, this reversal for Japan was caused by three fundamental things: (1) pressures on energy and other resources, which Japan is short on, (2) a slow-growing labor force caused by a low birth rate and almost no immigration, and (3) trade and foreign exchange issues.

In my view, as 2007 approaches, China will suffer from similar constraints on growth. Three major factors are behind this potential change. First, China is on the brink of hitting bottlenecks, particularly with respect to oil and other resources that could considerably constrain growth. Second, and ironically, China could be constrained by its labor force growth. In a land of more than a billion people, how can China be constrained by its labor force? In part, it is because of the one-child policy begun in 1979. But to understand the totality of this issue, one has to understand that China really has two labor forces: a mostly skilled labor force that lives along the coast and a largely unskilled labor force that lives inland. Third, China will face increasing trade and foreign exchange pressures, just as Japan did in the 1970s. In sum, China's growth over the coming decade will likely be slower than in the past decade, and India, which is less encumbered, is likely to grow faster in the coming decade than in the past decade.

The U.S. economy is in the midst of a 4.5-year expansion that is now reaching full employment. Moreover, it has been growing generally at a rate greater than its sustainable potential. Unless the growth rate is reduced to or slightly below its sustainable potential, the United States may experience a renewal of inflation. As a result, given a prolonged series of Fed rate hikes, there is a sense of inevitability that growth in the United States will slow. My forecast is for a slowing in U.S. real GDP growth to 2.9 percent in 2007 from 3.4 percent in 2006.

As the locomotive of global economic growth, the U.S. economy can affect other economies, notably those that rely heavily on exports, such as China, Japan, and Germany.

Globalization has doubled the world's labor supply during the past decade and a half as workers from the former Soviet Union, China, and India have entered the free market trading system. This doubling of the global labor supply has tended to hold down labor costs and prices in the United States. At the same time, however, the U.S. trade deficit has grown to an unsustainably high 6.5 percent of GDP as the United States has served as the primary locomotive for global economic growth.

To counter the mounting U.S. trade deficit, the United States could boost its national savings rate by lowering the Federal deficit, thereby lessening U.S. demand for foreign savings to finance domestic investment.

Furthermore, countries such as China and Japan that have trade surpluses with the United States could attempt to boost domestic demand, thus increasing their demand for U.S. exports. Finally, China could have more flexible foreign exchange rates, allowing the yuan to appreciate and thereby slowing growth of China's exports to the United States and increasing growth of U.S. exports to China.

Fed at a Crossroads

Unquestionably, the Fed is at a crossroads. First, it is in the midst of transitioning from the highly successful 18.5-year reign of Alan Greenspan to new Fed Chairman Ben Bernanke's reign. Second, the Fed must decide if further monetary tightening is needed in order to slow economic growth sufficiently to bring down elevated core consumer inflation.

Greenspan leaves a great legacy. In addition to dealing successfully with three major crises during his tenure (the 1987 stock market crash, the global financial contagion of 1998, and 9/11), his record also includes a remarkable 10-year economic expansion, strong growth, low inflation, low unemployment, high productivity growth, and strong business fixed investment. Yet in his own mind, Greenspan was most proud of two other things. He felt that his greatest legacy came from recognizing both the surprisingly strong productivity growth in the U.S. economy, associated with the information technology revolution and heavy business capital spending, as well as the tremendous increase in global competition in labor and product markets created by the collapse of Communism and the industrialization of China and India. These profound changes meant that the U.S. economy could grow faster with less inflation.

Under the best of circumstances, Greenspan would be a tough act to follow. And now is most decidedly not the best of circumstances. Since mid-2004, the Fed has been gradually reducing its monetary accommodation and more recently moving into "modestly restrictive" territory by raising its funds rate target from a 46-year low of 1.00 percent to 5.25 percent. The Fed must decide when it has tightened enough (but not too much) while its new chairman tries to establish his own anti-inflation credentials. Most importantly, the Fed must be mindful of the time lags associated with actions already taken.

At this point, the Fed must wrestle with three things: elevated core consumer inflation, contained inflation expectations, and confusion over future Fed intentions in the financial marketplace. The Fed has chosen the core personal consumption expenditures (PCE) deflator as its preferred measure of reported inflation. In June and July 2006, the core personal consumption expenditures deflator was increasing at a 2.4 percent pace, measured year-over-year, which is well above the Fed's unofficial "comfort zone" of 1–2 percent. To Fed policymakers, the risks of higher inflation outweigh the risks of slower economic growth. Note that new Fed Chairman Bernanke favors the formal announcement of an official Fed inflation target.

Fed Chairman Bernanke stumbled in his efforts to communicate with the financial markets soon after taking the helm at the world's most important policy institution. In congressional testimony on 27 April, for example, the new Fed chairman was perceived by investors as hinting that he might halt monetary policy tightening too soon. As a result, one closely watched measure of long-term inflation expectations, the TIPS (Treasury Inflation-Protected Securities) spread between the yield on 10-year Treasury issues and the yield on inflation-indexed government debt, widened to a recent high of 2.74 percentage points on 11 May. Subsequently, however, the new Fed chairman shored up his anti-inflation credibility with more hawkish remarks on 5 June, resulting in a narrowing in this TIPS spread to 2.53 percentage points soon thereafter on 13 June. Partly reflecting evidence of a slowing in economic growth, this measure of long-term inflation expectations narrowed further to 2.36 percentage points by the end of September 2006.

A discernible contrast is emerging between new Fed Chairman Bernanke and his highly successful predecessors Alan Greenspan (1987–2006) and Paul Volcker (1979–1987). In particular, Bernanke, a former professor of economics at Princeton University, wants to deemphasize the role of the Fed chairman in both monetary policy making and communicating with the public in favor of more emphasis on the institution itself. Bernanke's new approach stands in marked contrast to the approaches of both Greenspan and Volcker, who strengthened the role and effectiveness of the Fed chairman both within the Fed and outside and in relations with Congress, the White House, the markets, and the general public. In essence, Bernanke appears to be giving greater voice to his fellow 6 Fed governors and 12 Federal Reserve Bank presidents, an approach that is likely to confuse the markets, perhaps leading to greater stock and bond market volatility.

The importance of managing expectations cannot be emphasized enough. If the public starts to believe that inflation is picking up, businesses will raise prices in anticipation of future price increases. Consumers will demand higher wages for the same reason. Once all segments of the economy start to factor in higher inflation expectations, eliminating them can be extremely painful, as the 1970s proved.

Appendix A. Monetary Policy Transmission Mechanism

FOMC (seven Fed governors plus five voting Federal Reserve Bank presidents)

- Open market operations.
- Federal funds rate target.
- Discount rate (Fed governors).

Banking system (25 percent of total credit extended)

- Bank reserve pressures (BR/TR), where BR is bank borrowings at Fed discount window and TR is total reserves.
- Bank tradition against discount window borrowings because they are perceived as a sign of a bank's financial weakness.
- As a result, an increase in bank reserve pressures is signaled by an increase in the (BR/TR) ratio.

Capital markets (75 percent of total credit extended)

- Short-term interest rates.
- Longer term interest rates.
- TIPS spreads.
- Credit risk spreads.
- Stock market.
- Foreign exchange value of dollar.

Aggregate demand (time lag, approximately six months)

- Consumer spending (more than two-thirds of aggregate demand).
- Business fixed investment.
- Residential fixed investment.
- Government spending.
- Net exports.

Potential supply (output growth)

- Sustainable potential (trend productivity growth plus labor force growth).
- Resource utilization (labor, productive capacity).

Inflation (time lag, approximately 12 months)

- Core personal consumption expenditures deflator.
- Long-term inflation expectations (10-year TIPS spread).

This presentation comes from the 2006 Financial Analysts Seminar held in Evanston, Illinois, on 16–21 July 2006.

More from David M. Jones

This section presents the speaker's lively question and answer session with the conference audience.

Question: What constitutes a neutral fed funds rate?

Jones: A neutral federal funds rate is one that is neither stimulative nor restrictive with regard to economic activity. Chairman Greenspan was once asked if he could identify a neutral rate. His response was that he could not at that time but that he would know it when he saw it.

If I were to put myself in the position of the Fed chairman, I would say that right now, neutral is around a 4.50 percent federal funds rate. In my opinion, we are modestly restrictive at the current federal funds rate target of 5.25 percent and no longer neutral.

Question: What are the trade-offs associated with the Fed raising rates as a means of increasing the savings rate of the United States?

Jones: First, I would note that the U.S. savings rate is defined in terms of savings out of income and does not include capital gains on asset holdings, such as stock or real estate. If we raise interest rates to the point where we force consumers to cut back sharply on spending and increase savings, the danger will be that the U.S. economy will be pushed into recession. And because the United States is the locomotive for the rest of the world, so will the economies of other countries, particularly those that depend heavily on exports.

But it would certainly have the effect of reducing the trade deficit because it would pull down import growth relative to exports and reduce U.S. dependence on foreign savings. Perhaps a better approach would be less drastic reliance on increases in U.S. interest rates combined with policy changes abroad that would encourage other countries to grow faster through their stimulation of domestic demand so that U.S. export growth would start to pick up.

Question: How can a Fed chairman influence a country to encourage it to stimulate its own domestic demand?

Jones: It is very difficult. If a country has been successful with an export-oriented growth model, such as Japan, China, or even Germany, why should it change? But what if the United States as the global economic super power has to act alone as the main locomotive to slow down global growth? Clearly, the United States must raise interest rates more than it otherwise would, thereby threatening to push the U.S. economy into recession, which would, of course, have obvious negative consequences, particularly for export-driven economies.

So, the idea is that it would be best to encourage the sharing of the burden of reducing the large U.S. trade deficit and corresponding trade surpluses in major export-driven countries.

Specifically, the United States would follow a moderately restrictive monetary policy, combined with fiscal restraint, so as to slow growth in U.S. domestic demand to a more moderate pace, thereby slowing U.S. import growth and reducing the U.S. trade deficit. At the same time, surplus countries dependent on exports would follow a moderately stimulative monetary policy combined with some fiscal stimulus so as to boost their domestic demand growth, thereby increasing their imports of U.S. goods and services and reducing their trade surpluses.

China's Economy: Structural Strength, Cyclical Weakness

JIM WALKER

A close look at the recent upturn in Chinese economic activity leads to the conclusion that it is not sustainable. The growth cycle is weakening as commodity prices are rising and profit margins are being squeezed. The good news is that the current growth cycle, the first capitalist cycle in China, emanated from business investment that was generated in large part by the newly acquired right of the Chinese people to own private property. Investment is the key to a sustainable and high, but volatile, growth rate and ensures that the next cycle of growth in China will be characterized by even greater levels of productivity and efficiency.

Interpreting the economic data reported by the Chinese government is like trying to do a jigsaw puzzle blindfolded because so many contradictory messages emanate from the statistics, in part because the authorities constantly change the reported numbers, the definitions of the statistics, and how the statistics are calculated.

In this presentation, I will review the Chinese economy—its current status and future direction, particularly over the next 12–18 months. The signals from China are very clear, and they indicate a weakening of the growth cycle.

Fine-tuning into a weak manufacturing sector is dangerous, and the People's Bank of China is playing with fire.

Current Expansion

China's first truly capitalist growth cycle began in 2001 and continues today. It differs from the situation in 1994 and 1995 when China exploded in economic growth after Deng Xiaoping's "get rich is good" message. At that time, and previously, Chinese growth cycles were driven by the government's decision to stimulate growth through bank loans to state-owned enterprises. In the early

Jim Walker is chief economist at CLSA Asia-Pacific Markets, Hong Kong.

1990s, a growth sideshow that was created by manufacturing companies from Hong Kong moving into southern China materialized, but it remained just that, a sideshow, because it was under government control.

In 2000 and 2001, China incorporated private property rights into its constitution, and the impetus for growth began to emerge. Private property rights are the fundamental building block for economic growth. Once people have title to the property they own, they will use that property to support all manner of economic activity. As the Peruvian economist Hernando de Soto has said, when people own private property, they can unleash the capital that is inherent in their property through the banking sector's lending function.

Until 2000, the Chinese people had no notion of private property. They had no confidence that any investment they made would actually provide them with a meaningful return because of the ever-present fear of expropriation by the government. The addition of private property rights combined with China's acceptance into the World Trade Organization (WTO) in 2001 gave rise to the first capitalist cycle in China. By joining the WTO, a business rule book, already adhered to throughout the rest of the world, was put in place for Chinese companies. These two events created the driving force behind the current growth cycle. The result was the formation of thousands of new companies, which generated a massive number of competitors—officially, about 3,000, but unofficially, maybe as many as 5,000—in every industry; five years ago, there may have been a maximum of 200 or 300 competitors in each industry.

This explosion in business formation over the past few years may signal the beginning of the end if the theories proposed by Joseph Schumpeter are accurate. Schumpeter attributes business cycles to entrepreneurial activity. He has argued that at certain points in time, an innovation or invention occurs that initiates a new cycle of business formation. Eventually, through competition and bad decisions, the economic cycle disintegrates as these companies compete away profitability.

In China, no new invention or innovation has spurred the cycle but, rather, a new institutional framework—the framework of private property rights, which is probably more powerful than either invention or innovation. Inevitably, according to Schumpeter, such a massive swell of business formation destroys profitability in many companies within each sector and industry until eventually the weak companies go out of business.

By 2007, China should begin a significant economic slowdown, driven by a large number of companies going out of business and business investment drying up. As a result, economic activity will drop off. The GDP growth rate in 2007 is expected to be 3–5 percent. Over the course of the past five to seven years, GDP was officially in the 9–10 percent range, but in reality, it has probably grown slightly faster. The forecast, therefore, represents a fairly sharp drop but one that should not be too harmful. That China has economic cycles may come as a surprise to the rest of the world, and probably to the Chinese government as well, which still thinks that it can manipulate, or fine-tune, the economy through the cycle. That fine-tuning worked when the government dominated economic activity, but the private sector is now in charge.

The China Puzzle

Such signals as rampant wage inflation, skilled-worker job hopping, and falling profitability confirm that China is in the late-cycle stage of the boom. Typically, rampant wage inflation is not associated with China because China has an infinite supply of labor—at least that is what most of the newspapers have said for the past five years. Never has there been more nonsense written about a country than what has been written about China. China has a massive labor shortage. A labor shortage does not seem likely in a country of a billion people, but not surprisingly, not all of them are managers, technically skilled, or entrepreneurs.

The bulk of the Chinese labor force is unskilled and relatively ignorant and illiterate. Thus, China has run out of skilled workers. For the past few years, it has solved the problem by importing massive amounts of labor. One million Taiwanese now work in China in response to the Chinese skilled-labor shortage. None of these workers are cleaning streets, driving buses, or working as domestics. Rather, all of them are employed at the skilled and managerial levels in the Chinese economy. One million people equal 10 percent of the total work force of Taiwan. Taiwan, of course, does not have an infinite supply of skilled workers and managers either, so increasingly, workers in China are job hopping. Skilled workers, in particular, are able to secure new jobs for a 100 percent or higher increase above their current salaries. In the banking sector in China, average wage inflation is 30–40 percent a year. In the Guangdong province, the minimum wage for even unskilled labor has been rising 17–42 percent in 2006. Thus, few companies in China have no wage inflation. And the ones that do not have wage inflation are located either in the center or the west of the country and are using unskilled labor in a rather unproductive fashion.

Over the past 10 years, China has made huge inroads in trade with the rest of the world because of the competitiveness of its exports—a result of its cheap labor and low commodity prices. China is a manufacturing country, and manufacturers fare well when commodity prices are low. It is a different story altogether when commodity prices rise. About 60–70 percent of a Chinese manufacturer's total cost is raw materials, so when raw material prices double, and then double again, as has been the case over the past three years, profit margins are squeezed. Unfortunately, Chinese companies are not sensitized to declining profits and are in danger of falling prey to the same calamity that befell the rest of Asia in 1996 when companies did not rein in operations as profits dried up. Ignoring the deterioration in profits was the main cause of the Asian crisis in 1997.

The current phase of the economic cycle could extend for another 12 months, although renewed tightening may shorten this timeline. On 27 April 2006, the Chinese government raised the bank lending rate by 27 bps in reaction to a renewed acceleration in the Chinese economy, and it will not be the last tightening measure. The government is increasingly worried about the quality of growth because the reacceleration in production and investment activity has come entirely through the state sector. Another element of the economy that worries the government is property development because every manufacturer in China is now also a real estate developer, which is never a good sign in Asia. This manufacturer-turned-developer scenario occurred in the run-up to the Asian crisis, when many manufacturers in Thailand, Indonesia, Malaysia, and elsewhere became involved in the property market. Many of their speculative projects were never completed or sold. The same is likely in China over the next two years.

Fine-tuning into a weak manufacturing sector is dangerous, and the People's Bank of China (PBOC) is playing with fire. In 2004, when the government introduced an austerity program, it instigated a debate about whether China would have a hard or a soft landing that year. The reality is that China had no landing at all in 2004 because companies were making so much money that economic tightening did not mean anything to them; they just kept spending and investing. But today, as the government begins a new tightening trend, these same companies are no longer making money, and thus the newest tightening move is potentially much more damaging.

The real GDP numbers reported by the Chinese government are a waste of time. **Figure 1** shows a far too narrow channel of reported growth beginning in 2003. Real economies do not grow between 9 percent and 10 percent every quarter, every year; economic growth is much more volatile. China has, in fact, experienced much more volatile growth than has been reported. Confirmation that the GDP numbers are nonsensical can be found in the reported provincial GDP growth rates for 2005. An overwhelming 30 of the 31 provinces in China grew faster than the national average GDP of 9.9 percent reported for the year. Arithmetically, this is simply not possible, especially given that Hunan, a small province, is the only province reporting a slower growth rate than the national average. This example illustrates the difficulties in dealing with Chinese data.

The production data shown in **Figure 2** illustrate the reacceleration in the Chinese economy in the first and second quarters of 2006. It is important to note that it is a small reacceleration, which makes the PBOC's recent tightening move all the more worrisome. The government has used a sledge hammer—the increase in interest rates, which is usually a last resort—to send a big signal

Figure 1 Reported Real GDP Growth, 2000–2006

Year-over-Year Change (%)

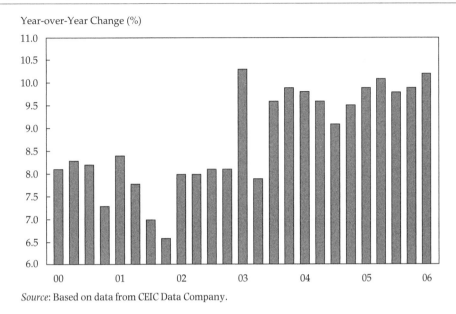

Source: Based on data from CEIC Data Company.

Figure 2 CLSA China Purchasing Managers' Index, Overall Index: March 2004–June 2006

50 = No Change from the Previous Month

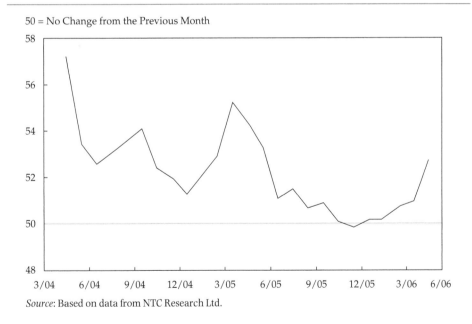

Source: Based on data from NTC Research Ltd.

to the borrowers and lenders of money. The message is "Stop, or we will make you stop." So, although economic growth in 2006 will still probably be about 9 percent, it will be much lower in 2007.

Even though reported GDP numbers do not show the cyclical nature of the Chinese economy, the Selected Consumer Goods series, as graphed over the

Figure 3   Change in Selected Consumer Goods Output (Units), 1994–2006

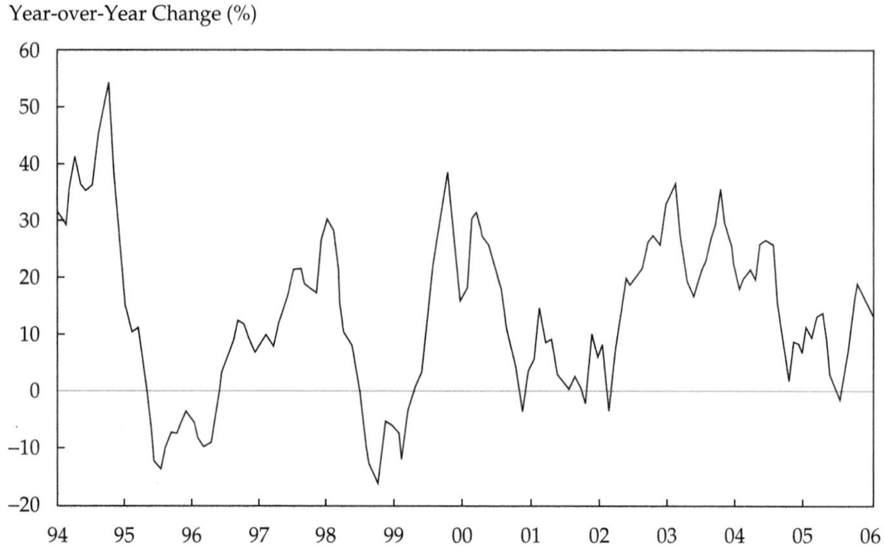

Year-over-Year Change (%)

Source: Based on data from CEIC Data Company.

past decade in **Figure 3**, does show definite cyclical behavior. Clearly, China has experienced annual growth rates in the 3–5 percent range, such as in the midst of the 1997 and 1998 recession in the Asian region, and the economy did not fall apart.

The muted nature of the current acceleration is obvious from a close analysis of manufacturing sector data. For example, China's Business Climate Index has trended lower since 2004. And the Internal Freight Volume series has not strengthened during the reacceleration, which is certainly a contraindicator. One reason that the manufacturing sector data lack buoyancy may be that strength in the economy is concentrated in the real estate sector, but the data bear further monitoring.

The economic cycle definitely peaked in 2004 and since that time has remained just slightly off that level of activity. Nevertheless, the economy has reaccelerated recently. External data, such as the Imports of Machine Tools series as well as the Foreign Direct Investment Growth series, demonstrate a recent upturn in the economy, albeit muted. Sentiment among Japanese foreign direct investors also peaked in 2004, although there has been an uptick in sentiment among Japanese foreign direct investment (FDI) industries over the course of the past two or three months. Thus, from the point of view of foreign investors, the economic environment in China is improving.

Although showing signs of strengthening, FDI into China is reluctant at best. Headlines tout significant FDI, and it is true that many commitments to invest in China are made, but investors often do not follow through on their

Figure 4   Monthly Contract Value vs. Utilized Amount of FDI, January 1998–March 2006

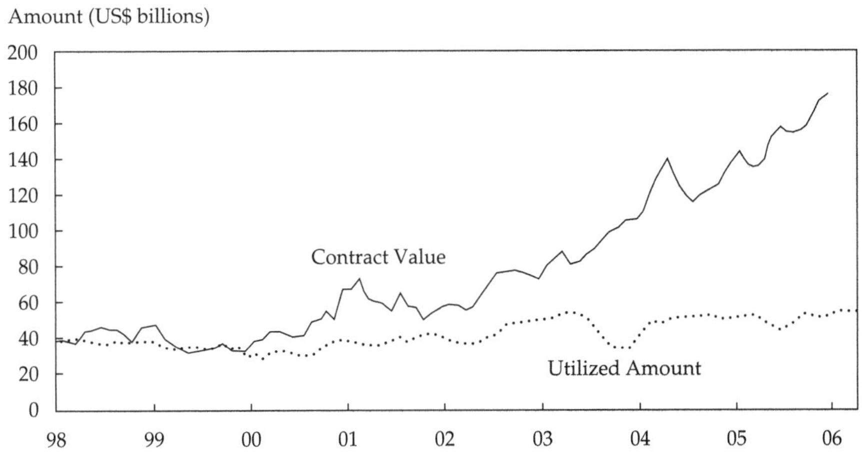

Source: Based on data from CEIC Data Company.

commitments. Utilized (or actual) investment in China is much lower than the contract (or publicized) value of investment, as illustrated by **Figure 4.** The utilized amount has remained fairly close to $50 billion over the past few years, which has to do with the absorptive capacity of the Chinese economy. It simply cannot digest more than this level of investment in a single year and may be unable to digest even that amount in the next couple of years.

The profit cycle also peaked in 2004, when Chinese companies' profits were up more than 40 percent year over year. In 2003, profits had likewise been quite strong, growing at a rate of approximately 40 percent year over year. But by the fourth quarter of 2005, the rate of growth in the profitability of Chinese companies was deteriorating rapidly. The drop in the profitability growth rate does not mean that these companies chalked up losses in 2005 but that their rate of growth in profits slowed. The consequence of this decline in profit growth is that these companies' investment plans will be negatively affected, which is a solid indicator that a slowdown is on the horizon.

In the A-Share Index, 17 of the 23 sectors reported year-over-year declines in profitability in the fourth quarter of 2005. Those that did not report slowing profits are, not surprisingly, in the oil and commodity industries. The potential for a profit margin squeeze is looming in China because Chinese companies do not like to raise prices because of the hugely competitive marketplace in which they operate and the fear of losing market share. Other countries in Asia have learned the hard way that market share is an extremely bad business model. Japan is a perfect example, and South Korea, a good example. This time around, China will learn the hard way that market share is a bad business model.

The Chinese government's Profitability and Industrial Enterprise Data series tell a different story, with both showing year-over-year growth of 27 percent in early 2006. Close scrutiny of the raw data reveals a 20 percent increase in the number of companies in the index over the past year, which raises concerns about consistency. In an effort to improve data comparability, at CLSA we have adjusted the companies included in the Industrial Enterprise Data series reported by the government. The result is that at the beginning of 2006, instead of a 20 percent year-over-year rise in profits as originally reported, the adjusted series indicates only a 6 percent increase in profits year over year. The series is reported as a 12-month moving average, but if it were a 1-month moving average, the rate of growth in profits would have dropped even lower—to 3 percent. The natural resource companies, who have benefited from much higher commodity prices, are included in this series, so all things considered, the overall profit picture is rather dim.

The margin squeeze is picking up speed as input prices are rising. The CLSA China Purchasing Managers' Index tracks input and output prices. If input prices are rising faster than output prices, then the result has to be a squeeze in margins, and the only option is to increase output prices. The profit squeeze is confirmed by data reported by the government showing raw materials and costs rising but the prices of finished goods remaining flat.

The Chinese consumer is participating in the reacceleration, but not wholeheartedly. Chinese retail sales, an undependable data series, show that consumption has picked up over the past few months, but the series itself is a weak indicator of the economic cycle. Consumer sentiment, or as it is known in China, the Satisfaction Index, indicates a positive feeling about the long term, but sentiment for the present is negative. Chinese consumer prices have stopped falling as fast as they had been, marking the beginning of the end of the disinflation cycle in China.

Monetary Factors behind the Boomlet

Monetary stimulation by the Chinese government in 2005 was primarily responsible for pushing the economy into a reacceleration. Chinese M2 growth reaccelerated in the middle of 2005 after the Chinese government revalued the renminbi (RMB) and suffered the consequences of a 2.1 percent revaluation. Curiously, the PBOC flooded the system with money with the goal of lowering market interest rates to dissuade more foreign capital from entering the country.

This strategy, however, backfired. Bank lending reaccelerated. The government had not anticipated that the Chinese business community, and especially local governments, would use the money pouring into the economy at this stage of the cycle. The PBOC realized in December 2005 that much damage had been done by its easy money policy and began to withdraw money from the system.

But as of April 2006, bank lending was still growing at a 29 percent annualized rate. Inevitably, more tightening is yet to come.

Evidence of Overheating

In 2004, when the Chinese government introduced austerity measures and concerns emerged about continued growth in China, CLSA created a checklist to indicate signs of overheating in the economy. The checklist has eight indicators, of which six are based on macroeconomic variables and two are based on microeconomic variables. The macroeconomic characteristics are

- fast monetary growth relative to history,
- rapid credit expansion relative to trend,
- adjusted resource gap (the current account of the balance of payments plus net FDI inflows),
- accelerating general inflation,
- rising asset prices with pressure building on the riskiest, and
- rising costs, particularly labor.

The microeconomic variables are corporate earnings and accounts receivable.

In 2004 when the checklist was created, only one of the indicators was flashing red. In 2006, four of the eight indicators are flashing red, and one indicator (the monetary variable) is mixed but moving toward red. Another indicator, rapid credit expansion relative to trend, can no longer be calculated because of the incomplete revision to nominal GDP in 2004. The four indicators that are flashing red are rising asset prices, rising costs including labor costs, corporate earnings, and accounts receivable. These indicators provide sufficient warning that China is in a particularly dangerous stage of its growth cycle. The profitability of Chinese companies is under grave threat.

China's Vulnerability

The roots of a nation's economic vulnerability lie in its dependence on commodities. An understanding of China's potential vulnerability can be gained from an examination of the economic history of the United States. **Figure 5** graphs two series: U.S. corporate profits as a percentage of national income and commodity prices. From 1947 to about 1971, commodity prices, proxied by

Figure 5   Corporate Profits as a Percentage of National Income vs. CRB Spot, 1947–2006

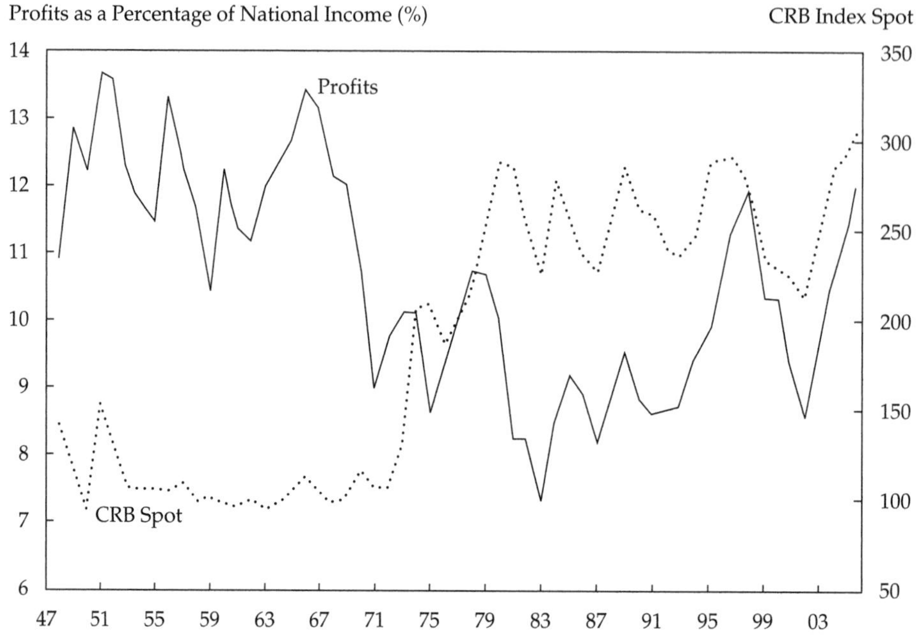

Profits as a Percentage of National Income (%)   CRB Index Spot

Note: Corporate profits as a percentage of national income is a seasonally adjusted annualized rate.
Source: Based on data from CEIC Data Company.

the Commodity Research Bureau (CRB) Index, were extremely low. During this same period, business profits contributed 12.5 percent of GDP. When oil prices escalated in the early 1970s, followed by rising prices of other commodities into the 1980s, the profit contribution to GDP fell from 12.5 percent to 9.0 percent. The late 1970s and early 1980s was the most difficult, most recessionary period of the last 50 years in the global economy, particularly in the United States, Japan, and Europe. The cause was high commodity prices in combination with bad central bank and government policy making.

The lesson to be learned is that profits and commodity prices do not move in the same direction; they move in the opposite direction. The United States was vulnerable to commodity prices because it was a manufacturing economy, as is China now. The economies most vulnerable to changes in commodity prices are those that are dominated by manufacturing. The United States was vulnerable in 1980 when 25 percent of its GDP was generated by manufacturing. China generates 42 percent of its GDP from manufacturing and is thus the most vulnerable economy in the world to high commodity prices. Higher commodity prices can mean only one thing—falling profits for Chinese companies.

Many of the economies in the Asian region are also heavily oriented toward manufacturing and are thus vulnerable to higher commodity prices. Nations in this category include Taiwan, Malaysia, Indonesia, Singapore, Thailand, and

Korea. For each of these nations, manufacturing contributes more than 25 percent of their respective GDPs.

Global Implications

If the economic engine of China falters, other nations will be affected to varying degrees. Should nothing change dramatically, rest assured that over the next two years, export prices, inflation, and interest rates will all rise because Chinese companies will be forced to raise prices. They have no choice. It is a very simple story. Chinese companies have no margins left.

China does not produce an export price series, but a proxy for this is the series that tracks import prices of goods going from China to Hong Kong, as shown in **Figure 6**. From mid-1997 to early 2004, import prices of goods going from China to Hong Kong were falling year over year, but since early 2004, prices have been rising. This trend has only just begun. Soon, the prices of Chinese goods imported by the United States, Europe, and elsewhere will also begin to rise.

A slowdown in China will have a dampening effect in 2006 and 2007 on the economies of other countries in the Asian region because the driver for regional exports has been domestic demand in China. If Chinese domestic demand takes a hit in the next couple years, then the rest of Asia will suffer as well and relatively more so than other parts of the world.

Figure 6   Price Index of Exports Shipped to Hong Kong, 1996–2006

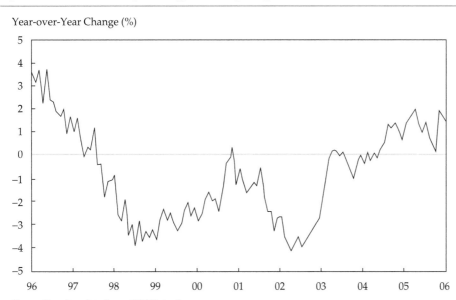

Year-over-Year Change (%)

Source: Based on data from CEIC Data Company.

The most exposed, most vulnerable countries to a slowdown in China are Korea and Taiwan because they are the most integrated into the Chinese investment story. In contrast, the economic driver in Southeast Asia is the export supply chain, and therefore, the United States is much more instrumental to the welfare of these economies than is China. Hong Kong is the least vulnerable to a slowdown in China because Hong Kong no longer operates as if it were a separate country and has been the biggest beneficiary of a structural shift within the Chinese economy—the opening of its capital accounts. Consequently, even during a significant slowdown in China, Hong Kong's economic performance should be surprisingly good.

At the present time, Japan is at the exact opposite end of the cycle from China. Japan is in the upswing phase of its economic cycle, and even with a slowdown in China and a recession in the United States, Japanese annual GDP growth should be between 2.5 percent and 3.5 percent for the next four to five years. Over the next two or three years, in absolute dollar terms, even with only about 6.0 percent GDP growth, Japan should contribute more to the Asian economy than China will.

In 2003 and 2004, Chinese demand produced about half the growth in Japan, although in absolute terms, exports to China were not that significant. Now that Japan's economic revival is strengthening, Chinese demand is less vital to its sustenance, which became obvious in 2005 when exports to China fell sharply and the Japanese economy did not miss a beat. So, a slowdown in China over the next several years should not make a difference to Japan as long as its domestic recovery continues unabated.

As for the United States, it is actually much more instrumental to China than China is to the United States. The United States is the end market for many goods that China produces, so the impact on the United States from a slowdown in China would be relatively immaterial.

Sustainable Growth

Japan is a good model of the level of economic growth that is sustainable, and fortunately, the Chinese government wants to follow this model. This desire and commitment are two of China's structural strengths. **Figure 7** depicts year-over-year growth in Japanese real GDP from 1946 to 1973. This is a typical growth pattern for a nation with an emerging industrialized economy. Over this 30-year period, the Japanese economy always maintained a growth rate above 4 percent, occasionally cycling up to 12 percent and even 15 percent. Economic cycles of this nature are normal, and China should follow the same pattern, as it has already begun to do over the past 10 years. As capitalism develops more profoundly in China, these cycles will become more pronounced. It is

Figure 7   Japan Real GDP Growth, 1946–1973

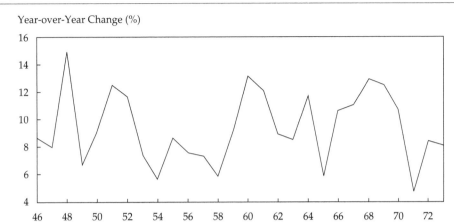

Year-over-Year Change (%)

nonsensical to believe that when China experiences an economic slowdown, its growth rate will drop from 10 percent to 8.5 percent. It is much more realistic to believe that the growth rate will drop to 5.0 percent before it swings back to the 10–12 percent range. Unfortunately, world markets do not seem prepared for such swings in Chinese economic growth.

Over the course of the next 20 years, China will probably not see two quarters of negative growth, which is good news long term for commodity prices and the establishment of China as a middle-income country but terrible news for the environment and other actors in the global economy. In each down cycle, Chinese corporate profitability will be rebuilt and enhanced. From each slowdown, China will emerge as a fiercer and more efficient competitor. Such slowdowns will also cause violent short-term fluctuations in commodity prices that will affect consumers and producers alike.

Conclusion

Investment, not consumption, is the driver of the Chinese economy. Efforts to encourage consumption will lead to lower growth and a damped cycle. If consumption becomes the driver of the Chinese economy, the average economic growth rate will fall from roughly 10 percent to 5 percent because growth rates associated with consumption are not as robust as growth rates associated with investment. The best scenario for China is to encourage saving, which will create investment and which, in turn, will maintain China's fast growth rate.

China is in the late stages of its first capitalist cycle, which has been ongoing since 2001. The creative–destructive process as articulated by Schumpeter is nearing its latter stages, and manufacturers are being caught in a pincer movement of rising input prices and flat output prices.

Over the next two years, the Chinese economy should consolidate as nonprofitable investment is weeded out. The cleansing side of an economic downturn leaves the strongest competitors to fight it out in the next cycle so that the productiveness and efficiency of the Chinese economy will be even greater in the future. Thus, the world will face an even stronger Chinese economic machine in the 2010s and 2020s.

This presentation comes from the 2006 CFA Institute Annual Conference held in Zurich on 21–24 May 2006.

More from Jim Walker

This section presents the speaker's lively question and answer session with the conference audience.

Question: Is China's financial system stable enough to handle the impending economic downturn, and what is the situation with nonperforming loans?

Walker: The state of the Chinese financial system is better than it was in 1995. The financial system has carved out, but not cleaned up, a lot of the bad debts from that period. But I am afraid that the risk assessment models are exactly the same as they were 10 years ago, which means that there is no risk assessment (no pricing of risk) by banks in China.

The problem is that the banks do not set interest rates. So, when times get tough for manufacturing companies, which has been the case for the past two years, and the banking sector doesn't want to expose itself to more risk, it lends to state-owned enterprises (SOEs). All of the lending over the course of the past year has gone to SOEs, provincial-government-related companies, or property developers. Recently, the quality of lending in the Chinese banking system has deteriorated dramatically, but Chinese banks see SOEs as a safe bet because they believe the government stands behind them.

So, I think the coming slowdown will produce a significant upswing in bad debts in Chinese banks, but it will not be nearly as bad a situation as in 1995. The system is stronger now.

Question: What is the amount of nonperforming loans in China at the current time?

Walker: The published amount of bad loans in the system, at the moment, is on the low side of reality but stated at roughly 8 percent of assets. China introduced a new international classification system recently that has 10 categories, with the fifth one being "Special Mention." The sixth through tenth categories cover doubtful debts, bad loans, losses, and the like. The Special Mention category is growing fastest.

So, although loans in this category are not considered bad loans, neither are they classified as good loans. This is a gray area indeed. If the Special Mention loans were to migrate into the bad debt categories, although I doubt all of them would, the capital in the Chinese banking system would be wiped out overnight.

Question: If China is forced to raise prices, what is the outlook for the country's ability to stay price competitive?

Walker: Because there are no good, consistent data on the issue, I have to turn to anecdotal information to answer the question. Already, low-end garment manufacturing has left China. The garment manufacturers are moving out of China as quickly as possible and relocating to Vietnam and the subcontinent countries. Basically, it is too expensive, especially in southern China, for low-end manufacturers to survive. So, the textile and garment industries, which have been a big part of the Chinese story over the past few years, have fled in search of lower-cost environments.

In those industries that require large amounts of raw materials, commodity prices are a major cost component, and competitiveness is all but destroyed already. Some companies we have spoken to have said that a 5 percent move in the RMB would cause them to leave China. This was before the 2.1 percent revaluation, and the RMB has moved another 2 or 3 percent since then.

Of course, competitiveness can be restored if growth slows down and companies consolidate, but at the moment, most companies are close to the edge. It is much cheaper now, in terms of input and labor costs, to be in just about any other Asian country than China. For example, the wage rates in Bangkok are half of what they are in Shenzhen and Shanghai.

Question: What is your outlook for China's currency over the next few years?

Walker: We anticipate a depreciation in the RMB over the course of the next two years because of the slowdown in the Chinese economy. If the economy is in trouble, the Chinese government will do anything it can to stimulate economic activity, and a cheaper exchange rate would be one way of doing that.

Long term, I suspect that the RMB direction is probably upward, but I say that with a great degree of caution, which is appropriate when making forecasts about the RMB. Recall that for most of the past 13 years, the Chinese have lost capital every year. It is only over the past three years that they have had a capital surplus.

Think of the Chinese economy as if it were a football. Air can be pumped into the football, but it can't escape because the valve contains it. Money can be pumped into the Chinese economy, but theoretically and practically, it is very difficult to get money out because of the closed capital account. Thus, no one really knows the true direction of the RMB until the capital account is opened. But I think the speed with which the Chinese government is opening the capital account indicates that the government is not at all confident that the RMB would appreciate.

Question: Could you comment on the connection between China and the U.S. dollar and the state of China's reserves?

Walker: China is not going to seek an appreciation of its currency versus the dollar any time soon. China has few investment opportunities other than U.S. Treasuries because it can't find the liquidity it needs in other markets. Certainly, the government is not going to move wholesale into euros.

China has about the lowest holdings of gold in its international reserves of any country on the planet, at about 0.2 percent compared with France at 20 percent.

Much of the rest of Asia holds gold positions in the low single digits, so China's gold reserve position is extremely low.

Question: Do the 2008 Olympics in Beijing play a role in the economic forecast for China?

Walker: The spending on the Olympic games in each of the five years leading up to 2008 will be less than 1 percent of China's GDP. The Olympics were extremely important in Korea, Australia, and Greece, where more or less the same amount of investment went into their facilities as will be going into China's facilities. The big difference, however, is that these countries have much smaller economies than China does.

So for China, Olympic spending really won't have much of an impact on the economy. In any event, I doubt that the government can stave off a slowdown until 2008 to benefit from any Olympic-related economic pickup. If it were an entirely state-run economy, it might be possible, but in the new capitalist China, I just don't believe it is.

PORTFOLIO MANAGEMENT

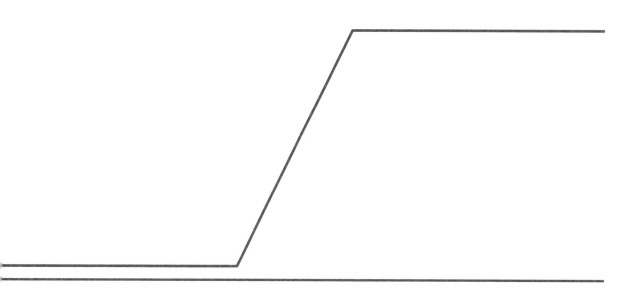

Challenges for the Next Generation of Investors

ABBY JOSEPH COHEN, CFA

Investors are coming to terms with new challenges related to the interconnectedness of national economies and financial markets. Globalization involves structural adjustments, including the growing importance of emerging economies, increased attention to climate change and other environmental issues, and a multitude of factors that drive cross-border capital flows. On a shorter-term basis, investors are facing several inflection points, such as (1) the deceleration of economic growth in the United States, which has long been the largest source of global economic demand, and (2) the end of the decades-long disinflation experienced in most developed economies.

The economic energy generated by individual nations can be expected to wax and wane, following time-honored cyclical patterns. But evidence also shows a clear rotation of economic energy from one region to another in a longer-term structural sense. In the increasingly interconnected global economy, these changes are accompanied by shifts in international trade balances, realignment of trading partners, repositioning of comparative advantage, redistribution of cross-border direct investment, currency fluctuations, and reallocation of assets in investment portfolios.

From a U.S. perspective, the next several years are expected to give witness to several economic inflection points, many requiring the keen attention of government policymakers. Following are six inflection points that are also likely to attract the attention of investors: (1) a shift in the source of incremental economic energy from the consumer to business investment and exports; (2) a reversal of the previously declining trend in inflation and interest rates; (3) the adoption by corporations of more conservative behavior in terms of accounting practices but a less defensive use of their large cash reserves; (4) a move to a more global context for decision making by corporations, investors, and regulators; (5) increased focus on the imbalance in the federal budget and trade accounts

> The increasingly global context for decision making is being adopted by investors and corporations alike. This movement is consistent with the theme of economic energy moving from the United States to other nations.

Abby Joseph Cohen, CFA, is chief U.S. investment strategist at Goldman, Sachs & Co., New York City.

and the longer-term pressures on budgets of state and local governments; and (6) a widening interest in environmental issues as they affect corporate management and investment decision making.

(1) Shifts in Economic Growth

Two points of inflection are currently under way. First, the global economy is showing new sources of vitality. Second, the sources of economic energy within the United States are shifting.

The United States has long been the world's largest economy. It has also been the fastest growing of the world's developed economies and has been the single largest contributor to incremental global growth since 2000. On the broader global stage, other nations are demonstrating enhanced economic vigor. After several disappointing years, some of this growth is coming from other large industrial economies, including Europe and Japan. These improvements are welcome and represent better balance in the global picture. Despite this revival, the currently smaller, but faster-growing, economies are adding more to global economic activity. These emerging BRIC (Brazil, Russia, India, and China) economies are cumulatively adding almost as much to global growth as is the United States.

Figure 1 displays the sources of global growth since 2000. Cumulatively, the BRICs have been the second largest source of incremental growth, and the four largest nations in the European Union (EU-4)—which have cumulative GDP almost as large as that of the United States—are trailing.

Over the next couple of years at Goldman, Sachs & Co., we expect the economic growth originating in Europe and Japan to become somewhat more robust. This change will benefit the United States because these other developed economies are the main foreign trade customers of U.S. businesses.

Incremental economic energy in the United States is shifting away from the consumer toward business fixed investment (BFI). Personal consumption spending exceeded 4 percent growth for several quarters but is decelerating toward the trend growth rate of about 3 percent. After almost four years of economic expansion, many households have already purchased new homes and furnishings and other major items, such as automobiles. A deceleration in consumption is a common cyclical occurrence but is expected to be somewhat exacerbated in this cycle, given the prior strength in these categories and because of the reduction in new mortgage equity withdrawals associated with somewhat higher interest rates and the slowdown in many residential real estate markets.

In contrast, the two sectors that are expected to enjoy solid growth are business fixed investment and exports. Within the United States, business fixed

Figure 1   Contributions to Global Growth, 2000–2004

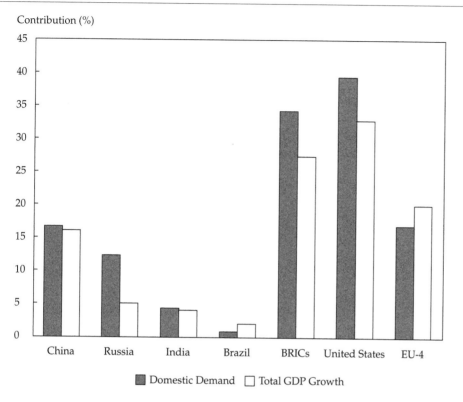

investment is the fastest growing sector and exports is the second fastest. Exports will benefit significantly from the anticipated acceleration in economic growth in European countries and Japan because these nations are the most important trade customers of the United States outside North America.

(2) Reversal in Inflation Trends

For the past two decades, disinflation (prices increase but at a decelerating pace) or outright deflation (declines in prices) has existed in many economies. But inflation is now on the rise in most countries. Although this reversal is to the relief of some—such as policymakers in Japan, who have worried about deflation for many years—most policymakers and investors are contemplating the potential pitfalls of rising inflation. Core inflation (i.e., inflation stripped of transitory components) troughed in the United States about two years ago. Even so, inflation likely presents only a mild threat to the U.S. economy. Following the long-lasting secular disinflation and the associated reduction in long-term inflation expectations, it is unlikely that the United States is about to move into

Figure 2   Year-over-Year Change in Unit Labor Costs, 1982–2006

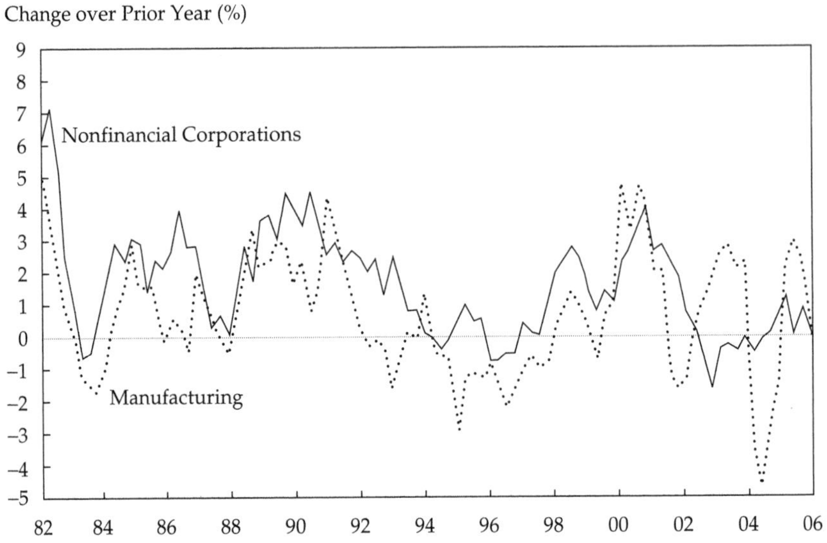

Change over Prior Year (%)

Note: Data from 2Q 1982 through 4Q 2005.

a dramatic reflation. Some upward drift in prices is likely and is increasingly reflected in market interest rates.

The main reason core inflation appears under control in the United States is the moderate pace of increases in the cost of labor. Labor costs account for about two-thirds of total business costs.

Figure 2 shows that unit labor costs (ULCs) in the United States have begun to rise. ULCs are a combination of increases in cash compensation and the potential offset from increased worker productivity. Productivity growth has been at high levels for several years, largely because of substantial business fixed investment in productivity-enhancing technology and other equipment. On average, compensation grew at about a 3 percent annual rate, as did productivity, leading to no change in unit labor costs between 2001 and 2005.

The currently low unemployment rate of about 4.5 percent suggests some tightness in labor markets, and wages and salaries have begun to rise at a slightly faster pace. Looking forward, it is expected that some, but not all, of these compensation gains will be offset by rising productivity. Labor costs will likely rise but at a pace dramatically below that seen during the 1970s and 1980s.

Another element of total compensation expense, the cost of benefits, does raise concerns because it is rising at a dramatically faster pace than wages and salaries and cannot be offset by productivity gains. These benefits are predominantly health care related and are growing in almost every developed economy, at a double-digit pace in some. This acceleration of inflation in health care benefit costs is expected to be a long-term phenomenon, and it may have a potentially dramatic impact on retiree-related expenditures by corporations

Table 1 Commodity Returns and Forecasts, GSCI

Item	Current Weight	Return 2003	2004	2005	12-Month Forward Forecast
GSCI	100.0%	20.7%	17.3%	25.5%	9.5%
Energy	74.3	24.6	26.1	31.1	10.0
Nonenergy	25.7	12.2	0.7	12.2	8.0
Industrial metals	9.3	40.0	27.5	35.8	10.0
Precious metals	2.3	19.5	5.6	18.6	5.0
Agriculture	10.1	6.6	(20.2)	2.4	8.0
Livestock	3.9	0.0	25.5	3.5	8.0

and government employers. In the United States, the main retirement benefits issue is likely to be health care, not defined-benefit pension programs or Social Security. Indeed, the retiree health care programs of S&P 500 Index companies are estimated to be underfunded by about $400 billion, compared with a more modest $85 billion underfunding for the same companies' defined-benefit pension liabilities. But the more serious policy issue may be that employers have scaled back or eliminated retiree health care programs, shifting the burden to their workers or, perhaps, to government entities. Anecdotal data suggest that programs for the future retirees of state and local governments are less well funded than are most corporate plans.

One final observation on inflation relates to commodities. The notable rise in commodity prices since 2003 has led to considerable attention to this area. We note, however, that energy and other commodities combined are about 10 percent of all business costs in the United States, even at today's elevated price levels. The aggregate economic impact is far less than that of unit labor costs. Furthermore, we believe that several key commodity prices have approached or exceeded equilibrium levels and that future price increases will be more moderate. The Goldman Sachs Commodity Index (GSCI) is economically weighted, based on actual use in the economy. The expectation is that energy-related inflation over the next 12 months, as shown in **Table 1**, will be approximately 10 percent compared with 31 percent in 2005. This deceleration helps explain why headline inflation has been less worrisome for 2006 even while core inflation is moving somewhat higher.

(3) Corporate Behavior

U.S. companies, and those in many other developed economies, are in solid financial condition. For example, the past years have been favorable for margin enhancement and cash generation. As a result, balance sheets have been strengthened and return on capital has risen. We also note that corporations are following more conservative accounting practices and investing excess cash—not just for defensive purposes but also to enhance future growth. These strong cash positions may also be viewed as good ballast should economic conditions deteriorate.

More Conservative Accounting

We believe that corporate accounting in the United States is now tighter than it has been in several years. These accounting enhancements reflect actions taken by regulators, shareholders, and corporate managers in response to external demands and their own proclivities. The U.S. Securities and Exchange Commission has taken dramatic steps, such as requiring CEO and chief financial officer certification of financial statements; mandating reconciliations of GAAP and non-GAAP measures; shortening deadlines for 10-K, 10-Q, and 8-K filings; and assessing internal controls. The Financial Accounting Standards Board has been actively addressing key accounting areas by assessing the value of goodwill and other intangible assets, outlining the accounting for asset retirement obligations, defining financial instruments as debt or equity, enhancing pension and other postemployment benefit disclosures, capturing off-balance-sheet activities, and mandating the expensing of employee stock options.

In general, companies' financial statements for the years from 2003 to 2005 showed more disclosures and fewer write-downs than in earlier years. In 2002, write-offs were an unprecedented 140 percent of reported earnings, reflecting a "catch-up" from earlier years, but write-offs are now less than 10 percent a year.

Strong Balance Sheets

Cash on the balance sheets of U.S. companies remains at robust levels. Ratio analysis of balance sheets reveals that companies are healthier than they have been in many years. Data for the S&P 500 are mirrored in the results for the broader corporate sector in the United States, as seen in the National Income and Product Accounts. **Table 2** shows total cash on the balance sheets of S&P 500 companies from 1993 to 2005. In 4Q 2005, these companies reported aggregate cash of $2.5 trillion on their balance sheets. Please note that even in 2002—a period of near recession in the United States—balance sheets were also cash rich.

Table 2   S&P 500 Cash and Cash Equivalents, 1993–2005
(trillions)

Year	Including Financials	Excluding Financials
1993	$0.6	$0.2
1994	0.7	0.2
1995	0.8	0.2
1996	0.9	0.2
1997	1.0	0.3
1998	1.1	0.3
1999	1.3	0.4
2000	1.4	0.4
2001	1.6	0.5
2002	2.0	0.6
2003	2.1	0.7
2004	2.3	0.7
1Q 2005	2.2	0.7
2Q 2005	2.1	0.6
3Q 2005	2.1	0.7
4Q 2005	2.5	0.8

Sources: Based on data from Standard & Poor's, FactSet Research Systems, and Compustat.

So, for the past several years, U.S. companies have enjoyed solid balance sheets and have used them for a variety of purposes, which has benefited shareholders, employees, and retirees.

Move away from Defensive Uses of Cash Reserves

Cash as a percentage of market capitalization for the S&P 500 is approximately 22 percent, compared with the historical average of 10–12 percent. Stated differently, when an investor buys the average S&P 500 share, about 22 percent of that purchase is cash, suggesting that equity ownership is more defensive than in the past. (The percentage of cash is about one-half that level if financial companies in the S&P 500 are excluded from the calculation. Even so, the pattern of dramatic increases in cash levels is the same.)

Between 2001 and 2005, much of this cash went into bolstering cash dividend payments, but these increases have begun to decelerate. Hence, the dividend payout ratio (the percentage of earnings paid to shareholders in cash) may soon peak, which makes good sense considering that the aggregate cash payout ratio has returned to normal levels from the depressed payouts of the late 1990s and that corporations are using their cash for other, less defensive purposes. Before I describe these other uses, please note that cash has also been applied to prefunding of pension liabilities, thus improving the balance sheets of some corporations, especially those in such troubled industries as autos.

Move toward Capital Expenditures, Acquisitions, and New Ventures

Companies do not engage in capital spending because they have cash but because demand is driving them to increase productive capacity. **Figure 3** compares the aggregate growth in U.S. industrial production with the growth in three components of business fixed investment: computer and peripheral equipment, communications equipment, and semiconductor and related equipment. These sectors have been the main recipients of corporate investment. Growth in capital expenditures in these sectors has exceeded that of all other sectors.

The ultimate benefit to long-term economic expansion is stronger than that suggested by the dollars of investment because of the deflation in the prices of some of these goods; consider that the growth in the actual units of technology products and other productivity-enhancing equipment available for workers to use has been stronger than the dollar growth. For example, the prices of such items as semiconductors, PCs, and telecom equipment have been declining. As a rule of thumb, the annualized increases of 10 percent in dollar expenditures

Figure 3   Change in Industrial Production, January 2003–April 2006

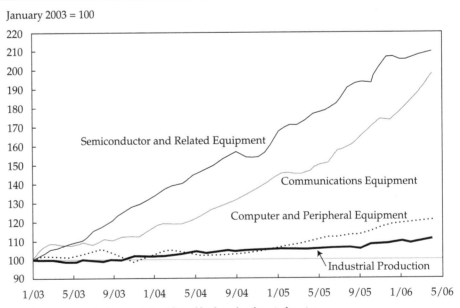

Note: Industrial production excludes selected high-technology industries.
Source: Based on data from the U.S. Federal Reserve Board.

in these categories have led to 20 percent growth in the equipment available for workers to use and have led to their productivity being bolstered.

Cash is also being used for financial purposes other than dividend increases. These uses include share repurchases, leveraged buyouts, and mergers and acquisitions (M&A). M&A activity has increasingly become cross-border in nature. The consolidation of global industries has been ongoing for several years. Although it slowed dramatically from 2002 to 2004, these cross-border flows are picking up again. Some of the regulatory impediments to global consolidation, such as the Glass–Steagall Act, have now faded. This regulatory change, in combination with the perception of strong growth opportunities in markets and production opportunities in other nations, has further hastened the pace of cross-border investment by corporations in the form of foreign direct investment, as distinguished from portfolio flows.

(4) Global Context for Decision Making

The increasingly global context for decision making is being adopted by investors and corporations alike. This movement is consistent with the theme of economic energy moving from the United States to other nations and with the significant increases in global flows of not just tradable goods but also capital. As capital increasingly flows back and forth across borders, regulators and accountants face a significant challenge in adapting to this new reality and its inherent reporting complexities.

Surge in U.S. Foreign Direct Investment

U.S. capital flows abroad have been strong for more than a decade. Over the past five years, they have been exceptionally vigorous, reflecting the improved confidence of U.S. corporate leaders and strong corporate balance sheets. **Figure 4** compares U.S. companies' foreign direct investment (FDI) with net U.S. flows into foreign public equity markets. Much more capital crosses borders in the form of corporate decision making, or FDI, in such projects as greenfield expansion and new factories than in the form of financial asset investment. For decades, the largest single FDI target for U.S. corporations was Europe, but now, much incremental FDI is going to Asia.[1] This movement parallels the changes in net new flows into financial assets, which were also previously directed primarily to Europe.

---

[1] Existing European operations of U.S.-based companies continue to receive substantial FDI in the form of reinvested profits.

Figure 4   U.S. Capital Flows Abroad, 1994–2004

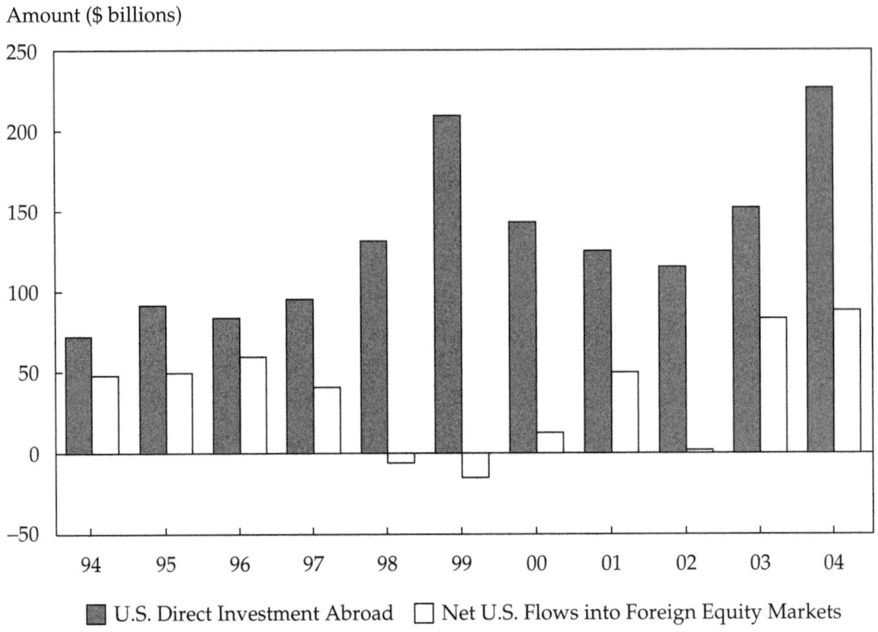

Amount ($ billions)

■ U.S. Direct Investment Abroad   □ Net U.S. Flows into Foreign Equity Markets

Source: Based on data from the U.S. Department of Commerce.

Capital Flows into and out of the United States

In the 2003–05 period, U.S. net flows into foreign equity markets exceeded the previous record set in 1993. Much of the incremental flow was targeted to Japan and selected emerging markets, and there was lessened relative interest in the markets in the larger economies in Europe. For 2003, 2004, and 2005, U.S. net flows into all European equity markets were $19.9 billion, $52.7 billion, and $46.5 billion, respectively. Compare that with the net flows into the Japanese equity market alone for the same years of $41.1 billion, $33.2 billion, and $40.0 billion, respectively.

Interest has grown in the equity markets of emerging Asia as evidenced by net flows for the same years of $28.9 billion, $5.5 billion, and $26.2 billion, respectively. But enthusiasm for emerging markets was actually higher in 1993, on a percentage basis, than it is today. In 2005, U.S. investors invested a net $126 billion outside the United States, roughly double the 1993 amount. The markets in 1993, however, were less than half their current size. In 1993, roughly 50 percent of U.S. mutual fund investment was directed toward foreign markets, and about half of that was in the world's smallest markets. For example, the two favorite foreign markets of U.S. investors in 1993 were Mexico and Hong Kong. In 1993, Hong Kong had higher net inflows from the United States than did Japan, which was the world's second largest market at that time and had 10 times the market capitalization of Hong Kong.

This historical review is important for the following reason: In 1994 and 1995, the U.S. Federal Reserve Board and other central banks began to raise interest rates, which significantly curtailed liquidity. The markets most adversely affected by the change in monetary policy were the equity markets in Hong Kong and Mexico, which declined far more than did their U.S. counterparts. And U.K. gilts declined more than U.S. Treasury securities. Today, as investors contemplate the consequences of higher interest rates and lower liquidity from current levels, a similar pattern may emerge. That is, markets other than those in the United States may be the most affected and experience larger rises in volatility as a consequence of changes in global monetary policy.

Although U.S. capital flows abroad remained vigorous throughout the past several years, capital flows into the United States slowed dramatically after 2000. The so-called bubble years of 1999 and 2000 were the peak of FDI in dollar terms into the United States, as shown in **Figure 5**. This FDI took the form of foreign acquisition of assets in the United States, propelled by large mergers in financial services and other industries, and the construction of new facilities in such industries as autos. At the time, European companies were keen on opportunities in telecommunications, and European investors were major participants in telecommunications issues in both the U.S. equity and fixed-income markets. In 2004, FDI to the United States was relatively modest compared with earlier years, but it represented the largest amount of FDI targeted to a single

Figure 5   Capital Flows into the United States, 1994–2004

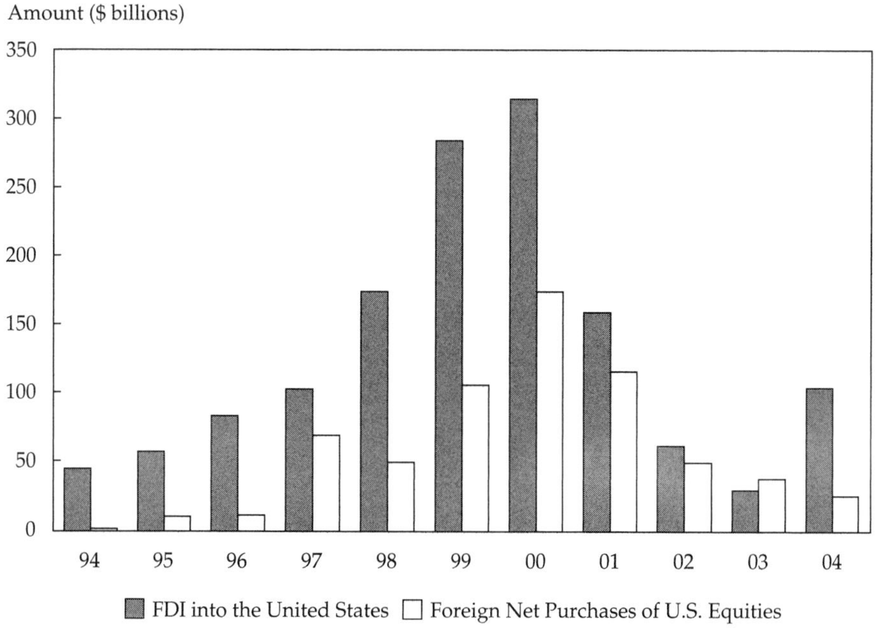

Source: Based on data from the U.S. Department of Commerce.

country that year. Other than in 2002, the United States has been the largest recipient of global FDI for many years.

Foreign Involvement in U.S. Public Markets

The U.S. public equity market is mainly a domestic market with only about 12 percent ownership by non-U.S. investors. Net foreign acquisitions of U.S. equities were less than $80 billion in 2005, well below the levels reached in 2000 and 2001 of $175 billion and $116 billion, respectively. Foreign investors in U.S. stock markets do not have a particularly good track record with regard to timing; they were largely absent from 2003 to 2005, a period of strong equity market performance.

In notable contrast to the equity markets, U.S. fixed-income markets experience much greater participation by foreign investors, who own 26 percent of the corporate bond market and 47 percent of the Treasury market. Therefore, the impact of changes in interest rates or currency on foreign investment in the United States is more likely to be observed in the fixed-income markets than in the equity markets.

Japanese investors are by far the largest group of foreign owners of U.S. Treasury securities, which has been the case for many years. In early 2006, more than 30 percent of the foreign holdings of U.S. Treasury securities were in the hands of Japanese investors. Japanese-based financial institutions have found U.S. Treasuries, offering yields of 4–5 percent, to be quite attractive relative to Japanese government bonds, which have yielded less than 1 percent. The Treasury securities are often converted into retail products and sold to individual investors in Japan. Chinese investors are the second largest holders of Treasury securities, owning 15.4 percent of total foreign holdings, up from 6.1 percent in 2001.

The third largest owner of foreign-held U.S. Treasuries is U.K. investors, who held 8.6 percent of the total in 1Q 2006, an increase of more than 80 percent over the previous two years. Most of the recent inflow into the U.S. Treasury market from the United Kingdom does not appear to be coming from U.K. corporations (which, some suspect, might be driven by changes in pension accounting practice) but, rather, from investment offices based in London that manage money for petroleum-exporting countries. The flow-of-funds data provided by most government authorities are not based on whose money is being invested but, rather, on where the money is being managed. We suspect that the dramatic inflow of petrodollars into the U.S. Treasury market may also explain Alan Greenspan's "conundrum" in 2005 when he observed that energy prices and inflation expectations had risen but that Treasury yields were flat to down. The explanation to the puzzle may be that as energy prices were rising, the number of petroleum dollars available to be recycled was increasing.

Much of this flowed into the U.S. Treasury market, keeping yields under good control.

(5) U.S. Economic Measures Out of Balance

A longer-term economic and market view must be predicated on the sustainability of a situation. For example, we often consider the sustainability of economic growth, linked to such factors as trend growth in productivity and the trend in secular inflation. Similarly, we also must examine whether equilibrium is achievable on other metrics.

Some of these economic measures remain out of balance and could provide impediments to growth and markets in the coming years. For example, the U.S. budget deficit, despite strong economic growth and tax revenues, has improved only modestly from prior years. Likewise, the U.S. trade deficit has grown wider, as has the current account deficit. These two, however, also reflect the relatively strong growth enjoyed in the United States, especially when compared with that of the lackluster export markets, especially in Europe.

Budget Deficit

The federal budget deficit has worsened since the late 1990s but is currently well within the norms for most industrialized nations. **Figure 6** graphs the annual budget deficit in dollar terms and as a percentage of GDP. Note that the GDP estimate for 2006 is $300 billion, which is a large figure, but it is only about 2 percent of GDP.[2] Thus, the United States is one of the few nations abiding by the constraints adopted by members of the European Union under the Stability Pact! Nevertheless, with the U.S. economy as strong as it has been, the budget deficit could be smaller. At present, the U.S. administration has certain tax reduction and budget spending priorities that are preventing a more noteworthy reduction in the deficit.

The current budget situation is not a problem. The longer-term view, however, is more worrisome, especially if the pace of economic growth and revenue generation slows. In a few years, members of the unprecedentedly large Baby Boom generation will retire in large numbers. This change will negatively affect income tax revenues and put upward pressure on transfer payments.

Trade Deficit

The analysis of trade patterns, and the imbalances that arise, cannot focus on a single country. Trade and foreign exchange, by definition, involve at least two

---

[2] The latest CBO estimate for 2006 is $260 billion.

Figure 6   Federal Budget Balance, 1967–2006

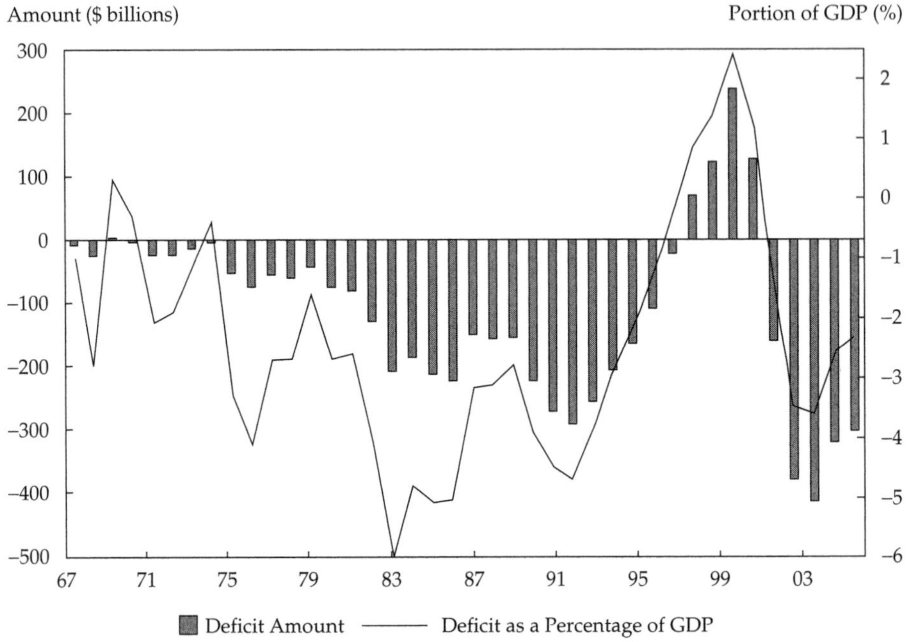

Note: Data for 2006 are estimated.
Source: Based on data from the U.S. Department of the Treasury.

parties. In this increasingly global economy, trade relationships may span many countries. **Table 3** displays several of the nations with which the United States trades. The most important trade partners are the United States' neighbors in North America—Canada and Mexico. Of course, there is some muddiness in the accounting because of the complexity of the trade relationships. Consider, for example, that automobile engines produced in Michigan are exported to Canada and put into vehicles that are then exported back to the United States. It is a challenging data-reconciliation process for the government economic bureaus in the region.

Outside North America, the most important trading partner of the United States is Europe, which is, by far, the largest customer of U.S. tradable goods and services. Although it receives little attention, the stagnation in U.S. exports to Europe since 2000 is responsible for a large portion of the increase in the U.S. trade deficit. The export slowdown is directly linked to the relatively meager GDP growth on the European continent and the commensurate lackluster demand for U.S. goods. GDP growth in the large European nations was little more than 1 percent for an extended period, business investment was anemic, and there was little demand for technology and capital goods—the primary exports of the United States to other developed economies. During the second

Table 3   Share of U.S. Foreign Trade, April 2005–March 2006

Location	U.S. Exports Amount (billions)	Share	U.S. Imports Amount (billions)	Share
North America	$341.6	36.5%	$476.7	27.6%
European Union	190.9	20.4	315.6	18.3
Japan	56.7	6.1	139.6	8.1
Central/South America	75.9	8.1	127.6	7.4
China	45.4	4.9	252.3	14.6
Korea	28.8	3.1	43.8	2.5
Total	$934.8	100.0%	$1,725.0	100.0%

Source: Based on data from the U.S. Department of Commerce.

half of the 1990s, in an environment of robust capital expenditures, 50 percent of the revenues of U.S. technology companies were generated outside the United States, and 85 percent of that came from Europe. As economic vigor returns to Europe, many exports from the United States to Europe should be positively affected, helping reduce the U.S. trade deficit, all other things being equal. Even so, other categories of previously strong U.S. exports to Europe, including agricultural products and airplanes, may continue to face structural trade issues.

The trade relationship with China often attracts the most discussion but often simplistically focuses only on the bilateral trade between the two countries. After all, the largest source of the U.S. trade deficit is the imbalance with China. But consider this: The United States has a $207 billion trade deficit with China; therefore, China has a $207 billion trade surplus with the United States. But China does not have an aggregate trade surplus at this time. That is, China has an aggregate $200 billion trade deficit with its trading partners other than the United States. What is the significance of this situation? This circle of economic demand may be a positive factor for global growth; the willingness of the United States to import from China creates demand for Chinese products, which creates Chinese jobs, which stimulates Chinese demand for goods and services, including demand for items outside China. Thus, the U.S. trade deficit with China has benefited not just China but also other nations that export their goods to China.

(6) Environmental Awareness

Environmental awareness is taking hold in markets around the world and is a matter not just for investors but also for corporations.

Increase in ESG Investing

Environmental sensitivity, social responsibility, and governance (ESG) is gaining momentum in terms of investor interest. Investors are paying attention to which companies are good citizens, not just by their words but also by their deeds. In 2003, U.S. portfolio managers with assets under management totaling $600 billion publicly stated their desire to emphasize environmentally sound investing. That number has grown to almost $4 trillion in 2006.

The markets are responding by pricing securities in a way that reflects this interest. Several investment vehicles facilitate such investment. One choice is mutual funds with a related investment goal. According to the Social Investment Forum, 200 funds were dedicated to socially responsible investing in 2003. Perhaps more importantly, many professional managers, without necessarily adopting a pure ESG mandate, are increasingly incorporating environmental and other issues into their fundamental analysis. Another alternative for investment is exchange-traded funds.

Insurance and reinsurance, both policies and investments in the companies that provide them, may be additional vehicles. The demand for protection from weather-related property damage, health-related risks caused by pollution, and directors' and officers' liability for inadequately addressing climate change threats will likely increase, as will the ability to transfer and share the risk of loss from weather-related incidents. And finally, there are markets that allow trading in carbon emissions by placing a value on these emissions and ultimately facilitating a cap-and-trade approach to reducing carbon emissions. These are still young markets, but they have the potential for significant growth in both Europe and the United States.

Fiduciary Responsibilities

For investment managers and pension sponsors, fiduciary responsibility comes first. Pension fund managers must focus on providing strong returns for plan participants. Until recently, environmentally aware investing did not typically generate returns above market benchmarks. In some cases, the returns to these strategies were below average, which may be attributable to the markets not being efficiently priced along this dimension. But as more investors pay attention to ESG issues, the so-called eco-efficiency premium, allowing strong relative returns, may become increasingly large and statistically significant.

Competitive Position

Companies are awakening to the benefits and opportunities associated with incorporating ESG policies into strategic planning as well as to the risks associated with ignoring ESG issues. Reputation, competitive position, and new product development are a few of the opportunities available to ESG-aware companies. Companies viewed as environmentally friendly, even within troubled industries, are likely to see their reputations enhanced. Companies that are better able to adapt to a "greener" world will have a competitive advantage over those companies that cannot, or will not, adapt. And companies that can develop new products or technologies to efficiently reduce the emission of greenhouse gases from existing products or processes will almost assuredly experience increased demand.

The risks of ignoring ESG issues include damage to a company's reputation, lack of preparedness for regulatory changes, potential future liabilities, a reduced competitive position, and a possible negative impact on business operations. The obvious candidates for careful study include participants in such industries as energy, chemicals, transportation, and utilities. Furthermore, many other industries may find that they are affected by climate issues, including insurance, travel, tourism, and construction.

Energy Intensity Gap

Figure 7 illustrates the energy intensity gap between developed and developing economies. Energy intensity is the amount of energy used per unit of GDP. The

Figure 7   Energy Intensity Gap between Developed and Developing Economies, 2003

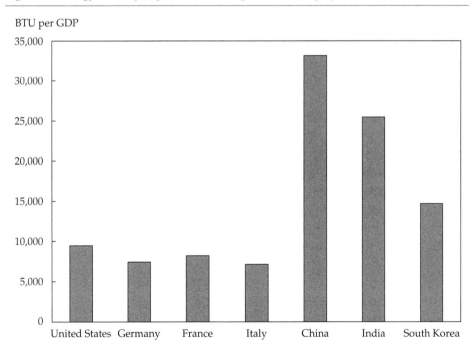

Notes: BTU stands for British thermal unit. GDP is calculated in U.S. dollars.
Source: Based on data from the U.S. Department of Energy.

United States is the world's largest user of energy, but it also has the largest GDP. This intensity metric allows a rough comparison of how efficiently nations use energy. For example, the energy intensity of the United States is not much different from that of other developed nations. It is somewhat higher but not because of industrial processes but because of Americans' ownership of larger autos and the tendency to drive them longer distances.

The more interesting gap in energy intensity is not between developed nations but between developed economies and so-called emerging economies. The energy intensity of China, India, and South Korea is much higher than that of the major developed economies. One possible explanation is the sector differences in the composition of the economies. Developed economies have outsourced much of their manufacturing, which tends to be energy intensive, to the developing economies. The developed economies have a larger service component in their GDP, and these activities tend to be less energy intensive. Nevertheless, an important question is whether the industrial processes and electricity generation in the emerging economies are sufficiently energy efficient and use clean energy sources. The emissions of carbon and other pollutants tend to be much higher, per unit, in developing economies.

Conclusion

Globalization is accompanied by a transfer of economic growth between regions and industries. The current cyclical shift to a slower growth trajectory for the U.S. economy will be somewhat offset by the recovery in some other industrial economies as well as the secular gains in several emerging nations. The period of dramatic global disinflation and declines in interest rates is over, but it is unlikely to be quickly followed by a period of worrisome inflation. Central banks have become less friendly but will not soon adopt extremely restrictive policies. Liquidity, still easily available in many economies and markets, will likely become less ample, and there will be shifts affecting the cost of capital. Capital flows and trade patterns will become increasingly global and multidimensional; bilateral analysis will be incomplete and misleading. Finally, decision making will increasingly be set within a global context, whether it deals with regulatory matters, accounting practices, environmental issues, or other forms of corporate governance. Companies, in general, will operate globally and think globally because opportunities for growth, and such issues as climate change, are not contained by borders.

This presentation comes from the 2006 CFA Institute Annual Conference held in Zurich on 21–24 May 2006.

More from Abby Joseph Cohen, CFA

This section presents the speaker's lively question and answer session with the conference audience.

Question: What is your outlook for the U.S. equity market vis-à-vis the equity markets in Europe and Asia?

Cohen: My colleagues remain enthusiastic about Japan. We see true structural improvement there because the banking system has recovered and domestic demand in the economy is improving. The return on equity (ROE) of Japanese companies, which has already doubled, will move somewhat higher. ROE in Japan is currently about 8 percent, still well below the 16–18 percent in the United States, but has room to easily grow. Corporate governance is much improved in Japan, and we expect that returns from the Japanese market will be in the mid-teens in yen terms. We expect equity returns in the United States and Europe to be below those in Japan. My forecast for the S&P 500 is 10–12 percent a year in 2006 and 2007. Emerging markets in Asia are likely to generate good long-term returns, given the solid growth expectation for their economies, but share prices are also expected to become more volatile.

Question: Are the discount rates used by pension fund sponsors overly optimistic?

Cohen: The discount rate is one of the few inputs for which companies have very little maneuvering room because it typically is driven by the AA corporate rate. It is an almost paradoxical situation that rising interest rates, and the discount rate, cause a decrease in pension expense so that the overall funding status of pension plans improves—at least in accounting terms. My colleague Michael Moran examined the discount rates used by each of the S&P 500 companies with defined-benefit pension plans and found only minimal variation.

The input to pension accounting that investors should emphasize in their analysis is the long-term expected return assumption on plan assets. A few years ago, the range of expected returns was concentrated between 12 percent and 14 percent a year. This is now down to single digits, with some companies using an expected return assumption as low as 6–7 percent and very few using an assumption above 9 percent.

Question: Could you comment on the information technology sector in the United States?

Cohen: In general, we are keen on the information technology sector because many U.S. technology companies have turned their attention away from the so-called commodities in technology and toward differentiated products. A commodity is something that sells on global markets on a fungible basis; for example, consumers don't care if DRAM (dynamic random access memory) is made in South Korea or South

Dakota. Instead, U.S. technology companies have been investing heavily in research and development—as have U.S. biotechnology companies—and these companies will benefit from the trend in the global economic growth of capital spending. So, technology companies represent one of our most favored sectors in the U.S. stock market at this point.

Question: How big is the risk that a decline in U.S. housing prices combined with a rise in mortgage rates will cause a decline in private consumption?

Cohen: Even if real estate markets weaken, as we expect, consumption spending is unlikely to turn negative. Personal consumption growth in the United States typically ranges between 2 percent and 4 percent and is rarely negative, even during recessions. In real estate, the main factor is location. The United States is a very large economy with many different real estate markets. Some of them are overpriced, but most are not. The overpriced markets appear to be those that are experiencing a large influx of people seeking second homes or vacation properties. The potentially troubled markets also tend to be communities where lending institutions have not been as careful as they should have been in evaluating borrowers. About 25 locations around the United States fit these parameters, and most of them are located in the states of California, Florida, Texas, and Arizona.

The factor to be watching with regard to the economic impact of a weaker housing market is "mortgage equity withdrawals." To the extent that mortgage interest rates are no longer falling and home prices are no longer rising, the opportunity for mortgage equity withdrawals has now been reduced. In the past, about 15 percent of the withdrawals were used to finance consumption. Much of the rest was used to pay down higher-rate debt, such as earlier mortgages or credit card debt, which led to improvements in the balance sheets of many U.S. households.

Most of the mortgage dollars that were borrowed over the past three years were borrowed in the form of conventional fixed-rate mortgages in which households locked in very low mortgage rates for the next 20–30 years. These households will not be affected by higher market interest rates. Instead, the households who used more exotic forms to refinance were typically lower middle income. Their goal was not to improve their balance sheet but to minimize their monthly payments. This is the group of consumers about which we have concerns. These are the same consumers who will be most affected by the rise in energy prices because of the increased expense of heating or cooling their homes or filling up the tank of their automobiles. The anticipated reduction in the growth rate of U.S. consumption is going to come from primarily lower-middle-income households.

Investing in a World of Rapidly Changing Geopolitical and Economic Trends

MARC FABER

A transfer of wealth is under way from the West—the United States and Europe—to Asia as evidenced by the current account balances of countries in these regions of the world. The impending industrialization of Asia has vast implications for geopolitical alliances, commodities demand (particularly oil), and investment strategy. As investments, financial assets should take a backseat to commodities as the global economy's expansionary phase begins to lose stamina in light of rising commodity prices, inflation, and interest rates.

Over the past five years, we have seen an extended period of global expansion, but certainly, the expansion cannot last forever. So, how much longer will it last? Is it extended by the emergence of a new world economic power? Is inflation a concern? And how do shifting alliances and geopolitical pressures affect the outcome? To explore these questions, I will begin with a description of the current expansion, highlighting its several unusual features. I will then discuss geopolitical trends, U.S. monetary policy, shifting global economic power, and China's influence on the global economy and markets. Finally, I will conclude with some observations.

Current Global Expansion

The current economic expansion began in November 2001 and is now about five years old. Compared with previous post–World War II expansions, the current expansion has several unusual features. First, this expansion has been greatly influenced by China and, to a lesser extent, India as well as the former USSR satellite countries. These countries are now major factors in the global

> When a nation's economic expansion is driven largely by consumption, as is the case in the United States, the nation suffers a loss of competitiveness versus nations whose growth is driven by strong investment activity and capital spending, as is the case in China.

Marc Faber is managing director of Marc Faber Limited, Hong Kong.

economy because they have become not only producers of goods and services on a global scale but also consumers. As producers, their impact on certain sectors of the global economy has been deflationary because of their cost efficiency and high productivity, but as consumers, their impact on such sectors as commodities and raw materials has been inflationary.

The current economic expansion is also unusual because for the first time in the history of capitalism, the global economy is experiencing synchronized growth. In the earliest days of capitalism under the colonial system of mercantilism, the industrialized countries of the West were interested simply in extracting raw materials from their colonies. They would bring these raw materials home for processing and return them as consumer goods to the colonies to capture a substantial profit. Hence, the colonial system kept a lid on the growth of the colony nations. When colonialism expired at the end of World War II, communism and socialism emerged to support growth and production in only limited sectors of the economy, such as capital goods (especially military hardware). And after 1989 when the communist system unraveled, synchronized global growth was not possible because of successive periods of depression in Latin America and recessions in Japan and North America. Fortunately, developed and developing nations alike are now joined in a web of symbiotic relationships that support their own respective modes of economic growth.

As a by-product of synchronized global growth, commodities have become a recognized asset class, another unique feature of this present expansion. The United States is showing strong growth, as defined by consumption; China is showing strong growth, as defined by production; and India, Latin America, and Russia, whose growth is largely fueled by rising resource prices, are similarly booming. Obviously, this concerted pattern in global growth has had a massive impact on the demand curve for most commodities, essentially resulting in a higher equilibrium price. Although commodities played a role in previous expansions, particularly in the 1970s, the commodities of interest back then were mainly precious metals (gold in particular) and oil. In the current environment, virtually all commodities have earned a place at the asset allocation table.

Another feature unique to this expansion is that the poorer countries, the newly emerging economies, are financing the richer, developed nations. Historically, the opposite has been the case. For example, in the 19th century, European capital financed the construction of canals and railroads in the emerging U.S. economy. And in the 20th century, U.S. and European capital financed economic development around the world. But now, the United States has a growing trade and current account deficit offset by growing trade and current account surpluses, most notably in the Asian countries. These Asian countries are thus financing U.S. consumption through the purchase of U.S. Treasury and agency securities. This situation has never existed before.

Finally, another unusual factor in this recovery is that all asset markets have risen since October 2002. Developed and emerging stocks, commodities, real estate, art, collectibles, and even wines have appreciated, as have bonds until recently. It is unthinkable that in the long run, commodity and real estate prices will rise along with bond prices because the former markets are indicators of inflation and hence bad news for bonds.

Global Geopolitical Trends

Two themes dominate current geopolitical trends: (1) increasing demand for Middle East oil and for a broad spectrum of commodities by rapidly developing Asian nations and (2) increasing political tensions tied to shifting diplomatic alliances driven in large part by the twin demands for oil and other raw materials.

Clearly, the pace of growth and rapid infrastructure changes in China make this nation the focal point for analysis of geopolitical trends. Of note, tensions between Japan and China have worsened in recent years as Japan and the United States have continued to strengthen their strategic alliance, thus pushing China much closer toward Russia. Five years ago, China and Russia formed the Shanghai Cooperation Organization with the central Asian republics of Uzbekistan, Kazakhstan, Kyrgyzstan, and Tajikistan. The purpose of the organization is to promote trade and national security in the region, but it does not encompass a formal defense treaty. The four observing nations of Mongolia, Pakistan, India, and Iran are scheduled to join the organization in June 2006. China is obviously concerned about and interested in central Asia because of the several-thousand-mile shared border with these countries, not to mention China's appetite for resources, which are plentiful in central Asia.

Russia is also interested in central Asia because it has always considered the nations in this region to be within its sphere of influence, which has heightened tensions between the United States, China, and Russia. The Shanghai Cooperation Organization issued a statement following its meeting in June 2005 whereby it demanded that the United States begin to withdraw its bases in central Asia. Russia, China, and India are interested in furthering ties with Iran, which would be much easier to do without U.S. troops in close proximity. Iran is already a large trading partner with Russia, especially in military hardware, and China and India are interested in developing Iran's oil resources. India has, with the approval of Pakistan, which is unusual, agreed to build a pipeline between India and Iran to pipe natural gas and oil to India. China already has a pipeline to Kazakhstan, which it would like to extend to Iran. Obviously, the United States would be concerned about such a development.

As Asia becomes almost entirely dependent on Middle East oil, Taiwan has become strategically important because of its location adjacent to the major shipping lanes. Japan, South Korea, and Taiwan import 100 percent of their oil, and 75 percent of these oil imports come from the Middle East. Until 1994, China was basically oil self-sufficient, but because of its rapidly growing demand, China has now become the world's second largest consumer of oil. Because oil going to China must travel by tanker through the Strait of Formosa, situated between mainland China and Taiwan, China feels vulnerable to the threat of disruption in its supply, which could potentially come from Taiwan or its allies. Thus, China will never allow Taiwan to become an independent country.

As the demand for commodities rises, so do diplomatic tensions, according to the theory of war cycles. For example, commodity prices declined after 1980 along with diminishing international tensions as the Cold War abated. The dissolution of the USSR and the failure of communism in the late 1980s actually resulted more from collapsing oil prices in 1985 and 1986 than from President Reagan's Star Wars program. And the Russian economic crisis in 1998 occurred after oil prices collapsed between 1996 and 1998. As a result, the resource-producing nations lost traction in the global balance of power and are only now regaining that power.

Conversely, when commodity prices rise, as is happening now, countries become concerned about obtaining sufficient, reliable supplies of needed commodities. Most wars can be attributed to some sort of commodity shortage or to another commodity-related cause. Therefore, consistent with the theory of war cycles, rising commodity prices lead to increasing national tensions and eventually to war. During periods of war, commodity prices tend to rise almost vertically, and as a result, all major commodity price peaks have occurred during or at the end of wars.

As geopolitical tensions continue to increase globally in the tug of war between the United States' need for oil to fuel consumption and China's need for oil to fuel economic growth, military expenditures will rise, budget deficits will increase, and government debt will increase. This has happened in the past, and it appears to be happening again.

U.S. Monetary Policy

U.S. Federal Reserve Board Chairman Ben Bernanke is concerned about asset price deflation and the potential it holds for an economic depression like the ones in the United States and Europe from 1929 to 1932 or the one in Japan from 1989 to 2003, when stocks and real estate depreciated for 14 straight years. Bernanke is prepared to combat falling asset prices with so-called extraordinary measures, such as printing money.

Figure 1   MZM as a Percentage of GDP, 1984–2005

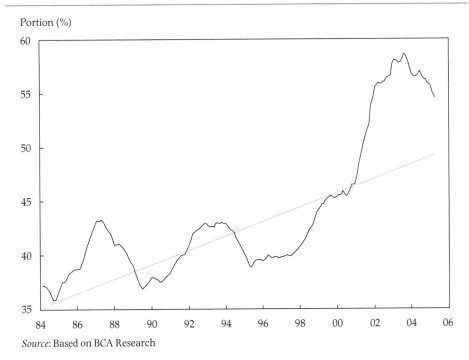

Source: Based on BCA Research

At the end of the 1990s, the United States was in the midst of a capital spending boom and a stock market boom. Both came to an end in March 2000 with the NASDAQ falling by 70 percent and capital spending (concentrated in the telecommunications, media, and high-tech sectors) dropping like a rock. To combat this potentially deflationary scenario, the Fed began to pursue an ultra-expansionary monetary policy. Although U.S. money supply, measured by money of zero maturity (MZM) as a percentage of GDP, grew steadily starting in the early 1980s, it really exploded after 2000, as shown in **Figure 1**, as the fed funds rate was cut from 6.5 percent in 2000 to 1 percent in 2003. But despite 16 subsequent interest rate hikes, which began in June 2004, at a fed funds rate of 5 percent, an expansionary monetary policy is essentially still in place—evidenced by the fact that broad measures of U.S. inflation (not core consumer price index [CPI]) show that inflation continues to accelerate.

Total U.S. debt as a percentage of U.S. GDP has risen dramatically recently. In 1980, total credit market debt was 130 percent of GDP; now, it is 320 percent of GDP. At this level of debt to GDP, true monetary tightening would be out of the question. So, Bernanke has no other option but to print money because an asset decline in the United States equal to, for example, a drop of 10–20 percent of the average home price or 30–40 percent of the stock market would lead to a very severe recession and extensive problems throughout the financial system.

If asset prices fell dramatically but the debt level stayed the same, debt to GDP would balloon, causing serious discomfort in the U.S. economy.

Credit market growth also signals that monetary policy is still effectively expansionary. In the first quarter of 2005, nonfinancial debt increased by $2.5 trillion, which is a good bit more than the second quarter 2004 increase of $1.7 trillion. In fact, total credit was 39 percent higher in the fourth quarter of 2005 than it was in the second quarter of 2004, when the current period of Fed tightening began. In other words, the Fed has increased interest rates, but credit market growth is not slowing. In fact, credit market growth is much higher than it was in 2004—hardly a sign of tight monetary policy. Moreover, asset prices continue to trend upward. If money really were tight, this would not be happening.

Although these measures indicate that monetary policy remains expansionary (i.e., not tight enough), money supply growth in the United States has responded to the ratcheting up of the fed funds rate by slowing substantially, as shown in **Figure 2**. Non-U.S. official dollar reserve growth tells the same story because it too has slowed over the past couple of years, but not by enough.

In 2005, in the United States, total credit market debt grew by $3.3 trillion and GDP grew by $751 billion. Outstanding debt is growing at a

Figure 2   Yearly Percentage Change in MZM, 1984 to 29 May 2006

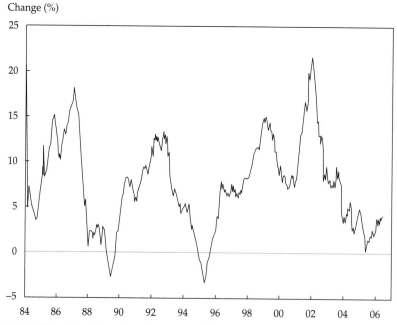

Note: MZM includes M1, savings deposits, and all money market mutual funds (individual and institutional).
Sources: Based on data from the Board of Governors of the Federal Reserve System and Oak Associates Ltd.

much faster rate than GDP, and the impact of that increase on real economic activity has been diminishing over time. Eventually, printing money has no direct impact whatsoever on the economy and is simply passed through to the asset or currency markets. A peculiarity of the current U.S. expansion is the imbalance that has developed in the credit markets. Nearly 80 percent of new credit creation was for housing-related activity. In the 1990s, home mortgage borrowing increased by an average of $250 billion annually; it is now growing at more than $1 trillion annually.

Real estate assets as a percentage of disposable income are at an all-time high. Although the growth in real estate assets is "off the charts," the growth in household net worth is reaching a new high, but not by much. In fact, the growth in household net worth is no higher than it was in the late 1980s. The refinancing boom of recent years, which resulted from artificially low interest rates, has encouraged households to borrow to fuel consumption in lieu of improving their net worth. Arguably, the housing slowdown has commenced. The refinancing index is down, and buying attitudes are depressed. In addition, homebuilding stocks peaked in July 2005, with some already off 50 percent from their highs. Housing affordability is also down, and soon there will be a drop in what I call "life affordability," which will have a dampening effect on U.S. consumption. Consequently, the U.S. economy is quite vulnerable.

The asset inflation associated with printing money pervades the attitudes of consumers and investors. In the 1960s, wages rose as a result of expansionary money policies, and in the 1970s, commodity prices rose. Of course, the beneficiary can also be equities, bonds, real estate, and so forth. In the presence of asset inflation, consumers come to believe that it will be a permanent feature of the economic landscape. For example, if a consumer's home is worth $100,000 today, then in a year's time, the consumer reasons that its value must appreciate to $120,000, and so on. Asset inflation leads households to save less from current income because they see the appreciation in their savings and in their homes. Effectively, the household savings rate drops, as shown in **Figure 3**. From an average savings rate of 9 percent in the 1970s to 6 percent in the 1980s to 4 percent in the 1990s, it has moved to less than 2 percent in recent years. Of course, artificially low interest rates do not encourage savings either, which has certainly been the case in the past couple of years.

Shifting Global Economic Power

The U.S. expansion is a product of consumption growth, not capital spending. And capital spending in the United States, both as a percentage of corporate profits and as a percentage of GDP, is depressed. When a nation's economic expansion is driven largely by consumption, as is the case in the United States,

Figure 3   U.S. Household Savings Rate, 12-Month Moving Average: 1960–2006

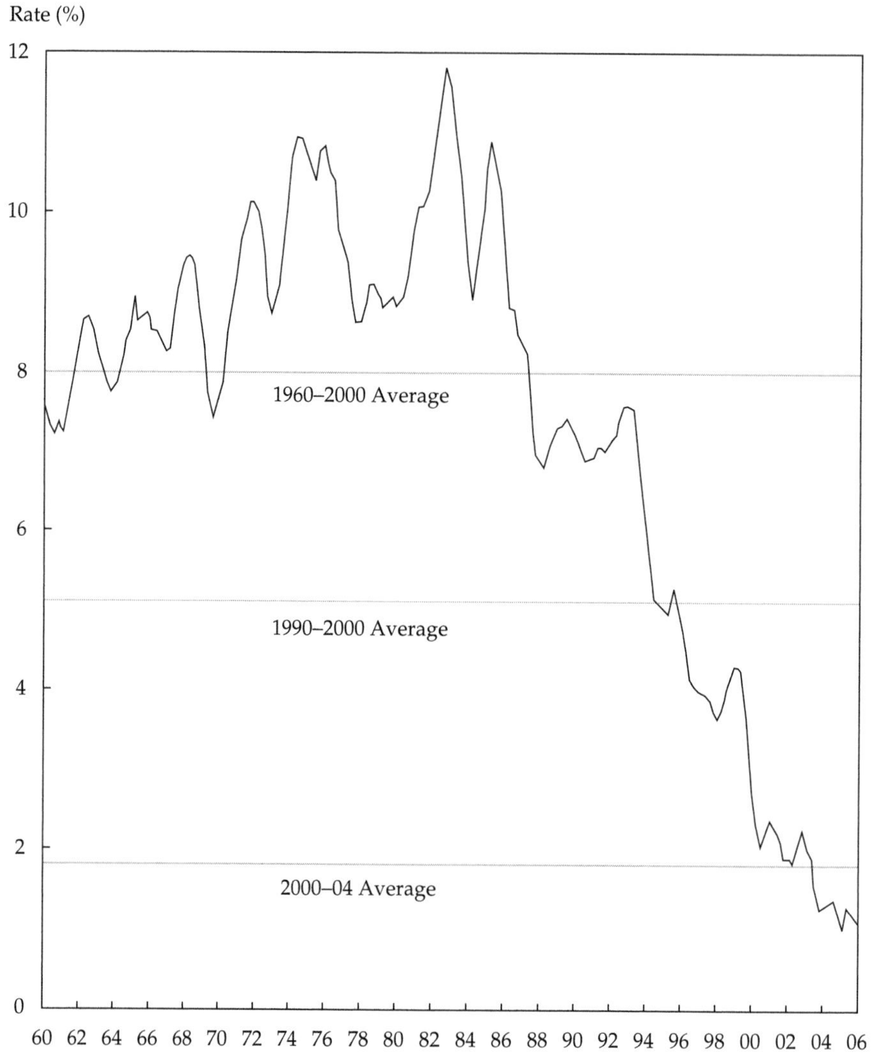

Rate (%)

1960–2000 Average

1990–2000 Average

2000–04 Average

60 62 64 66 68 70 72 74 76 78 80 82 84 86 88 90 92 94 96 98 00 02 04 06

Sources: Based on data from Thomson Financial Datastream and Dresdner Kleinwort Wasserstein.

the nation suffers a loss of competitiveness versus nations whose growth is driven by strong investment activity and capital spending, as is the case in China. China has a much smaller economy than the United States does but a capital spending rate almost as high as that of the United States. The equivalent of $1 billion of capital spending on infrastructure in China goes farther than it does in the United States or Switzerland because the Chinese government owns the land and labor costs are much lower. Therefore, capital spending in real terms is larger in China than in the United States.

A nation's competitive position can easily be measured by its exports as a percentage of global exports. Based on this measure, the United States is losing competitiveness because it is a net consumer, and China is gaining competitiveness because it is a net producer. This situation leads to a growing trade deficit for the United States with China and a growing trade surplus for China with the United States.

Although China's trade surplus with the United States is in excess of $100 billion annually, do not be misled to think that China does not import. At the same time China is running a trade surplus with the United States, it has a growing trade deficit with its neighboring Asian countries as well as with other countries around the world. Today, China, not the United States, is South Korea's largest customer, with South Korea's exports to China growing at more than 20 percent a year. And Japan is exporting less to the United States while exporting more to China. Japan's exports to greater China, which includes Taiwan, Hong Kong, and the mainland, are now larger than those to the United States. To be sure, China's vast consumer economy is stimulating the economies of other Asian nations. And although the United States maintains trade deficits with nearly every nation in the world (including the Asian nations), China has emerged as a strong engine of growth, sharing this honor with the United States.

The optimists in the United States point to the trade surplus in services as an offset to the trade deficit in goods, but the amount of the surplus has been insufficient over the past 15 years to wipe out the trade deficit in goods. The trade surplus in services has benefited over the past few years from declining interest rates, which has kept net interest payments to foreigners relatively flat, but it will soon experience a trend reversal. With interest rates rising, interest payments owed by the United States to foreign holders of U.S. assets will jump from about $140 billion annually to $200 billion annually.

Also of interest is the negative U.S. net asset balance, which has collapsed over the past five years as a percentage of GDP. Non-U.S. investors now own $9 trillion in assets in the United States, and U.S. investors hold the equivalent of $6 trillion in assets overseas. This negative $3 trillion net asset balance continues to grow each year and now represents 25 percent of the United States' $12 trillion economy. Although the net asset balance turned negative as far back as 1987, it began to deteriorate badly after 2001, when the United States began to implement an ultra-expansionary monetary policy. Until 1998, the U.S. current account deficit equaled about 2 percent of GDP, but now, it is closer to 7 percent. In other words, the current account deficit has tripled. An optimist may say it does not matter if a country has a current account deficit of 7 percent, but if it triples again to, say, 21 percent of GDP, then the story will change. Considering the financial position of the United States as a whole, it has definitely deteriorated.

Clearly, if a country (such as the United States) has chronic, growing trade and capital account deficits and a region (such as Asia) has steadily improving trade and capital account surpluses, then a transfer of wealth is taking place. Not only is it taking place in terms of financial accounting, but it is also taking place through the transfer of technology and skill building each time production is outsourced to China or services are outsourced to India. Outsourcing creates employment and generates capital spending, and ultimately, it has a growth multiplier effect on the Asian economies and a negative impact on the U.S. economy.

The outcome of the economic power shift to Asia and away from the West is that it will lead to currency weakness. The world economy is based on the U.S. dollar, euro, yen, Chinese Renminbi (yuan), and gold or precious metals. Over time, the four paper currencies will depreciate against the other Asian currencies because of the pending transfer of wealth to Asia. In addition, each of the paper currencies will depreciate against precious metals. The U.S. position is that China's trade surplus with the United States is a result of the artificially low exchange rate between the two nations' currencies. So, China has carried out a modest revaluation, what I would consider a cosmetic revaluation, but this revaluation is unlikely to be the answer to the trade imbalance.

China's Influence

Wages in China and India compared with those in the United States are quite low. In China, per capita wages are equal to 2.5 percent of U.S. per capita wages, and in India, 1.6 percent of U.S. per capita wages. Assume China's currency doubles in value against the U.S. dollar. If US$1 equals 8.28 yuan now and it appreciates by 100 percent, the U.S. dollar's value will depreciate to about 4 yuan. Then, wages in China will be approximately 5 percent of wages in the United States and Europe. Even with such a significant currency strengthening, whether from a revaluation or something else, production and investment activity will not flow back from Asia to Europe and the United States.

In addition, China has an excess labor reservoir because of a very low level of urbanization. In Europe and the United States, urbanization rates are 95–98 percent, but in the Asian region and in India, the urbanization rate is closer to 30 percent. China's urbanization rate has increased from 29 percent in 1996 to 37 percent in 2005. Nearly 20 million people in China move from the countryside to the cities every year, steadily feeding the labor supply and ensuring that labor costs will not rise dramatically in China.

China runs a net positive trade balance and has been doing so for the past 10 years. Looking back 20 years at the long-term pattern, China has been increasing its imports at about the same rate as its exports. In 2002, monthly Chinese imports were $12 billion. At the present time, monthly imports are

$65 billion, hardly supportive of accusations that China is pursuing unfair trade policies.

In the anticipated wealth transfer between the United States and Asia via their respective trade and current account balances, something has to give. As stated earlier, that "something" is the value of the U.S. dollar, which can be expected to depreciate against the Asian currencies; alternatively, as has happened since 2002, Asian assets could appreciate relative to U.S. assets. In other words, the stock markets of emerging Asian nations, which have been outperforming the S&P 500 Index, and real estate in Asia are likely to appreciate further. In fact, the asset class for the future will be real estate in such countries as India, which has an underdeveloped real estate market, and Vietnam, which is just now becoming a full-fledged capitalistic system and is about 10 years behind China. Such investment opportunities are sprinkled liberally through Asia.

The Chinese economy is often dismissed as being relatively small. But the physical markets in China are enormous and have significant growth potential. China now has more than 420 million mobile phone subscribers and 90 million motorcycles. And China is experiencing deflation in many sectors of the economy, which is leading to greater demand. For example, the price of the cheapest car has dropped from the equivalent of about $20,000 five years ago to $3,700. At a price of $20,000, maybe 1 million households could afford a car, but at $3,700, 50 million households can afford one.

China's share of world mineral production in 2003 is shown in **Table 1**. In most minerals, China is already ranked number one. China's demand for copper was 6 percent of total world production in 1990, 12 percent in year 2000, and now is more than 21 percent. China is the largest user of iron ore at 27 percent of the world's production. And remarkably, the per capita consumption in China of all raw materials is still very low. For example, in China, consumption of copper is just over 4 pounds per person compared with 16 pounds per person in the United States, aluminum consumption is 4 kilograms per person in China compared with a little more than 20 kilograms per person in the United States, and oil consumption is just under 2 barrels per person in China compared with about 22 barrels per person in the United States. Thus, the demand for raw materials in China will inevitably increase as China moves at a faster pace toward a capitalist economy.

As economies become increasingly industrialized, the demand for oil rises rapidly. The industrialization of the United States caused per capita oil consumption to rise from 1 barrel to 27 barrels annually from 1900 to 1970. The industrialization of Japan from 1950 to 1970 and the industrialization of South Korea from 1965 to 1990 caused per capita consumption of oil to increase from 1 barrel to 17 barrels in each country. In China, per capita oil consumption currently stands at 1.7 barrels, and in India, at 0.8 barrels. Once China and India have fully emerged as industrial powerhouses, they will experience a sharply

Table 1   China's Share of World Mineral
Production, 2003

Commodity	Percentage	Rank
Fuels		
Coal	45%	1
Oil	4.7	6
Industrial minerals		
Cement	42%	1
Fluorspar	55	1
Rare earths	85	1
Metals		
Aluminum	18%	1
Antimony	89	1
Copper	12	2
Gold	8	4
Lead	18	2
Magnesium	45	1
Molybdenum	24	3
Silver	12	3
Steel, crude	23	1
Tin	32	1
Tungsten	83	1
Zinc	22	1

Source: Based on data from the U.S. Geological
Survey.

rising demand for oil. Urbanization, a phenomenon Asia is now experiencing, also leads to rising energy consumption.

Observations

In light of my discussion, several observations are in order.

Observation 1: Financial assets are not attractive investments.

Commodity prices have a much greater upside than financial assets. **Figure 4** shows that adjusted for inflation, commodity prices are still relatively low. After a protracted period of falling prices, on an inflation-adjusted basis, in 2001, commodities reached their lowest level in the history of capitalism. Up 100 percent now from that low point, the rising world demand for commodities is

Figure 4   S&P Commodity Index Adjusted for Inflation by CPI, 1969–2006

Note: Data as of 31 December of each year.

making itself known. Each commodity cycle lasts 45–60 years and has been identified as part of the Kondratieff wave phenomenon. These waves are not business cycles but commodity and price cycles. Riding the front of the wave are rising commodity prices, which eventually spur rising consumer prices and rising interest rates. Riding the back of the wave are falling commodity prices, which eventually trigger falling consumer prices and falling interest rates. With a 45–60 year cycle, each wave—rising or falling—takes 22–30 years. If the low in commodity prices, the turn in the wave, was in 2001 and it is now 2006, the Kondratieff wave is 5 years old. Hence, the 5-year-old bull market in equities—as well as the bond market—is vulnerable to reversal.

Also a concern is that at cycle turning points, volatility significantly jumps in all markets and big corrections are common. At the last turn in the cycle, which was in the early 1970s, the price of gold dropped from $195 to $103 between 31 December 1974 and 31 August 1976; it then proceeded to move up another eight times before the cycle peaked in the early 1980s. The Dow Jones Industrial Average (DJIA) plummeted 40 percent in 1987 before rising another eight times. The best environment, of course, for financial assets and bonds, in particular, is a period of falling commodity prices and interest rates; when the opposite occurs, financial assets take a beating. It appears a new cycle is beginning, which suggests higher commodity prices and interest rates, which in turn, is bad news for financial assets.

Observation 2: An investment in the physical commodity is preferable to an investment in the shares of commodity producers.

As the prices of commodities rise and the balance of power in the world shifts from industrialized to resource-producing countries, workers in the resource-producing nations will seek and get more concessions from their employers. In addition, the road to compromise will lead to meaningful supply disruptions and a generally unfavorable climate in the respective sector, which will put undue pressure on shares.

Observation 3: The price of oil will continue to rise.

My view is that oil demand will double in Asia to 40 million barrels per day in 10–12 years. Oil demand in Asia ex-Japan has risen from roughly 6 million barrels a day to about 17 million barrels a day over the past 20 years (1986 to 2005). Japan and the rest of Asia, with a population of 3.6 billion, or 56 percent of the world's population, together consume 22 million barrels of oil a day. In comparison, the United States consumes 22 million barrels a day and has a population of only 300 million. Regardless of how much oil the suppliers produce, production will not be able to keep pace with demand. Therefore, oil will never return to $12 a barrel.

Observation 4: Bonds are a bad investment.

Bond yields vis-à-vis oil prices can be divided into three phases: 1960 to 1980, 1980 to 1999, and 1999 to the present. In the first phase, the bond yield rose from 4 percent to more than 15 percent and the price of oil trended up as well. In the second phase, the price of oil and bond yields, or interest rates, fell—from 15 percent to 6 percent. The third phase is characterized by diverging performance between the two measures: The price of oil has risen dramatically to a high of $75 a barrel from a low in 2002 of $20 a barrel, and interest rates have steadily fallen. This divergence is most unusual.

In my view, the commodity markets are right. Although the demand for commodities may slow, the structural demand for commodities, particularly from China, given the supply constraints, has caused the demand curve for commodities to shift to the right. When India's economy begins to really expand, the curve will shift to the right once again. The structural demand for commodities, combined with the easy monetary policy of the Fed, means that eventually interest rates and inflation will be much higher than any of us can imagine. I am always asked what the best investment is. If I were instead asked what the worst investment is, I could easily respond; it is the U.S. 30-year Treasury bond.

Observation 5: If an investor must buy financial assets, buy equities.

Figure 5 is similarly divided into three phases and shows the 10-year U.S. Treasury yield and nominal GDP growth. In the first phase, from 1962 to 1980, the bond yield was below nominal GDP and coincided with accelerating inflation. In the second phase, between 1980 and 2002, a period of disinflation, interest rates, proxied by the bond yield, were above nominal GDP growth. From 2002 to the present, the bond yield has once again been below nominal GDP growth, which suggests that inflation may again be accelerating. This hypothesis is supported by other economic variables that I have discussed, such as an expansionary monetary policy on the part of the United States, rising commodities prices, and increasing global demand for commodities, particularly oil. Therefore, if forced to buy financial assets, I would rather be in equities than in bonds for the long term.

Observation 6: Gold is an excellent long-term investment.

Just like the equity markets, different sectors in the commodities markets move at different times. Right now, gold is relatively cheap compared with oil. Gold can definitely rise more, particularly in the midst of an expansionary monetary

Figure 5   Ten-Year Government Bond Yield and Nominal GDP Yearly Percentage Growth, 1962–2006

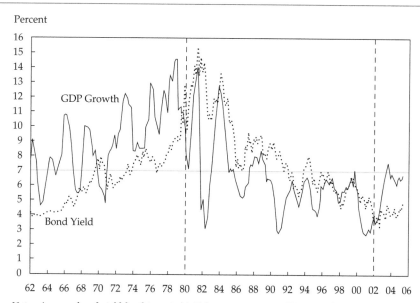

Notes: Average bond yield for this period is 7.1 percent; average GDP growth is 7.3 percent.
Sources: Based on data from the U.S. Department of Commerce, Bureau of Economic Analysis, Board of Governors of the Federal Reserve System, and Oak Associates Ltd.

policy because gold becomes the primary holder of value. At this global economic juncture, gold is a better investment than, say, industrial commodities, which would likely come under pressure if a recessionary period were to ensue from the next upsurge of the commodities, inflation, and interest rate wave.

Another way to look at the value of financial assets is in respect to gold. For example, in 2000, the value of the DJIA could buy 45 ounces of gold; today, it buys 18 ounces of gold. In other words, even though the DJIA has advanced, it has not advanced as much as gold. My view is that if governments, in particular the United States, print enough money, then money will depreciate in real terms and against hard currencies. So, if the DJIA triples in value to 33,000, I believe that gold will rise to $5,000 or $6,000 an ounce and that the value of the DJIA will buy only four or five ounces of gold. And if the Fed continues to unabatedly print money and the DJIA reaches 100,000, its value will then equal only half an ounce of gold.

This presentation comes from the 2006 CFA Institute Annual Conference held in Zurich on 21–24 May 2006.

Developments in Asset Allocation Modeling

LUIS M. VICEIRA

The "traditional" approach to designing policy portfolios assumes that expected returns, risk, and real interest rates do not change over time so that short-term and long-term risk properties of asset returns are the same. Thus, target asset allocations are the same regardless of investment horizon and remain constant over time. The "modern" approach, in contrast, recognizes that expected returns, risk, and real interest rates may change over time. This view creates a wedge between the short-term and long-term risk properties of asset returns and implies that target allocations may vary with investment horizon and over time. One implication of this view is that short-term bonds may not be the "safe asset" for long-term investors.

In this presentation, I will discuss the design of policy portfolios for long-term investors.[1] To do so, I will begin by looking at the traditional and modern approaches to policy portfolio design. I will then address return patterns over time and the other side of the coin, risk.

> For investors with longer investment horizons, the "safe" investment, T-bills, is not very safe because it leaves investors with an exposure to changing real interest rates.

Traditional Design

In the traditional approach to the design of policy portfolios, the investor starts by formulating a set of capital market assumptions (e.g., beliefs about risk premiums, interest rates, and risk itself) and then assumes that the risk–return trade-off is constant over time. In other words, the investor assumes that bonds have, say, an expected return of 2 percent in excess of the return on Treasury bills and that this expected excess return will remain constant in the future, regardless of economic conditions.

Based on that assumption, the investor formulates the policy portfolio with a target asset allocation by seeing how much each asset class contributes to

---

[1] Note that this presentation is based on Campbell and Viceira (2005).

Luis M. Viceira is an associate professor of business administration at Harvard University, Cambridge, Massachusetts.

expected excess returns relative to risk in the policy portfolio. When that step is done, the investor can decide on the specific allocations. One way to formalize this analysis is to use the mean–variance approach because it indicates what kind of tilts the capital market assumptions are introducing into the target policy portfolio. The investor can then adjust these allocations depending on other constraints and for "risk outside the model."

The key point is that in the traditional approach, no distinction is made between short-term and long-term risk properties of asset returns. One set of numbers summarizes risk at all horizons. And the underlying belief is that the target asset allocation should be constant over time and independent of investment horizon.

Figure 1 is an illustration of this traditional approach, with expected return on one axis and risk on the other. Suppose an investor is trying to allocate among stocks, bonds, and cash. The investor formulates his or her capital market assumptions, which then indicate where these three asset classes are on the return–risk spectrum. Based on that analysis, the investor considers all portfolios that combine stocks and bonds so as to find the optimal mix. Then, depending on the degree of risk aversion, the investor includes cash—perhaps none for the risk tolerant, perhaps a good bit for the risk averse. The point is that the policy portfolio is independent of the investment horizon and that cash is seen as the safe asset regardless of the investment horizon.

Figure 1   Risk–Return Trade-Off, Traditional View

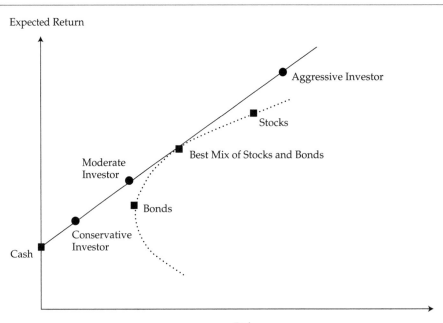

Modern Design

Some institutions have been experimenting with policy portfolio design, what I call the "modern approach." Some large endowments, large foundations, and large pension funds have adopted a practice by which they revise periodically their capital market assumptions. Accordingly, they also revise the target allocations for their policy portfolios. These revisions are based on their belief that investment opportunities, real interest rates, and expected returns on equities and bonds change over time. Thus, they change their policy portfolios over time too. Note that these institutions are making gradual changes in their policy portfolios. It is not a tactical asset allocation program, which calls for high-frequency trading in and out of asset classes. They are periodically revising their capital market assumption based on current market conditions and introducing gradual changes to their policy portfolios.

Return Patterns

Because these changes in the policy portfolio depend on changes in expectations about returns, it is important to look at history to see how these patterns change over time. Changes in nominal dividend growth and nominal earnings growth are generally driven by changes in inflation and have been stable over 10-year periods in real, inflation-adjusted terms. For example, dividend growth per share (DPS) in the S&P 500 Index over the past 10, 30, or 84 years has been, in nominal terms, 4.0 percent, 5.8 percent, and 4.4 percent, respectively, as shown in **Table 1**. It was on the high side for the past 30-year period because this period captures the high inflation of the late 1970s and early 1980s. In contrast, in recent times, it has been in the 3.0–3.5 percent range. It is the same story for EPS. In nominal terms, it has been, respectively, 6.7 percent, 6.5 percent, and 5.0 percent for the same 10-, 30-, and 84-year periods. Earnings may be negatively affected in the short term, but they always end up catching up with inflation. So, when projecting future dividends or earnings growth,

Table 1 Dividend and Earnings Growth of S&P 500, Periods Ending 2004

Period	DPS	EPS
10 years	4.0%	6.7%
30 years	5.8	6.5
84 years	4.4	5.0

Figure 2   S&P 500 Price/10-Year Average Earnings, 1881–2005

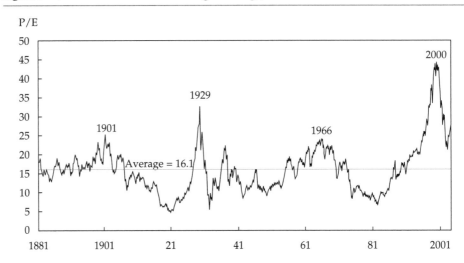

an investor can reasonably use long-term historical values, unless the investor believes things have changed significantly from the past.

P/E multiples also need to be examined when making capital market assumptions. **Figure 2** shows the ratio of the price of the S&P 500 to the 10-year moving average of earnings from 1881 to 2005. By this measure, the P/E of the S&P 500 averaged a little more than 16 times in this period. Big jumps from this average occurred in 1901, 1929, 1966, and 2000, but in general, the P/E moved slowly around the average.

If you are someone who thinks that the P/E multiple of the market will revert to its 100-year average, then you must ask yourself what has to happen for it to revert in, say, 10 years. The answer is that either the denominator must grow (i.e., earnings) or the numerator must fall (i.e., prices). So, earnings would have to grow at their long-term average of 5 percent a year, or 60 percent in total, over the next 10 years while stock prices stay flat. Alternatively, prices would have to fall by 40 percent, as in 1929, 1966, and 2000, to get back to the average. Of course, a combination of growth in earnings and a fall in prices could also happen. This type of thinking is precisely what modern portfolio policy design has in mind.

The dividend/price (D/P) multiple, shown in **Figure 3**, is another factor to be examined. For the 1881–2005 period, it averaged 4.5 percent. And again, by and large, it has hovered around the average, although it is currently at roughly 1.7 percent. When making predictions, one needs to decide whether D/P will remain below its historical average or will mean revert, with resulting implications for dividend and price movements.

Figure 3   S&P 500 10-Year Average Dividend/Price, 1881–2005

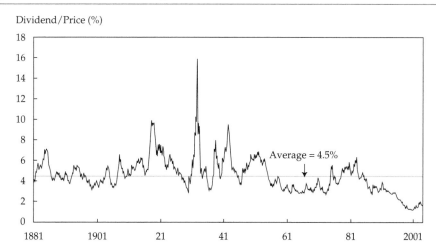

Dividend/Price (%)

Average = 4.5%

Table 2   Future 10-Year Real Rates of Return
When Stocks Are Purchased at
Alternative Initial P/E Multiples,
1871–2004

Initial P/E Range	Return
Cheapest 20% (5.6×–10.1×)	11.6%
Second 20% (10.1×–12.7×)	8.1
Third 20% (12.7×–14.9×)	6.8
Fourth 20% (14.9×–17.9×)	4.1
Most expensive 20% (17.9×–26.6×)	4.7

In fact, the level of multiples provides important information about prospective returns. **Table 2** reports the subsequent 10-year real return on the S&P 500 for different current P/E ranges. On average, when the market is cheap (P/E range of approximately 6 to 10 times), it does very well for the next 10 years. When the market is expensive (P/E range of approximately 18 to 27 times), it does not do well. Right now, the market is in the most expensive category, unfortunately. The same pattern holds for dividend yields, or D/P, shown in **Table 3**. That is, when markets are expensive based on dividend yields, returns over subsequent periods are below average.

This type of analysis forces investors to consider how their expectations for risk and return and how their allocations to various asset classes might change over time depending on how expensive or cheap the markets are. This analysis can be extended in the following manner. Consider just three projections based on what has happened over the past 30 years: 1975 to 2004. In 1975, the

Table 3   Future 10-Year Real Rates of Return
When Stocks Are Purchased at
Alternative Initial Dividend Yields,
1871–2004

Initial Dividend Yield Range	Return
Cheapest 20% (9.9%–5.8%)	10.1%
Second 20% (5.8%–5.0%)	7.8
Third 20% (5.0%–4.2%)	7.4
Fourth 20% (4.2%–3.4%)	5.8
Most expensive 20% (3.4%–2.7%)	4.3

dividend yield was about 5.0 percent. EPS growth over the past 30 years has been about 6.5 percent, and the P/E multiple has expanded by about 1.7 percent a year. Thus, the total return per year during this period, in nominal terms, was about 13.2 percent.

An investor could repeat this exercise by looking at the current yield on stocks, which is around 1.7 percent, and inserting his or her own views about the other two components of expected stock returns—EPS growth and changes in P/E multiples. For example, one could reasonably assume that the kind of hyperinflation seen in the late 1970s and early 1980s will not happen any time soon. So, reducing expectations for nominal growth of EPS from the historical 30-year average of 6.5 percent to 5.0 percent may be reasonable.

The critical question at this point becomes: What will happen with P/Es? If the investor thinks multiples will remain at their current level of about 26 for the next 10 years, then the return expectation is 6.7 percent (5.0 percent earnings growth plus 1.7 percent dividend yield). But if the investor thinks multiples will double again, then about 2.0 percent a year from multiple expansion needs to be added as a source of return. And finally, if the investor thinks multiples will contract down to their historical level, then multiples contraction will be a subtraction from the expected return. For example, if the institution expects that multiples will go from 26 to 16, then it must subtract about 1.7 percent a year from returns on an annual basis over the next 30 years, which would produce an expected return of 5.0 percent. If that is the investor's view, then it would probably make sense to reduce the allocation to equities. Note that this action does not mean that the investor is trying to time the market on a tactical, short-term basis. Rather, the investor is simply trying to base his or her actions on a plausible scenario for expected returns in the foreseeable future.

In a world of low expected returns, managing the risk exposure becomes more important than ever. The institutions I referred to previously manage their risk exposures by slowly moving their target asset allocations. Basically, they believe that there is some low-frequency, slow-moving asset return predictability. That is, they are not timing the market in the sense of predicting what it will do over the next month, but they may have a sense of what will happen over the next 10 years. As a result, they change their asset allocations accordingly.

Conditional Risk

In traditional asset allocation analysis, investors use constant, or unconditional, expected return assumptions based on long-term historical patterns for risk and return for each asset class. In the model described herein, investors establish conditional return expectations that may be different for each time period. This view of return, accordingly, forces investors to take another look at the traditional approach of measuring risk as the unconditional volatility and correlation of asset returns. Specifically, if there is predictability in asset returns, then not all of the unconditional volatility of asset returns should count as risk because part of this volatility is caused by predictable changes in asset returns. Risk should be measured by the conditional volatility of asset returns at the investor's horizon. For example, depending on the investment horizon, stocks may be less or more risky and bonds may be more or less risky. Similarly, cash may be riskless at certain horizons and risky at others. The point is that what we call a "term structure of the risk–return trade-off" exists, as described in Campbell and Viceira (2005), and accordingly, the optimal policy portfolio (the target policy portfolio) might be different across investment horizons.

To capture horizon effects on risk, we used a simple, flexible statistical model that essentially describes the dynamic behavior of asset returns. We used a well-known model from time-series econometrics—a first-order vector autoregression model, or VAR(1) model—and applied it to asset allocation analysis. The idea is simple. Start with the set of asset classes that you are interested in. Then, add a set of variables that you think is relevant for forecasting returns, such as P/E and D/P, the level of interest rates, or the slope of the yield curve. These are all variables that seem to have some forecasting power for stock and bond returns. Once you have this information, construct forecasts of returns by regressing each asset class return on its own lagged value, the lagged values of other asset returns, and the lagged values of the return-forecasting variables. The model is then used to extract the volatility and correlation structure of asset returns at different horizons. The technical details are included in an appendix to Campbell and Viceira (2005).

Figure 4 plots the annualized standard deviation of real (or inflation-adjusted) returns for horizons between 1 year and 50 years for four investment strategies. The first is an all-equities strategy, and the second represents a five-year constant-duration bond portfolio strategy. The third strategy is to be fully invested in T-bills. The final strategy is to buy and hold bonds with maturities equal to the investment horizon. Notice that when the risk–return trade-off is

Figure 4   Annualized Volatility of Real Returns across Investment Horizons

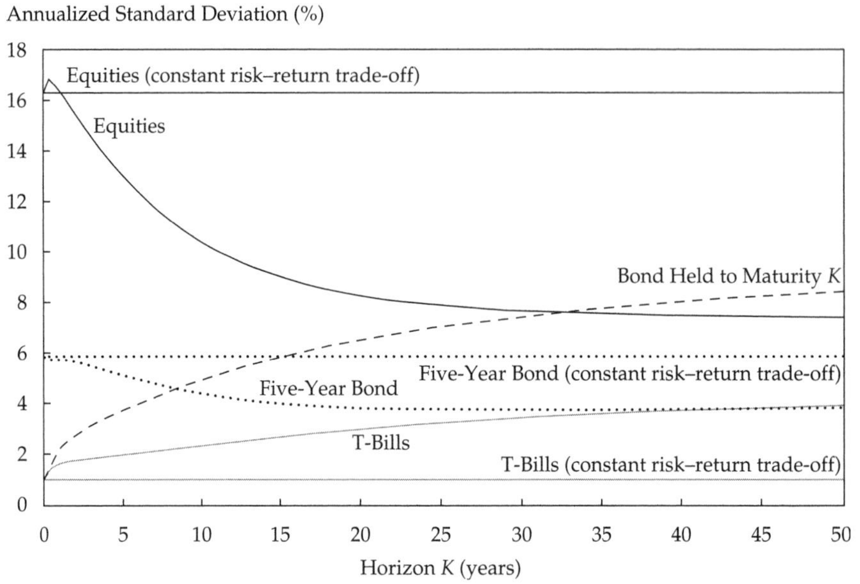

Annualized Standard Deviation (%)

Horizon K (years)

constant (i.e., when future returns are not predictable and interest rates are constant), the annualized standard deviation of real returns is independent of investment horizon and should be the same at short and long horizons. Under the traditional approach to asset allocation, one would use this constant level of risk, which corresponds to the horizontal lines in the plot. But this figure tells a completely different story. Over a short-term horizon, equities have a 16 percent annualized standard deviation, but for a 20-year horizon, they have approximately an 8 percent standard deviation. This level of risk is still quite significant and fully contradicts the claim that stocks are riskless in the long term. But it does represent a reduction in risk at long horizons relative to short horizons. This reduction in risk is caused by stock return predictability, or mean reversion. Thus, the gradual tendency of stock returns to exhibit mean reversion reduces the risk of stocks for investors who have long-term horizons relative to those who have short-term horizons.

Figure 4 also shows that volatility for a five-year constant-duration bond strategy declines as the horizon increases, but not as much as for equities. Two partially offsetting effects are responsible for this pattern. First, a steepening of the yield-curve forecasts positive bond returns in the future, which creates long-term mean *aversion*, or an amplification of volatility at long horizons. Second, an increase in nominal interest rates causes bond prices to decline immediately. But over the long term, nominal interest rates exhibit a mean-reversion pattern, which ultimately reduces volatility. This mean-reversion effect dominates the mean-*aversion* effect of yield-curve steepening, resulting in this pattern of slowly declining volatility in bond returns. The net effect is that bonds are less risky at long horizons.

Compare this pattern with that of T-bills, for which annualized standard deviation increases with the investment horizon. Because this result is completely counterintuitive, it must be explained. Certainly, T-bills provide a good hedge against inflation risk because their short-term maturity implies that their rates adjust frequently and quickly reflect changes in expected inflation. But the downside of this frequent adjustment is that T-bills do not protect against unexpected declines in real interest rates. The reinvestment risk of T-bills is actually quite pronounced at long horizons and causes the volatility of T-bill returns to increase from 1 percent a year for short horizons to 4 percent a year for long horizons. As tangible proof, consider the situation of those who retired in the early 1980s with their investment funds in short-term investments yielding in the high teens. These pensioners, who have a 20- to 25-year horizon, have come to realize their exposure to fluctuations in real interest rates the hard way because significant declines in real rates (and not just inflation) during the 1990s and early 2000s hampered their ability to spend out of the principal of their investments.

A similar analysis explains the risk of buying and holding a nominal bond to maturity. With bonds, investors receive regular coupons. But the purchasing power of those coupons depends on how inflation moves in the meantime. Buying and holding bonds subjects an investor to inflation risk. Figure 4 shows that over long horizons, inflation risk is quite pronounced.

As can be seen in **Figure 5,** an interesting correlation pattern exists between equities and a constant-duration bond portfolio for varying investment horizons. At short horizons, the correlation of stocks and bonds is quite low. But for medium investment horizons, the correlation becomes quite large. Perhaps even more surprisingly, for very long investment horizons, it declines significantly. The question is: What is driving these changes? Over the intermediate term, the correlation increases dramatically because of the effect of changes in the discount rates, which tend to move stocks and bonds in the same direction. When nominal short-term interest rates increase, bond returns fall at once but stock returns react with some delay, which explains the low short-term correlation of stocks and bonds. Over an intermediate-term business cycle, however, stocks respond in the same manner, causing a significant increase in their correlation. Over long horizons, economic growth has a far greater impact on stock returns than discount rates. As a result, the return patterns diverge again.

A similar case can be made for the correlation between stock returns and inflation. Over short horizons and intermediate horizons, stocks react negatively

Figure 5   Correlation between Equities and Five-Year Bond Portfolio across Investment
Horizons

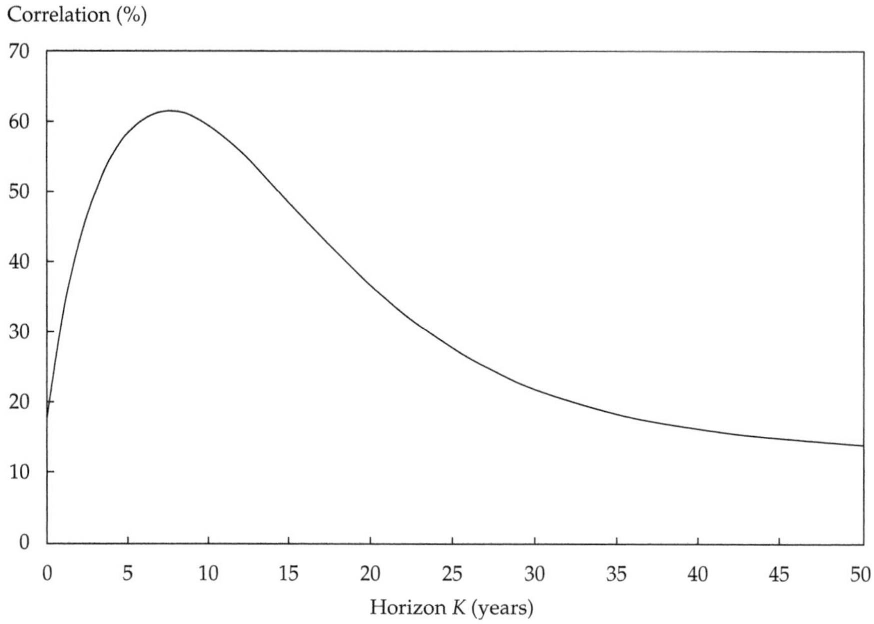

to increases in inflation risk. But over longer horizons, as earnings and dividends adjust for the effects of inflation, stocks become a good inflation hedge.

Thus, for investors with longer investment horizons, the "safe" investment, T-bills, is not very safe because it leaves investors with an exposure to changing real interest rates. The safe asset for a long-term investor thus becomes a bond that matches his or her investment horizon and whose coupons and principal adjust with inflation. In the United States, Treasury Inflation-Protected Securities (TIPS) probably constitute a good proxy for this safe asset. At the same time, the "risky" investment, stocks, appears to be less risky for two reasons. First, long-term volatility in stock prices is less than short-term volatility. Second, stocks provide a better hedge against inflation.

Conclusion

I conclude with some caveats about my analysis as well as some final thoughts. First, the caveats. The dynamic properties of stock and bond returns are extremely difficult to estimate accurately. Thus, asset allocation recommendations under any asset allocation approach (traditional or modern) are sensitive to how the model characterizes future movements in stock and bond returns. Consequently, investors should be aware of this uncertainty and should trim back extreme positions in stocks and bonds that may be suggested by a particular model.

Nevertheless, empirical evidence shows that the volatility and correlation structure of asset returns can change across investment horizons. These patterns have important implications for portfolio allocations among cash (or T-bills), stocks, and long-term bonds. Real interest rate risk (or reinvestment risk) tilts the composition of minimum variance portfolios at long horizons toward long-term inflation-indexed bonds and away from T-bills. The large positive correlation of bond and stock returns at intermediate horizons and the declining volatility of stock returns at long horizons create bias in the composition of risky portfolios toward stocks and away from long-terms bonds at long horizons. Investors thus might want to adopt policy portfolios whose target allocations vary with their investment horizon and with changing long-term capital market conditions.

This presentation comes from the 2006 Financial Analysts Seminar held in Evanston, Illinois, on 16–21 July 2006.

References

Campbell, John Y., and Luis M. Viceira. 2005. "The Term Structure of the Risk–Return Trade-Off." *Financial Analysts Journal*, vol. 61, no. 1 (January/February):34–44.

———. 2006. "Strategic Asset Allocation for Pension Plans." In *Oxford Handbook of Pensions and Retirement Income*. Edited by Gordon L. Clark, Alicia H. Munnell, and J. Michael Orszag. Oxford: Oxford University Press.

More from Luis M. Viceira

This section presents the speaker's lively question and answer session with the conference audience.

Question: Proposed accounting changes are predicted to make year-over-year liabilities much more volatile for U.S. corporations. Should corporations be looking at one-year time horizons based on that change?

Viceira: If a corporation is sponsoring a pension fund, it has a very long horizon and, therefore, needs to think accordingly. A properly chosen 100 percent allocation to fixed income will certainly hedge liabilities that are derived from accrued pension obligations. But this means that the corporation will now have to fund out of operations future pension obligations as they accrue. These obligations typically grow with productivity and inflation, and over long horizons, stocks tend to grow with productivity and inflation.

It is not entirely clear to me that stocks should be completely discarded from the investment portfolio of a traditional pension fund. Moreover, I am not sure that adopting a 100 percent fixed-income portfolio in a traditional defined-benefit pension fund is in the best interests of the shareholders of the corporation sponsoring the plan, as Bill Sharpe and Jack Treynor pointed out 30 years ago.[2]

Question: For correlations modeled out 50 years, doesn't that put a lot of stress on the data period for which you are making your estimations?

Viceira: Absolutely. That's why we look more to the 20- to 25-year horizon. I don't think we can see much beyond that.

Question: Have you looked at the long-term volatility of TIPS?

Viceira: In my view, TIPS are the truly riskless asset. If you are an investor with a 10-year horizon, you can buy a 10-year TIPS, and that TIPS will save you from an inflation risk that can be quite large over 10 years. It also saves you from real interest rate risk because you now fix the real interest rate. So, this is truly the safe asset—not cash. But keep the trade-off in mind. TIPS have much lower yields.

Question: What questions would you ask your clients to determine what their actual risk preferences are in the context of the time horizon concept?

Viceira: You need to understand what their liabilities are and what their needs are. For someone who is 60 years old and thinking about retiring now, we know objectively that he or she has a 20- to 25-year horizon. How much does this person want to leave

---

[2] For pension fund investing, please refer to Campbell and Viceira (2006).

to his or her children, and how much does he or she intend to spend? If the client doesn't need it all, his or her risk tolerance increases immediately.

Question: Should you be looking at expected earnings rather than trailing realized earnings?

Viceira: You have to base your analysis on projected earnings. The problem is how to project earnings 10 years into the future. I have found that regardless of how you analyze earnings history, it is a remarkably consistent story. Over long periods, earnings consistently grow at a 3 percent real, 5 percent nominal, rate.

So, yes, you want to use earnings projections, but the best projections should be guided by the historical experiences just cited. If you think that our future experience will be different from our past, then by all means use your projected earnings.

Asset Allocation for High-Net-Worth Investors

DAN DIBARTOLOMEO

The asset allocation process for private clients is affected by a unique set of parameters that includes taxes, illiquid assets, a multiplicity of asset locations with varying tax treatments, and qualitative goals and preferences. The traditional mean–variance methodologies successfully used by institutional investors are unable to construct an "optimal" portfolio in the context of a high-net-worth investor. The analytic hierarchy process, which incorporates qualitative as well as quantitative factors, offers an alternative approach to private client asset allocation.

This presentation is based in part on the recently published Research Foundation of CFA Institute monograph *Investment Management for Taxable Private Investors*, which I co-wrote with Jarrod Wilcox, CFA, and Jeffrey E. Horvitz (2006). First, I will briefly discuss a few issues related to asset allocation for private clients. Second, I will describe an asset allocation tool recently borrowed from the operations research field called the "analytic hierarchy process." This tool is a nonparametric, nonoptimizing approach to asset allocation that is appropriate not only for high-net-worth individuals but also for funds of hedge funds and other investors who need a qualitative overlay in their decision-making process.

> To systematically convert the feelings, beliefs, and goals of wealthy investors into straightforward risk and return preferences for use as inputs in a classic mean–variance optimization is an impossible task.

The Challenge of the Private Client

The individual investor, from the point of view of the investment manager, brings to the table a number of special challenges. To meet these challenges, managers must resort to creating a customized solution, using a nontraditional methodology, or making a qualitative judgment. Several private client characteristics that prove particularly challenging are the uniqueness of each

---

Dan diBartolomeo is president of Northfield Information Services, Inc., Boston.

client's goals, direct and indirect costs that threaten the wealth-building process, spontaneous requests to liquidate assets, multiple asset pools or locations, and lack of investment knowledge and sophistication.

The overriding challenge facing managers of private client assets is heterogeneity: No two individual investors are alike, and each wants an investment program that is customized to his or her particular set of circumstances and life goals. First and foremost—in terms of investment performance—heterogeneity completely characterizes the issue of taxes: capital gains tax, income tax, gift tax, and estate tax. How does a manager efficiently and effectively tackle this degree of heterogeneity? The private client conundrum, unfortunately, is that the fundamental theories underpinning investment management (modern portfolio theory and the capital asset pricing model) assume not only no transaction costs but also no taxes. Private client managers thus have to meet the needs of a diverse client base with widely varying financial goals and personal preferences. Accordingly, the private client manager's asset allocation task is extremely complex and requires a sophisticated analytical process to arrive at a satisfactory and appropriate outcome.

Net returns, not gross returns, build wealth. And as the old saying goes, it does not matter how much you make; it matters how much you keep. Many forces combine to reduce gross wealth accumulation, including transaction costs and management fees; income, capital gains, and estate taxes; inflation; and consumption. If each of these costs is not controlled in a rational way, the ability of the high-net-worth investor to build and preserve wealth will be severely limited. For example, disparity in consumption rates among family members can be a major source of dissension within a family and can create a burden for joint enterprises, such as family-owned businesses. Consumption can be distinguished from spending in that consumption destroys wealth. Spending does not always result in consumption; cash may be spent to acquire an asset, such as a Rembrandt painting, that will, in turn, build wealth.

Varying rates of consumption present a problem not only for family members but also for private client managers. A peculiarity of the very high-net-worth private client world is the spontaneous desire to liquidate investment assets to enable consumption or spending. For example, a client may think nothing of calling his or her manager to ask that $10 million be made available tomorrow to buy a yacht. This phenomenon occurs quite unpredictably, and for managers seeking to run optimal portfolios, it can be very annoying.

Only a small percentage of wealthy individuals have a staff of investment experts and consultants to advise them. Some very high-net-worth clients may have a family office staffed by a combination of professionals and administrators, but the most common adviser is the family accountant. Therefore, investment firms must realize the extremely large fiduciary responsibility they assume when dealing with private clients. Managers must undertake to educate their private clients about the economic ramifications of investment policy decisions in an after-tax context—particularly the pros and cons of active versus passive management. Frequently, an active strategy will not provide a higher after-tax return than a passive, or index, strategy. In advising their clients, managers often find themselves faced with a conflict: support their own bottom line by recommending an active strategy or watch out for their client's best interests by recommending a passive strategy.

Rethinking Finance Theory in a Private Client Context

If the market can be considered relatively efficient in the presence of transaction costs, it seems all the more efficient after the large bite of taxes. Taxes create such a tremendous drag on performance that an active manager has to produce an outstanding pretax return to compensate for them. Although active managers can almost always minimize the negative impact of taxes by considering them in investment decisions, active managers almost always ensure an unsatisfactory result by ignoring them.

One strategy that can add value in the context of a taxable portfolio is the pursuit of tax alpha, which can be achieved through tax deferral and risk control. Over time, a tax-alpha strategy can add wealth for high-net-worth investors more reliably than an active strategy that ignores taxes. In the high-net-worth world, think taxes first, risk second, and active alpha third.

In the institutional realm of traditional optimization and utility theory, extensive analysis is needed to establish the appropriate level of investment aggressiveness. Because of the intricacies of utility theory, high-net-worth investors, who are not typically investment experts, struggle to quantitatively articulate their preference functions. The finite and complex lives of individuals make the expression of economic utility via simple utility functions quite challenging.

Other basic theoretical tenets that are thoroughly applicable in the institutional world, such as Markowitz mean–variance optimization, the capital asset pricing model, option valuation theory, and stochastic growth theory, fall short of the mark when applied in the private client world. These models oversimplify the issues of private clients.

Private client managers who use Markowitz mean–variance optimization should keep a couple of things in mind. First, all inputs, such as expected return, correlation, and volatility, need to be in an after-tax form. Second, most institutional investors state their performance goals and risk preferences relative to a benchmark. Individual investors generally prefer to measure risk and return in an absolute sense because they pay taxes on absolute gains and losses, not on benchmark-relative gains and losses. (It is difficult to pay for a child's college education with "relative" money.)

Another concern in applying mean–variance optimization in a private client world is estimation error. Mistakes in estimates used in the asset allocation process can have grave consequences because to correct these errors, to rebalance a taxable portfolio, is very expensive as a result of capital gains and transaction costs. Therefore, advisers must develop and strictly follow a risk management policy that will control for potential errors in the asset allocation process that may subsequently require a costly correction.

Any asset allocation process for individuals should include alternative assets, such as real estate or art. It is not unusual for wealthy individuals to own brick-and-mortar real estate (e.g., a hotel or shopping mall) or a limited partnership interest in an office building. These investments can represent major portions of an individual's total wealth, but because of their illiquid nature, they can be hard to value and thus difficult to put into the traditional optimization model.

A technical issue that can complicate the asset allocation process is the asymmetries in the tax code. These asymmetries may skew the mean–variance distribution of the after-tax return. For example, only certain types of losses can be netted against certain types of gains. To the extent that these asymmetries exist, optimizing on an after-tax basis can be very tricky; the result is a nonnormal return distribution.

Probably the biggest issue for the high-net-worth investor related to the Markowitz mean–variance optimization process is that it is a single-period model. The model incorporates only two concepts of time: now and forever. The model cannot express this week or next month, when a tax payment is made or due. Therefore, reconciling the real world of taxes to Markowitz optimization is not a trivial task.

Performance attribution is also a challenge in private client portfolios. The high rebalancing costs associated with these portfolios make the statistical analysis of past performance difficult. A monthly performance attribution on an institutional portfolio can encompass, for example, 60 data samples. Compare that large number of inputs with the typical number for a high-net-worth portfolio, where frictions are numerous and tax costs are large. From one month to the next, so few changes may occur that the data samples will not be independent. Consequently, the degree of path dependency is so high that most attribution methodologies simply do not work.

The capital asset pricing model (CAPM), one of the building blocks of investment theory, assumes that there are no trading costs and no taxes and that each investor is a Markowitz mean–variance optimizer. In this model, investors differ only in their aversion to risk. The CAPM implies that an index fund holding the entire market of risky securities at their respective market weights will be more efficient than any other portfolio. A limited amount of research has been done on the type of passive portfolio that would be most efficient on an after-tax basis, but unfortunately, the extant literature only scratches the surface in exploring whether the CAPM holds up in an after-tax world.

Option valuation theory, such as the Black–Scholes model, assumes cost-less, continuous rebalancing of a hedge, which is not realistic in a taxable environment. The continuous gains and losses that result from maintaining such a position can wreak havoc in a private client portfolio. But individual investors can benefit from a basic understanding of option valuation theory because it accurately expresses the right, but not the obligation, of the individual to sell a security at a loss to create a tax benefit. The value of this option is tied directly to the variance of the security. Institutional investors attempt to neutralize the variance of individual securities, but individual investors can benefit from asset-specific risk in that it enables a robust tax-loss harvesting strategy.

Stochastic growth theory, which provides the framework for the life-cycle investing approach discussed below, shows that when discretionary wealth is maximized in each period away from the investor's shortfall point, or desired floor on wealth, median long-term total wealth is maximized. The investor's desired level of risk, as supported by the stochastic growth theory model, must be adjusted for the reality of taxes and consumption. Stochastic growth theory holds only over long time horizons, a fact that conflicts with the mortality of individual investors.

Life-Cycle Investing

Individual investor preference functions not only differ among individuals; they change as the investor grows older, undertakes or sells a business venture, enters or exits relationships, or has children and grandchildren. A private investor's financial goals and personal objectives are continuously evolving. In comparison, institutional investor preference functions change slowly, if at all.

The risk tolerances of individual investors change with age as well as with wealth and must be revisited continually. These changing risk tolerances have the potential at any time to cause the current asset allocation to become out-dated. A life-cycle mutual fund, a relatively new investment product, attempts to accommodate these shifting risk tolerances.

A key issue in building and preserving wealth over an investor's lifetime is how aggressive or conservative the investor should be in order to maximize long-term wealth subject to a shortfall constraint, or floor on wealth. This relationship can be expressed as

$$U = E\left[R^*(1 - T^*) - \frac{LS^2(1 - T^*)^2}{2}\right],$$

where

E = the expectations operator
R^* = pretax return
T^* = effective tax rate
L = ratio of total assets to net worth
S = standard deviation of pretax return

Let me reiterate that T^* is not the nominal tax rate. The nominal tax rate is rarely the effective tax rate. Many factors, alone or in combination, determine the effective tax rate, and it is the effective tax rate that affects the investor's ability to build wealth.

An investor defines the shortfall constraint as a percentage of the dollars he or she has today—perhaps 80 percent or 50 percent. The balance of the wealth, or the discretionary wealth, is committed to an investment strategy designed to maximize long-term growth after taxes. Within this framework, the investor prepares a life balance sheet. The life balance sheet lists all the investor's assets and liabilities, flexibly defined to include the present value of implied assets, such as lifetime employment savings, and expected expenses, such as college tuition, insurance, and estate taxes. Once all this information is pulled together on the life balance sheet, the manager can make an assessment of the appropriate level of investment aggressiveness for the investor.

The life balance sheet is central to the concept of life-cycle investing. The life balance sheet combines changes in the investor's age and wealth to get a single determinant of optimal aggressiveness. The model considers all the investor's assets and liabilities and all options available to the investor, such as increasing his or her savings rate or changing jobs, and then places a rough value on each and discounts each back to its present value to approximate the investor's net worth. The process is similar to calculating a debt-to-equity ratio for a company. This debt-to-equity ratio for an individual will vary through the individual's lifetime because certain expenses, such as college tuition, will drop off the balance sheet as they are paid and certain income sources, such as a pension, will increase in a present value sense as the individual reaches retirement age. The investor's net worth will also fluctuate because of changes in the market value of the investor's portfolio or changes in a career path. Using the life balance sheet, the investor can constantly refine the level of investment aggressiveness to suit his or her current life situation.

In the long run, the life balance sheet framework creates a time-varying risk aversion that causes the investor to maximize the median rather than the mean of future wealth, similar to a constant proportion portfolio insurance strategy. The basic idea of maximizing long-term growth but maintaining a wealth floor, or limiting the amount of wealth at risk, is consistent with the real world goals of individual investors. Even if an investor cannot describe every "implied asset" or "implied liability" on the balance sheet, this framework serves as an excellent conduit for a discussion of the investor's risk preferences.

Taxes and the Private Client

Taxes certainly complicate the management of private client assets. For instance, the manager must determine an individual's effective tax rate by looking at the definition of taxable amounts, the character of profits (such as ordinary income, short-term gain, and long-term gain), and the limitations on netting (i.e., what can be offset against what to compute the net amount subject to tax).

Tax Deferral

An investor's ability to defer paying tax on realized income is minimal, but deferring paying tax on unrealized capital gains is relatively easy and can provide significant value if done over a long period of time. To defer the realization of a gain for one year saves the investor the difference between the short-term capital gains tax rate (i.e., the investor's ordinary income tax rate) and the generally lower long-term capital gains tax rate. But if a capital gain is preserved for 5, 10, or 15 years, a meaningful benefit can be derived from tax-deferred compounding, otherwise known as tax alpha. And although federal taxes typically take a bigger bite out of an investor's income, state taxes matter too.

Often thought of as the classic tax strategy for building private client wealth, the deferral of capital gains becomes an increasingly valuable strategy as the investor ages. As an investor grows older and the probability of death increases, so too does the probability that the deferred gains will never be taxed at the prevailing capital gains rates. At an investor's death, his or her investments receive a "step-up" in basis to the market value at the date of death. The appreciation, however, is included in the valuation of the investor's estate. As part of the estate, the appreciation is taxed at the appropriate estate tax rate. The good news, however, is that only about 2 percent of the U.S. population is subject to estate tax. The other 98 percent pays no estate tax.

The 2 percent of the U.S. population who pay estate tax do so because of inadequate estate and wealth transfer planning. Today, an estate tax liability is basically an optional tax. If an individual has sought and taken the advice of a knowledgeable trusts and estates attorney, estate tax should be avoidable. Currently, the estate tax rate is just under 50 percent, so it is extremely important for individuals with a high net worth to consider planning appropriately. In 2006 and 2007, the estate tax rate will be 46 percent and 45 percent, respectively, applied to the amount of the estate exceeding $2 million, the estate tax exclusion.

Part of the lore about tax deferral is that it operates as an interest-free loan from the government: If tax is not paid now, it will have to be paid in the future. That notion is just wrong because when the tax is finally paid, the amount of tax owed will likely be much higher than the amount of tax owed today—the reason being that the amount of the tax deferral is invested in the interim and the earnings on that amount will eventually also be taxed. Tax deferral is much more like a limited partnership in which the government is a silent partner. Tax deferral allows for faster wealth accumulation through faster compounding, which leads to greater tax revenues for the government. Obviously, the government realizes this fact; otherwise, the option to defer would have been removed many years ago.

Choosing not to defer the realization of taxable income is also an appropriate strategy when the investor believes that the applicable tax may be raised. Tax rates are not fixed. The history of income taxes in the United States shows that rates fluctuate based on the prevailing political and economic winds. Currently, rates are relatively low, but no guarantee exists that they will remain low.

Alternative Minimum Tax

In recent years, the alternative minimum tax (AMT) has garnered a great deal of attention. When the AMT was established by the Tax Reform Act of 1969, it was designed to affect only 800 very wealthy families who paid no taxes at all. Unlike the income tax brackets, which are indexed to inflation, the nominal income level at which the AMT becomes effective is not indexed. As a result, increasing numbers of U.S. households are paying the AMT. One of the preference items used in determining whether an individual is subject to the AMT is investment income. Of importance is the size of investment income relative to earned income: The larger the percentage of investment income, the more likely that the AMT will apply. Basically, the AMT levies an extra tax on investment returns that otherwise would be subject to a lower, or zero, rate of tax, such as the income on certain tax-exempt bonds.

Tax Treatment of Asset Classes

Different asset classes are subject to different tax treatment, which should be considered in the asset allocation and asset location decisions. In private client portfolios, asset allocation and asset location are really two sides of the same coin. As mentioned earlier, asset location—for example, an asset inside a tax-sheltered retirement account—is a critical factor in the overall asset allocation decision.

Equities

The two sources of income generated by equity investments—dividends and capital appreciation—are now taxed at the same rate, although this is a relatively new development. A dividend must be a "qualified dividend," which is an ordinary dividend paid after 2002 by a U.S. corporation or a qualified foreign corporation. In addition, the investor must meet the holding period rules. Qualified dividends and capital gains are taxed at 15 percent if the applicable regular income tax is 25 percent or higher and at 5 percent if the applicable regular income tax rate is lower than 25 percent.

The determining factor, however, in the effective tax rate of an equity portfolio is the degree of cross-sectional dispersion in the holdings. Compare a diversified equity portfolio with a portfolio of Treasury bonds, for example. A Treasury bond portfolio generates a gain or a loss, but not a mixed bag of gains and losses with the potential to offset each other. In contrast, a diversified portfolio of equities generates both gains and losses. This cross-sectional dispersion arising from diversification among industries and companies facilitates a strategy of tax-loss harvesting and tax deferral. The effective tax rate on a diversified equity portfolio is thus a function of the cross-sectional dispersion of equity returns. Therefore, an asset class that has a high degree of dispersion, such as small-cap stocks, will have a lower effective tax rate than one that has a low degree of dispersion, such as large-cap stocks.

Fixed income

At the present time, taxable interest on fixed-income instruments is taxed at the highest marginal ordinary income tax rate. Because tax-exempt bonds are subject to the AMT, the possibility of being subject to this additional tax must be considered when making taxable and tax-exempt bond allocations. And remember that capital gains on municipal, or tax-exempt, bonds are taxed in the same way and at the same rates as capital gains on other investments.

The taxable equivalent yield is a useful measure only if a municipal bond is likely to be held to maturity. Although the income on a bond may be tax exempt, the capital gain on the bond, if it is sold prior to maturity, is taxable. The taxable equivalent yield is more often accurate for a short-term bond than for a long-term bond because the short-term bond is less apt to be sold prior to maturity. Thus, the effective tax rate on municipal bonds can vary tremendously depending on the maturity of the bond. The effective tax rate is, in fact, close to zero for a short-term bond, whereas the effective tax rate for a long-term bond sold prior to maturity equals the applicable capital gains tax rate. This analysis, of course, assumes that a net gain is realized and not offset by a capital loss from another investment. Therefore, a long-term municipal bond is much closer to a long-term taxable bond in terms of effective yield than is apparent at first glance, which is one reason why taxable/tax-exempt spreads at the long end of the yield curve are much narrower than they are at the short end of the curve.

Mutual funds and REITs

Mutual funds and REITs (real estate investment trusts) share a couple of tax traits that should be given careful consideration in the asset allocation and asset location process. These entities pass capital gains through to their investors but not capital losses. They also pass along unrealized or "embedded" capital gains, triggering an accelerated capital gains tax liability for their investors.

Hedge funds

Hedge funds as an asset class often look surprisingly attractive because after-tax volatility is considerably lower than pretax volatility. But most hedge funds are highly tax inefficient because the vast majority of their returns comes from short-term gains. An issue to consider before putting high-net-worth investors into hedge funds is whether the hedge fund manager maintains separate pools of assets for high-net-worth investors and tax-exempt entities. Clearly, the investment goals of these investors are not the same, so a strategy that is tax efficient and thus conforms to the goals of the high-net-worth investor is probably in conflict with the goals of the tax-exempt investor.

Hedge funds, of course, charge high fees. A problem for high-net-worth investors, who commonly diversify across many managers, is the combined performance fees charged by multiple hedge funds. The combination forces a very high effective fee structure. For example, if an investor has two hedge fund managers and one does really well and the other does rather poorly, the net result may be a breakeven situation in terms of postfee performance. Because the investor has to pay a 20 percent performance fee to the manager who performed well, the effective fee rate on the investor's total hedge fund allocation can be quite high and thus reduce the overall performance.

Real estate

Often, high-net-worth investors have a large portion of their wealth in illiquid assets, such as a family business or real estate. Real estate provides significant tax benefits but is not liquid. Another concern with real estate is local risk. An investor is more likely to own real estate near his or her home, which increases exposure to a slowdown in the local economy. If a significant portion of an investor's portfolio is invested in such illiquid assets as real estate, the investor must plan ahead to ensure that sufficient liquid assets are available to pay unexpected expenses, such as estate tax, so as to avoid a forced "fire sale" of assets.

Tax-sheltered savings accounts

In the United States, tax-sheltered savings accounts, such as IRAs, are tremendously popular investment and savings vehicles. The tax-sheltered feature changes the effective tax rate for any asset class that is located in these accounts. Thus, assets in tax-sheltered accounts must be analyzed differently from assets outside these accounts.

These accounts can be characterized in one of two ways. One type of account, such as the traditional IRA or 401(k), affords the investor tax-deductible contributions if certain income qualifications are met, but the withdrawals are taxable. The second type, such as the Roth IRA, operates with contributions of currently taxed income but allows tax-exempt withdrawals. The central feature of both types of account is that all income earned in the account, including dividends, interest, and capital appreciation, compounds tax free for an extended time period.

The investor's view on future tax rates affects the selection of the tax-deferred account. If the investor believes the general level of tax rates will rise or that he or she will be in a substantially higher tax bracket after retirement, when penalty-free withdrawals from a traditional IRA can begin, the investor's preference may be to pay tax now. Thus, the investor would make contributions to a Roth IRA rather than to a traditional IRA. Income limitations on these tax-sheltered savings accounts, however, often prohibit high-net-worth individuals from participating in them.

Several asset location strategies can wring the maximum benefit out of tax-sheltered accounts. For example, place heavily taxed asset classes, such as taxable bonds, and tax-inefficient asset classes, such as equity mutual funds, inside tax-sheltered accounts. Also, use tax-sheltered accounts as much as possible for rebalancing purposes to avoid the capital gains tax that can be triggered by reducing the equity allocation and increasing the fixed-income allocation. Always ensure, however, that liquidity sufficient to meet unexpected expenditures is maintained outside tax-sheltered accounts because of the high penalties for early withdrawal.

The presence of taxes can dramatically change the traditional view of asset allocation for private client assets. Thus, private client managers must remember that each asset class inside a retirement account differs from its taxable counterpart because their effective tax rates are vastly different. Also, the taxable/tax-exempt bond decision should always take the AMT into account if the investor might be subject to the AMT. Lastly, managers should recognize that an asset class that has a high degree of cross-sectional return dispersion, such as small-cap stocks, offers the greatest opportunity for tax deferral.

Concentrated Stock

Frequently, private client portfolios have a large, concentrated position in a public or private company, often acquired through inheritance or an entrepreneurial venture. The decision to diversify this position can have serious tax consequences for the investor. Therefore, any transition strategy used to diversify the concentrated position must weigh the tax cost associated with liquidation against the benefits of a diversified portfolio. A manager cannot simply liquidate a private client portfolio and initiate an entirely new portfolio. The manager must formulate a tax-rational transition strategy.

The typical concentrated stock scenario can be illustrated by a situation that my firm experienced about 10 years ago. A client walked through the door with a $600 million investment in a single stock with a zero cost basis. The position resulted from the tax-free merger of the client's private company and a public company. The client understood that having $600 million, the entire wealth of his 30-member extended family, in the stock of a company that his family no longer controlled was highly risky. At that time, the long-term capital gains rate was 20 percent, so simply liquidating the stock would have obligated the client to write a check to the IRS for $120 million, which no one but the IRS would have deemed a desirable outcome.

One approach to the problem would have been to construct a costless collar by writing a call and using the proceeds to buy a put. The collar truncates the risk of the concentrated position: Although the benefit of holding the stock in a rising market is limited, the risk of holding the stock in a falling market is limited as well. This approach is a holding action at best; it does not solve the problem of how to liquidate the position with minimal tax consequences. Another approach would have been to use a prepaid variable forward, which is basically a variation on the costless collar using OTC derivatives. The problem with the prepaid variable forward, however, is that it can be expensive to maintain.

The strategy we chose for our client was a leveraged complementary fund. The idea is simple. The manager margins a block of stock to "cash out" the concentrated position, then shorts either index futures or an index exchange-traded fund to bring the beta of the position back to what it was before the stock was margined, and then invests the newly acquired cash in a complementary fund.

The complementary fund should be a diverse portfolio of very volatile stocks chosen to neutralize the factor exposures of the concentrated position. The goal is not to pick stocks with high expected returns but to pick stocks solely on the basis of high expected volatility. If a stock performs well, it can remain in the portfolio, but if a stock performs poorly, it can be sold to realize a tax loss. In this manner, the concentrated position can gradually be liquidated so that realized capital gains are offset by realized tax losses in the complementary fund.

The proceeds from the sales of the concentrated stock are reinvested in the complementary fund. This process continues until the concentrated position is entirely liquidated and the margin arrangement is gradually unwound. This strategy worked quite well in the case of our client. In the period following the implementation of the complementary fund, the market was exceptionally volatile, so within two years, the concentrated position was reduced to 8 percent of the family's total portfolio without the family's having to pay any capital gains tax.

Analytic Hierarchy Process

Private clients have complex lifestyle and investment preferences. To systematically convert the feelings, beliefs, and goals of wealthy investors into straightforward risk and return preferences for use as inputs in a classic mean–variance optimization is an impossible task. High-net-worth investors' preferences may encompass multigenerational issues, such as preserving intergenerational purchasing power, or may involve high-profile charitable endowments. Reducing such complex factors to quantitative risk and return preferences is very difficult.

For the past several years, my firm has addressed this problem by using a nonparametric technique called the "analytic hierarchy process" (AHP). The AHP methodology arose from the operations research literature. It was designed as a nonparametric way to make complex, but often qualitative, decisions in a robust, consistent fashion. Thomas Saaty, a professor at the University of Pittsburgh, developed the AHP (for more information, see Saaty and Vargas 1994) to improve complex decision making and to identify and weight selection criteria. For example, General Motors Corporation used the AHP in making its decision to build a new assembly plant for the Saturn Corporation in Tennessee. The AHP has the capability to concurrently evaluate a number of qualitative factors. In the case of General Motors, these factors included labor availability and skill level, location of highways, location of suppliers, and local taxation.

The beginning point for applying the AHP in an investment context is a series of multiple choice questions posed to the individual investor. For each evaluation criterion, the AHP creates a comparison matrix. The upper triangle of the matrix holds the relative ratings (from 1 to 9, with 1 being the highest) of the alternatives—asset classes or fund managers. The diagonal of the matrix is composed of 1s because every asset class or fund compared with itself equals 1. In other words, if A is 9 times as good as B, then B is 1/9 as good as A.

When the comparison matrix has been filled, the matrix's first eigenvector contains the weights to be assigned to each choice. In this application, the weights are applied to the asset class or manager allocation for that criterion. The portfolio weights for each criterion are then averaged in a form of "importance" weighted average score. Basically, at my firm, we create a matrix that represents how we believe each asset class or fund manager under consideration might fit the investor given the investor's answers to the multiple choice questions about his or her key attributes. In practice, any preference can be determined using the multiple choice format, and questionnaires can be easily administered online. My firm has had excellent success building AHP asset allocation models for private clients with a variety of wealth levels.

The AHP can be operationalized in the following manner. The investment management organization's expert in asset allocation determines which asset classes are available to its clients. The expert develops and weights the questions used in the AHP to determine a suitable portfolio for each client. Then, the expert rates the relative attractiveness of both members of every possible pair of asset classes with respect to their suitability within that portfolio, given every possible response to each question.

To illustrate the application of the AHP, think of an investment universe of only three asset classes—stocks, bonds, and cash. And assume that only two attributes are known about the investor—age and income. A typical set of age ranges might be younger than 25 years, 25–35, 35–50, 50–65, and older than 65. A typical set of annual income ranges might be (dollars in thousands) less than 50, 50–100, 100–250, and more than 250. Next, decide the relative importance of each attribute. Is the relationship 10/90, 50/50, 90/10, or another value? Then, compare all possible pairwise combinations. For example, are stocks or bonds more attractive if the only attribute known about the investor is that he is less than 25 years old? Is the less attractive choice 1/2, 1/3, or 1/5 as attractive as the more attractive choice? Are bonds or cash more attractive if the only attribute known about the investor is that her income is between $100,000 and $250,000 a year? Is the less attractive choice 1/2, 1/3, or 1/5 as attractive as the more attractive choice?

The key criterion in AHP decision making is relative comparative value, but the way in which relative value is determined is totally arbitrary. It can be based on a firm's internal analysis of expected risk and return and historical correlations or on a survey of the relevant population—for example, 25-year-olds or individuals with income between $100,000 and $250,000 a year. The important factor is that an organized way to express an opinion on the relative value of different asset classes for different investors is developed and followed.

The AHP creates a portfolio for each question by forming a matrix that compares the suitability of each fund with that of each other fund. The principal component for the comparison matrix is the portfolio that is most suitable for that question. The recommended portfolio is then determined by weighting the portfolio outcome for each question. The resulting AHP portfolio of asset classes can be used as a benchmark for fund allocation. Alternatively, an actual portfolio can be implemented with index or active funds using the AHP portfolio weights.

The AHP portfolio is not intended to be "optimal" in terms of traditional mean–variance methodology. The key outcome of the AHP is suitability of the portfolio in meeting the needs, wants, and preferences of the investor. Portfolios designed by using the AHP actually come relatively close to the traditional efficient frontier portfolio. The starting points of the two approaches differ, however: For the AHP, it is the individual, and for mean–variance optimization, it is the market and the efficient frontier. In other words, the AHP is an investor-centric (as opposed to a market-centric) technique. More information about the AHP and its application to investment decision making can be found in Khaksari, Kamath, and Grieves (1989), Bolster, Janjigian, and Trahan (1995), and Saraoglu and Detzler (2002).

Conclusion

Appropriate asset allocation for high-net-worth investors requires significant intellectual effort to synthesize the investor's goals with the opportunities available in the market. Major contributions in sound theory and best practice have been made in recent years to address the unique requirements of taxable investors. Asset allocation and security portfolio strategies, such as tax-loss harvesting and the use of a leveraged complementary fund, can reliably generate economically substantial tax alpha. And the analytic hierarchy process can be used effectively in investment management to broaden the context of asset allocation in meeting the complex needs and preferences of private investors.

This presentation comes from the Asset Allocation: Alpha and Beta Investment Strategies conference held in Marina del Rey, California, on 6–7 April 2006.

References

Bolster, Paul J., Vahan Janjigian, and Emery A. Trahan. 1995. "Determining Investor Suitability Using the Analytic Hierarchy Process." *Financial Analysts Journal*, vol. 51, no. 4 (July/August):63–75.

Khaksari, Shahriar, Ravindra Kamath, and Robin Grieves. 1989. "A New Approach to Determining Optimum Portfolio Mix." *Journal of Portfolio Management*, vol. 15, no. 3 (Spring):43–49.

Saaty, Thomas L., and Luis G. Vargas. 1994. *Decision Making in Economic, Political, Social, and Technological Environments with the Analytic Hierarchy Process*. Pittsburgh: RWS Publications.

Saraoglu, Hakan, and Miranda Lam Detzler. 2002. "A Sensible Mutual Fund Selection Model." *Financial Analysts Journal*, vol. 58, no. 3 (May/June):60–72.

Wilcox, Jarrod, Jeffrey E. Horvitz, and Dan diBartolomeo. 2006. *Investment Management for Taxable Private Investors*. Charlottesville, VA: Research Foundation of CFA Institute.

More from Dan diBartolomeo

This section presents the speaker's lively question and answer session with the conference audience.

Question: Has your firm experienced any bumps along the way in applying the AHP?

diBartolomeo: Yes, one perplexing situation that we confronted comes to mind. We tested our questionnaire in Japan because we have a few clients there. One question we asked was, What is your time horizon for this portfolio? The universal response was six months, whether the investor was 20 or 90 years old. So, we rewrote the question: How long before you expect to spend this money? Now, the answer changed from six months to 20 years. Again, the response was the same regardless of the age of the investor.

We were puzzled. So, we decided to go back to these investors to ask what they thought the first question meant. Their interpretation of the question was, How long do you plan to remain a customer of the financial services firm? The moral of this story is that you have to be extremely careful and deliberate in selecting and wording the questions that you use.

Question: Many investors expect higher capital gains taxes in the future. So, is now a good time to realize capital gains?

diBartolomeo: Clearly, the decision is a trade-off. The conventional wisdom is defer, defer, defer. But if you think capital gains taxes are going to rise, then it may be sensible to take some gains now and pay the tax. Many sophisticated optimizers are available to analyze this trade-off, but it can also be done with a fairly innocuous, simple approach presented in the Research Foundation of CFA Institute monograph.

Question: How effective are life balance sheets in guiding asset allocation decisions?

diBartolomeo: Using a life balance sheet approach to inform the asset allocation decision makes a lot of sense. The biggest problem for investment professionals dealing with high-net-worth investors is the inability to articulate how conservative or aggressive an investor ought to be.

I remember a conversation with the CEO of a large asset management firm who asked me to specify the "right" amount of tracking error for his clients. My response was that he and his team would have to make that call. The problem in the high-net-worth world is that the client doesn't have a clue. A fellow who just sold his business for $3 million doesn't know how to gauge his level of aggressiveness in the market.

As positive an approach as it is, the life balance sheet concept is not easy to execute. Many factors have to be considered. How do you value the option to save more? How do you value the option to spend less? Nevertheless, the life balance sheet approach provides a relative measure of a sensible degree of aggressiveness or conservatism and how that degree of aggressiveness or conservatism ought to evolve through time.

A common misconception is that an investor becomes more conservative as he or she gets older, but the truth in that piece of conventional wisdom is closely tied to an investor's level of wealth. Many wealthy, very elderly investors, given their wealth transfer and other goals, should be as aggressive as possible. In my experience, the life balance sheet concept, although not the easiest tool to implement, can be a powerful guide.

Trends in Portfolio Structuring

Investment professionals rely on four fundamental asset categories to build portfolios. Traditional models of diversifying risk among these building blocks tend to let systematic risk dominate the risk profile. Recent trends in portfolio structuring seek to better balance active and systematic risk by increasing the diversification options and changing the proportions of active and systematic risk in the portfolio, which often requires lifting constraints on the use of shorting, leverage, and derivatives.

Recent trends in portfolio structuring tend to focus on modifying traditional portfolio management to manage risk more effectively. To place these trends in context, it is useful to review some basic principles.

Portfolio Structuring Principles

Four fundamental investment building blocks are typically used in structuring an investment portfolio:

- debt,
- ownership (of equities, commodities, real estate, and so forth),
- numeraire (or currency exposure), and
- derivatives contracts (exposures driven by relationships with underlying securities or indices).

These building blocks generate various systematic exposures, including exposure to equity markets, interest rates (duration), credit or default risk, optionality (volatility), foreign exchange, commodities, and real estate. Within

Finding pure alpha strategies is not easy, and some observers question whether the capacity is available to take large exposures, whether in absolute return strategies or derivatives positions.

Roger G. Clarke is chairman of the board of Analytic Investors, Inc., Los Angeles.

these exposures are various tilts (or alternative betas), including tilts caused by equity styles (such as value and growth), market capitalization (size), momentum, industry or sectors, countries, market volatility, liquidity, inflation, and individual securities.

Having identified the four building blocks of a portfolio and the various exposures and tilts that portfolios are prone to, investment professionals follow several principles in building portfolios:

- Carefully identify sources of risk and return.
- Unbundle systematic risk exposure from active risk exposure.
- Diversify risks.
- Balance risks with expected returns.

Decomposition of Total Risk and Return

The total return of a portfolio can be divided into three components: (1) riskless return, (2) systematic risk premiums, and (3) active returns. The two associated risk components in such a decomposition are categorized as systematic risk from broad market exposure (or beta) and active risk (or alpha) from active management.

Systematic risk

Systematic risk (or beta) is generally created by passive exposure to asset classes or sectors. Such exposures embody the sources of long-run risk premiums. All investors can earn these risk premiums simultaneously. Little skill is required, and the cost of implementation is low. The Sharpe ratios (risk premium/volatility) for bearing this type of risk usually fall in the 0.2–0.4 range. For every 10 percent of volatility taken on by an investor, roughly 3 percent of risk premium can be expected.

Table 1 provides information on volatility and Sharpe ratios for several types of systematic risk over the past 26 years. For example, the return spread of international equities over T-bills was 5.4 percent with 16.7 percent volatility, making the Sharpe ratio 0.32 for that period. In contrast, the Sharpe ratio for U.S. equities over T-bills was 0.47. The Sharpe ratio for the value-to-growth spread was 0.24, and the small- to large-cap spread was 0.01. The credit spread of corporate over government bonds in the fixed-income area was about 60 bps with a Sharpe ratio of about 0.23. Interestingly, there did not seem to be much risk premium in the foreign exchange market, which in this case was based on the Europe/Australasia/Far East Index relative to the U.S. dollar.

Determining the amount of systematic risk to put into a portfolio is the traditional task of strategic asset allocation for institutions and constitutes the framework in which most of us have labored over the years.

Table 1   Systematic Risk Relationships, 1979–2005

Asset Relationships	Return Spread	Volatility	Sharpe Ratio
Equity			
International equity/T-bills	5.4%	16.7%	0.32
U.S. equity/T-bills	7.2	15.3	0.47
Value/growth	2.4	10.1	0.24
Small/large cap	0.1	10.8	0.01
Fixed income			
Short-term bonds/T-bills	1.6%	1.7%	0.91
Long-term/short-term bonds (term)	1.4	2.6	0.55
Corporate/government bonds (default)	0.6	2.6	0.23
Foreign exchange (FX)	−0.3%	8.4%	−0.04

Active risk

Active risk is created by active management of the asset class or sector exposures or by individual security selection. By actively choosing exposures different from a benchmark, managers hope to generate relative returns (alpha). To generate extra returns consistently over time, managers must be skilled, although statistically distinguishing skill from luck in the short run is not easy.

A major difference between systematic and active risk is that within a closed universe of securities, active risk is a zero-sum proposition. Whereas all investors who have exposure to broad equity market risk can earn the systematic risk premium, not all investors who are actively managing exposures in a market can earn positive relative returns simultaneously. Those who earn relative returns through active management profit at the expense of other investors who lose. Some investors will outperform while others will underperform such that the combination results in the average market return.

Another difference between the two types of risk is that, although active risk typically makes a smaller contribution to the total risk in a portfolio than does systematic risk, the cost of active management is usually higher because it is skill based. Information ratios (alpha/active risk) of successful active strategies can exceed 0.5.

Active return is typically driven by security selection and the active timing of systematic risk exposures. The drivers of security selection may be diverse but are often based on (1) business strategy or valuation, (2) momentum, (3) change in creditworthiness, or (4) arbitrage or some particular event. The active timing of systematic risk exposure includes such strategies as (1) global asset and currency allocation, (2) duration management, (3) style management, and (4) industry or sector rotation.

Putting Together an Investment Strategy

Typical investment strategy objectives include the following:

- Earning long-term risk premiums above the riskless rate through exposure to systematic risk (beta). Managers usually seek to diversify among various sources of risk premiums and across economic scenarios.
- Capturing additional return from active management. Here, managers seek to diversify among sources of active returns. Managers spend substantial energy to increase information ratios by broadening the investment opportunity set, reducing the impact of constraints on the portfolio, or improving forecasting ability.
- Building well-structured portfolios for an efficient trade-off between risk and return. Achieving this objective requires that the manager find an effective balance between systematic and active risk in the portfolio. Managers may choose to scale risks to equalize volatilities between the parts of their portfolios. Scaling risks typically entails the use of cash to lever low-volatility assets or delever high-volatility assets.

To separate or unbundle alpha and beta risk, managers need more flexibility in their management strategies than a typical long-only manager has. First, they need the flexibility to take short positions so they can reduce the systematic risk exposure in their long positions. Second, the use of derivatives is often necessary to unbundle systematic and active risk. For example, if a manager's portfolio is structured with both long and short positions to exploit the spread, derivatives overlays allow the manager to add back into the portfolio systematic risks that may have been neutralized. Third, managers may need more flexibility in structuring their capital through the use of leverage to balance the risks in the portfolio.

Dimensions of Diversification

Besides identifying, choosing, and balancing risks, managers must also diversify risks. Many developments in portfolio structuring today, particularly for hedge fund and fund-of-funds management, rely on several basic dimensions of diversification:

1. imperfect correlation,
2. breadth of application,
3. unequal volatility,
4. contribution to variance, and
5. risk scaling through leverage.

Imperfect correlation

Portfolios achieve better diversification with imperfectly correlated assets, and the less the correlation, the greater the reduction in volatility.

Breadth of application

As the number of securities in a portfolio increases, so does its diversifying capacity. As shown in **Figure 1**, adding even a relatively small number of imperfectly correlated securities to a portfolio can have a substantial effect on volatility. The less correlation that exists among the assets added, the more dramatic the volatility reduction. If a portfolio's assets have a common correlation, such as stocks that share broad market risks in addition to their individual risks, the reduction in volatility is limited because of the correlated systematic risk reflected in the portfolio.

Unequal volatility

When managers combine assets with different volatilities, volatility is reduced and the effect can be dramatic, as shown in **Figure 2**, which combines the effect of low correlation with differences in volatility. The effect is created primarily by

Figure 1   Effect of Additional Assets on Diversification Benefits

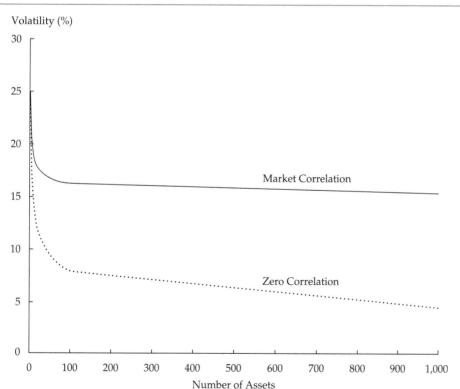

Figure 2   Effect of Combining Low- and High-Volatility Assets

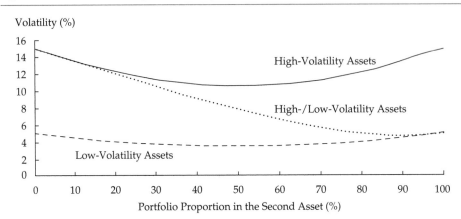

the unequal volatilities rather than the diversification benefits of low correlation. But as the figure also indicates, the manager has to have a fairly high proportion of the portfolio in the low-volatility asset before the combination of high and low volatilities has its full effect.

Contribution to variance

When active risk is added to the systematic risk in a portfolio, the systematic risk tends to dominate because of its greater volatility. Furthermore, even when the proportion of active management increases, its contribution is not substantial as long as its level is modest relative to the volatility of systematic risk. Thus, with 2 percent active risk, the portfolio continues to behave much like an index fund, even when 100 percent of the portfolio is actively managed. When the active risk increases to 4 percent, the portfolio behaves more like a traditional long-only fund. Not until the active risk is increased to 8 percent does active management have a substantial effect on the volatility of the portfolio. This result occurs because volatility is a nonlinear function. When a small component of volatility is combined with a much larger component of volatility, the larger component dominates disproportionately. Note that less than 5 percent of the total volatility in an enhanced index fund and less than 15 percent of the total volatility in a traditional long-only fund are contributed by active management.

Risk scaling through leverage

Applying leverage allows a manager to equalize volatilities between two disparate assets before using them to diversify a portfolio. **Figure 3** offers a graphic example of leverage used to scale risk to parity. The horizontal axis is the leverage ratio. Thus, at zero, the manager uses no leverage. The target volatility, as shown in the figure, is about 12 percent. One asset has a volatility of 15 percent (high volatility); the other asset has a volatility of 5 percent (low volatility). To

Figure 3   Risk Scaling through Leverage

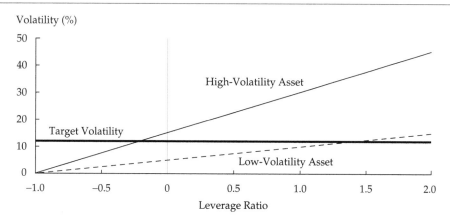

lower the high-volatility asset to the target volatility, the manager must add cash; to raise the low-volatility asset to the target volatility, the manager must leverage or short cash. By bringing the volatility of these two assets to parity, the manager can mix them for better diversification and not worry that the higher-volatility asset will dominate the risk profile. The manager can create the same effect by mixing assets of different volatilities and then aggregating the combined cash positions into a new leverage position that achieves the same total volatility. Some portfolio structures, however, may not allow leverage to be aggregated and require that it be done within individual assets positions.

For example, risk scaling is often useful in building funds of funds because managers achieve the best diversification if they construct portfolios with assets that have roughly equal volatilities. But leverage is often required to create such parity at the individual fund level within each manager's portfolio, instead of doing it at the total fund level.

To illustrate the effect of risk parity, **Figure 4** shows that in a portfolio consisting of 50 percent low-volatility assets and 50 percent high-volatility assets, risk parity allows 50 percent of volatility to be contributed by the low-volatility assets. Without risk parity, the low-volatility assets contribute only about 10 percent of total volatility to the portfolio. Thus, the sources of risk are not very balanced. Similarly, the maximum Sharpe ratio can occur whether or not risks are scaled to parity, but without scaling, risks are unbalanced and the maximum Sharpe ratio is not achieved unless the portfolio consists of 80 percent low-volatility assets.

Portfolio Building Blocks and Risk Exposures

Each individual security carries some amount of both systematic and individual risk. Combining securities in a portfolio helps diversify away much of the

Figure 4   Risk Parity for Balancing the Contributions to Total Volatility

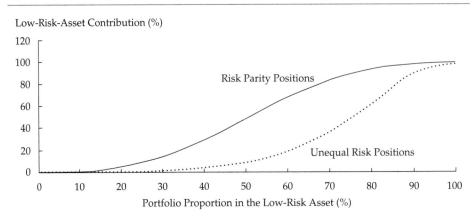

individual risk, leaving mostly systematic risk. Actively managing individual security positions and the timing of systematic risk exposures creates active risk. Systematic sources of risk are usually correlated with each other, although not perfectly. The more diversity a manager can get in systematic risk exposures, the better the diversification.

For large portfolios, managers prefer that risks come from multiple sources, but large portfolios need to access substantial capacity and preferably at relatively low cost. Among the active sources of risk, managers also want diversification. They prefer mixing strategies with as little correlation as possible with each other and with little systematic risk. Ideally, they would prefer strategies having adequate capacity for their needs while achieving all these goals at reasonable cost. Finding strategies with these characteristics usually requires looking at managers with the ability to take short positions, use leverage and derivatives, and execute cost-efficient transactions. Note that systematic risks tend to have high to medium correlation with each other, but fortunately, many sources of active risks tend to have relatively low correlation, depending on the underlying strategies. Thus, investors can usually add active risks into a traditional portfolio without increasing the portfolio's risk profile significantly. Nevertheless, historically, investors have tended to take less active and more systematic risk in their portfolios, perhaps because they have somewhat lower confidence in their ability to choose managers who have positive information ratios.

The traditional institutional portfolio structure has tended to be long-only and actively managed with the majority of assets invested in stocks and bonds. Systematic risk tends to dominate, and active risk makes a relatively minor contribution to total risk. Among traditionally managed pension funds and endowments, systematic risk is driven mostly by the portfolio's equity exposure.

Decomposing Portfolio Risk

To illustrate the risk profile of a traditional portfolio, consider an actual long-only institutional portfolio that is benchmarked to 60 percent equities and 40 percent fixed income. About 90 percent of the risk in this portfolio comes from the systematic risk in the benchmark; active risk constitutes only 10 percent of the portfolio's total risk. This is not to suggest that 90 percent of the total return comes from systematic risk exposure but that systematic risk contributes about 90 percent of the portfolio volatility. Further analysis shows that 95 percent of the total risk is driven by the equity portion of the portfolio and only 5 percent is driven by fixed income, a pattern consistent with mixing two different types of assets that have disparate volatilities. When one considers only active risk, the composition of risk in this portfolio is even more polarized, with 98 percent of the active risk coming from active management of stocks and only 2 percent coming from active management of bonds, reflecting both the higher allocation to equities and the higher relative active risk in the equity portion of the portfolio.

The active risk in this portfolio comes from two sources: (1) active security selection and (2) active asset allocation. This particular portfolio shows that 85 percent of active risk is contributed by active security selection and that 15 percent is contributed by tactical asset allocation away from the benchmark, using its current composition.

If one assumes that a traditional portfolio has an average Sharpe ratio of 0.3 for systematic risk exposure with 10 percent total volatility, then the portfolio should earn about 3 percent in risk premium from passive exposure to long-run systematic risk:

$$\text{Sharpe ratio} \times \text{Systemic volatility} = \text{Risk premium};$$
$$0.3 \times 10.0 = 3.0\%.$$

In addition, if one assumes that the portfolio is actively well managed—that is, its managers are generally good and generate a 0.5 information ratio (IR) with 2 percent active risk—then the investor may expect another 1 percent in additional return from active management:

$$IR \times \text{Active risk} = \text{Active return};$$
$$0.5 \times 2.0 = 1.0\%$$

Combining the expected long-term systematic excess return with the expected long-term active return suggests that the portfolio should pick up about 4 percent above the underlying riskless rate:

$$3.0 + 1.0 = 4.0\%.$$

The current efforts in portfolio structuring seek to enhance returns above the expected 4 percent by encouraging institutional investors to consider portfolios other than this traditional long-only, equity-dominated structure. Some of the motivations include the following:

- Declining equity returns and decreasing interest rates are putting tremendous pressure on the funding ratios of pension plans as well as on the overall returns of endowments and foundations, thus leading them to search for other ways to increase portfolio returns.
- Systematic equity risk dominates the risk profile, creating an unbalanced risk profile.
- Derivatives contracts make it possible for managers to separate systematic and active risk.
- Managers see the negative impact of portfolio constraints (such as the inability to take short positions) on expected active returns.
- Technology facilitates better risk management systems and new ways of trading.
- The development of relatively market-neutral investment strategies accommodates the separation of active and systematic risk.

Portfolio Structuring Trends

Several current trends can be seen in portfolio structuring. One trend is to increase the diversification of systematic risks by expanding the choice set of asset categories. Opportunities to diversify beta include real estate, private equity, global bonds, emerging markets, high-yield bonds, Treasury Inflation-Protected Securities (TIPS), and commodities. Such alternatives allow investors to improve risk–return trade-offs and to rely less on high exposure to the equity risk premium.

Another trend has been the decoupling of active and passive risk exposures using three tools in particular — shorting, derivatives, and leverage. Specific risk-separating strategies include active currency overlays, global asset allocation, market-neutral strategies, and absolute return strategies. Managers seek more active risk components to help them achieve greater diversification and change the proportions of active and systematic risk in portfolios. One way to do this is to combine physical assets and derivatives positions, typically using a derivatives overlay plus some underlying physical assets. Both the physical assets and the derivatives overlay can be managed either actively or passively, and the physical assets can be invested in different markets from the derivatives exposures. The combination can then be used to access both systematic and active risks.

Exhibit 1   Alternative Portfolio Structures

Physical Assets	Derivatives Overlays		
	None	Passive	Active
Passive	Index funds of physical assets	Synthetic index funds with or without specific tilts, passive currency hedging	Active tilt strategies, active asset allocation, active currency hedging
Active	Traditional long-only active management of physicals, long–short or market-neutral strategies	Enhanced index funds, alpha transport strategies, passive currency hedging	Multiple alpha strategies actively managing both physical assets and derivatives overlays

Exhibit 1 presents some combinations of physical assets and derivatives that are commonly used.

Use of Hedge Funds

Hedge funds are often considered as a means of bringing more alpha into a portfolio. Few hedge funds, however, generate pure active risk. Many hedge funds carry their own component of systematic risk, and managers need to consider a hedge fund's systematic exposures when using hedge funds to add alpha. According to Partners Group of Zurich, 80 percent of the volatility in the Hedge Fund Research (HFR) Index can be explained by the following factors:

- large-cap stocks,
- large-cap/small-cap spread,
- serial correlation in returns,
- MSCI emerging markets, and
- global bonds.

Thus, a manager who puts money into the HFR Index in a quest for alpha will also add systematic risk into the portfolio.

As data from Morgan Stanley illustrate in **Table 2**, the average beta found in certain typical hedge fund strategies is clearly nontrivial. Furthermore, the range of systematic risks both among hedge fund strategies and over time is quite large. Thus, if an investor places money with a particular hedge fund to get active returns, the investor cannot be certain how much systematic risk might come along and how it might vary over time.

Table 2   Equity Betas for Selected Hedge Fund Strategies

Strategy	Average Beta	Range
Long bias	0.51	0.28 to 0.75
Event driven	0.21	0.04 to 0.55
Discretionary trading	0.11	−0.05 to 0.27
Convertible arbitrage	0.02	−0.13 to 0.13
Fixed-income arbitrage	−0.01	−0.17 to 0.10
Systematic trading	−0.09	−0.47 to 0.72

Source: Based on data from Morgan Stanley.

Separating Alpha and Beta

The concept of separating active and systematic risk is theoretically attractive. There is no particular reason that an alpha source needs to be bundled with a beta source. But finding pure alpha strategies is not easy, and some observers question whether the capacity is available to take large exposures, whether in absolute return strategies or derivatives positions. Substantial use of derivatives overlays raises issues of counterparty risk exposure as well as limits on the credit allocation by counterparties. The management of cash flows can also become an issue because parties need to settle derivatives positions from time to time.

When deciding how much systematic risk to take on, an investor might ask the following questions:

- What objectives does the fund need to meet?
- What is the investment time horizon?
- How important is the path of returns over time (i.e., the impact of short-term volatility)?
- How large are the expected risk premiums?
- How reliable are the expected risk premiums over time?
- How much diversification is possible?

Investors considering active risk might ask additional questions:

- How confident am I in my ability to pick skilled managers?
- What is the capacity of the market to absorb the fund's need for alpha?
- What is the cost of acquiring alpha?
- How effective is the risk management process?
- How will I educate the board and committees about the characteristics of active risk management?

- How well does the board deal with the emotions of periodic losses that inevitably accompany active risk?
- How do I balance a risk allocation perspective with a traditional asset allocation perspective?
- Will active managers meet the fund's requirements for transparency?
- How will I monitor active managers?
- How do I protect against the possibility of tail risk or meltdown scenarios?
- How do I reduce the risk of fraud and counterparty default?
- Can traditional constraints be adapted to accommodate the use of derivatives, shorting, and leverage?

Active management against an index can be pictured in what might be called the "triangle of active management," which consists of three components: (1) alphas, or expected returns, which distinguish one security from another; (2) relative weights, or how assets are allocated in a portfolio; and (3) actual or *ex post* returns. Each of these three points of the triangle is important relative to each of the other points. On the one hand, the quality of a manager's signal as measured by the information coefficient reflects a manager's skill at predicting actual returns. On the other hand, the extent to which the manager's forecasts are transferred into relative portfolio weights is measured by the transfer coefficient. These two legs are critical drivers of the *ex post* performance, determined by the extent to which relative portfolio weights correspond to the relative *ex post* returns of securities.

Managing the Transfer Coefficient

The Grinold (1989) formulation of the fundamental law of active management (see the following equation) suggests that the success of active management as measured by the information ratio depends on the quality of the manager's information and the breadth of application. In effect, it is an attempt to indicate the total amount of return that an investor might expect from the information set:

$$IR = \frac{E(R_A)}{\sigma_A} = IC\sqrt{N},$$

where
$E(R_A)$ = expected portfolio active return
σ_A = portfolio active risk
IC = information coefficient
N = breadth

The information coefficient measures the quality of the information, and N is the portfolio breadth. The information ratio, the expected return per unit of risk, is a product of those two components. The implication is that the manager needs good forecasts and then applies them as broadly as possible to maximize the information ratio.

Such a relationship quantifies the maximum amount of return that an investor can expect from a given amount of information used to make forecasts. In reality, however, most portfolios include constraints that prevent them from realizing the full value of the available information. Subsequent work by Clarke, de Silva, and Thorley (2002) showed that the relationship can be modified to reflect the amount of information transferred into actual portfolio positions using the transfer coefficient:

$$IR = \frac{E(R_A)}{\sigma_A} \approx TC \times IC\sqrt{N},$$

where TC is the transfer coefficient.

The transfer coefficient is measured as the correlation between the forecasted attractiveness of a security and its relative weight in a portfolio (adjusted for risk). Portfolios with more binding constraints tend to have lower transfer coefficients, and portfolios with lower transfer coefficients tend to have lower expected information ratios and lower expected returns given the amount of active risk incurred.

Common constraints in portfolios are the following: no short selling; industry or sector limitations; position limits on individual securities; limitations on such characteristics as size, dividend yield, and price to book; and limitations on turnover. All such constraints affect a manager's ability to structure a portfolio to best reflect the information content in the manager's security ranking system.

Consider the example shown in **Table 3**. The full set of constraints requires the portfolio to be long-only, industry and sector neutral, and market-cap

Table 3   Impact of Constraints on Transfer Coefficient

Item	Transfer Coefficient
All constraints imposed	0.33
Constraint removed	
Industries *or* sectors	0.35
Sectors *and* industries	0.42
Market capitalization	0.47
Long-only	0.68

Notes: Full constraint set equals long-only, industry and sector neutral, market-cap neutral, position limits ±3 percent of benchmark, beta equal to market. Security ranking equals book to price ratio. Target tracking-error volatility equals 4 percent.

Figure 5   S&P 500 Unconstrained: Transfer Coefficient = 0.98

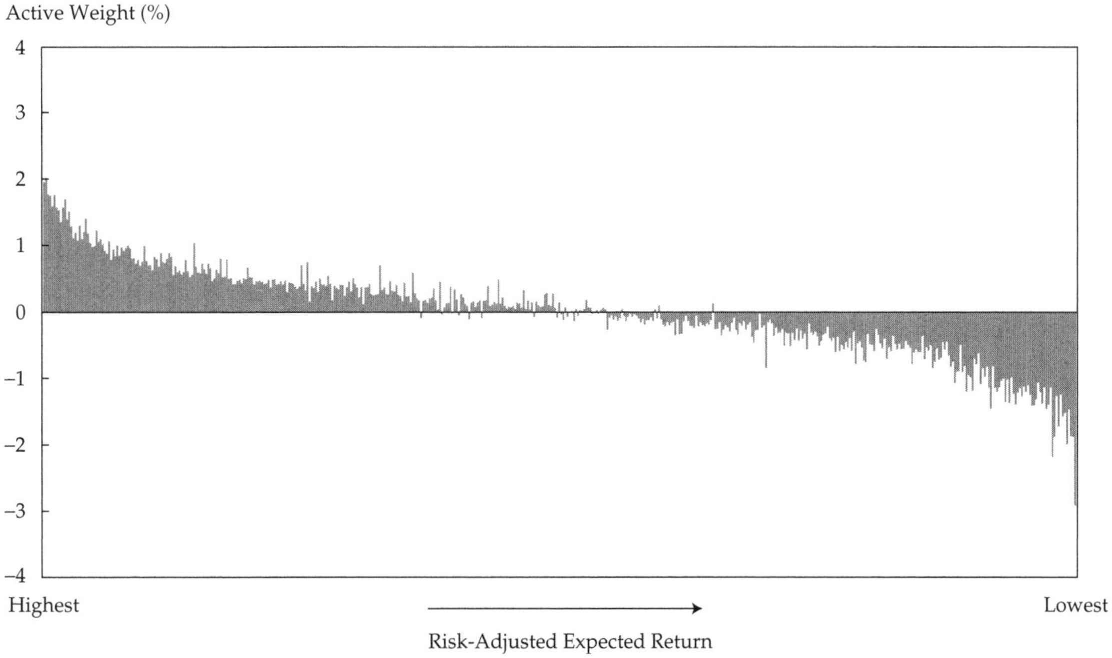

neutral with position limits within ±0.3 percent of the benchmark and to have a beta equal to the market. This is a fairly typical portfolio structure for a long-only manager, and the resulting transfer coefficient for this portfolio is 0.33. Therefore, about one-third of the potential added value for this information set is actually being transferred into the portfolio positions. By going down the list and removing constraints one by one, the transfer coefficient gradually rises until, with just the long-only constraint applied, the transfer coefficient is 0.68. With no constraints at all, the transfer coefficient would, in theory, be 1.0.

To demonstrate the insight of the transfer coefficient and the effect of constraints on its value, **Figure 5** shows an active portfolio relative to the S&P 500 Index with no constraints and a transfer coefficient of 0.98. Based on the active weights in the portfolio (sorted by their risk-adjusted expected returns), the portfolio is overweight in assets with positive expected alphas and underweight in assets with negative expected alphas. By adding a long-only constraint, as shown in **Figure 6**, the transfer coefficient is reduced to 0.58 and the patterns become much choppier. But the portfolio is still generally overweight in assets with positive expected returns and underweight in assets with poor expected returns. Unfortunately, sorting the overweight and underweight positions by market capitalization rather than alpha, as shown in **Figure 7**, shows that most of the underweight positions are in the large-cap stocks. This result mimics the

Figure 6   S&P 500 Long-Only Constraint: Transfer Coefficient = 0.58

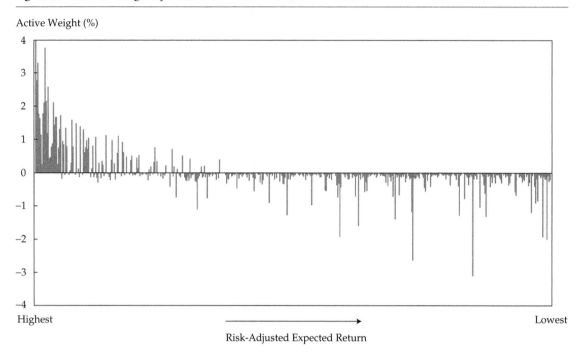

Figure 7   S&P 500 Long-Only Constraint: Market-Capitalization Sorting

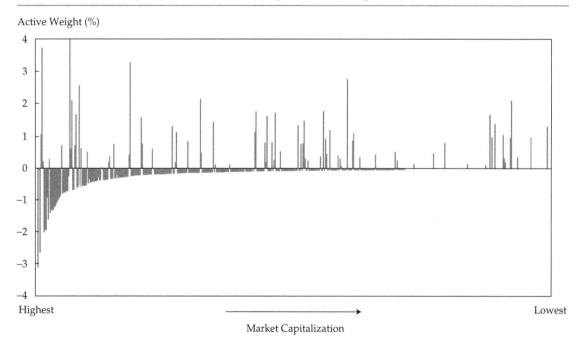

condition of most institutional portfolios with a long-only constraint. They tend to have a small-cap bias because they cannot underweight small-cap assets effectively, so most of their underweight positions are in the large-cap area. Therefore, when small caps outperform large caps in the index, many active managers tend to outperform not because they are particularly good at security selection but because they tend to have a small-cap bias against a capitalization-weighted index.

To counter this tendency, managers are using strategies that relax the long-only constraint. A 120/20 strategy, for example, allows the manager to go long 120 percent market exposure and short 20 percent, thus relaxing the short side enough to underweight some of the smaller-cap stocks and allowing the portfolio to be more risk balanced across the signal. Such a variation on the traditional long-only strategy (100/0) allows the transfer coefficient to move from 0.51 to 0.63 in the example with a resulting increase in expected alpha.

Conclusion

Recent trends in portfolio structuring are motivated by a desire to improve portfolio diversification, better balance the mixture of systematic and active risks, and increase performance in a lower-expected-return environment. Managers are trying to identify active and systematic risks more clearly, diversify among the sources of risk more effectively, focus on risk exposures rather than just accounting values, attend more closely to risk budgeting, reduce constraints (particularly the long-only constraint), and install overlay applications using derivatives for alpha transport strategies in multiple layers to use the underlying capital more effectively.

This presentation comes from the 2006 Financial Analysts Seminar held in Evanston, Illinois, on 16–21 July 2006.

References

Clarke, Roger, Harindra de Silva, and Steven Thorley. 2002. "Portfolio Constraints and the Fundamental Law of Active Management." *Financial Analysts Journal*, vol. 58, no. 5 (September/October):48–66.

Grinold, Richard C. 1989. "The Fundamental Law of Active Management." *Journal of Portfolio Management*, vol. 15, no. 3 (Spring):30–37.

More from Roger G. Clarke

This section presents the speaker's lively question and answer session with the conference audience.

Question: How would you suggest measuring the risk to portfolios of assets that are not valued on a daily basis, such as private equity and real estate?

Clarke: Real estate and private equity are not priced continuously in liquid markets, so they appear a lot less volatile than they would be if there were an open market where prices were determined frequently. Investors tend to deal with this limitation in two ways as they consider their risks and configure their asset allocations. They either increase the historical risk parameters for these assets, or they place constraints on the amount invested in such assets while optimizing everything else.

Question: Is it possible that active risk resulting from seeking alpha is noise?

Clarke: It is hard to even talk about alpha without first defining what we mean by beta because we tend to think about alpha as what's left over after we subtract the beta contribution from the total return. We try to build mental constructs to help us understand the world, and part of that framework is to describe what the beta portion is. How one describes the beta portion will affect whether the alpha portion might be thought of as noise. The alpha risk is certainly real because we see its effects in the *ex post* returns. The question is whether we can measure it very well and what difference it makes in our decisions.

Unfortunately, as we become more quantitatively oriented in terms of our risk measurement, we may be fooled into thinking there is more precision than actually exists. We deal in a world of uncertainty. We know only what has happened in the past, and the linkage between past and future is not always tight. We seem to observe a lot of nonstationarity. Therefore, we should not be fooled by depending on too much precision in our risk models. New frameworks may be full of unknowns and instabilities that may only be clarified through experience. That may be the true source of noise, and it is not easy to capture fully.

Question: Do you see any long-term trends for achieving the optimum information ratio?

Clarke: There is probably no solution that will always be optimal. Performance trends seem to be somewhat episodic. Sometimes, the majority of our active, long-only institutional managers seem to be outperforming; at other times, they seem to be underperforming. Such perceptions are probably determined by how we measure performance against the investment universe.

In the hedge fund universe, capacity issues will probably have an impact on how much alpha is available. For example, if all investors moved to market-neutral investing and then tried to get their broad market systematic risk exposure through a derivatives overlay, finding alpha would probably become more difficult.

The crowded environment might get a little more difficult, but these things ebb and flow. There will be periods when hedge funds will look terrific and other periods when investors will wonder why they bothered with hedge funds. This will be an issue for investment committees. When the equity market has 25–30 percent returns and hedge funds are delivering 12–15 percent because they do not have full market exposure, investment committees will have to deal with the regret of having less equity exposure and using strategies that have periods of underperformance compared with equities as the best performing asset class for the period.

Question: How do you measure the ability of derivatives-related strategies to contribute to a portfolio if the traditional framework does not apply?

Clarke: The convenient thing about most overlay strategies is that they are pure value-added strategies. Thus, to the extent that traditional overlay positions do not require a lot of underlying capital directly, the portfolio earns a pure active return from those derivatives positions, which adds to the underlying portfolio performance.

Consider currency overlay strategies. Once the active return is calculated, the investor can determine whether that conforms to expectations. Will the investor be happy if the number is simply greater than zero, or does it need to be scaled for some amount of risk? For example, suppose the average active risk for a currency overlay manager is 2 percent. If the target is an information ratio of 0.5, the investor would expect the manager to add 100 bps over time. You might evaluate the manager relative to the 100 bps expectation given the active risk involved, not just whether the active return is positive.

Asset Growth and Its Impact on Expected Alpha

For years, researchers have acknowledged, but poorly understood, the relationship between capacity and alpha. A model has been developed that clarifies the relationship and identifies the two drivers that have the greatest effect on capacity: information ratio and costs.

Capacity refers to how much money a firm can manage effectively in an active investment strategy.[1] Firms such as Barclays Global Investors put great effort into addressing this issue, and my purpose is to describe the framework that we use in our own internal discussions. To begin, however, I will posit two assumptions: (1) Active investment strategies have limits to their capacity. Such limits may vary from strategy to strategy, but all strategies are prone to capacity limitations. (2) Managers must have a clear understanding of capacity before they can manage the effects of capacity.

> A goal for most firms is to move beyond rules of thumb and develop models that actually measure the limitations on capacity and the behavior caused by those limitations.

Prior Research on Capacity

Prior research on capacity has included *ad hoc* pronouncements and general observations, historical backtests, and academic research.

Ad Hoc Pronouncements and Observations

Ad hoc pronouncements and general observations include all the rules of thumb that practitioners have developed through years of experience and informal observation. For example, industry veterans have observed that once firms manage more than 2 percent of market cap, they no longer outperform. Thus, if the U.S. equity market has a cap of roughly $10 trillion, then the implication

---

[1] This presentation is based on Kahn and Shaffer (2005).
Ronald N. Kahn is a managing director at Barclays Global Investors, San Francisco.

is that no firm can actively manage more than $200 billion of U.S. equities successfully. As for all such rules of thumb, however, they apply to certain managers better than others. For example, one rule of thumb will not apply equally to Warren Buffett and to a statistical arbitrage manager. Therefore, a goal for most firms is to move beyond rules of thumb and develop models that actually measure the limitations on capacity and the behavior caused by those limitations. One attempt at such measurement is the historical backtest.

Historical Backtests

Historical backtests involve building portfolios based on (historical) monthly alpha forecasts and tracking them through time. But because transaction costs increase as the assets under management increase, it affects returns delivered to investors.

The problem with backtesting, however, is that it relies on historical performance, which makes it hard to change assumptions. Furthermore, historical backtests will show that slow-moving ideas that work well historically have a lot of capacity. But this is a backward-looking view. It is not the right way to analyze capacity. An approach is needed that starts in the present and projects forward.

Academic Research

For a long time, academics did very little work on the relationship between capacity and alpha. Recently, however, more researchers have been trying to understand market anomalies, and some studies try not only to understand a particular anomaly but also to determine whether managers can exploit it.

Chen, Stanzl, and Watanabe (2002) examined the effects of costs on the profitability of size, book-to-market, and momentum strategies, and Korajczyk and Sadka (2004) conducted a similar study that examined momentum in particular. Most such studies, unfortunately, use overly simple approaches to building portfolios, such as ranking stocks by momentum, ordering them by deciles, and then examining the performance of the deciles by subtracting one from another, perhaps the top decile minus the bottom decile. They might also control for other factors, but their basic portfolios are based on deciles, created without regard to the cost of trading.

An earlier study that I find interesting is by Perold and Salomon (1991) in which they tackled capacity head-on. They defined capacity as the amount of assets that generated the maximum dollars of alpha. The problem with their approach is that it is very top down. They imposed certain assumptions and considered the results. They did not build from the bottom up. Nevertheless, they do offer an important insight—the likelihood that a maximum dollar amount of alpha exists.

Model of Capacity

Because of the flaws of these prior approaches, we have built a model to help us understand the driving forces behind capacity limits and to improve our ability to manage capacity. Before discussing the value of the model, however, I will point out its shortcomings.

First, it extrapolates beyond our experience. This is, unfortunately, a given in capacity studies because we are always asking the question, What would our performance be if we were managing more money than we are today? If we manage $50 billion now, how will we do managing $100 billion in the future?

Second, the model ignores important market issues, such as regulatory limits, the implications of triggering poison pills, and short availability. These issues are difficult to model.

Third, the model ignores the relationship between liquidity and skill. As the portfolio gets bigger, the manager will take more positions in the most liquid stocks because those are the ones that the manager can buy and sell. But the manager may not be as good at picking big, liquid stocks as he or she is at picking small stocks. The model does not address this issue.

Despite the shortcomings, I believe the model is useful because it captures many key effects, and it provides a context in which to understand its shortcomings. The model is simple, and the real world is complicated. That said, I prefer using simple models and adjusting their outputs to the complications of reality rather than trying to build all those complications into the model itself.

The model begins with the basic concepts of active return, expected active return, and active risk, represented in the three equations below:

$$\theta = r_p - r_B,$$

where active return, θ, equals return on the portfolio, r_P, minus return on the benchmark, r_B;

$$\alpha = E(r_p - r_B),$$

where expected active return, α, equals the expected return on the portfolio minus the expected return on the benchmark; and

$$\omega = \text{StDev}(r_p - r_B),$$

where active risk, ω, equals the standard deviation of the active return.

Another key concept to the model is the information ratio, which is the ratio of expected active return to active risk—that is, the ratio of alpha to omega.

We can use the information ratio as either an *ex post* or *ex ante* construct. For the purposes of this model, we consider it *ex ante*. The model is designed to determine capacity constraints in the future.

The information ratio itself comes in two forms—intrinsic information ratio and implemented information ratio, which are related through the transfer coefficient (TR).[2] The intrinsic information ratio (IR_{int}) captures the maximum achievable active return per unit of risk, ignoring transaction costs and constraints. The implemented information ratio (IR_{imp}) is the amount of expected active return per unit of risk after taking costs and constraints into account. Imagine building a portfolio by optimizing the trade-off between expected active return, active risk, and costs, subject to any relevant constraints. The implemented information ratio is the ratio of the alpha of that portfolio to its forecasted active risk. The transfer coefficient, which takes on a value between 0 and 1, quantifies the impact of these costs and constraints. We can express the relationship, known as the fundamental law of portfolio management, between these three variables as follows:

$$IR_{imp} = IR_{int} \times TR.$$

We will need three additional concepts to understand the theoretical model: gross alpha, costs, and net alpha. We define these concepts in the equations below:

$$\alpha_{gross} = IR_{int}\omega TR,$$

where gross alpha, α_{gross}, equals the intrinsic information ratio multiplied by active risk multiplied by the transfer coefficient.

Therefore, gross alpha is the alpha that a fund can achieve and takes into account how constraints and costs impact portfolio construction.

In actually running that portfolio, we will incur costs, whose magnitude depends on turnover, τ, and typical round trip transaction costs, rtcost. These typical round trip transaction costs, in turn, depend on assets under management (AUM) and turnover—effectively, on the dollars traded per year. So, the complete expression for costs is as follows:

$$costs = \tau \times rtcost(AUM, \tau).$$

Thus, the larger the fund and the more it trades, the greater its costs. The net alpha is simply the gross alpha minus the costs:

$$\alpha_{net} = \alpha_{gross} - costs.$$

---

[2] For more on the transfer coefficient, see Grinold and Kahn (2000) and Clarke, de Silva, and Thorley (2002).

Theoretical Framework

To tie this all together, we express *ex ante* net alpha as follows:

$$\alpha_{net} = IR_{int} \times \omega \times TR(\tau) - \tau \times rtcost(AUM, \tau).$$

The intrinsic information ratio, which is an *ex ante* estimate, depends on a firm's research and available inefficiencies in the market. The transfer coefficient depends on turnover as well as on the constraints involved (such as long-only or long–short). We assume that the constraints are fixed for any particular analysis. The average trading cost depends on assets under management and turnover. The higher a fund's turnover, the higher its costs; and the round trip cost is a function of both assets under management and turnover. The costs of trading prevent managers from trading into their ideal portfolios. If managers could turn over their assets without limit, they could raise their portfolios' transfer coefficients significantly; thus, the higher the turnover, the greater the gross alpha.

The model is an excellent framework for understanding products and their capacity as well as for gaining insights into a variety of other issues, such as determining the optimal portfolio turnover for a given asset level.

In the context of this model, we define capacity as the maximum asset level that delivers the expected performance. Thus, the capacity is the maximum amount of assets that a firm can manage and still deliver the performance it has promised to its clients. Keep in mind two caveats when considering this definition of capacity: First, expected performance is an average, which means that actual performance will be lower than expected performance half of the time. Second, expected performance is not always clearly agreed on *ex ante* by investors and managers. I will discuss expected performance as if it were a precise number that all parties have agreed on, but such precision seldom occurs.

Sample Application

Now that we have established a theoretical framework, I will apply it to a specific example. In this case, I will use a typical U.S. equity mutual fund with the following characteristics:

- The fund is long-only.
- It takes 5.0 percent active risk.
- Investors expect an average active return before fees of 1.4 percent.

Figure 1   Transfer Coefficient vs. Annual Turnover

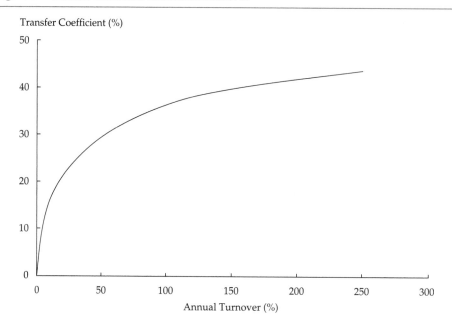

- The intrinsic information ratio is 1.2.
- Before constraints and costs, the fund can deliver an average alpha of 6.0 percent (i.e., 5.0 percent active risk multiplied by 1.2 percent intrinsic information ratio).

First, consider the transfer coefficient as a function of annual turnover, as plotted in **Figure 1**. As one can see, the transfer coefficient reaches an inflection point at around 60 percent annual turnover. Only at a very high rate of turnover (in excess of 200 percent) does the fund's transfer coefficient approach 50 percent. Note that it will never reach 100 percent because the manager will always be faced with the long-only constraint.

We developed the transfer coefficient model by running a large number of backtests. For these backtests, we were not concerned with performance. Rather, we were trying to determine how many ideas we could incorporate into our portfolio for a given amount of turnover.

Average Trading Costs

To model average trading costs, we assumed—based on available evidence—that costs tend to rise with the square root of assets under management and turnover. In **Figure 2,** average trading costs are plotted as a function of annual

Figure 2   Average Trading Costs vs. Annual Turnover for a Fund with $10 Billion in Assets

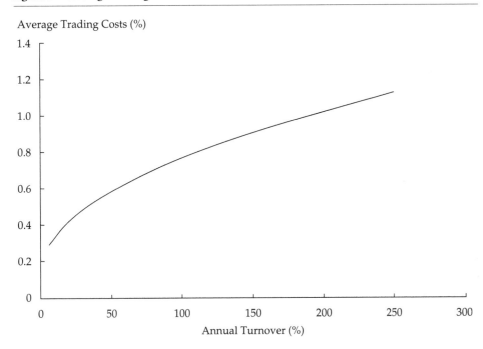

turnover. The figure shows that a $10 billion fund with 100 percent turnover will incur average trading costs of about 0.75 percent.

At this point, one needs to recognize that the previous two figures are somewhat offsetting. That is, in Figure 1, the transfer coefficient (and thus gross alpha) increases as turnover increases. The transfer coefficient increases in this manner because high turnover allows the manager to get as many ideas as possible into the portfolio. But as Figure 2 shows, as turnover increases without limit, costs also increase without limit.

As shown in **Figure 3**, depending on the assets under management, all funds have an optimal level of turnover that maximizes the net alpha the fund can deliver to clients. For our example fund, at $20 billion under management, optimal turnover is about 50 percent. If turnover exceeds that amount, the increase in the cost of trading will outweigh the increase in the transfer coefficient; if a fund's turnover falls below 50 percent, the loss in transfer coefficient will outweigh any savings in trading costs.

Given the optimal turnover level for a given amount of assets under management, we can specify all the remaining parameters in the model. **Figure 4** illustrates these results by showing how gross and net alpha relate to the expected alpha of 1.4 percent. Note that costs do not vary much with assets. The model assumes that we take costs into account as portfolio size increases.

Figure 3   Optimal Turnover to Maximize Net Alpha

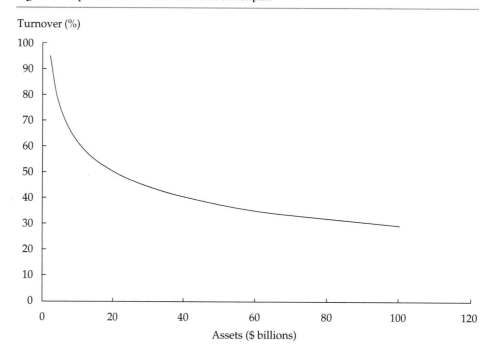

Figure 4   Optimal Net Alpha

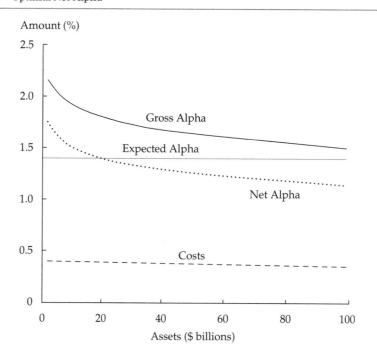

In other words, as assets go up, less trading occurs. Therefore, monitoring costs may provide little insight into the limits of capacity.

Also note that performance erodes because gross alpha erodes. As portfolios increase in size, costs and constraints increasingly prevent the firm from getting its ideas into the portfolio.

Finally, the portfolio shows a slow decay of net alpha. Recall that the fund's investors expect an alpha of 1.4 percent. For asset levels above $20 billion, net alpha drops below expected alpha. As a result, $20 billion is the capacity limit.

But notice that, although managing asset levels beyond capacity leads to eroded performance, the effect is modest. In going from $20 billion to $100 billion of assets under management, we lose only about 25 bps of net alpha. Therefore, poor performance is not necessarily a warning sign of capacity problems.

Figure 5 addresses the impact of suboptimal portfolio management—specifically, building portfolios without regard to cost. It assumes that a fund begins by managing $2 billion with 75 percent turnover. As assets rise to $20 billion, $40 billion, and $60 billion, the fund keeps turnover at 75 percent, ignoring the growing costs of trading. When the fund reaches $50 billion, suboptimal portfolio management has reduced alpha from 1.26 percent to 0.99 percent, a loss of $135 million a year to its clients. A key conclusion to draw from this analysis is that with optimal portfolio management, asset levels have a surprisingly small impact on alpha. But suboptimal portfolio management leads to a steep drop in net alpha with growing asset levels.

Figure 5   Impact of Suboptimal Portfolio Management

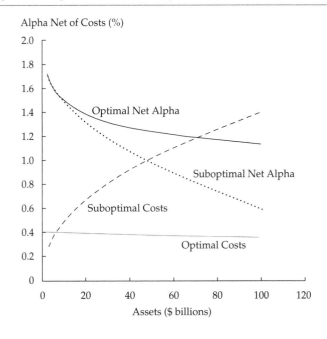

Sensitivity Analysis

Figure 6 considers the sensitivity of capacity to changes in the information ratio and trading costs. The base case information ratio is 1.2. Panel A illustrates the sensitivity of our results to that assumption by analyzing the impact if the intrinsic information ratio is actually 1.4 or 1.0 instead. If the information ratio increases from 1.2 to 1.4—an increase of about 15 percent—capacity goes

Figure 6   Sensitivity to Information Ratios and Trading Costs

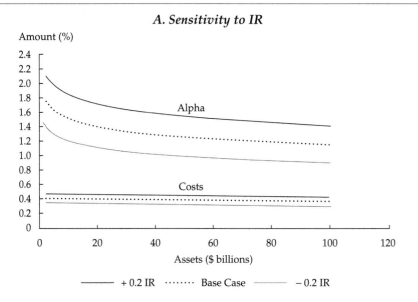

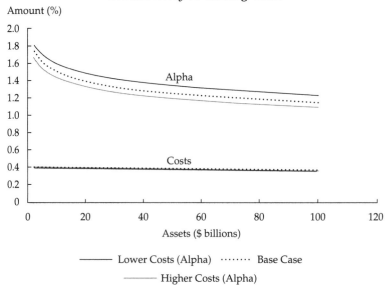

from $20 billion to $100 billion. (Recall that we define capacity based upon when net alpha decreases to the expected alpha of 1.4 percent.) Thus, a 15 percent adjustment in an input assumption increases capacity by a factor of 5. In contrast, if the information ratio decreases from 1.2 to 1.0, capacity drops from $20 billion to $2 billion, which means that capacity decreases by a factor of 10. The intrinsic information ratio is little more than an educated guess, yet even small changes in it cause significant changes in capacity.

Panel B presents a similar analysis of sensitivity to trading costs. If trading costs rise or fall by 20 percent from the base case, net alpha falls or rises, respectively, by 50 percent and 100 percent. Capacity is also quite sensitive to transaction costs, although not as sensitive as it is to information ratios.

This sensitivity analysis shows that we cannot estimate capacity with much precision, although we can identify a probable range. We have also learned that capacity is more sensitive to inputs than is expected alpha. For example, if a fund assumes an information ratio of 1.4, the analysis indicates that capacity for the fund should be $100 billion. But if the true information ratio turns out to be 1.2 instead of 1.4, the fund's capacity is actually $20 billion instead of $100 billion. So, instead of delivering 1.40 percent alpha at $100 billion, it delivers only 1.15 percent. By exceeding its capacity by a factor of 5 (quite a large amount), the fund will fail to deliver 25 bps of alpha (a much smaller amount proportionally). Thus, the effect on capacity is much greater than the effect on expected alpha.

Practical Issues

Several factors impinge on the effectiveness of the model, and we must consider them when applying the model to an actual portfolio.

Extrapolation issues
We cannot extrapolate cost models far beyond our experience. Consider a fund that is currently managing $1 billion and is contemplating how much alpha it could deliver if it were managing $200 billion. Because such an increase is well beyond the fund's experience, it cannot accurately predict the impact of such a large increase in assets on trading costs. Probably the best way to address extrapolation issues is to repeat a capacity analysis every year and use the results mainly to determine appropriate asset growth over the year.

Borrowing limitations
Long–short portfolios may face limitations on their ability to borrow stock. We can mainly analyze such limitations on an *ex post* basis.

Liquidity/efficiency trade-offs

As a fund's assets under management increase, the fund takes its biggest positions in the most liquid stocks. But the most liquid stocks are likely to be more fairly priced, thereby diluting the fund's ability to generate alpha.

Market reaction to poor performance

Despite the fact that poor performance is not necessarily a sign that a fund has gone beyond its capacity, many participants in the market believe it is. Therefore, if a fund has gathered considerable assets to manage and then experiences poor performance, it is likely to lose assets.

Practical limits

Position size may be constrained by such factors as regulatory issues and poison pill provisions.

Theoretical limits

I have defined capacity as the maximum asset level that delivers the expected performance, and the model asserts that alpha decays slowly with asset levels. Figure 4 implies that dollars of alpha increase without limit. Nevertheless, the Perold and Salomon (1991) assertion of a maximum potential dollars of alpha still seems reasonable. At some large asset size, then, net alpha should drop more quickly.

Competition

Funds must share capacity with competitors who follow the same ideas. As funds succeed, and gather assets, they also gather competitors trying to copy them.

Conclusion

Despite the limitations imposed by real world conditions, the model offers several benefits. It helps investment managers develop intuition about limits on capacity, understand the factors that are important as assets increase, and decide on effective tactics for controlling asset growth and capacity.

The model can help investment managers go beyond their current practices for monitoring capacity, such as monitoring performance and realized gains. It shows them the value of monitoring risk budget allocation, portfolio management, and exposure to alpha. And beyond that, it shows them how to manage the two drivers that affect capacity: information ratios and costs. The model shows them that they can increase their information ratios by increasing skill and breadth. It also shows them the value of exploring trading strategies that reduce costs, thereby increasing the alpha they can deliver to their clients.

This presentation comes from the 2006 Financial Analysts Seminar held in Evanston, Illinois, on 16–21 July 2006.

References

Chen, Zhiwu, Werner Stanzl, and Masahiro Watanabe. 2002. "Price Impact Costs and the Limit of Arbitrage." Working paper, Yale School of Management (February 26).

Clarke, Roger, Harindra de Silva, and Steven Thorley. 2002. "Portfolio Constraints and the Fundamental Law of Active Management." *Financial Analysts Journal*, vol. 58, no. 5 (September/October):48–66.

Grinold, Richard C., and Ronald N. Kahn. 2000. "The Efficiency Gains of Long–Short Investing." *Financial Analysts Journal*, vol. 56, no. 6 (November/December):40–53.

Kahn, Ronald N., and J. Scott Shaffer. 2005. "The Surprisingly Small Impact of Asset Growth on Expected Alpha." *Journal of Portfolio Management*, vol. 32, no. 1 (Fall):49–60.

Korajczyk, Robert A., and Ronnie Sadka. 2004. "Are Momentum Profits Robust to Trading Costs?" *Journal of Finance*, vol. 59, no. 3 (June):1039–1082.

Perold, Andre F., and Robert S. Salomon, Jr. 1991. "The Right Amount of Assets under Management." *Financial Analysts Journal*, vol. 47, no. 3 (May/June):31–39.

More from Ronald N. Kahn

This section presents the speaker's lively question and answer session with the conference audience.

Question: Does the modest impact on alpha derive from the fact that you use the square root function?

Kahn: If transaction costs were higher and if they rose more rapidly with assets under management, there would be more impact, less capacity, and a steeper drop-off. The evidence that I have seen indicates that until the numbers get quite large, the square root function works reasonably well. If trading volume is very high, such as half a day's volume, the square root works less well. So, the model does break down at some point.

Question: Can a fund dilute impact and lower transaction costs if its strategy is not sensitive to execution speed?

Kahn: The model includes the idea of speed in how the transfer coefficient depends on turnover. In our example, moving from 60 percent annual turnover to 200 percent turnover increases the transfer coefficient from about 30 percent to 40 percent. For a high-turnover strategy like statistical arbitrage, 60 percent annual turnover would lead to a very small transfer coefficient (much less than 30 percent). Moving to 200 percent turnover would represent a big improvement in transfer coefficient. This is how we embed the speed of ideas in the transfer coefficient.

Question: Does a relationship between breadth and size exist?

Kahn: Yes. With broader strategies, a fund can manage more assets. The strategies that lead to capacity problems are those that have little flexibility, such as strategies that require deciding which of a limited number of stocks the fund likes and then deciding to invest in those stocks in equal proportions.

In contrast, assume a fund is investing in the Russell 1000 Index and has an alpha forecast for every stock. Breadth allows a manager to say, "In principle, I like Stock A more than Stock B, but once I take the cost into account, I would actually rather have B than A."

Breadth offers a fund flexibility and the room to express many of its ideas. Breadth also helps a fund achieve a higher intrinsic information ratio because of the opportunities to diversify across ideas.

Question: When you calculate average trading cost, do you consider the price impact? And considering that the U.S. equity market allows for all sorts of strategies that require many different assumptions, how can you build a portfolio based on your model?

Kahn: Regarding the first question, we take price impact into account. Price impact is, in fact, why costs increase with asset levels and turnover.

Regarding the second question, the sample portfolio I described does not look like any of our own products. But we have analyzed all of our products, whether they are large cap or small cap, U.S. or international, long-only or long–short. The model applies to any product.

For example, when we analyze our small-cap products, we assume higher average costs because we know that trading small caps costs more. If a product is driven by high-frequency signals, we consider that in the transfer coefficient. We built flexibility into the model. Our assumptions are based on an optimization process and a transaction-cost-aware process. We can use the model with complicated and simple portfolios.

Question: Will your model work as well for a manager who has other duties, such as marketing and client service, besides the management of a portfolio?

Kahn: The short answer is no. The model assumes that someone is actively managing the portfolio and that the management process is very aware of transaction costs. Most portfolio managers are stretched by various responsibilities, whether they are visiting clients or handling internal matters. In a small shop, the manager has little choice other than to wear many hats. Large shops should have enough resources to allow the portfolio manager to focus on the portfolio itself.

Question: Can your model be applied to the work of a passive manager?

Kahn: The framework is very general and could be applied to some aspects of passive management. For example, a passive manager is not likely to fully replicate an index consisting of thousands of instruments, so the fund will take on tracking error. But the manager probably gives less thought to the amount of turnover the fund should have or whether to increase turnover or how to relate that turnover to the amount of active risk he or she is taking on. I think this sort of analysis can help a passive manager. It can also help the manager build a tracking portfolio.

Question: Can lower turnover alone increase capacity?

Kahn: No. I believe there is an optimal amount of turnover. But slow-moving ideas generally do have higher capacity.

Question: If your model indicates that as assets get bigger turnover comes down, do active managers at Barclays abide by this model?

Kahn: We do not apply this model continuously, with each dollar in requiring a corresponding drop in turnover. Rather, we consider a portfolio over time, and as assets grow, we adjust the turnover level periodically.

One challenge in using the model is determining our current information ratio. Given all the uncertainties with respect to the inputs to the model, we probably experience stickier turnover than the model would suggest.

Question: Can a firm determine the optimal level of institutional management in relation to a certain proportion of nonmanaged assets?

Kahn: I have examined that issue, but it is difficult to model because of the variety of competitors and products that overlap in a space. For example, assume that a long-only product and a long–short product both invest with similar ideas in the same areas. They do not overlap 100 percent, but they do eat out of the same trough, which makes it difficult to determine overall capacity for the space.

RISK MANAGEMENT

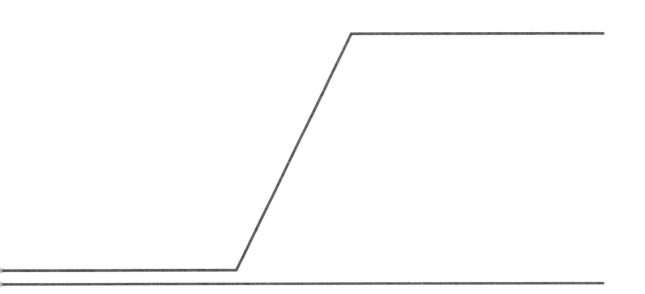

Risk: The Hottest Four-Letter Word in Financial Markets

PETER L. BERNSTEIN

The future is uncertain, so we can never know what will happen. Indeed, risk would not exist if we could correctly anticipate the future. But rather than reacting blindly to adverse—or even favorable—events, investors can prepare themselves for the future by imagining plausible outcomes. As opposed to the notion that risk management is only about the calculation of probabilities, I assert that risk management is *quality* decision making in the face of uncertainty. Thus, investors must live with the inevitability that their decisions will sometimes be wrong.

Investing is unlike many other fields of endeavor because uncertainty is lodged in its heart. When we think we know the future, we are setting ourselves up for trouble. Trends are not destiny. We are no more able to extend smooth lines into the future than a sailor can observe what lies ahead on a choppy sea. The safest risk management system is to view uncertainty as a constant rather than a variable and to take those variables out of the measurement system. Bill Sharpe recently said that, in general, it is dangerous to think of risk as a number. The problem we all face is that many scenarios can unfold in the future. Elroy Dimson defined risk in a way that I like: More things can happen than will happen. It is a profound, thoughtful, and helpful definition. When you add it all up, it really means that we do not know what will happen, but this definition frames risk in a way that is useful for thinking about the problem.

> We measure the risk that we know, but the real concerns are the risks that we do not know or what happens if the measurements that we make are wrong.

The Known and Unknown

I am increasingly concerned with how the risk management business today focuses so intently on the tools of risk measurement—probability, normal curve

Peter L. Bernstein is president of Peter L. Bernstein, Incorporated, New York City.

sampling, regression to the mean, mean–variance. To me, risk management is not about measurement at all. It is about how we make decisions and only incidentally about the math we use in making those decisions. If we stare at just the models and equations, we lose sight of the mystery of life—we lose sight of the unknown. There would be no such thing as risk if everything were known. If only a finite number of things could happen, risk would not exist. Even the most brilliant mathematical genius will never be able to tell us what the future holds. *What matters in thinking about risk is the quality of the decisions we make in the face of uncertainty.*

Pascal's wager offers the ideal model for making decisions. Blaise Pascal, the celebrated 17th century French mathematician and philosopher, was the first person to develop the idea of probability, so the genesis of risk management begins with Pascal. He spent half his time leading an unsavory life and half the time being very ascetic. In the end, he came to the conclusion that he must give up the sinful life and retire to a monastery. While in the monastery, he asked himself the following question: "God is, or God is not?" He said that reason cannot answer this question—an important statement to come from a mathematician. He said belief in God is not a decision. I cannot wake up one day and say, "Today I will believe in God," or "Today I will not believe in God." It does not work like that. The answer to Pascal's question comes from within, but you can decide how you will live your life. You can act as though there is a God, or you can act as though there is not a God. This is your choice. If you act as though there is a God, you lead a life of virtue. If you die and you find out that there is no God, well, you gave up a few things but you lived a good life. Look at it from the other point of view. Suppose you act as though there is not a God and lead a life of sin and lust, and then you die and discover there is a God; you are in big trouble. Thus, Pascal argued that the better bet, the better wager, is to behave as though there is a God. So, in many instances, the consequences of decisions must outweigh the probabilities. Even outcomes with small probabilities may have big consequences, which is the primary reason why I say that there is too much focus on measurement. If you get lost in the measurement process, you forget the consequences.

Knowing the probabilities is insufficient for making decisions where outcomes are dependent on preceding events. In other words, probability works when you are at the roulette table in that prior knowledge of where the ball landed has no consequence on future spins by the croupier. Probability does not work terribly well in life if one event is the consequence of a preceding event and thus the events are not independent. It is like the difference between roulette and poker. Probability is great when you are at the roulette table, but when you are sitting at the poker table, a lot of other considerations come into play, such as reading the faces of the other players. In real life, events are not independent of each other; in real life, consequences are what matters. To be technical, the expected utility of an outcome seldom equals the mathematical expectation of that outcome.

Why do I put so much emphasis on this? Why do I talk about what we know and what we do not know? The risks that we know are relatively easy to manage. I am going to cross the street against the light. I have a pretty good idea what that risk is, so I can make a decision about it. We are running an investment management firm, and the chairman of the U.S. Federal Reserve makes a comment about inflation risks increasing. We know how to deal with that.

The risks we know are relatively easy to manage, and the risks we know are also easy to measure, which is why measurement is so nice. We diversify. We set limits to our strategies. We use sophisticated measurement tools. But the devil is in the fat tails, which do not lend themselves to measurement or prescribed responses because, in most instances, we do not even know what those risks are. We did not know on 10 September 2001 what the primary risk of the next day would be.

When we accept that we do not know the future and that we will never know the future, we must realize that, with certainty, from time to time some of our decisions will be wrong. There is no way a person can always be right when nobody knows what will happen. So, we never know the precise probability of what will happen or, even as Elroy Dimson reminds us, the full range of probabilities we will face.

Consequently, surprise is an inevitability. Things will turn out not only differently from the way we expect but also even beyond our expectations. We are ignorant even about the magnitude and the shape of the forecast errors that we make. Thus, making decisions, choices, and forecasts must incorporate the consequences of being wrong. I do not want to sound like a gloom monger because being wrong can sometimes mean underestimating the good things that can happen. It does not necessarily mean that you are about to step on a piece of ice and slip and break your back. Good things can happen that you do not anticipate, and it is important to be prepared for those kinds of things too.

But this is the viewpoint from where I begin, and I think it dominates all other considerations of risk, including measurement: We measure the risk that we know, but the real concerns are the risks that we do not know or what happens if the measurements that we make are wrong.

What Can (or Will) Happen

There is another way of thinking about this problem. Another famed 17th century mathematician, Gottfried Leibniz, inventor of calculus (independent of Sir Isaac Newton), reflected on the fact that more things can happen than will happen. In 1703, Swiss mathematician Jacob Bernoulli wrote a letter to

Leibniz in which he said that we know the odds of throwing a seven instead of an eight with the dice, which is nice, but we do not know the probability that a man of 20 years will outlive a man of 60 years, which is a much more important thing to know. Bernoulli proposed to Leibniz that he study large numbers of pairs of men at the age of 20 and at the age of 60 to see how many of them die and then figure out the probabilities. Leibniz answered Bernoulli by saying that nature has established patterns originating in the return of events, but only for the most part. No model has an R^2 of 1.0. This is what we mean by uncertainty. We never know the future. We can only conjecture. Even in statistics we never accept a hypothesis; we say only that we cannot reject a hypothesis.

When we make decisions, we have to ask ourselves how reversible they are. If I am wrong, how easily can I get out of it? How much control do we have when decisions are irreversible or reversible only at a high cost, such as an investment in an illiquid hedge fund, real estate, private equity, or venture capital? If we make a decision that is difficult to reverse, the only thing that saves us is control: If things turn out badly and we have no control, we are stuck. For example, do not buy into a hedge fund where you have only limited visibility. And if you buy into a hedge fund with a lockup, the importance of transparency is even greater. You have to have some control if the decision is not reversible. How do we deploy portfolios when we do not know what the future holds? Harry Markowitz's answer was diversification. It is mine, too; diversification is an admission of ignorance about the future.

But what happens when the really unexpected strikes? What happens when something that nobody has talked about takes place? How do you respond to this? How do you deal with this? I give you, on the one hand, September 11. In many ways and in many places, responses were very impressive, not only at the highest level of government but also in such organizations as the NYSE. The event took place in the NYSE's backyard, and within a week, it was up and running again. There was a clear line of authority and some sense of organization that could deal with a totally unknown event of major catastrophic proportions. This tells you something about the decision-making process at the NYSE. I give you now, on the other hand, Hurricane Katrina. The authorities mishandled Hurricane Katrina and its aftermath in New Orleans, even though it was something that could have been anticipated.

Every organization should sit down and discuss at some length what it should do, who would be in charge, and how the line of authority would run if another Katrina or September 11 were to occur. This is not a matter of mathematics. This is not a matter of probability curves and the like. It is, in essence, an organizational matter, a management matter, but one that is of overwhelming importance and worth more time and effort than what kind of risk management system the organization uses in terms of measurement. Consider these relevant questions:

- How will the organization function?
- Where are the lines of authority?
- Where are the lines of communication?
- What backup facilities, if any, are in place?

Source of Uncertainty

More things can happen than will happen. But why? What is the source of uncertainty? Centuries ago, a day's activities consisted primarily of hunting, fishing, and gathering. In a world where hunting, fishing, and gathering are the primary activities, the only source of economic uncertainty is the weather. No one can change the weather, so people pray and dance—those are the only forms of risk management available under those circumstances. Everything is God's will or the will of the fates.

Now, we move into modern times. Things begin to change. Trade expands. Businesses have to move ships across water, and the ships can sink. The industrial revolution was much less dependent on nature than agriculture had been. As we move into the early stages of greater trade, we begin to invent things and make things. At the same time, across Europe, the Reformation and the Renaissance were beginning to happen, and they emphasize that human beings have free will on earth and have an opportunity to use it in optimal ways. This is a dramatic break with the long-term past and is the beginning of what we think of as modern times. Faith in God and faith in the fates are insufficient now. You have to have something more than that.

So, then, what is the underlying source of uncertainty in modern times? My answer to this question is game theory. Game theory, after all, is the granddaddy of behavioral finance. It is the evolutionary line from which behavioral finance comes. The most important insight came from the 1920s researchers John von Neumann and Oskar Morgenstern: Men and women are not like Robinson Crusoe, each individual making decisions independently of other individuals. (Pascal retreats to the privacy of his room and makes some thoughts about God is or God is not, but the majority of humans cannot live that way.) We have a much more complex decision-making environment.

Morgenstern and von Neumann emphasized the distinction between a real economy and a Robinson Crusoe economy. Crusoe controlled all the variables exclusively to obtain maximum satisfaction. All economic systems depend on production and technology, but the unique feature of capitalism is that it is about competition and combat. Buying and selling involve game-type decisions. What will a customer decide? What will the competition decide? What will the supplier decide? What will the employees decide? What will the politicians decide? What will our lawyers let us do? And all too often, what will the boss decide? All markets, including the capital markets, are highly interactive processes, and decisions that we make affect others, and their decisions affect us. The future value of the investment portfolio is not what somebody tells you will happen over the long run but what other investors will pay you for it at some future date. As Hurricane Katrina reminded us, nature is still a factor we must contend with, but essentially, risk in our world is nothing more than uncertainty about the decisions that other human beings make and how we can best respond to those decisions.

Albert Einstein wrote a letter to his colleague Max Born in which he said to Born: "You believe in a God who plays dice with the universe, and I believe in a God with complete law and order in a world that objectively exists." How should we, in the 21st century, think about this statement? Once we encounter risk, we are dealing with the basic questions of life. In the case of nature, I hope Einstein had it right: If law and order do not govern how nature works, then we are living in chaos and science is nothing but mumbo jumbo.

But for human beings, do we want a world where there is complete law and order, or do we want random variation—a roll of the dice? At first glance, I find the idea of a God who plays with dice repugnant. Everything is random—no cause, no effect. Every event is independent of preceding events—no power to influence outcomes, no meaning to anything. But suppose Einstein was right in this argument and there is complete order to everything. More things cannot happen than will happen; only the number of things that can happen will happen. Every event has a cause. Forecasting is easy because we know which button to push to get an outcome, but no money can be made in risk management in that environment. If Einstein was right and everything is law and order, then decisions are a waste of time. We have no control over our outcomes. Every action we take is determined by God's system, not by ours. Forget about deviations from normal and outliers, which are what make life exciting. What progress really comes from is filling the unoccupied spaces. Free will, our most precious attribute, would be null and void and meaningless. We would be God's prisoners rather than God's children.

Summary

Fortunately, I think Einstein was wrong when it comes to life. We do have free will. We can make choices. We do have some control over our outcomes, but we pay a price. We live in a world where complete law and order do not objectively exist. Our forecasts and our decisions can turn out to be wrong. Yet, without the risk that our forecasts can be wrong, without uncertainty, we cannot have free will; we cannot be free to make choices. But if uncertainty is our friend rather than our enemy, then let us treat it like a friend, with care, consideration, and attention to consequences.

This presentation comes from Defining, Measuring, and Managing Uncertainty: The CFA Institute Risk Symposium held in New York City on 22–23 February 2006.

More from Peter L. Bernstein

This section presents the speaker's lively question and answer session with the conference audience.

Question: What are some intelligent definitions of risk that you would encourage trustees of other people's money to use?

Bernstein: The conventional ones, such as standard deviation, semi-variance, and beta, are useful. And they are conventional for a reason. It is nice to have something like standard deviation—a definition of risk that is a number—because we can measure it. But volatility is very important no matter what because volatility is in your gut too. In a sense, volatility is an important measure of risk because it reminds us of uncertainty. But in another sense, I think volatility gets much too much emphasis.

Early on in my career, I stopped managing money and became a consultant. I met a manager who was responsible for a large family trust that, for a variety of circumstances, would not distribute its principal for a long time. So, the only thing that mattered to the beneficiaries was the income. This manager said to me that the way we should deal with this portfolio was to put it all in stocks and to the greatest extent possible grow the stocks because the only thing that mattered to this family was to have an income that would keep pace with inflation. He said he didn't care whether the stock market went up or down. In fact, he liked having it go down: If they had profits, that would make it less expensive to take capital gains and change from Stock A to Stock B.

If you are a long-term investor, if the fund you're managing exists into perpetuity, then we must not overemphasize volatility. In many instances, volatility will be a friend rather than an enemy. Indeed, I think the fascination with volatility leads to bad decision making. Success in equity investing must depend on an appetite for volatility. The smooth stuff is not where you make money. You're not going to get rich on Treasury bills. The ability to take risk and to go somewhere and have success depends on a set of human relationships just as much as it does on the mathematics of it.

In this instance, I think volatility is something that has to be straightened out at the beginning of the relationship as far as how much the investor can stand. The emphasis on smooth return, on smooth earnings streams, leads to bad things.

Question: Isn't it true that how tolerant an investor is of unexpectedly bad results won't be known until those bad results actually roll in?

Bernstein: It is essential to be up front and open about a possible adverse event—to try to understand it and be prepared for it. There are no easy or mechanical answers to it, but it is central to success. Certainly, until you have an event, a bad event or even a sensationally good event, you don't know how you're going to react. You may think you do, and people will tell you, "I can take this much," but whatever they say is only part of what will really happen. This should be an explicit element in the dialogue that goes on between manager and client—perhaps more important than performance measurement and appraisal.

Question: How much can an institution spend and still have some confidence that its capital will exist into perpetuity? Will institutions adopt this approach to measuring their own investment success?

Bernstein: The institution does earn something; that's why it has invested the money, so it should be able to spend at least some principal and still exist into perpetuity. How should this be measured? This question is pertinent now, when the income for most institutions is insufficient for what they either want to do or, in the case of foundations, have to do.

The reinvested earnings have some value. Research suggests that you could spend 130 percent of the income. Clearly, this is a number that's arbitrary, but it is in line with my presentation in that nobody knows whether it is too much or too little. Again, I think the useful thing is not the answer but the discussion.

If you are in a period when income return is larger (and in the old days it was larger), then maybe you begin to think about the problem a little differently or very differently. Nobody is going to come up with the right answer. You have to make these decisions, and they should be clearly laid out.

Question: What are the defects of the Sarbanes–Oxley Act of 2002, and what is its impact on risk?

Bernstein: If regulations get too tight, the bookkeepers will run the business. Modigliani and Miller postulated that a company's management put shareholders' interest first, the key assumption that makes the whole Modigliani–Miller concept work. What happened in the 1990s was that that notion got lost. Now, we have to pay the price, and the regulation that we are seeing is overcompensation. In theory, you don't need Sarbanes–Oxley. The players are all nice and clean and straightforward and transparent.

Question: What are your thoughts on Regulation FD?

Bernstein: I can't think of a reason to be opposed to it. Managers may have to be more transparent than they want to be, but when everybody gets the information in the same form and at the same time, that is the kind of environment that makes for efficient markets.

Question: What are the pros and cons of a policy portfolio?

Bernstein: I took up arms against the policy portfolio because we do not know what the future holds. I cannot accept the idea that in the long run stocks will outperform or underperform. We don't know that. Under those circumstances, why should I say an institution should be 40 percent in equities and that this is the strategic asset allocation into perpetuity? As a practical matter, we know that this isn't it forever; institutions do change their policy portfolios from time to time and for a variety of reasons.

There should be much more freedom about the policy portfolio because not only does the world change but also our view of the future evolves. Thus, this has to be an evolving process, not something that's set in stone. For example, we can forecast what the long-run risk premium will be, but not without using a lot of escape clauses that this is our best guess and this is what the numbers from today show, but we really don't know the answer for sure. The winners in investing have strong philosophies, but they also understand that the world will change and that what looks like value today will not be value tomorrow.

Risk Capital Allocation: Beyond Traditional Asset Allocation Approaches

BRIAN D. SINGER, CFA

A new paradigm of investment management is on the horizon, one that defines portfolios as bundles of risk to be managed dynamically with emerging technologies. Current investment management is locked at two extremes, with alpha-dominated alternative investing at one end and beta-dominated traditional portfolio management at the other. The new paradigm allows all managers to access all the opportunities and all the technologies between the two extremes.

Recently, I moved to London, a city filled with reminders of olden times and respect for longstanding traditions. On the banks of the Thames River is one of London's most magnificent and traditional buildings, St. Paul's Cathedral. Across the river from St. Paul's stands the Tate Modern, a museum containing one of the largest collections of art designed to test the boundaries of all things traditional. The only direct connection between St. Paul's and the Tate Modern is the Millennium Bridge.

I like to think that this scenario, this juxtaposition of the traditional and the alternative, represents the state of investment management today. Traditional investment managers reside on one side, alternative managers reside on the other side, and between the two flows a river of misunderstanding that is bridged only by a wonderful little walkway known as risk management.

Risk management has changed the way money is managed and will continue to do so in the future.

> Investment managers have relegated beta to the dustbin of finance. Alpha, they seem to think, is the only good. This is not a healthy development.

Evolving Investment Management

Peter Bernstein was one of the first financial thinkers to look over at our metaphorical St. Paul's and say that policy portfolios are obsolete, a declaration

Brian D. Singer, CFA, is general manager at UBS Global Asset Management, London.

that may overstate the point but that nonetheless recognizes several important changes in our understanding of investment management.

U.S. Equity Market Investment Regimes

Since the end of the 1940s, the United States has experienced four distinct investment regimes: 1949–1966, 1967–1981, 1982–1999, and 2000–2005, shown in **Figure 1**. Each of these regimes is characterized by distinct aspects of investment management history. Thus, the first period, 1949–1966, was largely a monolithic bull market that was punctuated by the electronics boom. Annualized return during these years was 14.7 percent, and risk (standard deviation based on monthly logarithmic returns) was 11.7 percent. It was during this period that much of the research was done on asset management and modern portfolio theory. These concepts, especially asset allocation and portfolio diversification, were applied in the following years (1967–1981), which constituted a period of extreme volatility; the annualized return was 7.1 percent, and risk was 15.3 percent. The real return during the period was essentially zero, but modern portfolio theory provided a wonderful opportunity, and a number of firms began to make a mark.

Figure 1   S&P 500 Index Total Returns, January 1949–December 2005

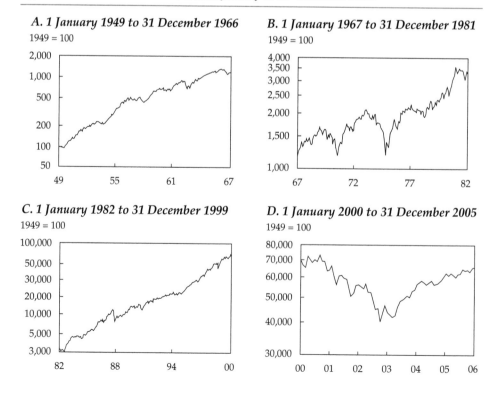

Having learned the concepts of portfolio diversification and asset allocation, the industry entered the next period (1982–1999), which constituted another monolithic bull market that ended in the dot-com bubble and its bursting. The annualized return was 18.5 percent, and risk was 15.0 percent. Unfortunately, having learned the concept of asset allocation, investors applied it. They diversified their portfolios only to learn that they should have invested only in equities. Not only that, they should have been in U.S. equities. Even more specifically, they should have been in growth equities. And more specifically still, they should have been in Cisco Systems and Intel Corporation and forgotten the rest of the market. Therefore, asset allocation did not do investors a lot of good. Two interesting developments during this period were the growing emphasis on alpha and skill and the nascence of hedge funds. Even more interesting was the growing dichotomy between passive managers and skill-based managers, a dichotomy that is now seen almost entirely in favor of skill-based managers. The current period, beginning in 2000, with an annualized return of –1.13 percent and risk of 15.32 percent, is dominated by the application of skill seeking (or alpha-based investing). Everyone is going after skill, and no one wants to invest in no-skill, boring beta.

Since 1925, the bond market has generally exhibited two secular trends, shown in **Figure 2**. A bear market ran into the beginning of the 1980s.

Figure 2   Ten-Year Treasury Bond Yield, Monthly Average: 1925–May 2005

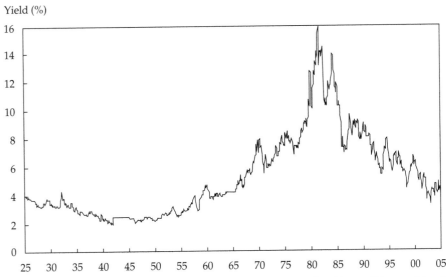

Note: Data from 1925 to 1956 represent the unweighted average of yields on all issues of bonds outstanding during 1925–1956 that were neither due nor callable in less than 10 years. Data from 1957 to May 2005 represent the 10-year Treasury bond yield monthly average.
Sources: Data from 1925 to 1956 were obtained from the U.S. Federal Reserve; data from 1957 to 31 May 2005 were obtained from Leuthold Group.

Then, Paul Volker (U.S. Federal Reserve Board chairman at the time) burst the bubble, inflation came down, and the market became more stable. Since the 1980s, investors have experienced a significant secular bull market in bonds. Today, investors are dealing with fears of a low-return environment, and the equity market has declined significantly. From its peak, the S&P 500 Index has declined by 45–50 percent. The NASDAQ has declined by about 75 percent. Unfortunately, investors did not begin responding to the low-return environment until after the market had declined. Bond yields are running at 4–5 percent, and investors are concluding that they are in a relatively low-return environment. From my perspective, investment managers have relegated beta to the dustbin of finance. Alpha, they seem to think, is the only good. This is not a healthy development.

Periodic Advances in Asset Management

During its history, our industry has experienced periodic leaps that have often used new technologies to achieve superior investment performance for clients. In the early 1970s, investors began thinking about total return. They stopped holding bonds to maturity, and they stopped buying equities for dividend purposes, which, until that time, had been a dominant factor in the investment process. As investors focused on total return, investment performance began to increase—but so too did business performance for those firms that were the early adopters. As the early 1980s dawned, global diversification and asset allocation moved to the forefront, and their value as risk management tools became apparent. Firms that adopted these tools early in the trend experienced superior performance, and other firms eventually caught up, as is typical when a new trend becomes apparent in a competitive environment. In the 1990s, specialization and the search for alpha led to the next surge in performance, which has brought us into the midst of a new leap forward—one dominated, I believe, by what I call "assimilators."

Assimilators are investment managers who combine alpha sources into customized solutions based on such client needs as return objective, risk appetite, and time horizon. Investment banks were the early adopters of these techniques. In the past 5 or 10 years, risk management has developed tremendously as a tool for understanding and modeling complex securities. A few years ago, most investors used third-party providers of risk management, and all these providers offered essentially the same models. Thus, no investor achieved a significant edge over the others, based on their risk management skill. Today, however, the situation has changed dramatically. Asset managers, investment advisers, plan sponsors, institutional investors, and ultra high-net-worth individuals are all beginning to adopt sophisticated risk management and value-at-risk techniques.

In addition, financial engineering has been a tremendous boon for the industry. When derivatives first entered the investment scene, they tended to carry a negative connotation. Too many practitioners assumed that the purpose of the derivatives market was to find unsuspecting individuals, charge them high commission rates until they had been tapped of all their money, and then move on. Often, unfortunately, the negative connotation was well earned. But the derivatives industry has grown a lot since then. The Bank for International Settlements recently released a study indicating that the notional size of the over-the-counter derivatives industry is $250 trillion, which indicates growth of more than 200 percent in the past five years. Such robust growth and size indicates that portfolio managers and investors now have available a powerful tool for managing risk more effectively than ever before. Rather than the blunt tools of asset allocation from a generation before, managers now have access, through new technologies and the rich derivatives market, to much more precise tools for modulating risk exposures.

Hedge funds have done a tremendous service to the industry by allowing managers greater flexibility. When clients invest in a hedge fund, they provide the manager with the flexibility to invest however the manager wishes. Additionally, the manager does not even have to report performance to any standard industry or consultant databases. On the traditional side, however, clients tie managers' hands behind their backs and then say, "Go compete." Traditional managers often are not allowed to go short, are not allowed to use derivatives, and are tied to a benchmark by a 2 percent tracking-error restriction. Yet no one seems to see the irony in treating these two types of managers with such massive discrepancy. Figuratively speaking, the Tate Modern is on one side of the Thames, St. Paul's on the other side, and no Millennium Bridge connects them.

The increasingly sophisticated use of leverage is another advance currently improving the capabilities of the industry. I am not referring here to the sort of leverage that was used to do complex and levered transactions that could take municipal institutions down at inappropriate times. Firms are now able to use leverage to manage the amount of market and nonmarket risk that their investors take. In fact, the industry has had these tools for quite some time, but regulators have restricted their use. And regulators do so because they do not understand entirely how these tools can be used for beneficial purposes. The result is that regulators try to slow things down, and asset managers are trying to move as fast as they can to provide their customers with the best possible performance by utilizing these powerful techniques.

Responding to Current Market Developments

The traditional structure that consultants and asset management firms use to organize their businesses are another deterrent to improvements in the industry.

Consultants and asset managers build their businesses as silos: the equity silo, the bond silo, the U.S. silo, the European silo. They even have an alternatives silo, which is everything that will not fit into the other categories. All of these silos are simply groupings of assets that do not necessarily offer any functional value other than to provide an artificial way of organizing one's thoughts (and business). The result of this lack of forward thinking is that investors have been forced to accept extremes in investment strategies.

At one extreme are the nonmarket or skill-based managers, consisting of hedge funds that are purportedly market neutral. These managers offer alpha through security exposure. Risk, and the potential for reward, are inherent in the managers' individual security selection decisions. At the other extreme are the passive managers, such as index funds and traditional, actively managed portfolios. These managers offer beta through market exposure, particularly the risk and reward potential of markets and asset classes. In between these two extremes lies a vast, unexploited land full of opportunities to add value.

The industry has responded to this situation in a variety of ways. First, in a low-return environment, it has biased policy portfolios toward higher-returning assets. One of the ways to do this is to incorporate such assets as real estate, timber, and private equity that have an illiquidity premium. Thus, if two assets have the same underlying economic and fundamental drivers but one is liquid and the other, illiquid, the liquid asset is obviously more attractive, so, investors bid up the price on the liquid asset while the illiquid asset remains lower in price and, thereby, provides a higher return at the same economic and fundamental exposures. Regardless of whether such reasoning makes sense, investment managers are indeed clamoring for illiquid asset classes.

The predominant response, however, is to expose plan assets to more active risk. To achieve this, firms are seeking skill or alpha-intensive investing. They are also seeking absolute return, market-neutral strategies. And finally, they are loosening, if only slightly, their restrictions on tracking error. Uncorrelated risk, it seems, is the only good. Unfortunately, this attitude is indicative of an industry that is flailing about.

A More Dynamic Model

One of the great contributions made by Friedrich Hayek (the Austrian economist who received the Nobel Prize in 1974) was to transform the established way of thinking by attacking the myth of the given. He broke down rigidly conceived models of human knowledge so that a more dynamic exchange of knowledge could occur. I would like to honor his efforts by challenging the financial dogma of the past century so that we can make real progress as we enter the 21st century.

To begin, consider alpha and beta. Alpha is skill, and everyone is clamoring for skill. Yet, skill is not, on average, well compensated. In fact, after each interested party takes its share of the action, alpha is actually negatively compensated. Beta, on the other hand, is market risk. Beta is easy to find because every asset has market risk. Every asset is a claim on the income-generating capability of society. Therefore, every asset provides a market risk and is compensated, on average, for that market risk. Such characteristics should not be cast aside just because alpha is the hot item today.

Policy portfolios are not obsolete, but beta management—the concept of managing betas relative to benchmarks—constrains portfolio management. By embracing all the sophisticated tools currently available for risk management and by managing assets relative to liabilities, the industry can begin to perceive that benchmarks are becoming an outmoded asset management tool. For example, many defined-benefit pension plans are actively trying to hedge their liabilities. To do so, they are using swaps and buying long-duration bonds, which does not make particularly good sense because in many instances, especially where rates are today, such plans end up hedging liabilities but not defeasing them. Defined-benefit pension plans are, in essence, moving from an environment of uncertain success to one of almost certain failure. They are locking in their hedges but not defeasing future liabilities.

Portfolios as Bundles of Risk

The state-of-the-art solution involves separating portfolio management into aspects of risk management—market risk, defined in reference to liabilities, and dynamic risks. These dynamic risks arise from security selection, currency management, and the altering of market risk over time. Also, increasing breadth enhances portfolio efficiency and can be accomplished, in part, by shortening the investment horizon into multiple horizons and by changing the asset mix over time through dynamic beta management. For the liabilities, the recommendation typically is a neutral-policy asset allocation in which neutral beta exposure not only hedges but also defeases liabilities. Thus, a solid portfolio policy generates a long-term return, which allows clients to meet future liabilities.

Unfortunately, most investors continue to maintain a dichotomous view in which alpha resides at one extreme and is unrelated to beta at the other. We prefer to think of both alpha and beta simply as risks. With this perception in mind, we manage beta actively by setting market exposures to capture compensated market risks while avoiding uncompensated risks. We also manage alpha by selecting exposures to capture uncorrelated opportunities across markets, currencies, and securities.

An entire host of risks comes together in a portfolio, and investors have learned to characterize those risks as value/growth or as large cap/small cap and so on. But they are simply a package of risks that are sometimes compensated and sometimes not. Thus, the new risk management paradigm removes the old boundaries and constraints of asset management silos and allows traditional managers access to all of the same strategies that hedge fund managers are now allowed to use—going long and short, using derivatives and leverage, or using whatever strategies and assets are most effective for earning the best returns.

As far as I am concerned, risk is risk, and using terms like "alpha" and "beta" only muddles sound investment thinking. I prefer to consider portfolios as bundles of risk exposures.

The New Paradigm in Practice

To put this new model into practice, we must think in terms of allocating risk capital. In this way, a portfolio can be categorized according to the different managers used, or portfolios can be categorized as various asset classes. But no matter how the individual components are categorized, the flexibility exists to manage composite portfolios very effectively. In this framework, clients can use any of the emerging strategies they deem appropriate. As we loosen the constraints, we find that different managers bring different risk exposures, depending on the assets and how they manage them. Sometimes, managers bring risk exposures that are compounding; sometimes, they bring risk exposures that are offsetting. But whatever the exposures are, risks can be reduced to security selection risk, market selection risk, and currency selection risk.

In these endeavors, derivatives have enabled us not just to leverage but also to eliminate uncompensated risks and concentrate on compensated risks. In doing so, we are able to take no more risk than we took 5 or 10 years ago while earning greater compensation for taking that risk. That greater compensation comes from greater breadth and a higher transfer coefficient, which means a higher information ratio in relative return space or a higher Sharp ratio in total return space. But it takes economies of scale to be able to build out the tools and technologies that enable us to manage the risks of a broadly diversified portfolio—to download daily the individual securities, whether they are equities, bonds, structured products, credit swaps, or credit-default swaps. We bring them into a portfolio, evaluate them, and then determine which risks we actually want. It takes a firm with real breadth and access to a lot of different alpha sources, management styles, and asset classes to follow the new paradigm. It requires a concentration on the exact sort of alpha diversification desired, and doing so creates an environment in which we can manage dynamically to desired risk exposures.

All of these strategies and developments require that investment advisers and clients evolve. It is not enough to establish investment guidelines and then hope that the manager beats a benchmark. We are introducing fundamental changes to the risk space of our broadly defined portfolios every three or four months. We are adding new derivatives capabilities, new short capabilities, new emerging strategies—all of which we have been vetting internally and determining when and how to introduce them to a portfolio. That requires a lot of trust between the client and the investment adviser. It also means that the relationship evolves from being advisory to being collaborative in nature.

My intention is to break down every constraint that has been placed on traditional managers and move both alternative and traditional managers to the middle ground where they all have the flexibility to do their best in managing portfolios, generating alpha, and doing so at the lowest possible risk. In effect, I would like to push the industry to build a Millennium Bridge that allows the Tate Modern of alternative investing to work directly with the St. Paul's of traditional investing.

Because we now have the means to manage portfolios that are more appropriately directed at the liabilities, we are increasingly managing in an asset/liability space. Therefore, we consider beta in reference to those liabilities. All assets and liabilities begin in terms of a large covariance matrix that is sourced at the same set of economic and fundamental drivers. Thus, as we change our views about the relationships between assets and liabilities, the covariance matrix that includes those assets and liabilities also changes. We then look at the assets themselves as a number of risk exposures that can be related to the risk exposures of the liabilities.

Conclusion

A new environment in portfolio management is on the horizon, and that new environment is all about risk management. Certainly, this new way of considering investments presents challenges that some firms and investors will have difficulty adapting to. For those who can adapt, however, the coming environment offers many opportunities.

The first and most fundamental challenge is the need for increased flexibility, a quality not necessarily encouraged in the established paradigm. It is integral, however, with the coming paradigm. Next, firms need to define beta in less narrow terms. They need to consider beta with respect to liabilities and think about systematic and nonsystematic risks. In fact, they need to be prepared to redefine the market itself. Most investment professionals—academics in particular—define the market as the S&P 500 because the S&P 500 offers large quantities of data going back not just years but generations. The availability of data induces us to define the repository of that data as the market itself. But the S&P 500 is not the market. It is an actively managed portfolio that has been dictated in advance with certain selection criteria. I am unwilling to sign on to that paradigm because I assert that the market portfolio is the collection of every claim on the cash flows that society can generate, including my human capital, including the buildings in which we work and meet and live, and including my ability and the ability of others to leverage that capital. The market is *not* the S&P 500, and it is wrong to think of it in that manner.

A third challenge of the coming environment is the need to educate all the essential parties: plan sponsors, asset managers, consultants, ultra high-net-worth individuals, and decision-making committees. These parties are, for the most part, stuck in the old paradigm, and they need to actively learn about new tools, new techniques, and new ways of looking at investment risk. After becoming educated about this new paradigm, these parties will become aware of new risks to measure and manage, such as administration risk, operational risk, and accounting risk.

By responding to these challenges, the investment community will find itself discovering a new range of opportunities.

First, success will follow those who are able to assimilate all of these risk management tools into one portfolio context. That will be the primary aspect driving investment and business performance. Second, expertise in portfolio construction—particularly management of risk dimensions—is paramount. Third, hedge funds have pioneered the use of the new tools; therefore, firms should take advantage of that expertise by using hedge funds and adopting their strategies. Finally, firms will discover that giving greater consideration to liabilities will provide value not only to plan sponsors and beneficiaries but also to society in general.

All the distinctions that existed in this industry are blurring, and they are blurring quickly. Those who can adapt most quickly to the new paradigm will be the ones who gain the most.

This presentation comes from the 2006 Financial Analysts Seminar held in Evanston, Illinois, on 16–21 July 2006.

More from Brian D. Singer, CFA

This section presents the speaker's lively question and answer session with the conference audience.

Question: Under the assimilation concept, how do I lay off risks for smaller portfolios?

Singer: A firm cannot do what I am suggesting unless it has a large asset base to build the team needed to manage a risk orientation and bear the fixed costs required to build out the risk systems. Only larger firms will be able to pull this off. The smaller boutique firms will need to concentrate on specific capabilities for capturing opportunities in the marketplace. The middle-tier firms will find themselves in the most difficult situation.

UBS Global Asset Management is a relatively large firm, but it manages numerous smaller portfolios. No matter the size of their portfolios, all clients think they are big clients. They often come to us with the initial demand that we manage their assets separately. We tell them that we can do that if that is what they require, but they will not get the best service our shop can provide because we work best as a collective vehicle. We try to convince them that moving into the collective vehicle is the best decision they can make.

Question: If you move them into the collective vehicle, how do you accommodate your last point about greater consideration of liabilities?

Singer: The vehicles can be liability structured. The fact that the liabilities exist suggests that using derivatives, such as swaps, to target the liability risk exposures in the portfolios allows us to have a core from which to manage in a consistent manner. We probably need three or four different core portfolios that we can manage against those liabilities. In fact, we will soon announce liability indices that are based on these types of risk factors, so, they are much more consistent in the way we manage portfolios. The bottom line is to choose some derivatives-structured products. We have spent the past 10 years building out the risk system and the last 2 or 3 years building out the tools for asset/liability investment solutions that enable us to manage the systematic risk exposures to the liabilities.

Question: Do you define risk using standard deviation?

Singer: Most risk systems, if they are going to be effective, are basically standard deviation with a normal-distribution orientation. It is possible to create models capable of handling fat tails, but difficulties arise when trying to manage the convexity of portfolios. Therefore, I prefer a simple risk system based on normal distributions that provides me with an input to the decision-making process. Ultimately, however, all risk management is done in qualitative terms, and it is in that qualitative manner that we bring in such issues as convexity.

In my own shop, we have embedded convexity in the portfolio because the potential for tail risk is greater today than it has been for a while. I perceive numerous reasons for the heightened risk, but I will mention two in particular that are event risks in the portfolio. On the positive aspect of the tail, we are in the midst of a demographic shift that creates an incentive for the integration of emerging and developed economies that has never existed before because the shift is occurring at a time when capital and goods flow freely across borders. The demographic change creates a level shift in the productivity of the economy, and I believe that investors cannot accommodate that type of level shift appropriately. The shift, therefore, creates the potential for a positive-return tail that is unanticipated in certain areas.

On the other end of the spectrum is something that we have been following for several years: avian flu. Most of us consider avian flu high risk but low probability. But a serious epidemic like avian flu is not low probability; it is rather a likelihood. Therefore, we have been structuring our portfolios to insure against that type of tail risk. It is one way of bringing in convexity.

To extend the example, we have long exposure to emerging market equities and short exposure to emerging market debt through credit-default swaps. Thus, if a positive event occurs that evolves over time, we believe that equities will do well but that debt does not have much scope for positive performance. In contrast, if a major event, such as avian flu, occurs, emerging markets in both equity and debt will be decimated. Therefore, we perceive an asymmetric risk exposure for which we have embedded an option into the portfolio. No risk system in the world is going to characterize that situation as convexity, but it is a convexity that arises from qualitative thinking. We build convexity in such a way that we are not just buying insurance because the event may not happen for 10 years, and by the 10th year, we will have paid so much in insurance premiums that we will receive no payout.

Question: What system do you have in place to measure the efficacy of what you are doing with this new paradigm?

Singer: We do not use an external performance attribution system. Instead, we use an internal performance attribution technique that we have built our own system around. We also specify the benefit to portfolio construction and performance from our qualitative overlay of market behavior considerations, especially in reference to our fundamental valuation.

EQUITY INVESTMENTS

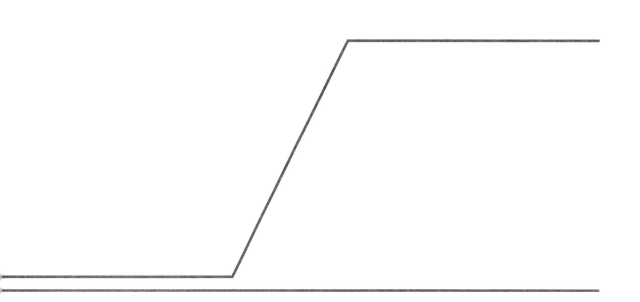

Conversation with a Money Master

BILL MILLER, CFA

Bill Miller, CFA, is chairman and chief investment officer at Legg Mason Capital Management, Inc., and was named "The Greatest Money Manager of the 1990s" by *Money* magazine. In this question and answer session, Fred H. Speece, Jr., CFA, interviews Bill Miller about his insights into portfolio management in general and value investing in particular.

Speece: You have an impressive long-term track record as a portfolio manager. Given today's very efficient and sophisticated market, do we still have room for stock picking?

Miller: When we discuss market efficiency, we run into a semantic issue about what exactly is meant by the term "market efficiency." At Legg Mason, we believe that the markets are pragmatically efficient, which means that they are extremely competitive and usually beat most active managers. For example, fewer than 35 percent of large-capitalization managers beat the market in the recent 12-month period ending 30 June 2006, just under 30 percent in the past 5 years, about 20 percent in the past 10 years, and about 22 percent in the past 15 years. So, on average, the market has beaten 70 percent or more of all active managers in time periods longer than one year. Managers should start out with the belief that if they are trying to actively manage money and outperform the market, the odds are against them.

Nevertheless, the market has room for active managers. Passive management does *not* give investors the return of the index; it gives them the return of the index less costs. So, the longer they have their money passively managed, the greater their underperformance will be relative to the index. One of the arguments against active management is that it underperforms. But passive management underperforms every year, forever. And the wedge between

> 100 percent of the information you have about any business reflects the past, and 100 percent of the value of that business depends on the future.

Bill Miller, CFA, is chairman and chief investment officer at Legg Mason Capital Management, Inc., Baltimore.

the index return and the investor's return gets wider. To have a prayer of outperforming, an investor must have some active management.

In the current market, one of the changes, in my opinion, is that the advent of hedge funds has made the market highly informationally efficient in the short run. The result is an opportunity for "time arbitrage," which means that by lengthening the time horizon for thinking about a company's results three to five years out rather than one year out, you can increase the probability that you will outperform. Put somewhat differently, in a market that's informationally efficient in the short term, thinking three years ahead is likely to be more effective than thinking three to six months ahead. This assumes that the investor is fundamentally oriented, not technically oriented, where short-term price trends drive behavior.

Speece: You are a value manager. How do you define value?

Miller: We take our approach to value directly from the textbooks. The value of any investment is the present value of the future free cash flows that are going to come from that investment.

What makes us different is that most value managers don't value assets that way. They'll use a wide variety of practical heuristics—like P/E, price to book, and price to cash flow. They'll use all kinds of historical metrics. They'll do all kinds of things to try to assess value, but they're not actually doing the pure, theoretical value. So, part of what we do in our shop is use all of those heuristics but also take theory and apply it to a wide variety of investments.

Most value investors weight past data *very* heavily. As I tell our analysts, 100 percent of the information you have about any business reflects the past, and 100 percent of the value of that business depends on the future. So, it is only to the extent that the future resembles the past, or maps onto it in some kind of systematic way, that historical data are useful for assessing value.

Speece: Investors hire you to take risk in order to enhance return. Your approach to risk taking has been compared with that of Earl Weaver, former manager of the Baltimore Orioles baseball team. What is your definition of risk?

Miller: What Earl Weaver said is that more games are won on three-run homers than on sacrifice bunts. I think that is right. Part of what people insufficiently distinguish, or confuse, is the difference between frequency and magnitude—that is, how often you're right or wrong versus how much money you make when you're right and how much money you lose when you're wrong. Most people look for a high batting average—a high frequency of being right. And most of the time when they do that, they have what is known in philosophy as a "high epistemic threshold." They need a lot of information and a lot of stuff to convince them that they are right.

As a result, they focus on how often they are right and not on how much money they make when they are right. They might make 10–20 percent when they are right. But then, of course, they've got to reinvest. Mathematically, if they make one significant error, it will offset a lot of instances where they were right.

We focus not on our batting average, to continue the baseball metaphor, but on our slugging percentage. So, if we have a few investments where we make 5 or 10 times your money—or as we did in Dell and AOL, 50 times your money—that pays for a lot of mistakes. It pays for a lot of misses of 10 percent or 20 percent.

Speece: How does that approach translate into what your portfolio looks like today? Where is the swing for the home run?

Miller: Well, one thing that's interesting about today's market compared with historical markets is that the market is not offering valuation anomalies in which you can confidently invest with a really high expected rate of return. This is because valuation across industries is actually at about the 98th percentile. To put it differently, only about 2 percent of the time have valuations been less narrow than they are today. And so the problem is that you're not being paid to make big bets. The benefits are theoretically diminished because of the greater homogeneity across sectors and industries.

Speece: Do you view dividends and share repurchases as signals that companies use?

Miller: We have a huge interest in how companies allocate capital because we're long-term investors. Our turnover is 15–20 percent a year. So, our time horizon is five, six, seven years on average. And that's a distribution across things we've owned for 15–20 years and things that we've owned for a year or two.

But broadly speaking, how companies allocate capital is going to determine what our returns are going to be. And as Warren Buffett has noted, if you're the CEO of a company and you earn 15 percent on equity and have a zero payout ratio, and if you're the CEO for five years, you're going to allocate about half of the total equity capital that the company has generated in its history no matter how long that history is.

If you allocate it at a return above the cost of capital, you'll create value. If you allocate it at a return below the cost of capital, you'll destroy value. So, how a management allocates capital is critically important.

So as to dividends and share repurchases, the only thing we try to do with our companies is just inform them of certain mathematical principles. For example, one of the things we tell them is that if they pay a dividend, the rate of return that their shareholders will earn on that dividend, on average, is the market rate of return. It's paid out to all of these different shareholders. Broadly speaking, they will reinvest it, and they will not earn an excess rate of return—they'll earn the market rate of return.

On the other hand, if you repurchase your shares at a price below what the business is worth, then the shareholders will earn an above-average rate of return because the business is worth the present value of future free cash flows adjusted for risk and so on. So, if the company's shares trade at a big discount to what they're worth, management should be repurchasing shares. If the shares trade at or above what they're worth, management should be paying out dividends. And that's all that we try and make sure that they have in front of them. My colleague, Michael Mauboussin, has published a terrific analysis of this issue.[1]

Speece: Are earnings and quality of earnings important to you?

Miller: We hope and trust that our analysts are thinking carefully about the earnings that our companies are reporting and the quality of those earnings. We don't have any kind of a grid or any kind of a threshold with respect to quality of earnings because basically—and this is both a strength and a weakness—we tend not to pay much attention to earnings because, again, to go back to value, the value of the business is the present value of the future free cash flows.

So, we're basically looking at free cash flows. We're looking at them normalized, and we're looking at them reported. We're looking at all that kind of stuff. So, whatever the company's reported, whatever its accounting conventions are, we look through those to its free cash flows. And historically, I think that's served us well over the years. But it does have its downside because in a lot of cases, we tend to underestimate historically the impact on companies that kind of run fast and loose on the accounting side.

For example, some companies use gain-on-sale accounting. We would say, "Well, we understand gain on sale. So, who cares? We can look through that and convert it to portfolio accounting; we can make adjustments." But guess what? Whenever companies convert from gain-on-sale accounting to portfolio accounting, their stocks collapse. So, we finally learned that just because we can see through it doesn't mean that other people are thinking about it the same way.

Speece: Do you use a valuation model for setting a price target?

Miller: We use a multivariate model. So, we use every valuation methodology known to anyone who's ever done this. If there's any evidence at all that it has value, we will use it. It can be very simple historical correlations. It can be DCF (discounted cash flow) models, DDMs (dividend discount models), or LBO (leveraged buyout) models. Actually, LBO models are probably in the current world a little more effective than some of the other models, given the short-term nature of the market and the heavy influence of private equity. So, we tend to put a little more weight on that than we have historically.

Speece: Because the private equity segment is so big and so active that the players cannot find enough private companies, they are coming into the

---

[1] See http://www.leggmason.com/funds/knowledge/mauboussin/Mauboussin_on_Strategy_011006.pdf.

public markets. Is the traditional spread between private valuation and public valuation narrowing?

Miller: It's narrowing slowly. Part of the reason private equity is so active is that public market valuations are so attractive. At the current financing rates, there are a lot of businesses going private. When PETCO announced it would be going private at a 49 percent premium, it's important to understand that the private equity guys think that they're going to earn an excess rate of return on *that*.

There are all kinds of deals where the private equity guys have picked these things off, and even without taking them public again, they have been able to earn pretty good returns just by flipping them to other private equity guys. So, I think public market valuations are really attractive—especially in the big-cap range, partly because the mega caps are too big to take private.

Speece: Perhaps money managers spend too much time analyzing the mathematics of the valuation models and not enough time analyzing company management. Do you find talking to corporate managers to be a useful tool?

Miller: It's more effective the longer your time horizon is because in the *short* run, I don't think that you gain a lot by talking to management. Management is constrained by Regulation Fair Disclosure (Reg. FD) in the very short run. And if you're new to following the company, you don't have a context for understanding how that particular CEO or CFO has behaved in the past. I think if you've owned a company for 3, 5, 10 years and had a lot of extensive contact with the management, you can learn a lot from the nuances in the way in which management answers questions, the way they think about strategy, and so forth.

I agree with Buffett totally when he says that ignorance is not a virtue in our business. So, any source of knowledge, any source of information, is useful as long as you understand its pluses and minuses. What these companies do is try to put the best spin or face on their situation. Rarely will managements tell you how bad things are.

But you understand that going in. So, you're really trying to understand how they think about the business and how their views may have changed in recent years.

For example, a couple of years ago, Amazon.com was down around $7–$8 a share, and we were the biggest shareholder other than its chairman, Jeff Bezos. So, one night at dinner, I asked him, "Jeff, what kind of things are you spending your time on these days?" And he said, "Oh, it's different from last year when I spent a huge amount of time on our financial situation—on our cash flow. These days, I'm spending it on the customer experience."

I thought, "That's really good." What that told me was that he was no longer worried about the way the business was developing—the financial situation. To put it in simple terms, he had been playing defense during the prior 12 months. Now, he could switch from playing defense to playing offense.

Well, the stock price was telling you that Amazon was still playing defense. So, that was really important information as we thought about that investment.

Speece: When you meet with corporate managers, do you have an agenda or do you let the talk roll and look for windows of insight?

Miller: It's actually all about insight, but it's about *long-term* insight. So, to take an example, Hank McKinnell from Pfizer came in to see us, and he brought his entire management team, including the chief medical officer. And we're not major shareholders of Pfizer; we have a few-hundred-million-dollar position. It's not one of our really big positions.

But one of the things that he talked about was the nature of the R&D pipeline in the pharmaceutical industry. And the reason we'd been underweight pharma for years was that we were aware of the fact that the marginal productivity of that pipeline was in a steady fall for most of the past 10 years. That was part of the reason that the multiples contracted, because that, in essence, was a window into the future rates of return on marginal capital.

I asked, "What's different about the business; is there anything we should know? What is it that people don't understand?" And he said, "They don't understand that in the long-cycle nature of an R&D pipeline, the productivity of our R&D at the margin is turning up."

Well, if that's true, that's huge. So I asked, "Do you have evidence for that?" And he said, "Absolutely." And he gave data on how many typical drugs that go into Phase I make it to Phase II. It used to be that 40 percent in Phase I made it to Phase II. Now, almost 70 percent make it to Phase II because of new drug-discovery programs.

And then, subsequently, Pfizer reported, and it actually raised guidance, which is really interesting because it sold off the consumer products division, which was being valued more highly than the pharma division. And when it reported, it raised guidance moderately and referenced the pipeline. So, there's a lot of evidence now that it's turning up.

Pfizer has the lowest P/E of the big pharmas, to take a simple metric. And now it has the highest dividend yield, or certainly one of the highest dividend yields. Pfizer has announced that it is going to buy back $17 billion worth of stock. It didn't disclose exactly what it was doing with the dividend, but Pfizer gave a strong indication that dividend growth would be at least double digits.

So, how much can the valuation degrade from 13 times earnings—actually, 12 times next year's earnings? Well, I think the answer is not much—especially if the marginal productivity on capital is going up. And if the dividend is going to be growing at double digits starting out from a 3.5 percent yield and the valuation doesn't degrade, that is close to a 14 percent implied rate of return against an implied market rate of return of, say, 7–8 percent. That seems like a pretty easy one.

Now, the problem is that no one really cares about Pfizer right now. It has performed poorly over the past few years. So, everyone says, "There's no sense of urgency. Who cares?" But for us, it's all about implied rate of return relative to the market because that's where we'd want to put more capital now than we would otherwise.

Speece: So, you saw raising the dividends as a good signal?

Miller: Pfizer raised its dividend every year for a generation, but what is important is that the company believes it can continue to raise the dividend despite starting out with an above-average dividend yield.

When I first met John Neff 25 years ago, we compared portfolios. He said, "Your portfolio looks pretty good, kid. But where's your yield? It looks like it's below the market!"

I said, "John, I know you like above-market yield, but you know that an asset's value doesn't depend on how it pays out its return, unless you believe that the market systematically misvalues yield or you can allocate that return to earn a rate of return higher than the market can."

And he said, "Yeah, I believe both." So, I said, "Well, that's why you have a high yield in *your* portfolio. That makes perfect sense then." So, John was very rational even then, which is why he was a great manager.

Speece: A lot of big shareholders met with Kenneth Lay of Enron Corporation, and Lay lied to them. How do you protect against that?

Miller: The short answer is that you can't protect yourself against fraud. You can protect yourself slightly, maybe, against managements that dissemble or that you think aren't answering questions clearly. But Enron is a name that occupies a unique spot in our history because we bought Enron just before it went bankrupt. We had avoided it all the way up and all the way down, even though we were interested in the company. I had met with Jeff Skilling a few times. Enron was one of *Forbes* magazine's most admired companies, and Andy Fastow was regarded as the best CFO. But we always regarded it as being richly priced because no matter how quickly its earnings were growing, it actually didn't earn its cost of capital.

That was a red flag to us because that was the theme of the old W.T. Grant case back when I took the CFA exam about 25 years ago. It was one of the classic cases. So, it was clear that Enron couldn't keep doing that. But when it slowed its growth and it looked like it might earn its cost of capital or more, then we got interested.

When the stock got down to the mid-teens, we started to do some serious work on it, and we parsed off every hard asset (the pipelines, etc.) against the debt. We looked at all of the off-balance-sheet stuff. It was sort of opaque, but we knew what had gone into it. And we assumed that the equity in the off-balance-sheet partnerships was zero. But we also assumed that it could pay its debt.

We had all of the assets parsed off except for the trading operation, and we valued the trading operation in the twenties—assuming access to capital and assuming an investment-grade rating. So, to make a long story very short, we concluded that if it could maintain access to capital, it was a buy.

So, we bought it starting in the low teens—all the way down to about $3—and we put $300 million in it. And the reason I'm going on about it is that I think it's instructive about our process. This was in the fall of 2001—I guess it was post-September 11.

As we looked at it, we thought there was about a 10 percent chance that it was a zero. We didn't know of any fraud there, but we knew that, because of all the controversy, if Enron lost access to capital, it would be a zero.

And our view was, "OK, if it's a zero, can we still invest in it? How much can we invest in it if it goes to zero and with our overall portfolio, still beat the market?" And that's how we calibrated our position size in it. As it turned out, our average cost was probably $7, and we sold it at 80 cents.

We lost $300 million in 60 days—the fastest that we ever lost that kind of money in our history. But we still beat the market that year, so it wasn't a total disaster, but it was close.

Speece: For value investors, the biggest enemies are time, lack of patience, and "the value trap"—mistaking a dog for a value stock. You have said that you average down relentlessly. With that bias, how do you protect your clients' money against the value trap?

Miller: Almost every value trap is the result of people extrapolating past returns on capital and past valuations onto a different situation today. They say, "Oh, Toys 'R' Us' historical multiple was X. And now it's 0.8X, so there's an opportunity here." Or, "Look at what the pharmaceutical companies did for the last 50 years, and now they're cheap compared with that. So, now they're a good value."

The problem is that in most value traps, the fundamental economics of the business has deteriorated. And the market is gradually marking down the valuation of those to reflect the fundamental economic deterioration.

So, what we've tried to always focus on is, in essence, what the future return on capital will be, not what the past return on capital has been. What's our best guess at the future return on capital and how the management can allocate that capital in a competitive situation that is dynamic so that we can avoid, in essence, those value traps? We make a lot of other mistakes, but that one is not one that we make a whole lot.

Speece: A value trap that may be earlier in the cycle than the pharmaceuticals is newspaper stocks. One of your sister organizations, Private Capital Management, is a big owner of newspaper stocks. What is your take on that business?

Miller: The newspapers look like a value trap—or at least have appeared to be so over the past few years. Their long-term economics are under attack on a variety of fronts. The team at Private Capital knows these names as well as anyone and has a fabulous long-term record, so it's hard to be too critical of them because we don't yet know what ultimate rate of return they'll earn on their newspaper holdings.

Eastman Kodak Company (Kodak) is a name we own (they do, too, now, by the way) that is dealing with secular challenges brought on by technology similar to those facing the newspapers. One difference is that the move from film to digital is happening so fast that Kodak has had to move very quickly. This has been extremely challenging, but we think it is over the hump and that the next few years will be much better than the last few have been. The secular problems of newspapers are unfolding more slowly. That gives them more time to respond, but it's also permitted many of them to move too slowly, in my opinion.

I was at a presentation on new and old media a year or so ago at which Warren Buffett was also present. He raised his hand and asked, "If the internet had been invented first, do you think we'd have newspapers today?"

After some pondering, the answer came back, "No, I don't think so." And I recall Warren saying, "That's all you need to know about the future of newspapers."

Meg Whitman at eBay told me some time ago that its classified business was going really well, and she pointed out how much easier it is to navigate classifieds on the internet than it is via a newspaper.

And then there are movies. I think movie ads represent something like up to 10 percent of the ad revenue at some of the major newspapers. How effective are they at driving traffic versus trailers on the internet, for example? I think movie ads in newspapers are likely to decline pretty significantly. And I understand that Sony Corporation is looking at whether those ad dollars are really necessary in a connected world. So, the challenges are endemic.

And many of the newspapers trade at 8–9 times EBITDA (earnings before interest, taxes, depreciation, and amortization), or thereabouts, with declining circulation and declining or, at best, anemic organic revenue growth. So, why own them when you can buy Sprint Nextel at 5 times EBITDA with subscribers growing? After all, it's a subscription business just like newspapers.

Speece: Sometimes, an analyst will slide from *believing* something is going to happen to *hoping* it is going to happen, but the analyst, on whom you depend, does not realize that a slide has occurred. How do you help the analyst—and yourself—avoid that tipping point?

Miller: "Hope" is a deadly word. We pay close attention to the descriptions and the semantics of the analysts. When the word "hope" starts to appear in things, it's very bad. We want to see "I think," "I believe," even "I feel confident that" but not simply "I feel." When "I feel" or "I hope" start to crop up, emotions are taking over.

Speece: That verbiage can also be bound in Wall Street's sell-side research. Do you use that research and monitor their biases, or do you stick to your in-house research?

Miller: Today, I may scan sell-side research, but I read almost none of it. I pay attention to it only in relation to particular names that we know.

The incentive structure for most sell-side people is such that they neither structure their tasks nor describe what they are doing in a way that comports with what we are looking for. We do expect all of our analysts to know who the analysts with good reasoning are in a particular industry, sector, or company and to read their analyses.

Speece: You appear to rely heavily on your background in psychology and philosophy as an analytical tool in the investment business. Is that a fair characterization?

Miller: Everybody comes to the job with his or her own toolset, right? So, I don't have an MBA. I don't have any training in finance, which is probably obvious to most people when they talk to me.

I do have the CFA charter, which is the only thing that I was able to start with. But my technical toolkit actually comes out of analytic philosophy. That's what I bring to bear on the process, and I've found it to be very useful. But again, those are all the tools that I have.

I have adopted what Charlie Munger says. His view is that if you have a basic grounding in Psychology 101, Economics 101—most of the various disciplines—and you can combine them properly, they can provide you with all you need. I think that's mostly right. So, you don't need a great understanding of psychology. Psychology 101 works well.

Speece: Do you believe tracking error, benchmarks, and information ratios are good tools for the client?

Miller: Clients will ask us what benchmarks they should benchmark us against, and we tell them to use whatever they want. We are going to do what we do. We have a certain thing we are going to do, and however they want to evaluate us is fine.

We do try to make sure that our clients or potential clients understand our portfolio construction process, so the information ratio may be relatively more useful than tracking error or benchmarks. The information ratio may provide clients with a decent sense at certain points in time of how good the investment manager's process is.

If people care about tracking error, they should not hire us. We do not think or care about it.

Speece: You do not have a benchmark?

Miller: Our benchmark for Legg Mason Value Trust is the S&P 500 Index, but we do not construct the portfolio with any eye to the S&P 500 in the sense of overweighting, underweighting, or forecasting. If I have to have a position in each sector of the S&P 500, then what I know before the year even starts is that I will have exposure to the worst sectors of the market as well as the best. Why would I have a process that guarantees exposure to the worst sectors of the market? If I am in the worst sectors, it is because either I made a mistake or I chose to be there for the long term versus the short term. But over a three-year to five-year period, I want to have no exposure to what is really bad and maximum exposure to what is really good.

Speece: You have a very large separate account business, so your size may limit what you can do. How do you turn that facet into an advantage?

Miller: We've got about $65 billion in my group, and $40 billion to $45 billion of that is in a single product style. Fortunately, that's large-cap U.S. stocks, which has the advantage—or disadvantage—of being able to absorb a lot more than $45 billion. And because it was one of the worst performing sectors of the market in the last five years, it's one of the sectors with a high future expected rate of return.

We tell potential clients that it's good news and bad news where we are. The bad news is we are currently well behind the market because these names have performed poorly this year. The good news is that we can take double, triple, or quadruple whatever they can give us, and we think we'll do fine over the *next five* years. If the large- and mid-cap U.S. stocks looked like they did in 1999, then we couldn't do that well in absolute terms. But right now, we can take in almost unlimited amounts of money.

Speece: When you do a trade, how do you disguise it?

Miller: Our head trader has been with us for 15 years, and he is really good. We have a younger trading group that works with him.

In the early and middle years, we had a lot of trouble trying to, euphemistically, "train" our brokers not to give up our name to people. They learned that we imposed a high penalty for such deeds; basically, we gave them no business for a couple of years. But today, we do not have a problem in terms of people knowing too much about what we are doing.

Also, when we are buying, we tend to be liquidity providers to the market, as most value investors are. We are buying mostly what people do not want, and we are selling mostly what they do want. We tend to run against the tide with that, which makes it a bit easier.

Speece: We will now open questioning to the audience.

Question: Companies like Pfizer and Schering-Plough Corporation haven't done well recently, but I believe Fred Hassan, chairman and CEO of Schering-Plough since April 2003, can add value over time. What do you think?

Miller: We don't own Schering-Plough, but we do have a high regard for the CEO and what he's done previously. For us, it was a valuation call, not a management call.

Historically, concentration has paid off, but it doesn't pay as much right now. For any industry or sector, we typically want our analysts to collapse what they believe into the single best trade-off of risk and reward. So, ideally, we only want to own one or two names in any given group—not now, but historically. So, if we own Pfizer, we typically wouldn't own Schering-Plough and Merck & Co. and something else.

Question: Are you changing your process at all because of the issue of backdating stock options?

Miller: We're one of the largest shareholders of United Healthcare Corporation, and there's a backdating issue there. We've talked to the board members; we've talked to Chairman and CEO Bill Maguire; and we've talked to the lead investigator of the whole thing. And obviously, they can't tell us—because of Reg. FD—anything that they haven't told the world, but we kind of get a sense of what's going on.

We don't know how that's going to come out, except that our read on that particular situation—and I'm answering the question obliquely on this one—is that it's far from clear that there wasn't backdating.

It's a little bit like Microsoft Corporation. Microsoft had a policy of awarding options at the lowest price in any given quarter. So, if that's your policy, then backdating isn't an issue. In *this* case, Maguire had the authority to choose the date, so it's a bit murky.

But broadly speaking, we were well aware of the option dating situation—not backdating so much as just the fortuitous granting of options at low prices. So, it wasn't something that was secret. There were even some academic papers going back about six or seven years ago highlighting that.

We used to flip out at the repricing of options before there was an accounting penalty attached to it. And that drove us bananas—or at least it drove us bananas until we saw an academic paper that said when companies reprice options, they typically do it at or near the low. So, we said, "OK, it's like insider buying. We get it."

So, then when they'd reprice, we'd yell at them and then go buy the stock. And that worked pretty well.

Question: You seem to be relatively optimistic, or at least neutral, on the valuation of large-cap U.S. stocks, whereas many analysts see a somewhat bearish prospect for U.S. equities because, on a top-down basis, profit margins and macrolevels seem to be at all-time record highs. What is your view on the overall level of the U.S. equity market?

Miller: Our view is that reasoning from the macro to the micro tends to be very dangerous. Margins are at historical highs. I think it's actually very interesting because when you go back and look at what profit margins have been on a long-term basis, they are at historical highs, but the trend is up.

Grantham, Mayo, Van Otterloo & Co. LLC's Jeremy Grantham has this whole regression to the mean thing. And I have a systematic problem with that because the mean is not a stationary item. It migrates. So, if you can identify the mean and think it's stationary, then I'll buy it. However, I don't necessarily believe that.

Let me put it this way: U.S. mega-cap stocks are really cheap relative to U.S. small- and mid-cap stocks on a historical basis. They're also very cheap relative to their returns on equity and their reinvestment rates. You can see that, basically, reinvestment risk is what people are worried about in those things.

But take Microsoft's announced $40 billion buyback. That will tend, I think, to assuage people's concerns about reinvestment risk. And because Microsoft is a bellwether, a lot of other companies will probably follow its example. So, that's partly why we're quite bullish on U.S. mega caps.

And we're bullish on it for another reason. One of the markers, in my opinion, of a high future return is where the worst rate of return has been during the preceding five or six years. And it turns out that one of the worst things that you could have owned during the last five or six years has been U.S. mega cap. Everything else—small cap, mid cap, commodities, emerging, or what have you—has done great. Meanwhile, mega caps have done poorly.

Lots of people criticize Home Depot's Bob Nardelli or General Electric's Jeff Immelt, but all of these stocks have been cut in half. And meanwhile, their earnings have been doing fine. So, I think that's another marker of a likely high future return.

Question: In your long career of managing money, what was your biggest mistake, and did you learn any lesson from it that you can share with us?

Miller: Enron was my biggest dollar mistake. It was the most money—the most absolute dollars—I've ever lost in the shortest period of time.

The most egregious mistake I've ever made, I think, is one that I would be willing to bet that none of you here has ever made—or ever will make—in your entire investment career. Salant Corporation was an apparel company that owned the Perry Ellis brand at one point. We bought it in the early days in our fund, in the early 1980s, at around $10 a share.

Then, the U.S. Federal Reserve Board raised rates in 1984, and the economy slowed down a little bit. Salant ran into some problems—including foreign competition—and it went bankrupt. But we didn't sell it.

Well, then the company brought in a new CEO, and I met with him. At the time, the stock was at $1. This guy was a turnaround expert, and he told a great story. So, I thought, "Hey, this sounds pretty *good*. I like this." So we ramped up the position big time. The stock went from $1 to $30, so I felt pretty good about that.

But then in the late 1980s, he levered the company up to make acquisitions, and the Fed began raising rates again. The economy got worse, and the company went bankrupt for the second time. So, that CEO left and it brought in a new guy who said, "Oh, we can get rid of this debt. After all, we have good brands here, etc." So, I thought, "OK, I made 30 times my money the last time. Why not ramp it up and do it again?" So, I bought more of it, and it rose to $20 this time, if I remember correctly, before it went bankrupt again—for the third time—with us owning it.

Finally, I sold it, and we put a rule in place: Three bankruptcies and you're out.

Today, risk controls would prevent such a sequence. Risk controls must be appropriate to the sort of risks involved.

A senior manager at one of the biggest hedge funds in the world told me recently that risk control and risk management have assumed a dominant role because clients don't like volatility. Clients are paying high fees to avoid it. He said, "Three years ago, we bought McDonald's Corporation at $13 a share. When it went to $12, our risk management committee told us we had to sell it because it was down. It was down 10 percent and we had to sell it! We convinced them to let us keep it. Then, McDonald's tripled over the course of a few years after the company changed menu items and so forth."

What the risk management committee had done was take the risk management procedures that are appropriate to the global macro scene, currencies and so on, and applied them to individual securities. Such a misuse is plainly crazy. Nevertheless, and despite the fact that the fund has a great record, three years later, it has 35 lawyers and others monitoring risk control who will still try to sell the fund out of a stock if the stock drops 10–15 percent.

Question: Most of your funds have had little exposure to energy stocks, but most investors still see great value in energy stocks. Do you plan to change your view of this sector?

Miller: We are always thinking about all the things we've done wrong and all the things we ought to be doing in the future. We clearly missed the energy names in our portfolio.

We construct our holdings on the basis of a probabilistic scenario weighting. The error that I made was overweighting the long-term data relative to the short-term data—sort of the reverse of what behavioral finance says investors tend to do. Had I been more alert, I would have realized that every time we have what is, in essence, a global recession—especially one accompanied by a period when commodities are weak going into it—the demand curve will shift when the economy gets better and push commodity prices up. Based on history, this upward movement should last, at the shortest, 18 months and, at the longest, three to four years.

In fact, based purely on that call and the fact that on a pure valuation basis the odds favored it, one of our portfolio managers did overweight energy in late 2003. We almost did it in Value Trust, but then stocks moved up in December 2003, and I hate to pay up for anything, so I said forget it. So, I left some three-baggers on the table.

Question: What are some of the biggest mistakes plan sponsors make when hiring investment managers, and how can they be avoided?

Miller: Dick Strong, a good friend of mine who is now, unfortunately, out of the business, told me 20 years ago when we were first getting started that the only thing that matters to a plan sponsor is your most recent performance. He said that in every hiring competition, the manager with the best quarterly performance and the best annual performance will win 90 percent of the time. And that has been our experience.

First, plan sponsors tend to vastly overweight the most recent information. Suppose you are on the investment committee and you are looking at five managers. They all have great long-term records, but one of them has done great recently and also in the last year. Why wouldn't you hire that manager? Why would you hire the person who has done worse? If four managers continue to do worse, you're going to question why you didn't hire the manager who did best, right? Overweighting the most recent performance is the most common mistake. The correlated mistake is then to overweight subsequent recent performance.

Both mistakes arise, based on our experience, because plan sponsors tend to overweight performance relative to process. That is, they take the outcome of our process, which is our performance, and weight it a lot more heavily than they weight our process. Understanding the process, however, is a lot more important than recent performance. They think performance equals process, which, if true, is only true long term.

Question: In relation to dividends versus share buybacks, a year ago Dell was selling at 17 times book value of equity and stockholders' equity was going down every year because income was being used almost totally to buy back shares. How do you balance the dividend or the yield versus what the company is doing with the cash it is generating?

Miller: Dell has not covered itself with glory in its share repurchase program during the past five years. We owned Dell from about 1995 until early 2000, and then it collapsed. So, we bought a little bit back and then sold it. And then we were only in it again recently.

Dell has done what a lot of other tech companies have done—and this was its error—which was to systematically repurchase stock to "offset option dilution." Well, that's idiotic because what you're doing is effectively just a pure transfer from the public shareholders to the management and employees. And usually, if you're doing it that way, it's without regard to the rate of return that you're earning on that transfer.

So, I'm not going to make any excuses for that use of capital, which was far from optimal.

That's different from what it is doing now. Now, quite apart from the options thing, Dell bought back 2.5 percent of its stock last quarter. And we value Dell on our multifactor model at up to $40 a share. Our view is that if you buy back stock at its current price, you're earning big returns for the shareholders, and it's much better than a dividend at that level.

Also, when the company was buying back stock from the late 1990s up until a year or so ago, its founder and chairman Michael Dell never bought a share. Well, Michael's now buying the stock personally. And it's not like he needs more exposure to Dell. So, to me, that's a pretty good signal that this management understands what this business is worth.

I'm not sure that I answered your question. However, the wisdom of any share repurchase, in our view, always begins with, "What's the business worth? What's the present value of its future free cash flows?"

If a company is buying back shares below that value, then its management is adding value. If it is buying back shares above that value, then it is destroying value—all other things being equal.

Question: Do you see any value in the automobile industry? And how do you view the proposed alliance of General Motors Corporation (GM), Nissan Motor Co., and Renault?

Miller: We were a big shareholder in Chrysler Corporation back before it got sold to Daimler-Benz. And we've actually invested with Kirk Kerkorian a number of times—whether in MGM casino, MGM movie, or Chrysler. Typically, buying what Kirk is buying and selling when he's selling has been a pretty good strategy.

With respect to this particular go around, we bought GM bonds—the long bonds—in the Opportunity Trust. We did not buy any common stock, and GM stock has done great this year.

I think the proposed alliance with Carlos Ghosn and Renault is certainly really interesting, but it's unclear to us what long-term difference that would make. There are some interesting things going on in GM's pension plan where it's going to flip in about two years. So, it's going to start running in its favor, relatively speaking, although everything's relative. However, again, I think that some really interesting things are going on there.

We don't see a margin of safety sufficient to allow us into it right here. We have bought some Lear Corporation, by the way, in the Opportunity Trust, as well. And the GM bonds seem to me to be—even at 78 on the long-dated stuff—sort of a no-brainer. But the stock, I think, is less certain.

Question: Do you have any parting words of wisdom?

Miller: When I first got into the business, I met Bill Ruane, Warren Buffett's friend who ran Ruane Cunniff. Somebody asked him, "If you could give some advice about investing, what would it be?" And as Ruane related this story to me, he said, "I told the guy that if he reads *Security Analysis* [by Benjamin Graham and David Dodd] and *The Intelligent Investor* [by Benjamin Graham] and then reads all of Warren Buffett's annual reports, and if he really understands what they were saying, he will know everything there is to know about investing."

I thought about that advice for a number of years and agree with it, and then I heard this comment from two-time World Series of Poker champion Puggy Pearson: "Ain't but three things to gambling. Number one: knowing the 60/40 end of a proposition. Number two: money management. And number three: knowing yourself." This advice is succinct and encompasses all you really need to know about how to approach investing.

Here's why: Knowing the 60/40 end of a proposition means knowing when you invest that the odds are in your favor. However you compute the odds, the odds have to be in your favor.

Money management involves knowing how much you commit to that position. Will you commit 1 percent, 5 percent, 10 percent? I recommend the book *Fortune's Formula: The Untold Story of the Scientific Betting System That Beat the Casinos and Wall Street* (by William Poundstone). It is a far better way of thinking about asset allocation than mean–variance analysis.

Finally, knowing yourself means knowing your personal psychology and how you react to adverse circumstances.

This presentation comes from the 2006 Financial Analysts Seminar held in Evanston, Illinois, on 16–21 July 2006. Portions of this interview were previously published by Outstanding Investor Digest *(www.oid.com) and are reprinted here with permission.*

On Low-P/E Investing

JOHN B. NEFF, CFA

John B. Neff, CFA, was a portfolio manager at the Vanguard Group for 31 years, during which time he successfully managed the Windsor and Gemini II Funds. In this session, Fred H. Speece, Jr., CFA, asks Neff about his insights on equity investing in general and on low-P/E investing (his forte) in particular.

Speece: Is there room for stock picking in the market today?

Neff: Yes. I think the opportunities today are as good as they have ever been. I have continued to play the low-P/E game since I gave up my Windsor responsibilities, but I do it in a much more concentrated form. In my dotage, I actively manage my own money, a little charity money and some for my kids, and an individual retirement account, but it is a fair chunk of change. I typically own 8 to 10 stocks, which, of course, is the opposite of what you are supposed to have in the way of diversification. I buttress that allocation with about 30 percent in fixed income. So, if the wolf comes to the door, at least I have an anchor to windward.

Over the past 10 years, I have earned about 20 percent a year on my equities. I have not done as well so far this year, but the year is not over yet.

Speece: What are the enduring principles of investing?

Neff: Obviously, having a low P/E is the primary principle. Then, look for solid companies with strong fundamentals in strong, growing industries and hone your analytical prowess. A company's prospects should include fundamental growth of 7 percent or better. The company should not have cyclical exposure without a compensating P/E multiple.

Seek out companies on the "squash"—that is, ones that are making new lows. At Wellington Management Company, I would sweep the list of stocks making new lows each day and review *Value Line* each week, not for *Value Line's* opinion but for the 10 or 12 statistical yardsticks it provides. The new low list

> Look for solid [low-P/E] companies with strong fundamentals in strong, growing industries and hone your analytical prowess.

John B. Neff, CFA, is a retired portfolio manager, managing partner, senior vice president, and member of the executive committee at Wellington Management Company, West Conshohocken, Pennsylvania.

gives you one entry for consideration and *Value Line*, another. So, I would look for companies that were moving up the quality ladder.

Also, look for miscategorized companies. A current example of a miscategorized company is Lyondell Chemical Company, which is the fourth-largest chemical company in the United States but which also happens to own the eighth-largest oil refinery in the country.

Even if you have done a thorough analysis, sometimes you get surprised. And at times, these are good surprises, as in the case of what I call "free plus." For example, at Wellington, we owned Atlantic Richfield Co. when it discovered oil on the North Slope of Alaska. That discovery was not part of our analysis. We knew that Atlantic Richfield was looking all over the world for oil, but we did not know it was going to hit it big when it did. We also owned Tandy (now RadioShack Corporation) in the 1970s—one of the lesser-recognized growth stocks—and all of a sudden the market got excited about personal computers, which Tandy just happened to be merchandising all over the United States. That was not an original part of our analysis, and we didn't pay for that outcome—hence "free plus."

The other plus that you sometimes get is a buyout. Somebody else in the market wants to capitalize on the same virtues that you see.

Play to your strengths. Know your good plays and your not-so-great ones. I, for instance, don't own many technology stocks because of my limited technology knowledge.

Another good idea is to develop a curbstone opinion. Shop around the neighborhood, and ask family and friends about companies to get their perspective. With a curbstone opinion on top of basic fundamental analysis, you will be much more comfortable moving when you get the price opportunity. Match your opinion against what caused the stock's price to drop and you can easily determine if the timing is propitious for investment.

Speece: If instead of seeking low-P/E stocks of decent companies you were seeking high-P/E stocks of weak companies, couldn't you be successful by shorting them?

Neff: Certainly, it would seem so. One of the problems, though, is that if you short a stock and you are right, regardless of your holding period, you realize a short-term gain on which you pay ordinary income tax of 35 percent. In addition, if you short a future, regardless of your holding period, 60 percent of the gain is long term and 40 percent is short term. So, taxes are a problem, leading me to short infrequently.

Speece: How did you handle the periods when the market was not appreciative of your style?

Neff: Actually, it worked itself out, believe it or not. The first bad spell was the Nifty Fifty period in the early 1960s. During this time, the Nifty Fifty stocks were selling at P/Es in the low 40s. Their P/Es eventually fell to the low 20s, then to the low teens, and eventually to single-digit multiples in some cases. That meant that those growth stocks finally became out-of-favor stocks, and we loaded up with the likes of Tandy, Hospital Corp., and Browning-Ferris, among others.

By holding the line, we absolutely got killed in the 1971–73 period, but we eventually hit pay dirt with lesser-recognized growth stocks. We came blazing out of the aftermath of the early 1970s earning around 80 percent compared with the market's 40 percent, and we really recouped. So, ultimately, we just waited out the bad spells. And we repeated similar scenarios three or four times after that.

For instance, in 1980, oil was supposedly going to rise to $60 a barrel, and everything electronic was a hot item in the market. We did not do well that year. But those sectors got killed in 1981, and we did very well in the ensuing years.

Then, of course, came 1987. Equity market prices rose to 22–23 times earnings, and we built a 20 percent liquidity position in 1987; we simply could not find reasonably priced stocks to buy, so we fell behind in the first three quarters of that year. Following the famous crash in October 1987, we more than recouped our underperformance through 1988.

Then, in the early 1990s, the financial intermediaries went bust, or at least the market thought so. Thirty percent or more of our portfolio was positioned in financial intermediaries—thrifts, banks, and insurance companies. Shareholders complained that these financial intermediaries were all going to fail. Some did, but obviously they all did not, and they were eventually good investments.

Speece: How did your investors in the Windsor Fund react to these periods of underperformance?

Neff: Inflection points occur in the market, and around them performance can suffer, but you have to stick to your guns. We were a low-P/E fund, and that strategy was in the mutual fund charter, so the shareholders knew what they were getting. All we had to do was execute our strategy well. Obviously, the press would be on our back, particularly, when performance was not stellar.

Another bone of contention was when we, the low-P/E shooters, owned several of the big growth stocks from time to time, thus raising a few eyebrows. I'd even be questioned in the hallway about some of these positions. We owned Dell twice at single-digit multiples, and we also bought Home Depot, IBM, Xerox, Seagate Technology, Digital Equipment, and McDonald's Corporation when they reached single-digit multiples. So, we owned some genuine growth stocks after they were beat up badly enough by the market to meet our low-P/E hurdle.

Speece: The focus now is on tracking error and style adherence, which keeps managers from pursuing strategies perceived as "too different." Is this new way of thinking healthy for the market and investors?

Neff: No, it isn't healthy. Essentially, these tools enforce closet indexing. And it is hard to beat the averages (whatever average you are supposed to beat) if you cling to the index. So, managers should have some freedom to manage money intelligently. Nevertheless, funds (and managers) do need to be categorized. The client has investment needs and desires, and the manager has an obligation to deliver a service that measures up to these expectations in some fashion, be it low P/E or whatever measure is most appropriate for that client.

To give managers complete flexibility is also not necessarily healthy. Consider hedge funds, where investors often do not know what they are getting. Therefore, being somewhere between this highly structured closet index enforcement and total investment freedom is probably the best approach.

Speece: Do you think active managers can outperform the S&P 500 Index over extended periods?

Neff: The S&P 500 has not been particularly difficult to beat because it is not really an index fund but, rather, a managed fund. It is run by a committee, and the committee decides which equity securities are included. Consider the case of technology stocks in the late 1990s. At one time, the tech sector grew to represent about 34 percent of the S&P 500. So, in part because of large additions of tech stocks, this very large weighting provided an opportunity for investors to get on the other side of it and take advantage of that structure in the market. Frankly, the S&P 500 Index Committee gives investors a lot of opportunities.

Speece: Are dividends and share repurchases equally attractive to investors?

Neff: Yes, but yield is important, too. Citigroup, which was recently upgraded to AAA, is buying its own stock. If it is as undervalued as I think it is, this will be an awfully good return on capital. In addition, Citigroup increased its dividend by about 10 percent a year. A new chart in the *Wall Street Journal* on Mondays shows the Dow Jones Industrial Average companies ranked by estimated growth rate and P/E. Citigroup is at the top of the list with 10 percent growth and a P/E multiple of 10–11. But nowhere is its yield mentioned, and its yield is awfully good at 4.1 or 4.2 percent. It compares quite favorably with the average 2 percent yield of stocks and is almost as good as the yield on the long Treasury bond.

Our goal at Windsor was always to earn a total return (growth rate plus yield) of twice the P/E we paid, but that is hard to do these days. The lesser-recognized growth stocks typically had a 12 percent growth rate with a yield of 2–3 percent, which equaled a 15 percent total return. We bought them for 7.5 times earnings. Windsor's advantage at a return of 13.9 percent versus 10.7 percent for the market translated into 315 bps, of which about 200 came from superior yield. In other words, we had a portfolio yield about 200 bps better than market price for which we paid essentially nothing. In this same vein, Citigroup is now a buy, if I am right, on 10–12 percent growth simply because it is selling at about 10 times earnings.

Speece: What do you think of companies that are pouring their cash into buybacks and, in some cases, even borrowing money to repurchase stock rather than paying dividends or investing in the business?

Neff: The P/E of the stock is the determining factor. Coca-Cola Company and General Electric both repurchased stock at a high P/E, which didn't make any sense at all to me. If the company is trading at 25 times earnings, that is a 4 percent return on equity, which is really not very good. In the case of Citigroup and others, however, stock buybacks make more sense. Ultimately, the P/E and the price paid is the right yardstick for evaluating stock buybacks.

Speece: What is your opinion of money management firms not letting their analysts and portfolio managers meet with corporate management?

Neff: It is absurd. How can analysts do their job unless they spend time with management?

Speece: What is your take on corporate executives and ethics—on both the money management and corporate sides?

Neff: All things considered, the situation is good. But obviously there are outliers like Enron Corporation. It seems to me that as an analyst and investor you can protect yourself by meeting management and observing how they handle themselves. On balance, I think close to 95 percent of corporate management is on the level.

Speece: In what appears to be a momentum-oriented market, is low-P/E investing still viable?

Neff: Yes. There have always been camp followers. Ever since I've been in the business, the technicians have been around playing off the charts, playing the momentum game. But if you can get on the other side of that with solid fundamentals, it is just opportunity time.

All kinds of decent companies in decent industries sell at low multiples. Make your basic case—growth rate and earnings—and if in a year or so it is not materializing, then sell the stock, return to your analysis, and find another low-P/E stock. In following this strategy, usually not much is lost because the stock was so beat up when you bought it that you get your money back, or at least 95 percent of it back, and then you go on to the next one.

Speece: What do you do to protect yourself against the value trap?

Neff: You just have to be right on your fundamental analysis. If your analysis is wrong and the growth rate and earnings estimates don't materialize, then you need to be disciplined and get out of that stock and go on to the next one.

Speece: What is the difference between a value manager and a low-P/E manager?

Neff: Value is in the eye of the beholder. Low P/E is easily calculated and definitive.

Speece: What is your signal to sell?

Neff: As I've been saying, if an investment is not working, get out. If it is working and the market embraces it, sell into that technical strength as patiently as possible. At Windsor, we would model the expected growth rate and yield—total return—and, based on that return, determine the price that the stock should sell at relative to the market. As the stock approaches that price, we started selling.

Essentially, the portfolio usually had a 100 percent appreciation potential. I know that sounds a bit pushy, but we used it as a benchmark for when to start selling the stock. Generally, we would begin selling at 65 percent of the 100 percent and patiently sell into strength. Depending on how large a percentage of the stock we owned, we could be totally out of the stock by the time the price fell to about 40 percent of the portfolio's targeted appreciation potential.

Speece: Could you add more value with large-cap or small-cap stocks?

Neff: I am not smart enough to differentiate. I have never understood the press's intrigue with large cap versus small cap. We found opportunities in both areas and exercised them accordingly.

Furthermore, if you are alert, you can see somebody else's acquisition intrigue. And as a result, we got about two to three buyouts a year. The characteristics that attracted us, such as being a good company in a good industry and at a low price (P/E), would attract corporate purchasers as well.

Speece: How did you view debt when you were at Windsor?

Neff: It would bother us if a company had a lot of debt, and we would characterize it as a penalty relative to the P/E. Eventually, we would sell such a company simply because it was carrying so much debt.

Speece: Have hedge funds helped or hurt us?

Neff: The costs associated with hedge funds, both to the market and to the investor, are simply too great. The opportunity for gang warfare—particularly when a number of managers are chasing the same principle and thus owning the same individual stocks—sets the market up for a difficult time.

Remember the demise of Long-Term Capital Management? That situation was not caused by hanky panky, just by poor decision making. But now, superimposed on the probability that other funds will be making other bad decisions is the increasing likelihood that more and more funds will be engaging in hanky panky.

The basic problem is that hedge funds are taking too much off the top in fees. Remember the 13.9 return on Windsor versus the 10.7 return on the S&P 500? If we had been a hedge fund, that 13.9 would have been 11.2, and that is without a 1 percent a year management fee, which I did not figure into the calculation. Our basic management fee at Windsor was 16 bps. Compare that with where we are today. The top hedge fund manager made $1.5 billion in 2005. My point is that hedge funds are way, way, way too greedy, although generalizing about them is fraught with peril because the industry is filled with so many permutations.

Speece: Many endowments think they need to have 15 or 20 percent in hedge funds. Are they equipped to handle this kind of investment?

Neff: No, but not because of the endowment's internal shortcomings but because an investment of that size, through the leverage it entails, is more than a trillion dollars.

Speece: You earlier mentioned Lyondell. Is this a company you are looking at now?

Neff: Yes, I like Lyondell. It is a chemical company that was spun off from Atlantic Richfield in the late 1980s and is one of the United States' largest chemical companies. In the spin off, Lyondell got a refinery in Houston, which is the eighth largest in the country. Lyondell owns 58.75 percent of the refinery, and CITGO Petroleum Company, which is 100 percent owned by Venezuela, owns the other 41.25 percent.

The refinery was recently put up for sale for roughly $5 billion. If the sale happens, this company will go from being very highly leveraged—although it has paid down $1.7 billion in debt in the past 18 months—to investment grade.[1] When it is investment grade, it will begin to repurchase its stock, which is now around $21. Earnings will be $4 this year, so it is selling at about 5.6 times earnings and has a 4.1 percent yield. In addition to repurchasing its stock, Lyondell will also raise its dividend if the refinery sale goes through.

Speece: We will now open questioning to the audience.

Question: Why are you so confident that Citigroup is undervalued?

Neff: I like Citigroup because of its economies of scale and size. Obviously, it is a AAA credit, and the company has developed skills in many different areas. Although, in the United States, Citigroup does not have a big presence in retail banking, it is big in credit cards. I'm expecting about 10–12 percent growth.

If you are really asking how it can get a 20 percent return on equity, my answer is because it is good.

Question: Why don't other investors realize that?

Neff: One of the problems with Citigroup is the cloud that hangs over it from the Sandy Weill days when, quite frankly, its ethics faltered in terms of its Japanese private banking business, Enron, and so on. The company is paying a price for that, not only out of pocket but also in terms of its reputation. But Charles Prince has done a prince of a job to distance the company from the problems of the past. But a big question and the company's biggest challenge is whether Citigroup will lose its entrepreneurial edge by virtue of having to be much more guarded on the ethics side.

---

[1] On 16 August 2006, Lyondell purchased CITGO's 41.25 percent interest for $2.1 billion, including CITGO's portion of the refinery's debt.

Question: Some analysts believe P/E is not as important as price to cash flow. Do you look at price to cash flow?

Neff: Yes. I do look at price to cash flow. I have never been a fan, however, of EBITDA (earnings before interest, taxes, depreciation, and amortization). It seems to me that interest, taxes, and depreciation are legitimate business expenses, and an evaluation tool that ignores them has minimal value. I really would rather stick to low P/E.

Question: Can you comment on being the chairman of the Advisory Council of the CFA Centre for Financial Market Integrity?

Neff: The CFA Centre for Financial Market Integrity is an initiative by CFA Institute to address some of the less-admirable machinations and hanky panky going on in the global financial marketplace. The Centre's intent is to be a leading voice on issues of fairness, efficiency, and investor protection in global capital markets and to promote high standards of ethics, integrity, and professional excellence within the investment community.

Question: What do you think of the market today?

Neff: I think the marketplace is friendly and the economy is doing well. I am estimating $90 of S&P 500 earnings in 2007, up about 10 percent from 2006. It seems to me that the market has the ideal elements for solid corporate earnings. First, we have a decent growth rate, 3 percent or so constant-dollar GDP; good productivity at about 2 percent; moderate wage increases; moderating medical costs; and the ability to get some decent price increases.

If we keep the current P/E, a 13.5 multiple, that means 8–10 percent appreciation plus a 2 percent yield, which equals a 10–12 percent total return and which compares quite well with long bonds. I just cannot get too excited about alternatives right now.

Question: If you had to pick one important lesson, what would you pick?

Neff: That is a difficult question because there are so many lessons. But if I had to pick one, I would pick the low-P/E equity strategy. That is certainly the crux of it. There are so many stocks that meet this criterion. To effectively pursue this strategy, however, do not be afraid to take on a stock that is under market attack because your aim is to buy low P/Es in decent companies in decent industries. There are not too many outstanding industries, but there are many decent ones.

This presentation comes from the 2006 Financial Analysts Seminar held in Evanston, Illinois, on 16–21 July 2006.

FIXED-INCOME
INVESTMENTS

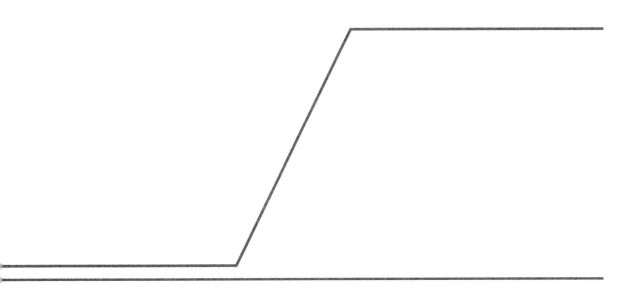

Credit Risk and the Link between Default and Recovery Rates

The U.S. high-yield bond market has grown dramatically in the past three decades, reaching more than $1 trillion in outstanding debt as of mid-year 2006. But little rigorous analysis has been done on what happens to the recovery rate over the credit cycle. Most models assume a fixed recovery rate, but a recent model that was tested using more than 1,000 defaulted bonds shows an inverse relationship between the probability of default and the recovery rate. Based on this model, several industries may be quite vulnerable to a high risk of default in the current environment.

$\mathbf{R}$isk, in general, and credit risk, in particular, have been brought front and center by the international banking supervisors who have endorsed the Basel II Capital Accord. By 2008, Basel II will be the paradigm used by most internationally active banking organizations for setting reserve requirements and determining capital adequacy as well as for measuring and managing risks, such as credit risk and operational risk. (Note that in the United States, Basel II will not be the paradigm for all banks, only the largest banks, but many medium-sized banks could opt to conform.)

Credit risk emerged in 1999 as a major focus in the international banking community after the first version of Basel II was released. As a result, two issues of primary importance that international banks and their clients are wrestling with are the probability of default and the loss given default (the credit loss incurred if an obligor of the bank defaults). Both measures are functions of default and recovery rates.

I will begin this presentation with an overview of current conditions in the high-yield debt market, including historical default rates and a historical perspective on the growth in the market. Next, I will review the previous

The latest incarnation of a distressed-debt fund is not only investing in distressed securities but also venturing into a new area called "rescue financing."

Edward I. Altman is director of the Credit and Debt Markets Research Program at New York University Salomon Center, Stern School of Business, New York City.

research in this area as well as the more recent empirical evidence on default and recovery rates and the links between them. And finally, I will conclude with a few comments on the industries considered the most vulnerable to default given the current environment.

Current Credit Conditions

The U.S. high-yield, or junk, bond market has grown dramatically in the past three decades. Drexel Burnham Lambert and Lehman Brothers began making fairly large inroads into this market in the early 1980s, but the market did not take off until the mid-to-late 1990s. Since the early 1990s, when the sector consisted of about $200 billion in outstanding debt, it has grown fairly consistently to more than $1 trillion in outstanding debt as of mid-year 2006.

A common way that a bond enters the high-yield sector is via the "fallen angel" route. That is, a company's situation deteriorates so badly that its debt is downgraded from investment to noninvestment grade. In May 2005, two huge fallen angels emerged as a result of the downgrades of Ford Motor Company and General Motors Corporation (GM) and significantly increased the size of the market. These two companies are now more important than ever to the credit markets. The bankruptcy of either company, but in particular GM, would have a huge impact not only on the U.S. economy but also on the world's economy because of these companies' global reach.

The rating agencies do a good job at the initial rating stage but a relatively poor job in monitoring and changing a company's debt rating over time (as documented by several studies) but not because the rating agencies do not know what they are doing. On the contrary, they know exactly what they are doing. One of the motivations driving the rating agency process is to have stable ratings. In other words, rating agencies operate with what can be called a "stability" objective. The agencies do not want to mistakenly change a rating from investment grade to noninvestment grade in a relatively short period of time and thus cause a reactionary shock in valuation with each change. As a result, the agencies' process almost mandates slowness in ratings changes.

Historical Default Rates

In the 1971–2005 period, the highest annual default rate in the high-yield bond market occurred in 2002, when it hit 12.8 percent. For the same 35-year period, the weighted average annual default rate was 4.65 percent. The markets quickly assessed the unprecedented default rate in 2002, and managers who lived through the 1990–91 two-standard-deviation market with default rates greater than 10.0 percent took risk management in stride. Nevertheless, yield spreads went up dramatically, with junk bonds selling at 1,000 bps over Treasuries—more or less the standard spread in the market. By 2003, the default rate had dropped to 4.60 percent, and by 2004, it had dropped to a very low 1.25 percent. Even though in 2005 the default rate rose to 3.37 percent (mainly because of a few very large bankruptcies), the market remained in a benign credit cycle, marked by low default rates, high recovery rates resulting from low interest rates, a generally healthy economy, and a massive amount of liquidity from traditional and nontraditional lenders (especially hedge and private equity funds).

In their calculations, most rating agencies use an issuer default rate (i.e., the number of issuers in default relative to the number of issuers outstanding). The default rate I prefer is dollar denominated (i.e., the dollars in default relative to the dollars that could have defaulted). The year 2005 serves as a good example of the difference between the two approaches. In 2005, the dollar-denominated approach produced a much higher default rate than the issuer approach: The number of issuers defaulting actually decreased from the prior year, but the par value of bonds defaulting increased from the prior year—from $11 billion to $36 billion. In 2005, 10 U.S. companies with a total of more than $1 billion in liabilities went bankrupt, including Delta Air Lines, Northwest Airlines, Calpine Corporation, Charter Communications (a distressed exchange), Delphi Corporation, and Winn-Dixie Stores. In contrast, in the three-year period from 2001 to 2003, 102 U.S. companies with more than $1 billion in total liabilities filed for bankruptcy. Thus, size is no longer a proxy for health.

The graph in **Figure 1** shows the quarterly default rate from 1991 to 2006. The six-year period from 1992 to 1998 was obviously a benign credit cycle. Some analysts believe another benign credit cycle started in 2003 and continued into 2004 and 2005. Note, however, the last two quarters in 2005, when the default rate in dollar-denominated terms escalated significantly. Has the benign credit cycle ended, or will it continue? (Note that the default rate in the first half of 2006 was a miniscule 0.4 percent.) Although interest rates are still relatively low, the economy is still fairly strong, defaults are still relatively low, and recoveries are still fairly high, much in the economy and the markets gives cause for concern. One major concern is a persistently low default rate in the midst of unusually high amounts of leverage in the riskier U.S. companies.

High-Yield Debt as Percentage of Total New Issues

Another reason I expect the default rate to continue to rise in 2006, and particularly in 2007, is illustrated in **Table 1**. In 2004 and 2005, the amount of new high-yield bond issues rated B− or below was more than 40 percent of

Figure 1   Quarterly Default Rate and Four-Quarter Moving Average, 1991–2006

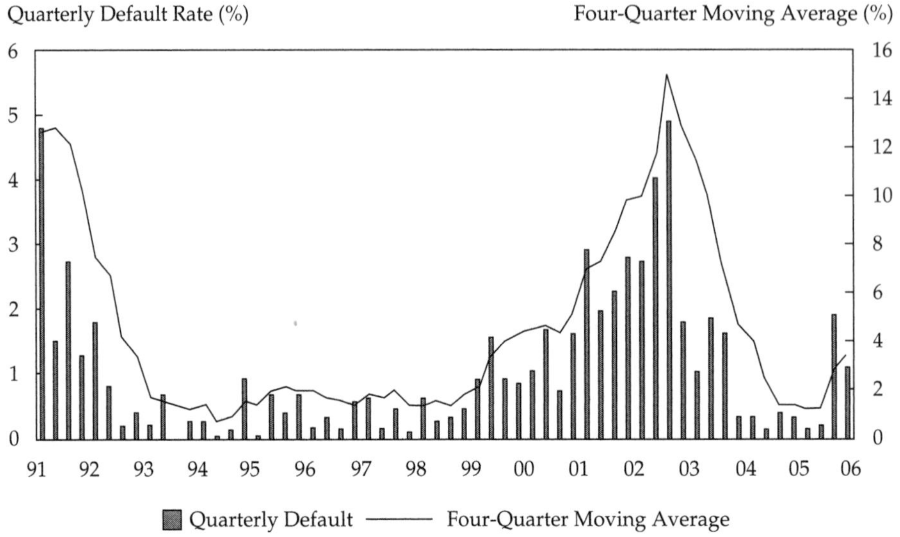

Table 1 New Issues Rated B– or Below as a Percentage of All New Issues, 1993–2005

Year	Amount
1993	26.0%
1994	22.0
1995	28.0
1996	26.0
1997	32.0
1998	38.0
1999	30.0
2000	31.0
2001	21.0
2002	21.0
2003	31.0
2004	42.5
2005	42.0

Source: Standard & Poor's.

all new bond issues, an unprecedentedly high percentage. In dollar terms, the impact is a little less dramatic, only 33–39 percent of the new issue market in each of these two years. The point, however, is that almost 20 percent of new issues in 2005 were rated CCC or below, which is also unprecedented.

A significant percentage of these new issues will default within four years, which means that 2007 is the likely target year for these defaults to begin.

Figure 2   Number of Bankruptcy Filings and Pre-Petition Liabilities of Public Companies, 1989–2005

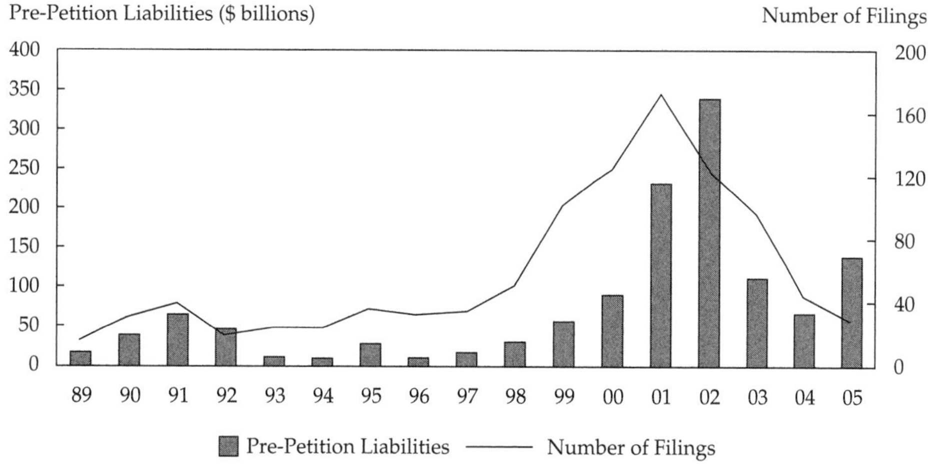

Pre-Petition Liabilities ($ billions) / Number of Filings

■ Pre-Petition Liabilities ——— Number of Filings

Note: Minimum $100 million in liabilities.
Source: Based on data from the NYU Salomon Center Bankruptcy Filings Database.

In addition, the private markets, particularly the leveraged loan markets, are exploding. So, the unparalleled rise of new issues in the weakest credit tiers of both the private and public bond markets indicates real problems in the not-too-distant future. **Figure 2** shows the number of bankruptcy filings and the amount of pre-petition liabilities of public companies from 1989 to 2005. In 2002, pre-petition liabilities amounted to $330 billion. Note that this 2002 spike in corporate bankruptcies occurred four years after a spike in 1998 in the new issuance of bonds rated B– or below, as shown in Table 1.

Growth in Defaulted and Distressed Debt

As an asset class, distressed debt has moved from a niche market to a major market in the past 15 years. More than 160 financial institutions currently manage funds with a dedicated strategy to public and private defaulted and distressed securities. **Figure 3** graphs the face value and market value of the U.S. defaulted and distressed-debt market. These measures include bonds trading in the public market and debt originating in the private market, such as bank loans, trade debt, private placements, and mezzanine debt. Before 1990, except for a few niche investors, institutional interest in the distressed-debt market was all but nonexistent. At that time, the market had about $300 billion in face value and $200 billion in market value and was composed mainly of leveraged buyout (LBO) financed companies that went bankrupt; more than 50 percent of the defaults in that period were LBO related. The average recovery rate was actually quite high at that time and followed on the heels of the boom period

Figure 3   Size of the Defaulted and Distressed Debt Market, 1990–2005

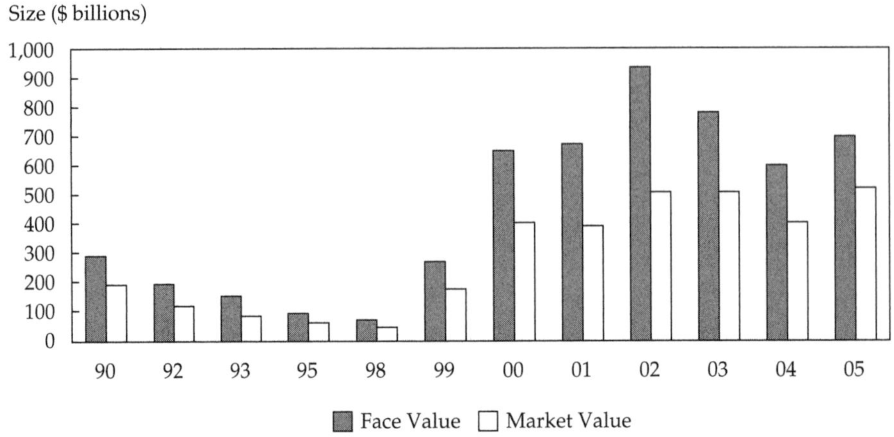

Source: Based on data from the NYU Salomon Center.

of the late 1980s. The market dwindled to a low in 1998. Then, in late 1998, Russia collapsed and Long-Term Capital Management imploded, both spurring a flight to quality. But in 1999, the market turned around and continued to grow until it reached a peak in 2002 at $940 billion in face value and about $500 billion in market value.

In 1999, only about $80 billion in par value was under management. Then, in the early 2000s, a tremendous amount of cash and liquidity entered the distressed market through newly created funds as well as existing funds with enhanced commitments to this market. Just as demand was increasing, supply began to fall until the market was reduced to $700 billion in face value but $525 billion in market value by 2005 and, respectively, $625 billion and $500 billion in mid-2006. Although the face value of the market in 2005 was almost $250 billion less than it was three years earlier (and more than $300 billion less today), the market value was $25 billion more in 2005 than in 2002 because of high recovery rates and the tremendous increase in prices of distressed and defaulted securities.

Performance and Demand

In 2003, one year after the peak in defaults, performance in the high-yield bond market was an outstanding 30 percent. Even more amazing was that bonds rated CCC and below returned 60 percent, and defaulted bonds earned an unbelievable 80 percent. Strong performance was also seen in 2004, with returns in the various high-yield and distressed sectors ranging from 14 to 20 percent. But in 2005, the average return of defaulted bonds and also distressed debt went up a measly 2 percent; overall market performance was only 2 percent. In contrast, the average distressed-debt hedge fund did better than the market (as measured by the Altman NYU Salomon Center Index of Defaulted Debt), producing returns of 8–10 percent.

Hedge funds in this distressed-debt space have reinvented themselves a number of times over the years. The latest incarnation of a distressed-debt fund is not only investing in distressed securities but also venturing into a new area called "rescue financing." Rescue financing is a lucrative way for a hedge fund to get involved with a company by lending at high interest rates or investing in the company's securities. On the one hand, if the company survives and prospers, the returns can be quite high. If things do not work out, however, the strain of the financing could contribute to the failure of the company. Debt-to-EBITDA (earnings before interest, taxes, depreciation, and amortization) ratios are now creeping up to the 5–7 times range, although they remain below the 8–10 times level reached in the LBO boom of the late 1980s. If these distressed companies have a hiccup in their cash flows or have trouble refinancing their debt—some of which is relatively short term—it could cause a big problem in the economy.

Distressed-debt hedge funds are now traveling overseas to Europe—the new frontier for this market—and have particular interest in German, Italian, and British banks' nonperforming loans. About 30 such hedge funds are now located in Europe, mainly in London and Frankfurt, and similar funds have been operating in Asia since 1997.

An area that is receiving more attention now than it has in the past is the equity of companies emerging from bankruptcy. Typically, these companies are not followed by the financial markets. The number of security analysts who follow such companies escalates as the company does well and declines as the company does poorly. So, when Wall Street forgets about these companies, the distressed industry picks up the ball. Of course, the poster child for this type of investing is Kmart. Kmart came out of bankruptcy with its equity priced at $17 a share before it rose to $150 or more a share.

Obviously, the potential for huge returns from rescue financing and distressed equity is quite attractive, and distressed-debt hedge funds are positioning themselves to take advantage of these situations. Unfortunately, not every distressed situation produces a winner. Consider the so-called Chapter 22 phenomenon—going bankrupt twice—experienced by U.S. Airways and more than 160 other companies since U.S. Airways paved the way.

Link between Default and Recovery Rates

Before discussing default and recovery rates, I must first define what these terms mean. As explained earlier, I prefer to use a dollar-denominated default rate in my research. And like default rates, recovery rates can be defined in various ways. The definition for the recovery rate that I prefer is the price that would be recovered if the securities that default were sold immediately after the default took place—literally, the closing price on the day of or day after the default. The rating agencies, credit default swap market, banks, and other financial institutions, however, have alternative definitions for the recovery rate.

Moody's Investors Service, Standard & Poor's, and the credit default swap (CDS) market define the recovery rate as the price of the bond 30 days after the default event. A CDS is basically an insurance mechanism, originally conceived of as a hedging device but now used quite often as an aggressive leverage play. The protection buyer pays a quarterly fee, or premium, to the protection seller in return for a contingent payment. This payment is equal to the "insured" value of the reference, or underlying, asset should a credit event, such as a default, occur prior to the termination of the contract—usually five years. But when a company is considered to be in distress, the quarterly payment convention is usually modified with an up-front payment.

A relatively recent, but important, development in the market is entering into a CDS to protect an investment or to speculate on its credit risk in synthetic securities. No longer must an investor own the actual security to buy or sell protection on it. When Delphi Corporation went bankrupt in the fall of 2005, it had bonds outstanding with a face value of $2 billion. Surprisingly, the amount of protection that was purchased and that investors sought to recover was $28 billion, compared with the $2 billion in the underlying.

In the case of Delphi, the investment banks agreed to participate in a Dutch auction to determine the price, or the recovery rate, of the bonds. As a result, during the 30-day postdefault period, a great deal of uncertainty surrounded the recovery rate of Delphi's bonds. The price went from $620 per $1,000 par value at the time of bankruptcy to as high as $740, back to $530, and finally settling at $630—close to the price at the time of bankruptcy. This type of speculation surrounding default events and recovery rates is adding to the uncertainty in the markets and forcing innovative responses to unforeseen circumstances.

Banks and other institutions calculate the recovery rate in yet another way. They define the recovery rate as the "ultimate recovery," which is the price of a security at the time a company emerges from its restructuring period, or from Chapter 11. This period averages about 18 months in the United States. When a company comes out of bankruptcy, as long as it reorganizes successfully under Chapter 11, its securities trade in the market until they are exchanged for new securities.

Little rigorous analysis has been done on what happens to the recovery rate over the credit cycle. Most models assume a fixed recovery rate. Indeed, the CDS market assumes a fixed rate. Most of the investment banks also use a fixed recovery rate, typically 40 cents on the dollar, which is the average price at default. This happens to be the price that I and others have calculated as the historical average recovery rate at the time of default.

Previous Research

Many academics and practitioners have written about credit models and default models and their assumptions about the relationship between the probability of default (PD) and the recovery rate (RR). PD and RR are absolutely critical variables for the credit markets and certainly for banks seeking to comply with Basel II. The first-generation structural models, such as the Merton model and its subsequent adjustments by a number of academics, treat RR as an endogenous variable that depends on the structural characteristics of the defaulted company. In these models, PD and RR are inversely related, at least theoretically.

The second-generation structural models, such as the one made into a popular credit tool by KMV Corporation, now owned by Moody's, treats RR as an exogenous variable independent of a company's asset value. In these models, PD and RR are independent. Next are the reduced-form models, which do not look at structural relationships but at the relationship between the recovery rate and a number of variables. Almost all of these models assume independence between PD and RR. The value-at-risk models that appeared in the late 1990s definitely assume independence between RR and PD and treat RR as constant or stochastic. More recent contributions to the literature have begun to question this independence. These models treat RR as stochastic, depending on a macro or supply factor, and consider PD and RR to be correlated, usually in a negative way.

The intuition that led to these latest studies is that default rates and recovery rates can be expected to vary over time in an inverse relationship. But why is it that when default rates are high, recovery rates are generally low and vice versa? In Altman, Brady, Resti, and Sironi (2003, 2005), we postulated that it was simply the supply and demand in the financial markets for the defaulted securities themselves that drive a security's price at any point in time. Likewise, we postulated that the state of the economy affects the supply and demand for a defaulted security as well as the overall supply and demand forces in the markets. Also affecting the supply and demand of a distressed security is the prospect for the success of the issuing company's Chapter 11 reorganization plan, given certain economic and market conditions.

Empirical Test of Default and Recovery Rates

Our empirical test used a database of more than 1,000 defaulted bonds. This database is maintained on a regular basis at the NYU Stern School of Business at the Salomon Center. We ran regressions using the database to observe the dollar-weighted recovery rate vis-à-vis the dollar-weighted default rate. The first

Figure 4   Dollar-Weighted Average Recovery Rates to Dollar-Weighted Average Default Rates, 1982–2005

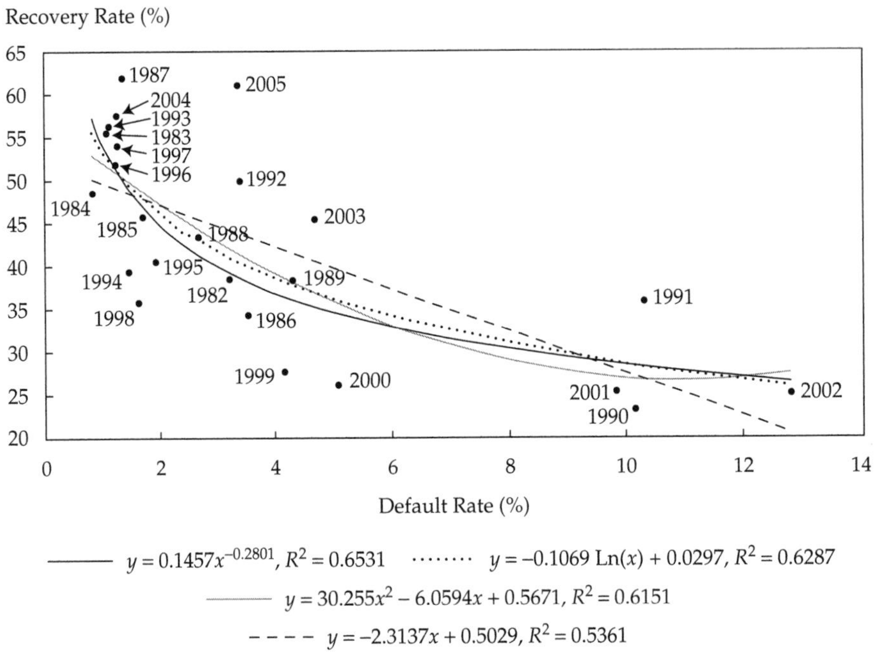

Recovery Rate (%)

$$y = 0.1457x^{-0.2801}, R^2 = 0.6531 \qquad y = -0.1069 \ln(x) + 0.0297, R^2 = 0.6287$$

$$y = 30.255x^2 - 6.0594x + 0.5671, R^2 = 0.6151$$

$$y = -2.3137x + 0.5029, R^2 = 0.5361$$

Source: Based on Altman, Brady, Resti, and Sironi (2005).

iteration of the test was a univariate analysis. The independent, or explanatory, variable was DR (default rate), and the dependent variable was RR. We ran four regressions in the first iteration—simple linear, loglinear, quadratic, and power functions. We found, as expected, a significant inverse relationship.

Figure 4 graphs the association between RR and DR from 1982 to 2005. The lines shown on the graph represent the four regressions in the first iteration of our test. The high-default periods of 1990, 1991, 2001, and 2002 are found in the lower right-hand quadrant. In almost all cases, with the one slight anomaly being in 1991, default rates were high (10–13 percent) and recovery rates were historically low (about 25 cents on the dollar). The data for 1993, 1996, and 1997 are found in the upper-left quadrant. Recovery rates were high in these years, and default rates were low. The R^2, or coefficient of determination, of the four regression lines shown in Figure 4 ranges from 54 to 65 percent. For a single variable to explain such a high percentage of the variation in another variable is statistically very significant.

The explanation for the inverse, but correlated, relationship between RR and DR is rather intuitive. When an industry hits hard times, many companies within that industry simultaneously fall on hard times. These companies are often forced to compete against each other when liquidating their assets so that the value of the assets is driven down and, ultimately, so is the recovery rate. For example, when several airlines file for bankruptcy at the same time, the resale value of their planes is much lower than under normal conditions. In 2001 and 2002, this exact situation occurred, not only with widespread failures within a single industry but also across many industries.

Notice the data points for 2003, 2004, and 2005. The model was reasonably successful at forecasting the recovery rate in 2003 and 2004. Then, in 2005, the forecasting ability of the model faltered. Although the default rate was a relatively low 3.37 percent and the recovery rate was a relatively high 61 cents on the dollar, 2005 was substantially off the regression line.

We believe 2005 was an anomaly for several reasons. First, the market was being affected by a tremendous amount of liquidity. Even though distressed-debt managers pursue other strategies, such as international, emerging equity, and rescue financing, their basic business is to buy and sell defaulted and distressed securities. Thus, because the default rate was low in 2005, the demand was that much heavier for any securities that entered the distressed market. Second, the default rate rose from 1.25 percent in 2004 to 3.37 percent in 2005. Any time the independent variable in a regression model spikes, the forecasting power of the model is weakened because the regression acts as a smoothing device for the historical relationship. Third, an unusually large amount of *secured* debt, both bonds and loans, defaulted in 2005. Because the average price of a secured security was high, the average recovery rate for the year was pushed higher than it otherwise would have been.

Although in 2005 our model performed poorly and it appears it will also do so in 2006, we continue to believe it has merit, particularly when the market returns to a more normal period based on company and market fundamentals. The forecasting ability of a model is, of course, quite important. The ability to forecast the recovery rate by estimating the default rate provides a tool for fund managers to value the individual securities in the market and for company managers to estimate the market value of their company both as a going concern and on the chopping block.

In the second iteration of our test, we used a multivariate analysis. This model incorporates other demand and supply factors, in addition to the default rate on high-yield bonds, the outstanding amount of high-yield or defaulted bonds, and the Altman NYU Salomon Center Index of Defaulted Bonds. The model also considers several macro factors, such as the level of and change in GDP and the S&P 500 Index. We found that the supply and demand variables explain about 90 percent of the bond recovery rate.

One variable that is critical in determining the recovery rate of a company's securities is the company's capital structure. Ironically, if a company has only senior bonds in its capital structure, that is bad news. A better investment strategy is to buy the senior securities of a company with a lot of subordinated debt. The holder of the senior debt is thus not at the bottom of the food chain. Subordinated debt in this instance is good news because a company with a complex capital structure probably has substantial assets financed by all the debt it issued. As a result, the likelihood of recovery on the senior debt is higher with the subordinated debt than without it.

Macro issues, although less explanatory, should not be ignored. Based on the experience of the past two U.S. recessions, one in the 1989–90 period and the other in 2001, high default rates in the high-yield bond market and the leveraged loan market were actually a leading indicator for the economy. On the surface, this finding seems to be counterintuitive. The more logical relationship might be that when the economy is growing, default rates are low, and when the economy tanks, default rates are high. So, the expectation would be for high default rates to be either a coincidental or lagging indicator vis-à-vis GDP. In fact, in these past two recessions, the default rate, measured in dollar-denominated terms, began to increase two to three years before the onset of the recessionary period.

Industries Vulnerable to Default

Several industries may be quite vulnerable to a high risk of default in the current environment. There is no secret about the plight of the automotive industry. Most of the auto parts manufacturers are already in bankruptcy, such as Dana Corporation and Delphi. Although not yet in Chapter 11, most of the other companies are in tough shape in terms of their costs as well as their ability to pass along the costs to the struggling auto manufacturers. The automotive industry encompasses many small companies and is likely to have more defaults.

Another industry to watch is the packaging industry—pulp, paper, and packaging. The economics in the industry are shaky, and the industry should see an increase in defaults. The commodity chemicals industry is making a bit of a comeback but probably still has some problems to overcome. And looking shaky again is the movie industry, which had a series of bankruptcies in the early 2000s that were refinanced (via LBOs) and resold.

Another round of telecom distress may also be ahead because of a huge amount of new leveraged financing in this industry. Although this round of financing is backed by better financial planning, the industry may experience more defaults.

The airline industry, of course, poses a perennial problem. And another industry perennially "in the soup" is retail, whose already strained margins may be devastated by any movement toward recession.

Conclusion

Default rates are still relatively low. The economy once perking along now shows signs of a slowdown, and the forces for a "perfect storm" are building on the horizon and are likely to batter the high-yield market in 2007 or 2008. Be careful. The markets are frothy. The yield spread required by investors in this market has, over the past 18 months, been ridiculously low compared with the risks. And this high-wire act continues as yield spreads remain far more than 100 bps below their historical average, even in the midst of new issue supply dominated by low-credit-quality deals.

This presentation comes from Defining, Measuring, and Managing Uncertainty: The CFA Institute Risk Symposium held in New York City on 22–23 February 2006.

References

Altman, Edward I. 2006. "Estimating Default Probabilities of Corporate Bonds over Various Investment Horizons." *CFA Institute Conference Proceedings Quarterly*, vol. 23, no. 1 (March):65–71.

Altman, Edward I., Brooks Brady, Andrea Resti, and Andrea Sironi. 2003. "The Link between Default and Recovery Rates: Theory, Empirical Evidence, and Implications." Working paper, NYU Salomon Center.

———. 2005. "The Link between Default and Recovery Rates: Theory, Empirical Evidence, and Implications." *Journal of Business*, vol. 78, no. 6 (November):2203–2227.

More from Edward I. Altman

This section presents the speaker's lively question and answer session with the conference audience.

Question: What is the likelihood that GM will enter bankruptcy?

Altman: My Z-score model currently rates GM as a CCC+ company (see, for example, Altman 2006). Based on work I and others did in the late 1980s using data from the rating agencies to generate default (mortality) probability tables, I would say the likelihood of a default by GM within one year is 15–20 percent and within five years, 47 percent. The CDS market is putting the odds at 23 percent for a bankruptcy within one year and 73 percent within five years, although this estimate was made before the announcement that Cerberus Capital Management agreed to purchase a majority stake in General Motors Acceptance Corporation.

Although my model's prognostications are not as dire as those of the CDS market, the current situation represents a sea change from that of just one year ago, when the topic was whether GM would be downgraded from investment grade to noninvestment grade.

Can GM turn it around? Absolutely, but management has to move quickly. One of the lessons we have learned about bankruptcy and risk is that companies, particularly large ones, face a great struggle in turning around their fortunes, particularly if the old management remains in place. The challenge for the old regime is the psychological hurdle of selling the assets they bought and firing the people they hired. If new management is brought in, a company stands a better chance of being turned around. But a bankruptcy, if it is going to occur, will occur more quickly under new management. Old management will protract the decision for bankruptcy as long as possible.

Question: When you first defined distressed debt, why did you adopt an additive rather than a multiplicative function?

Altman: First, an additive function is easier to interpret. Second, I observed that when a company issues debt and the spread it has to pay is greater than 10 percent above its risk-free rate, then that company is in trouble. Even if interest rates are relatively low, such as 3 or 4 percent, that means the company is borrowing at 14 percent. Given the typical profit margins of these companies, such a high interest rate will create a great deal of financial stress.

I've also learned over the years that when something works well, it is tough to make a change. And it doesn't make sense to change in this case because if we went to a different model, such as the multiplicative model, we would lose the time series that we have accumulated under the additive model.

That said, however, I believe a multiplicative model would work just as well. We have experimented a bit with a multiplicative model and have not found any meaningful differences between the two approaches.

The Evolving CDO Market

DOUGLAS LUCAS

The collateralized debt obligation (CDO) market has developed markedly in sophistication and complexity since the emergence of the first CDO in 1987. Because of this complexity, a way to categorize, and hence to understand, various CDO structures is needed. Equally important are understanding the benefits of attaining leverage in a portfolio via the CDO structure and CDO equity as well as the analysis of default correlation in credit portfolios.

Since the first collateralized debt obligation (CDO) was issued in 1987, the CDO instrument has developed into both a significant opportunity and a tremendous challenge for analysts and investors. A number of characteristics define a deal's structure and ultimately its risk-adjusted return. The structure can be cash or synthetic; credit protection can come from cash flow or market-value mechanisms; and the underlying collateral portfolio can be static or managed. In addition, another defining characteristic comes from the purpose for issuing a particular CDO: to remove assets from the sponsoring organization's balance sheet (a "balance sheet" purpose), to gather together and manage assets (an "arbitrage" purpose), or to facilitate the issuance of cheap equity-like capital (an "origination" purpose). Each CDO combines these characteristics—and more—in a distinctive structure that creates a unique analytical challenge in estimating the CDO's value and expected return.

> Improved credit features have kept investors interested in CDO debt, and fundamental characteristics have kept investors interested in CDO equity.

In this presentation, I will review the main issues related to cash CDOs: typical deal structures, credit quality, the virtues of CDO equity, conflicts of interest on the part of sponsoring organizations, default correlation, and the role historical data can play in modeling default rates.

Douglas Lucas is executive director and head of CDO research at UBS, New York City.

Cash CDO Background

The first CDO was issued on 29 September 1987 by Imperial Savings Association. The deal was managed by Caywood Christian (a subsidiary of Imperial), arranged by Drexel Burnham, and rated by Standard & Poor's. The structure's collateral, or underlying assets, was high-yield bonds, so the deal more specifically was a collateralized bond obligation (CBO). The collateral's cash flow to the CBO tranches was sequential pay. The deal used a market-value credit structure and was done for balance sheet purposes.

Since that modest beginning nearly 20 years ago, the CDO market has evolved into an assortment of complex structures with a confusing array of names. Very different names refer to the same type of CDO, and very similar sounding names refer to quite dissimilar CDO structures.

The best way to dispel confusion and understand the different types of CDOs is to analyze a CDO based on four attributes: the CDO's underlying assets, the liabilities of the CDO, the purpose of the CDO, and the CDO's credit structure. The following framework encompasses any CDO that has been created to date.

Assets

The collateral underlying a cash CDO falls into one of six primary categories: high-yield loans, high-yield bonds, high-grade structured finance, mezzanine structured finance, capital notes, and emerging market debt.

As mentioned earlier, the underlying assets of the first CDO were high-yield bonds. Distressed loans were introduced as collateral in 1988, and performing loans were introduced a year later, in 1989. CDOs backed by bank loans are more specifically known as collateralized loan obligations (CLOs).

By 1995, residential mortgage-backed securities (RMBS), commercial mortgage-backed securities (CMBS), asset-backed securities (ABS), and other structured-finance assets had been used as collateral for CDOs. Until 1995, annual issuance in the CDO market had never exceeded $2 billion, so even at this very low volume, the CDO structure already encompassed a great deal of asset diversification.

The increase in issuance between 1995 and 2000 was mainly propelled by the broader acceptance of high-yield bonds as CDO collateral. **Figure 1** shows a dip in CDO issuance from 2000 to 2002, attributable to negative conditions in the corporate credit market. When CDO issuance bounced back after 2002, it was not because investors became more comfortable with high-yield bonds but because high-yield loans became more important as assets underlying CDOs.

Figure 1   Annual Cash CDO Issuance, 1987–2005

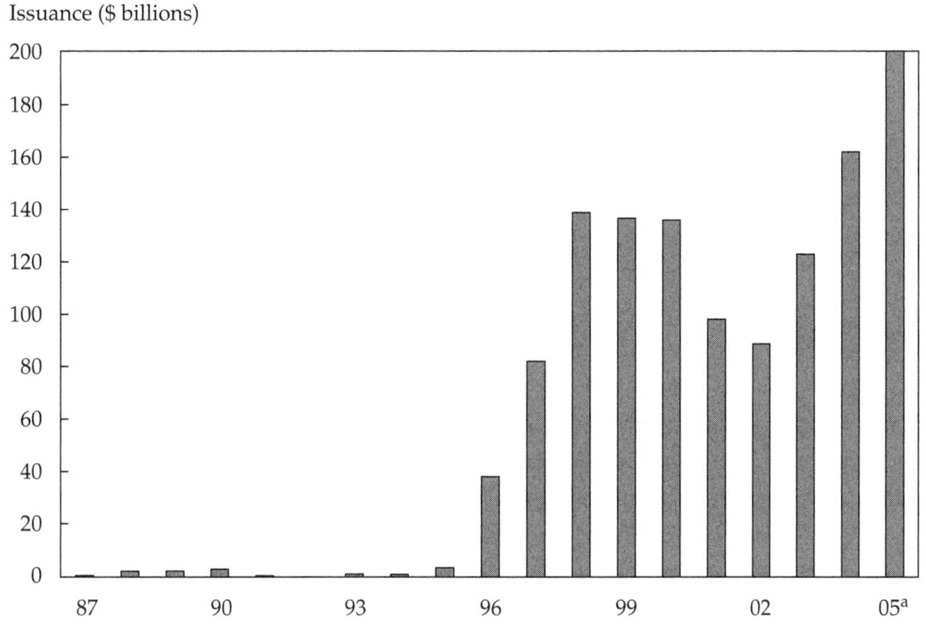

Issuance ($ billions)

ªIssuance for 2005 reached $280 billion.

Today, about half of cash CDOs are backed by high-yield loans, another 40 percent are backed by structured-finance assets, and 10 percent are backed by such asset classes as emerging market bonds, corporates, sovereigns, bank capital notes, and so forth.

Liabilities

All CDOs make use of tranching to place their debt and equity obligations in strict seniority to one another—from the most senior tranche, typically rated AAA, to the unrated equity tranche. Beyond that, a CDO's tranches can incorporate various structures, such as a fixed- or floating-rate coupon, a pay-in-kind (PIK) facility, short-term or long-term debt, a guarantee by a monoline insurance company (i.e., insurer of debt), and a delayed-draw or revolving note.

For example, a PIK facility allows the CDO to pay a current coupon with an increase in the par value of the CDO note in lieu of a cash payment. A delayed-draw note allows the CDO to issue notes and receive proceeds after a deal has closed in return for the payment of a commitment fee by the investor. And the revolving note is similar to the delayed-draw note except that proceeds can be repaid and redrawn upon as CDO assets mature and are repurchased.

Purpose

The third attribute that is important in evaluating a CDO is the purpose underlying its issuance. The two most common are balance sheet and arbitrage purposes. A third, less common, purpose is one that I call "origination."

A balance sheet purpose for issuing a CDO occurs when the sponsoring organization wishes to remove securitizable assets from its balance sheet to reduce required regulatory or economic capital or achieve cheaper funding costs. In this situation, the sponsoring party sells assets to the CDO.

The sponsoring organization of a CDO with an arbitrage purpose, typically an asset manager, is motivated by the desire to add assets under management. The investors in this type of CDO wish to obtain asset management services. The assets underlying the CDO are purchased in the marketplace.

In the case of an "origination" purpose for a CDO's issuance, collateral assets are originated specifically to be purchased by the CDO. In particular, this situation occurs when bank capital notes from a large number of smaller-sized banks are sold to a CDO coincidentally with its issuance. The collateral-issuing banks participate in order to gain cheap equity-like funding from the CDO structure.

Credit Structure

The fourth, and final, structural attribute of a CDO is whether it has a market-value or cash flow credit structure. In the former, CDO debt tranches gain their credit quality by ensuring that they can be retired by the sale of CDO assets. The market value of CDO assets must at all times be a multiple of CDO debt par. If the market-value multiple is violated, CDO assets are sold and CDO debt is retired.

In the more typical cash flow structure, after-default cash flow from the collateral portfolio is expected to repay CDO notes, which, of course, relies on assessment of how bad defaults and recoveries on the CDO's underlying assets can be. Performance triggers are in place to divert cash flow from the equity tranche to the debt tranches in order to increase the latter's credit quality.

Why CDOs Exist

Investor demand for CDOs is strong for a variety of reasons. One explanation is revealed by the butcher analogy: A butcher who buys chickens can either sell the birds whole or cut them into pieces. It turns out that selling chicken parts is a good deal for everyone concerned. The sum of the prices for the individual pieces is higher than the price the butcher would receive for selling a whole bird, and the purchaser gets to select a specific cut of chicken suitable to his or her tastes. Similar to the butcher, the CDO structure divides and distributes the risk of the underlying collateral to investors with differing appetites for risk. A typical CDO structure offers investment opportunities that range from AAA to BBB (or lower) debt instruments and a nonrated residual cash flow equity instrument—literally, something for everyone.

A second reason investor demand for CDO issues is strong is that buyers of CDO equity receive nonrecourse term financing with leveraged exposure to CDO assets. CDO equity provides nonrecourse financing because CDO equityholders own stock in a remote entity—the CDO—and are not liable for the losses of that entity. Asset financing is in place for up to 15 years, during which time it cannot be withdrawn, the rate cannot change, and under the cash flow credit structure, a forced liquidation of collateral will not occur. CDO debtholders provide the financing for the equityholders, and the equityholders sustain the risk of collateral asset payment delays and credit losses. Equityholders own a leveraged position in the assets of the CDO and receive all cash flows in excess of the debt tranche requirements and thus collect all the upside on the CDO's assets.

Contrast the investor's position just described with the comparable, but much less favorable, alternative of establishing a short-term secured financing arrangement with a local bank. In such an arrangement, financing rates can fluctuate and higher levels of security (or collateral) can be demanded by the lender. Furthermore, financing can be pulled at any time. Collateral can also be sold to meet what are effectively margin calls should the value of the collateral drop below a designated level. Lastly, the lender has recourse to the borrower if the collateral is insufficient to extinguish the bank debt. Clearly, CDO equity offers much more advantageous terms to the investor.

Debt investors like CDOs because they offer high rating-adjusted yields. The higher yield is primarily because of the liquidity premium and the inherent complexities of the CDO structure.

Another reason investors are interested in CDOs is because of the exposure they provide to a diversified portfolio of collateral, often of hard-to-acquire assets, such as bank loans and ABS assets. This characteristic is particularly touted in sales pitches to high-net-worth individuals and family offices—pitches heavily weighted toward the benefits of CDO equity.

Table 1 lists the most common types of cash CDOs issued in 2005. Arbitrage deals with a cash flow credit structure were by far the most common type of CDO, with high-yield loans being the asset class most frequently used as collateral. The table divides the CDOs that are backed by structured-finance (SF) products—ABS, CMBS, and RMBS—into high-grade and mezzanine credit quality. Typically, the collateral in a high-grade SF CDO is rated AAA to A, with an average rating of AA. Mezzanine SF CDOs are generally backed by A to BB

Table 1   U.S. Cash CDO Issuance, 2005

Purpose	Credit Structure	Assets	Share
Arbitrage	Cash flow	High-yield loans	30%
Arbitrage	Cash flow	High-grade structured finance	25
Arbitrage	Cash flow	Mezzanine structured finance	22
Arbitrage	Cash flow	Bonds, other	10
Origination	Cash flow	Capital notes	5
Balance sheet	Cash flow	Various	4
Arbitrage	Market value	Various	4

Table 2   Typical Arbitrage Cash Flow CDOs, 2005

Tranche	Percentage of Capital Structure	Rating	Coupon
CLO tranche structure			
Class A	77.5%	AAA	LIBOR + 26 bps
Class B	9.0	A	LIBOR + 75 bps
Class C	2.75	BBB	LIBOR + 180 bps
Class D	2.75	BB	LIBOR + 475 bps
Preferred shares	8.0	NR	Residual cash flow
High-grade structured-finance CDO tranche structure			
Class A	85%	AAA	LIBOR + 27 bps
Class B	8	AAA	LIBOR + 45 bps
Class C	6	AA	LIBOR + 60 bps
Class D	2	BBB	LIBOR + 270 bps
Preferred shares	1	NR	Residual cash flow
Mezzanine structured-finance CDO tranche structure			
Class A	55%	AAA	LIBOR + 27 bps
Class B	23	AAA	LIBOR + 45 bps
Class C	8	AA	LIBOR + 57 bps
Class D	5	A	LIBOR + 145 bps
Class E	5	BBB	LIBOR + 270 bps
Preferred shares	4	NR	Residual cash flow

assets, and they average BBB. Arbitrage cash flow CDOs represented 87 percent of total CDO issuance in 2005.

Example capital structures for the three most common types of CDOs are outlined in **Table 2.** Note that the preferred shares, or equity, tranche fluctuates among the deals from 8 percent in the CLO to 1 percent in the high-grade SF CDO to 4 percent in the mezzanine SF CDO. The higher the credit quality of the underlying assets, the smaller the equity tranche as a percentage of the total capital structure and the larger the AAA debt tranche.

Credit Quality

CDO debt credit quality is essentially a balancing act between asset risk and CDO structural protection. Neither the collateral nor the level of subordination alone dictates whether the CDO is worthy of investment for a given investor. Some of the best performing CDOs have been collateralized with the weakest credit quality assets. For example, CLOs backed by distressed loans have historically been top performers in the CDO market because rating agencies have required that a great deal of credit protection be built into the structure of these deals. The point is that CDO debt credit quality is determined by both asset risks and structural protections.

The primary risks associated with CDO collateral are defaults and recoveries following defaults. A high rate of default combined with a low rate of recovery can result from an undiversified portfolio, such as a portfolio with a concentration in a few industries or a few issuers. CDOs typically have stringent diversity requirements.

Two main types of structural protection exist for the cash flow CDO investor. One is related to subordination, and the other, to cash flow diversion. Subordination affects credit quality via the sequential application of collateral interest. The interest earned on collateral is applied first to senior tranches, then to junior tranches, and finally to equity. Likewise, subordination drives the sequential application of collateral principal to CDO tranches.

CDO debtholders are also protected by cash flow diversion via two coverage tests: the over-collateralization (OC) test and the interest coverage (IC) test. The OC test compares the par amount of performing assets with the outstanding balance of CDO debt. The result should reach a certain percentage depending on the type of collateral the CDO holds. Similarly, the IC test compares the interest generated by CDO assets with the interest payable on CDO debt. If the CDO fails either test, cash flow is diverted from the equity tranche and used to pay down debt-tranche holders until the failed test is cured. Only when the tests are again in compliance is cash flow allowed to go to the equity tranche.

Residual cash flow (i.e., cash flow not required to service CDO debt) has been allocated two ways in CDO structures. In the manner of the "old school," as practiced between 1987 and 1995, the residual was used either to buy more collateral or to pay down the debt tranches of the CDO. Excess cash flow in the "new school" approach, appearing after 1995, is paid out to equityholders.

The new school approach opens the door to a fundamental conflict between equityholders and debtholders. Under the old school approach, equityholders were not paid anything until all the CDO debt was retired, so equityholders, like debtholders, cared about the long-term credit quality of the collateral portfolio. Since 1995, some deals have been structured to generate large collateral interest cash flow. So, the cash flow in excess of that necessary to pay debt interest can be paid to the equity tranche, which significantly shortens its average life compared with those of the debt tranches, particularly in a CDO with high-yield collateral.

Once a seasoned CDO experiences a few defaults in the collateral portfolio and is in danger of failing the OC test because those defaulting assets are no longer counted in the numerator of the test ratio, the manager is faced with a potential conflict of interest. Suppose that several other assets in the collateral pool are trading at 30 cents on the dollar. Perhaps in a total-return portfolio, these assets would be sold and more expensive assets purchased. In the case of a CDO, however, selling these assets could cause the CDO to fail the OC test because the numerator of the test ratio would be reduced by the difference in the par value of the assets sold and that of the more expensive assets purchased.

Because the CDO manager typically owns some of the CDO's equity, the manager has a huge incentive to hold onto underperforming assets to keep cash flowing to the equity class. The opposite (a par-building trade) can also occur. The manager can sell an asset that is trading at par to buy an asset that is trading at 50 cents on the dollar, thus inflating the numerator in the OC test.

Some managers, particularly in 2000, 2001, and 2002, played both of these tricks. For example, an analyst at Standard & Poor's relates a story of a manager whose purchase of assets at 6 cents on the dollar in two CDOs caused the manager, as equity investor, to receive $2.5 million (versus zero) in cash flow in a single quarter. This type of abuse resulted in different levels of performance for different types of CDOs, hitting the high-yield CBOs particularly hard.

In the 2002 credit crunch, CBOs suffered a much worse fate than CLOs, with a commensurately large difference in the rate of downgrades between the two: 46 percent of CBOs were downgraded in 2002 compared with 8 percent of CLOs and 3 percent of structured-finance CDOs. The difference in the rate of downgrades between high-yield bond and high-yield loan CDOs is highlighted in **Table 3.**

Table 3 Cumulative Tranche Downgrades through December 2004 by Issuance Year

Instrument	1997	1998	1999	2000	2001
CBOs of high-yield bonds	95%	87%	87%	65%	29%
CLOs of high-yield loans	57	50	3	9	3

The reaction of rating agencies and investors was to seek change in CDO terms and structures. In 2003, investors demanded and got better credit quality CDO assets, higher-rated CDO assets, lower single-name risk limits, and prohibitions on investment in certain industries and certain ratings. Likewise, tougher rules on cash flow diversion were instituted so that haircuts for defaulted, downgraded, or cheap assets are now imposed in the OC test. A cap was also put on the cash that was distributable to the equity tranche, directing any excess cash to either pay down debtholders or to purchase more collateral. And lastly, the changes in 2003 resulted in higher subordination.

These improved credit features have kept investors interested in CDO debt, and fundamental characteristics have kept investors interested in CDO equity.

Virtues of CDO Equity

CDO equity has four positive attributes: Investors in the equity tranche (1) receive nonrecourse term financing (discussed earlier), (2) may earn a significant return even when CDO debtholders have lower-than-expected returns, (3) hold two options that further increase the value of their investment, and (4) hold a security with the potential to be part of a defensive investment strategy.[1]

Forgiving Nature of CDO Financing

A quick test demonstrates how forgiving the CDO cash flow structure can be to equityholders. Cash flows to the equity tranche and to the lowest debt tranche—BB debt—of a particular CLO structure were compared under varying default scenarios. In the test, both tranches were stressed by increasingly severe constant annual default rates (CDRs). Loan recoveries were set at 65 percent of par. In every CDR scenario, both tranches were priced to yield 15 percent. **Figure 2** shows that equity immediately begins losing value with increases in CDR. The debt tranche is unaffected until CDR reaches 6 percent. But even though debt is impaired, equity still has significant net present value because equity receives early distributions before the OC trigger is tripped and the structure denies cash flow to equity. In fact, above 10 percent CDR, equity has a higher return than debt. The bottom line is that CDO equity is not quite as subordinate as one might think.

---

[1] For more information on CDO equity, see UBS (2004a).

Figure 2   Equity and BB Debt Priced to Yield 15 Percent

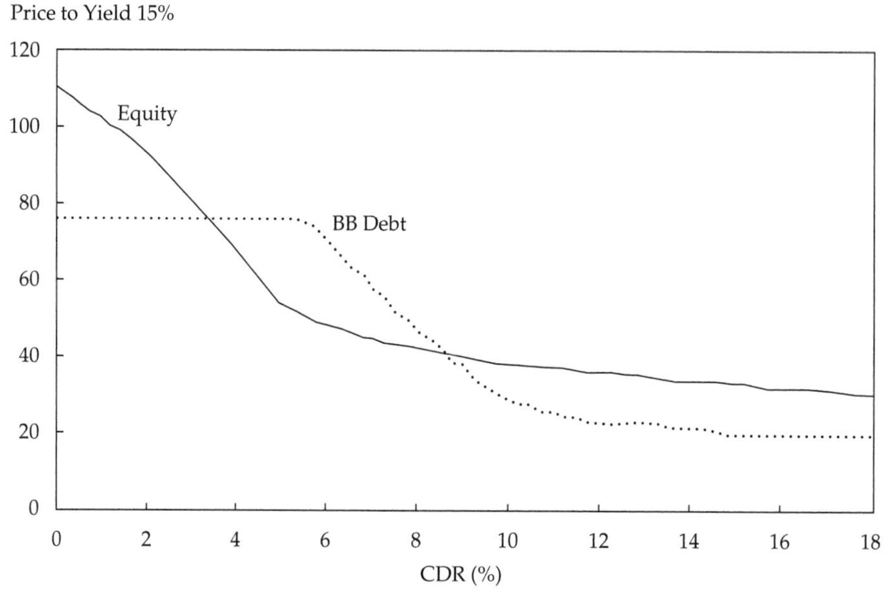

CDO Options

CDO equityholders also hold options on the *market value* of CDO collateral and on the *after-default cash flows* of those assets. The simpler to understand of the two is the market-value option. After a noncall period, CDO collateral can be liquidated. If proceeds exceed the cost of repaying debt and other expenses, equityholders benefit dollar-for-dollar. In fact, the option can be exercised by selling individual assets as well as by liquidating and unwinding the entire CDO. Otherwise, the market value of CDO collateral does not affect CDO equity distributions. In situations where the market value of the CDO portfolio has deteriorated, equityholders continue to receive payments, provided coverage tests are not violated.

The call option on the after-default cash flows of the collateral portfolio can be exercised by simply waiting to see how actual defaults and coverage tests interact to produce equity cash flow. If cash flow exceeds debt requirements, the equity tranche will gain dollar-for-dollar. If cash flow is insufficient to meet debt requirements, equity return is the same whether the amount of debt-service shortfall is great or small. The strike price of the market-value option is the amount necessary to retire CDO debt, and the strike price of the option on after-default cash flows is the amount required to service debt until the CDO fails the OC test.

As an optionholder, the CDO equity class is long volatility. The greater the market risk and the after-default cash flow risk of the underlying assets

Figure 3   After-Default Cash Flow Volatility

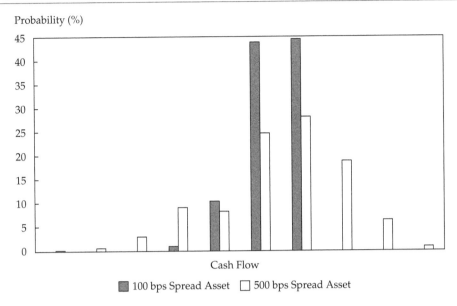

of the CDO, the greater potential benefit to the equityholder. **Figure 3** compares the after-default cash flow volatility of two collateral portfolios. The lower-quality collateral (Treasuries plus 500 bps) has higher volatility—that is, a wider distribution—of after-default cash flows (higher probability of large default losses and of higher cash flows). The higher-quality collateral portfolio (Treasuries plus 100 bps) has a narrower distribution. If the strike price, equal to the debt service, is $96, the riskier collateral has a greater probability of exceeding the strike price and providing a higher return for equityholders.

Defensive Investment Strategy

The investor who seeks a defensive investment strategy can benefit from the leverage provided by CDO equity. The investor has a choice: either invest fully on an unleveraged basis in the asset class that comprises the CDO collateral, such as an ABS or high-yield loans, or invest a smaller amount on a leveraged basis in CDO equity with the remaining funds invested in a safe-harbor instrument, such as AAA LIBOR floaters. For the same total initial investment, the two choices offer almost equal upside but a cushioned downside for the CDO equity/defensive asset combination.

Figure 4   Zero and Extreme Positive Default Correlation: 10 Credits, 10 Percent Default
Probability

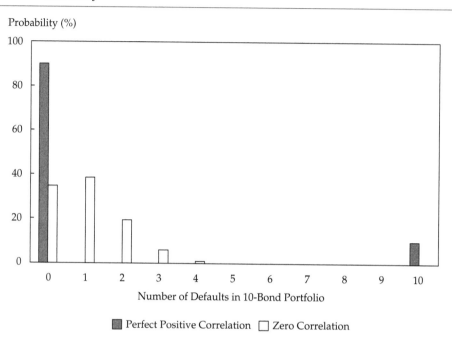

Default Correlation

Default correlation is the phenomenon that an obligor's default probability is affected by whether another obligor has defaulted.[2] **Figure 4** illustrates the contrasting scenarios of extreme positive default correlation and zero default correlation.

Suppose that 10 bonds from different obligors each have a 10 percent probability of default over a given period. This knowledge alone provides little information on the potential behavior of the portfolio. Perhaps, on the one hand, the relationship among the bonds is such that if one of the bonds defaults, they all default—a case of extreme positive correlation shown in Figure 4 by the distribution indicated by the two gray bars. Thus, a 90 percent chance exists that none of the 10 bonds default and a 10 percent chance, that they all default.

Perhaps, on the other hand, the bonds in the portfolio have zero default correlation, which means that the default experience for the bonds is similar to the results of rolling a 10-sided die 10 times and can be illustrated by the distribution depicted by the white bars in Figure 4.

---

[2] For more information on this topic, see UBS (2004b).

Figure 5   U.S. Corporate Rolling-Average Annual Default Rate, 1920–2003

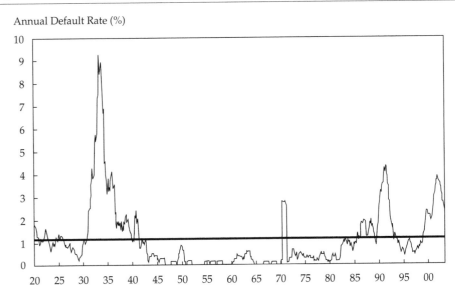

Figure 4 illustrates an important attribute of default correlation: Default correlation causes default-rate (i.e., the actual experienced rate of default) variability, as shown by the fact that the gray bars in Figure 4, illustrating extreme positive default correlation, are much more dispersed than the white bars, representing zero default correlation.

Figure 5 graphs the rolling-average 12-month default rate for U.S. corporate debt rated by Moody's Investors Service. The average default rate since 1920 has been 1.1 percent a year. People often make the assumption that default probability equals the long-term average default rate. So, when the actual default rate rises to 9 percent or drops to zero, they see it as an indication that default correlation exists because, as already mentioned, the variability of actual default rates around default probability indicates the presence of default correlation.

In Figure 5, the absolute difference between default probability (the average default rate) and the actual default rate averages roughly 1 percent. But this calculation depends on the assumption that the probability of default is constant. Instead, one could assume that the probability of default changes from year to year. One simple model is that default probability over the next 12 months equals the actual default rate of the previous 12 months. For example, in 1933 when 9 percent of corporate bond issuers in the United States defaulted, investors could have reasonably estimated default probability in 1934 at 9 percent. Under the assumption that default probability equals the actual default rate of the preceding year, the average absolute difference between default probability and actual default rate is reduced to 0.5 percent.

The effect of default correlation has been diminished merely because a better estimate of default probability has been used. Thus, if one were better able to predict default probability, there would be even less observed default correlation. And if one were perfect at predicting default probability, there would be no default correlation. The calculation of default correlation depends on the estimate of default probability, and default correlation only exists if one pretends that default probability does not vary. The alternative way to model defaults in a portfolio is to allow default probability to vary and pretend that default correlation does not exist.[3]

Consider the available sources of historical information that can be drawn upon to model default-rate and default-loss variability:

- default rates for rating cohorts formed from 1970 through 2005—for example, of all companies rated BAA on 1 January 1986, 1.33 percent defaulted in 1986, 0 percent in 1987, 1.68 percent in 1988, and 0.87 percent in 1989 (Moody's Investors Service 2005);
- year-by-year senior unsecured bond recoveries—for example, recoveries in 1991 were 51 percent of par and the standard deviation of recoveries was 25 percent.

At UBS, we like to simulate defaults in a portfolio by using actual historical default rates and actual historical recovery rates. For example, if we were looking at a diverse portfolio of BAA rated bonds with maturities of one year, we would use annual default rates from 1970 through 2005 as inputs into our simulations. Using different default rates captures the variability of default rates over time. The results of simulations using a default rate from any particular year captures the potential variability of portfolios created at that time.

Conclusion

The CDO market has evolved dramatically from its inception in 1987 with increasingly sophisticated deals. This presentation offered a way to categorize and hopefully understand the various types of CDOs that are sold today, explored the "virtues" of CDO equity, and finally, touched on the use of historical default rates to understand CDO portfolios.

This presentation comes from the Structured Credit Instruments conference held in New York City on 2 November 2005.

---

[3] The methodology was pioneered by CSFB in the mid-1990s.

References

Moody's Investors Service. 2005. *Default and Recovery Rates of Corporate Bond Issuers, 1920-2004* (January): http://www.lesechos.fr/info/medias/200050753.pdf.

UBS. 2004a. "Why Buy CDO Equity?" *CDO Insight* (31 December): http://www.iirusa.com/cdo/files/IIR_U2052_Lucas,%20Douglas%20UBS.pdf.

———. 2004b. "Default Correlation: From Definition to Proposed Solutions." *CDO Research* (11 August): http://www.defaultrisk.com/_pdf6j4/Default_Correlation_From_Dfnt_2_Prpsd_Sltns.pdf.

More from Douglas Lucas

This section presents the speaker's lively question and answer session with the conference audience.

Question: Who are the buyers of CDO equity?

Lucas: Hedge funds buy them as a way to be levered in the underlying assets via the CDO vehicle rather than via their own debt financing. Some insurance companies and banks purchase CDO equity. In the past two years, several asset managers have started funds that specialize in CDO equity.

Question: What are the internal rates of return (IRRs) for CDOs backed by the different asset classes? How do they differ?

Lucas: Prospective buyers of a CDO equity tranche are given a matrix of default rates and recoveries with an implied IRR for each scenario. But those numbers are calculated with a lot of hidden assumptions, such as the prepayment rate of underlying assets, collateral reinvestment rates, and the future path of interest rates.

The first request I received as a CDO analyst was to determine the historical return of CDO equity. There being no data, that was a very hard problem to solve. Over the years, in an attempt to address this question, analysts have computed monthly returns, Sharpe ratios, and return correlations with other assets for CDO equity. But how could monthly returns be calculated because no liquid market for CDO equity exists? These analysts were modeling the price of the CDO equity and its price volatility and then comparing it with the actual price volatility of other assets. Obviously, this is bogus.

But even if I did have historical market prices of seasoned CDO equity tranches, it would not have done me any good. CDO equity created five years ago is a product of asset spreads five years ago, CDO liability spreads five years ago, and the structure of the CDO five years ago. All of that has changed with time. Furthermore, for CDO equity that I may be offered today, I can explore asset spreads, liability spreads, and structure through cash flow modeling with a much better result than one found by reviewing how a CDO with completely different characteristics performed five years ago.

History can be helpful, however, in providing a record of the defaults and recoveries on assets like those in the CDO portfolio, which, in turn, can be put into a cash flow model of today's CDO structure. Then, I can think about which historical period provides the best proxy for my economic outlook over the next few years. This use of historical data in a current model is more instructive than the historical returns of outdated CDO structures.

Question: What information would be useful in bringing more transparency to the CDO market, especially in the middle-market loan sector?

Lucas: Transparency needs to be improved in two areas: the CDO structure itself and the underlying CDO assets. Over the past three years, great strides have been made in improving the transparency of CDOs. Intex Solutions has modeled the cash flow structure of almost all CDOs and updates their record of CDO collateral portfolios every month. Other vendors, such as Wall Street Analytics, are trying to provide the same service by using correlated default modeling. In addition, the Bond Market Association's CDO library compiles deal documents that are available to qualified investors and investment banks. As a result, I believe the transparency of CDOs, in terms of their structure, is very good.

Transparency in CDO assets is another story, particularly in the middle-market loan sector. Transparency in the middle-market sector is a real challenge primarily because the underlying transactions are private and so small that minimal data exist about them. Another example of a lack of transparency in the underlying transactions is structured-finance collateral, which is often hard to understand.

In periods of high default and distress, we've seen weaknesses exposed in certain CDO structures, particularly in managed deals. How might structures evolve to prevent this?

Actually, the solution has two parts. One involves the CDO structure, and the other involves how the CDO manager honors the CDO structure. Those are two different things. For example, I've discussed the ways the OC test can be manipulated. Many CDOs get done only because the manager purchases part of the equity tranche, which is the hardest tranche to sell. So, if a manager is willing to put his own funds into the tranche, it is easier to attract a banker.

You can point to many different people as contributing to the debacle in high-yield bond CBOs. You can point to managers who played the tricks of either avoiding the sale of depressed assets or intentionally buying depressed assets to build par. You can point to bankers who encouraged managers to buy into the equity tranche, creating the conflict of interest, because it was easier for the banker to sell CDOs in those circumstances.

You can point to the rating agencies because if the ratings had been more accurate and up to date, the arbitrage, in terms of the OC test, would not have been possible. In other words, if the manager couldn't find a B rated bond that was trading at 6 cents on the dollar because the rating agencies had already downgraded the bond to CCC, the manager would not have had the opportunity to add the depressed bond to the structure in the first place.

And you can even point to sell-side researchers who acted as cheerleaders and put the best face on everything that was happening.

Question: How are the different cash CDO structures currently trading?

Lucas: In general, spreads have narrowed a great deal over the past two to three years. Not all similarly rated tranches in different structures trade the same. For example, CLO debt trades at lower spreads than debt from SF-backed CDOs. And the spreads on CDO debt don't always follow the spreads on CDO assets. The relationship between CDO asset and CDO liability spreads is important because the difference dictates the amount of excess interest that can be thrown off by the structure, which ultimately attracts the equity investor to these deals.

As a result of the spread between assets and debt, there have been some times when it was inefficient to issue a high-grade structured-finance CDO and other times, but less often, when it was inefficient to issue a mezzanine SF CDO. By mezzanine, I mean having underlying collateral rated A to BB.

Question: Why do you believe distressed loan CLOs have performed so well?

Lucas: Even though the assets of a distressed loan CLO are obviously quite credit risky, CLO debt issues did very well because they had a lot of subordination underneath them and a lot of structural protection. Recall that the hallmark of a good deal is the balance between asset quality and structural protection. Although there have not been many of these deals—maybe six since the first one in 1988—they have done well for the debtholders.

The equityholders have also done well. Banks could move these assets at very low prices into the CDO structure and were willing to take a residual interest in the structures because of the resulting capital relief. Balance sheet CDOs are done for a couple of reasons. One is to remove the risk of the assets from the balance sheet. Some bankers were quite adept at getting rid of the riskiest assets in their portfolio.

Balance sheet deals are also done for funding reasons, such as the early middle-market loan CDOs. These deals had a lot of structural protection, and the arrangers of these CLOs were interested not so much in reducing risk but in funding loans. They made sure that the CLO structures would perform very well because the deals were important to their business and to their ability to continue making middle-market loans. Placing these loans into CLOs freed up their working capital to make more loans.

ALTERNATIVE INVESTMENTS

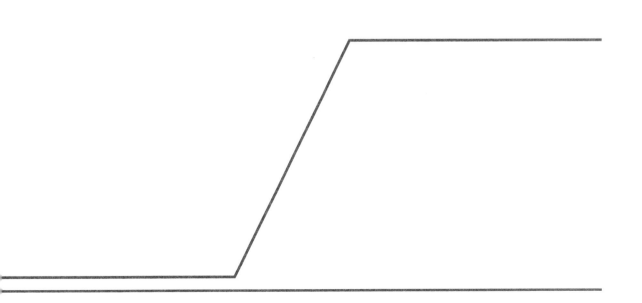

Irrational Exuberance Revisited

ROBERT J. SHILLER

Speculative bubbles have long been a feature of financial and asset markets, both in the United States and elsewhere. Although the bubble in the U.S. stock market collapsed in roughly 2000, housing prices now appear to be dramatically overvalued. Indeed, recent dramatic home price increases in the United States cannot be explained by fundamentals. Over the long run, real home prices may not increase by as much as investors expect today. Real estate is America's second largest asset class, and a new futures market now enables investors to hedge or to speculate against changes in residential home prices in 10 large U.S. cities, offering a portfolio diversification benefit provided the fledgling derivatives market flourishes.

Big market moves are historic events. And to understand historic events, a broad perspective is needed. We would not think of trying to understand the causes of World War II just in terms of changes in interest rates or inflation rates, and neither should we think of trying to understand events in the stock market in just such terms. As market observers, we need to understand more than just finance *per se*.

Understanding human psychology, culture, and institutions matters. Alan Greenspan's now famous phrase "irrational exuberance" is a good name for the variety of factors that has produced market excesses. I thought it was such a good term that in 2000 I wrote a book entitled *Irrational Exuberance.* I wish to talk about just what this term means. In particular, this presentation is about the psychology of the markets applied to the booms in the stock market in the 1990s and in the housing market just recently—essentially, a theory of bubbles based on all the perspectives I can muster from the social sciences. Finally, I will discuss new hedging vehicles for residential real estate.

> Bubbles are not purely psychological phenomena. They are an epidemic, and an epidemic requires contagion.

Robert J. Shiller is a professor at Yale University, New Haven, Connecticut.

The Psychology of Confidence

During a dinner speech on 5 December 1996, Alan Greenspan asked, "How do we know when irrational exuberance has unduly escalated asset prices?" As far as I can tell, that was the only time he ever uttered the words "irrational exuberance." He did not say there was irrational exuberance; he simply asked a question. Even though his words made no assertive statement, they spooked the markets. The Nikkei Index in Japan was open at the time and dropped 3.2 percent immediately on those words. Then, those words, and the reaction to them, spread around the world. I think the market response to his words more than the words themselves made "irrational exuberance" his most famous quote.

In the U.S. Federal Reserve's Economic Outlook of 20 October 2005, Chairman Ben Bernanke made the following statement about inflated home prices: "Although speculative activity has increased in some areas, at a national level, these price increases largely reflect strong economic fundamentals, including robust growth in jobs and incomes, low mortgage rates, steady rates of household formation, and factors that limit the expansion of housing supply in some areas." Bernanke is a very smart man, but based on this statement, he just does not get what is going on with home prices. In recent testimony, Bernanke did say that the clouds on the horizon are oil prices and home prices and that if home prices slow enough, it could weaken the economy. Note, however, no words about "bubble."

A bubble is a market situation in which news of price increases spurs investor enthusiasm. Thus, it is based on psychology and emotion. The bubble expands by psychological contagion from person to person, and this contagion is important. It brings in more and more investors who, despite doubts about fundamental value, find themselves drawn to the investment partly through envy and a gambler's excitement. Gambling behavior is part of human behavior, and anthropologists say it exists in every society and is an aspect of a human entrepreneurial spirit. My use of the word "gambler" could be provocative, but I am not criticizing gambling.

Bubbles are not purely psychological phenomena. They are an epidemic, and an epidemic requires contagion. An epidemic (bubble) can exist only if conditions favor contagion. For example, influenza, another contagious agent, tends to occur in the winter because people are inside more often than outside. Influenza is spread by droplets in the air, so when people are enclosed in a space, the contagion rate goes up. The contagion rate has to exceed the removal rate (the rate at which people recover from their illness), however, if an epidemic is to grow. One reason financial bubbles are mysterious is that their time pattern depends on the contagion rate of the enthusiasm, the spread of optimism and excitement for the market, and this contagion is hard to observe objectively.

The contagion rate is not just psychological. It depends on other things, such as monetary policy. The Fed can burst the bubble. It may not want to because of the collateral effects, but it has the opportunity to do so. Regulators in the past have stopped bubbles. After the Dutch tulip mania in 1637, authorities were aghast at what was happening and shut down the tulip markets.

I went on an expedition to find out who first defined the term "bubble." The earliest clear statement I could find was in an extraordinary book by Charles MacKay written in 1841 called *Extraordinary Popular Delusions and the Madness of Crowds,* which was a best-seller. I recommend it still today. In it, he talks about tulip mania, an event that occurred 200 years earlier. In describing the event, he uses vivid phrases: "Individuals suddenly grew rich," "A golden bait hung temptingly out before the people," and "They rushed to the tulip marts like flies around a honey-pot." As the bubble expanded, people who were not initially interested in the markets became interested, so it had elements of contagion. Then, MacKay writes about the inevitable bursting of the speculative bubble when the prices got too high. If prices get high, they are supported only by people's expectations that they will go up further, which cannot go on forever. A bubble has an inherent internal contradiction that brings it to an end. A bubble does not need any event to end it. It will end itself.

So, 1841 sounds like a long time ago, but for my scholarly perspective, I was not satisfied. I researched back to the tulip mania to find reference to a bubble. Old Dutch manuscripts of the time, however, do not include a definition of a bubble. But I did find evidence that hinted at one. A pamphlet from the year 1637, when the tulip mania bubble burst, contains a fictitious dialog between two men, Gaergoedt and Waermondt. Gaergoedt has just made a lot of money in the tulip market, and he is very proud of himself. He is talking to Waermondt, who is not in the tulip market. Gaergoedt talks expansively about the returns—10 percent, 100 percent, even 1,000 percent—trading tulips, and Waermondt is skeptical. He is worried that he is getting in too late. (Note that this was the very first big speculative bubble, and already it was obvious investors had to worry about getting in too late.) Gaergoedt just says some nonsense: "It's never too late to make a profit. You make money while sleeping."

One can picture the emotional response that Waermondt—a poor weaver who has been working all this time on his trade and never making much money—has to this kind of bragging behavior. Waermondt is uncomfortable because he knows logically that the boom might be coming to the end. He does not know what to do. Then, finally, he asks the question, "Do you know anyone who has become rich with your trade?" Gaergoedt gleefully gives him some examples. These stories seemed to convince Waermondt, and he seems ready to go into the tulip market, but he is saved by luck because Gaergoedt's wife comes in with news that the tulip market has just crashed.

That is the end of that pamphlet, but it is interesting that this writer from 1637 chose to explain the tulip mania in the form of a dialog because it illustrates the contagion as it works. It is word of mouth, person-to-person contagion. The human species is very empathetic; we feel others' feelings. The human species is also interconnected, and when we hear talk like this, it gets us emotionally involved, which is what happens in a bubble. I believe, but I cannot prove, that the writer of this pamphlet heard conversations like this in 1637 and made them the basis of the story. It is revealing of human nature. This same thing happens today.

Bubbles remain mysterious because they cannot be judged based simply on psychology. If it is just human psychology, then why don't we have a bubble all the time? That is always a difficult question. The theory of bubbles connected to the stock market has four elements:

1. precipitating factors, or what gets the bubble started;
2. amplification mechanism, the epidemic that gets the bubble to propagate;
3. cultural factors; and
4. psychological factors.

Precipitating Factors

Precipitating factors are the truly exogenous factors that begin to change the demand for stocks and start the epidemic on its path. A critical precipitating factor for the stock market boom of the late 1990s was the internet revolution. In the late 1990s, the internet was such a spectacular technological advance that it made people believe they were entering a "new era" and allowed them to think that stock prices could really soar.

Amplification Mechanism

The amplification mechanism propels the precipitating factors into irrational exuberance. The simplest amplification mechanism, as seen with Gaergoedt and Waermondt, is price to price. Prices start going up. It attracts attention. It spurs conversation and brings people into the market; they then buy and bid the price up more. The amplification mechanism can also be a price-to-GDP-to-price feedback. When the stock market is up, people feel optimistic and they spend more money, so the economy starts to boom. People see the booming economy, which encourages them to bid prices of stocks up even more. Finally, there is a price-to-earnings-to-price mechanism. When the stock market goes up, consumers spend more and corporate sales and earnings go up as long as costs are largely fixed. So, people can say that price was predicting the earnings growth. They believe that the reason the market is going up is because companies are doing so well when, in fact, it is all part of a cycle, albeit one that is self-limiting.

Cultural Factors

Cultural factors are the stories that surround the bubble. Stories are essential because humans are story-oriented animals. Listen to people on the way to and from a casino. Rarely are they talking about probability distributions or kurtosis or anything related to the science of gambling—probability and statistics. They are telling stories. They will say, "You know my friend? He went in. His wife told him not to go. But he did, and he won $10,000." That sort of story can justify a market boom. Many of these stories are stories about why the world is different this time. I call them "new era" stories.

Psychological Factors

To understand the vulnerability of markets to psychological errors, one has to understand the principles of psychology. One psychological factor is overconfidence. Most people (both men and women) think they are above average, and people have a tendency to believe in themselves, which is part of self-esteem. Another factor is the representativeness heuristic, which is a tendency to see patterns in data and expect them to repeat. Another factor is framing, which occurs when an individual lets his or her judgments be affected by the way a choice is presented, so people do not always judge things in a purely rational way. Finally, attention anomalies are mistakes that people make because of inattention. People get focused on one thing and miss the obvious.

Trends in the Stock Market

The stock market can be viewed from the perspective of bubble theory. The top line in **Figure 1** is the stock price from 1871 to 2005 corrected for inflation. It clearly has lots of ups and downs, with some ups that are quite sharp, such as the peaks in 1929 and 2000. These two peaks are cusp-shaped; they are classic bubbles. The market was increasing at an increasing rate, and then when nothing in particular happened, it suddenly turned. The bubble had its own end in sight.

The top line in **Figure 2** is the P/E for January 1871 to October 2005, and the bottom line is long-term interest rates. The P/E is computed using Graham and Dodd's 1934 definition, which is price divided by 10-year rolling-average earnings. In this period, one can see a few historic peaks, most notably in 2000. Also note that since roughly 1970, an inverse relationship seems to have existed

Figure 1   S&P Composite Real Price and Earnings, January 1871–October 2005

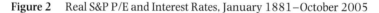

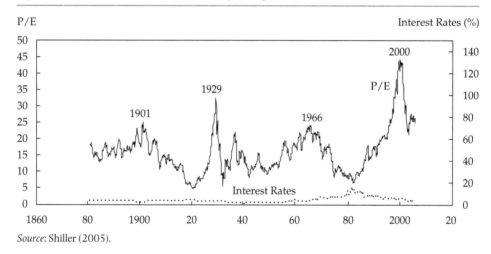

Source: Shiller (2005).

Figure 2   Real S&P P/E and Interest Rates, January 1881–October 2005

Source: Shiller (2005).

between interest rates and P/E. That relationship was talked about a lot around 2000; the so-called Fed model said that the frothy market was justified by the lower interest rates. Since 2000, that correlation has broken down, and also before 1970, there really was not a correlation. Thus, people seem to have been exaggerating the impact of interest rates on the stock market.

The stock market boom of the 1990s was a worldwide phenomenon. Brazil, China, France, Germany, the United States—all went up and down around the same time. Meanwhile, India, Japan, and South Korea did not share that same pattern, but even between 1998 and 2000, those countries all had dramatic booms. It seems as if the contagion reached these countries last, perhaps because the attention of people in these countries was on something else (e.g., the Asian financial crisis) and it took longer for the excitement to start there. Whatever the differences across countries, eventually the contagion spreads worldwide because the market culture is becoming worldwide more and more.

Figure 3 is a scatter diagram showing how P/E predicts future returns. Note that my colleague John Campbell and I showed an earlier version of this diagram to Alan Greenspan two days before he gave his irrational exuberance speech. A regression would not indicate a terribly good fit, but it is a good enough fit to suggest that there is something to this model. I see a negative slope to that scatter, and what it shows is that when the P/E has been high, subsequent returns have been low, and when the P/E has been low, subsequent returns have been high. For the years 1919, 1920, and 1921, the P/E was about 7—quite low—and the subsequent real returns were more than 15 percent a year. When the P/E has been high, say, 20–25 times, the subsequent 10-year returns have been just a little above zero. So, this relationship indicates that investors should expect low returns over the next 10 years because the P/E is about 25 times. Obviously, this is not a solid forecasting tool, but I still think that we are in exuberant times and that the market is still highly priced.

Figure 4 shows the One-Year Confidence Index, which I started calculating in 1989 based on a survey both of individual and institutional investors and

Figure 3   Subsequent Annualized 10-Year Return vs. P/E, 1881–1995

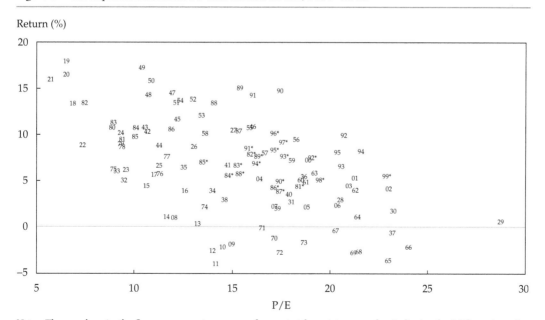

Notes: The numbers in the figure represent a year, and an asterisk next to a number indicates the 19th century. For example, 90* refers to the year 1890. P/E is for January of the indicated year.

Figure 4   One-Year Confidence Index: U.S. Six-Month Averages, 1989–2005

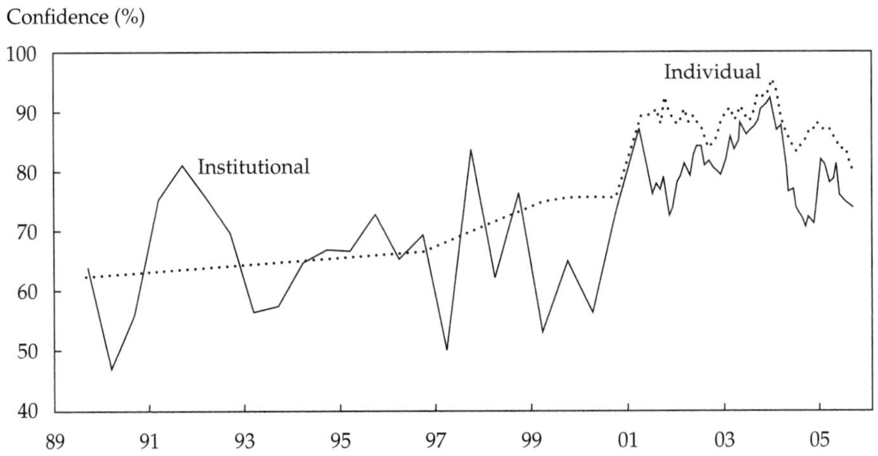

Note: Data for 2005 are through September.

which is now maintained by the Yale School of Management.[1] The index equals the percentage of people who think the stock market will go up over the next year. It rose rapidly through the 1990s both for individual and institutional investors, but after 2000, it either flattened out or began sagging slightly. Nevertheless, confidence is still high.

Figure 5 shows the Valuation Confidence Index, which is the percentage of investors who think the market is *not* overvalued. Interestingly, the percentage for both individual and institutional investors declined through the 1990s and bottomed out right before the peak of the market. After the market crashed, it shot back up again, which is maybe one of the best pieces of evidence that the stock market boom was a bubble.

Since 1996, I have asked the following question to individual investors: "Do you agree with the following statement: 'The stock market is the best investment for long-term holders who can just buy and hold through the ups and downs of the market.'" Surprisingly, the percentage of individual investors responding that they strongly agree did not grow through the 1990s, but it certainly declined afterwards. So, the experience of the declining market has weakened people's enthusiasm for the stock market.

Another question I have been asking is, "Do you agree with this statement: 'If there is another crash like October 19, 1987, the market will surely be back up to its former levels in a couple years or so.'" The percentage of investors saying they strongly agree has never been as high as 50 percent, but it grew through the 1990s and has fallen sharply since then. These opinions should

---

[1] For more information on the confidence indices, see http://icf.som.yale.edu/confidence.index/index.shtml.

Figure 5   Valuation Confidence Index: U.S. Six-Month Averages, 1989–2005

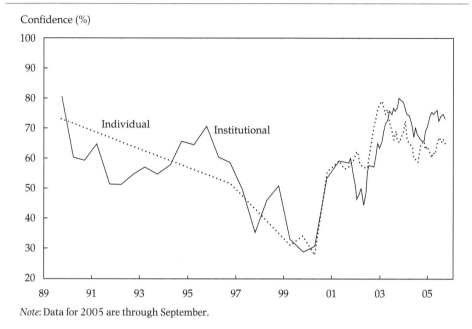

Note: Data for 2005 are through September.

not be changing so fast; people should know that the stock market has a history of more than 100 years, and the last few years do not add much evidence about the behavior of the stock market. People are focusing on the latest events, and they are changing their confidence in the market rather sharply.

Trends in Real Estate

Although the stock market bubble has burst, we are currently in what appears likely to be a housing bubble. This is significant. It is, in an important sense, a new phenomenon. Since 1980, I have been counting (using electronic searches) the times the phrase "housing bubble" appears in newspapers. The phrase was not used at all before 1987. Then, it began to appear right after the stock market crash in 1987 but died out again. It suddenly reappeared in 2002.

We have entered a speculative phase, and now, a lot of people think we are in a housing bubble. Many people are buying real estate today because they think real estate prices will go up for a while. This mentality, of course, propels the bubble, for a while.

Regulators should pay attention. Nontraditional mortgages have helped fuel the housing boom. We have seen a deterioration in lending standards and a proliferation of adjustable-rate mortgages (ARMs) and option ARMs. People with very small down payments are buying houses, and too many of them

Figure 6   Long-Term Trends in Single-Family Homes, 1890–2005

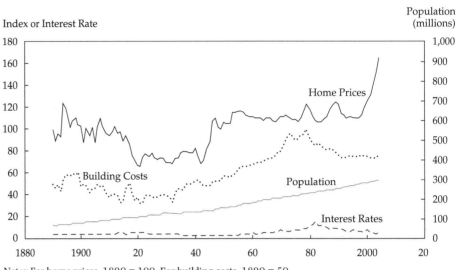

Notes: For home prices, 1890 = 100. For building costs, 1890 = 50.

are considered lower income or have poor credit histories. Unfortunately, the regulators do not move fast.

Because no long historical time series for home prices exists, I had to create one, shown in **Figure 6**. I looked at every price index for homes to try to get a quality control price index—pricing a standard home, which is not constant over time because homes have gradually gotten bigger over the past century. I found a number of series, but I had to fill in gaps to create this index. Notice that starting in 1890, home prices in real terms did not grow much until 1997, when they started shooting up—apparently a bubble period.

Back in the 1950s, economists reasoned that home prices are driven by building costs. They found that the change in real home prices very roughly mirrored the change in building costs. But that relationship seems to have broken down; recently, no correlation exists between the two. Furthermore, the jump in home prices cannot be explained by population increases because the population has been growing steadily—with no sudden jump after 1997. Finally, interest rates cannot explain the sudden increase in home prices after 1997 because interest rates have been on a rather steady decline since the early 1980s, with no sudden move down after 1997. Therefore, I think the increase is psychological.

Home prices have not gone up in real terms over long periods of time. Thus, a house has not been a great investment, unless, of course, one has a sufficiently high valuation of the "dividends" the house pays in terms of housing services.

Figure 7   Home Prices and Real Interest, 1890–2005

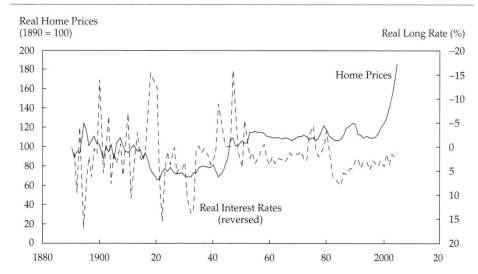

Why haven't home prices gone up? The price of a house relates mostly to its structure. And houses are getting cheaper to build, not more expensive, because of technical progress. In 1890, homes were handmade by skilled artisans. Now, people can purchase modular, prefabricated homes, circumventing the skilled artisans. Land has been getting more expensive, but if a person wants a house and does not care where it is, land can cost almost nothing. The population spreads out into formerly rural areas, taking the pressure off of prices in city centers.

Why do people believe home prices will do well in the long term? I think it is partly because of inflation confusion: Homes cannot be split like shares when they become highly priced, and so the rise in nominal home prices caused by inflation is much more apparent than the rise in stock prices. Another possible explanation is popular perceptions of the decline in real interest rates. I constructed a long-term real interest rate series back to 1890, shown in **Figure 7**, and compared it with the same home price series shown in Figure 6. But popular perceptions notwithstanding, declining real interest rates actually cannot justify the home price boom today. Real interest rates have been declining since the early 1980s (note the inverted scale), but they do not match up well with home prices. I separately tested the relationship between government expenditure and home prices and found no meaningful relationship. And remarkably, the unemployment rate shows no correlation with real home prices. The United States had two high periods of unemployment (the 1890s and the 1930s), and neither of those periods experienced a decline in real home prices. Finally, people are now saying that the boom in housing prices cannot deflate because no recession looms on the horizon.

Figure 8   Ratio of Shiller Home Price Index to Rent of Primary Residence Index, 1913–2004

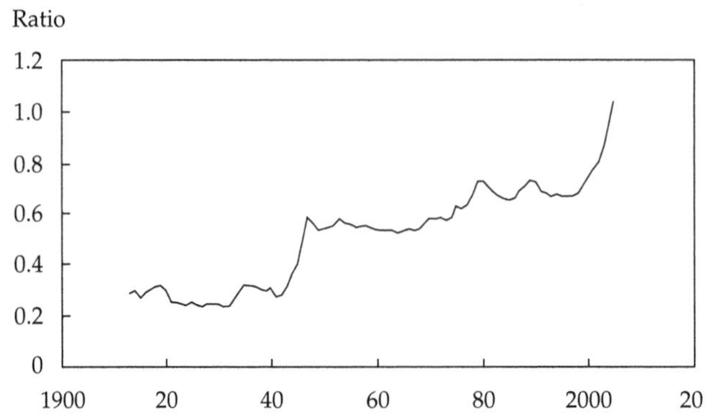

Another factor to examine is rental prices. Since 1913, real rents of primary residences, as reported by the U.S. Bureau of Labor Statistics (BLS), have gradually declined. Thus, home prices have gone up recently without any concomitant increase in real rents. But rents are different from home prices. A renter does not have any speculative interest in the property, but the buyer does. **Figure 8** shows the ratio of my home price index to the BLS rent index, which can be thought of as the P/E for housing. Since 1913, this ratio has exhibited a strong uptrend. Some have criticized the BLS rent index for not accounting properly for quality change, but at the very least, the available data do not show that recent home price increases are justified by rent increases.

Eichholtz (1997) computed a housing price index that went back to 1628, which includes the tulip mania, for the upscale Herengracht neighborhood of Amsterdam. Although it has shown boom and bust cycles, it has not shown an uptrend. If I were to ask people what they thought the return on housing should be in a glamorous metropolitan area, a lot of people would answer even better than the stock market—say, 10 percent a year. Think about it. Amsterdam has been a booming metropolis since 1628. It was the financial center of the world in the 1600s. It ought to have done well. Could it have done 10 percent a year since 1628? No. Compounding 10 percent a year for 370 years would produce a total return of 443,031,891,418,593,000 percent, which would bring us beyond the galaxy—not possible. Real prices have actually doubled in 350 years, and that is only a 0.2 percent increase a year. Thus, this beautiful downtown section in Amsterdam has not changed in price adjusted for inflation.

Why can someone buy an apartment there today and pay the same price as in 1628, adjusted for inflation? Because people do not have to live there. Other locations are competing with the Herengracht neighborhood. Amsterdam is now spread out over a huge area and is continuing to spread. Prices are not going to go up in the center because people can go somewhere else. It is

Table 1   Long-Term Expectations for Housing Appreciation, Los Angeles
         and Milwaukee

City/Measure	1988	2003	2004	2005
Los Angeles				
Mean	14.3%	13.0%	22.5%	22.7%
Median	10	8	10	9
Milwaukee				
Mean	7.3%	11.7%	13.4%	13.6%
Median	5	5	5	7.5

elementary supply and demand, and that is why home prices will not go up strongly in real terms over long periods of time.

Expectations of future price appreciation, however, are quite different. I asked homeowners in Los Angeles and Milwaukee the following: "On average over the next 10 years, how much do you expect the value of your home to change each year?" The results are shown in **Table 1**. These are extraordinary expectations, especially because home prices are already high. Milwaukee had lower expectations until recently, so what I think is happening now is the bubble has gotten so much publicity that even in Milwaukee people are getting optimistic.

I then asked people whether they agreed that real estate is the best investment for long-term holders, who can just buy and hold through the ups and downs of the market. In Los Angeles, more than 50 percent said they strongly agree. But as I have just demonstrated for real home prices in Amsterdam over a 350-year history, real estate has about a 0 percent real return in the long run. These survey respondents do not know that. In Milwaukee, however, respondents seemed more rational; only about one-third thought that real estate is the best long-term investment.

Hedging Vehicles for Real Estate

According to the Federal Reserve Board, real estate owned by households is the second largest asset class in the United States, valued at $21.6 trillion in the fourth quarter of 2005. But until recently, unlike for stocks and bonds, investors could not hedge real estate risk efficiently. Many investors are exposed to real estate risk because it is concentrated in one geographical area, and especially for ordinary retail investors, real estate may be the biggest part of their portfolios. Many are hoping to use this "asset" when they retire, but it may be in one of these volatile sections.

Various attempts have been made to develop hedging vehicles for real estate. The first such attempt was in London in 1991. The London Futures and Options Exchange (London Fox) started trading property futures in 1991 on U.K. home price indices. It was a cash-settled futures market, but it lasted only a few months because the volume of trade was disappointing, eventually leading to London Fox officers making fraudulent trades to inflate the volume of trade.

Around 2002, a futures market in U.K. housing began: City Index and IG Index. These are spread-betting firms in London, and they have some trading of home price indices in the United Kingdom, but they are not very successful. In 2004, Hedgestreet.com set up an online trading site aimed at retail investors with price indices for single-family homes. As far as I can tell, it is not a big success, although it just announced that it is teaming up with the Chicago Board Options Exchange to develop new products.

In May 2006, the Chicago Mercantile Exchange (CME) opened a futures market based on the S&P/Case–Shiller Metro Area Home Price Indices, which were originally developed in the 1980s.[2] Cash-settled futures are available in 10 U.S. cities, as is a national composite index, with the highest weightings given to New York (27 percent), San Francisco (12 percent), and Chicago (9 percent). The futures are traded on CME Globex. The value for each contract is 250 times the value of any index. With the opening composite index at $231, the value of one futures contract is $57,750. So, a homeowner wishing to hedge a $570,000 house could sell 10 contracts for a complete hedge. The CME has also created an options market, based on the same home price index.

These new markets may start slowly and grow, but as people get used to liquid markets for home prices, they should garner more and more interest. Perhaps within a few years, investors will be hearing on the news that New York closed up 2 points and Los Angeles closed down 2 points, just like the stock market. The cash market for homes is inefficient right now. It has very strong momentum compared with the stock market, not at all the random walk that financial theory describes. I hope that the housing market will become more like the stock market and that investment professionals will have the opportunity to participate in these markets on behalf of their clients on a global scale.

This presentation comes from Defining, Measuring, and Managing Uncertainty: The CFA Institute Risk Symposium held in New York City on 22–23 February 2006.

---

[2] Editor's note: Professor Shiller is a co-founder of, and stockholder in, MacroMarkets LLC, the producer of a series of home price indices that are licensed to the CME and that form the basis for the futures contracts referenced in this article.

References

Eichholtz, Piet M.A. 1997. "A Long Run House Price Index: The Herengracht Index, 1628-1973." *Real Estate Economics*, vol. 25, no. 2 (Summer):175–192.

Shiller, Robert J. 2005. *Irrational Exuberance*. 2nd ed. Princeton, NJ: Princeton University Press.

More from Robert J. Shiller

This section presents the speaker's lively question and answer session with the conference audience.

Question: Who would naturally be on the long side of a futures trade given that so many individual investors, in particular, are already long real estate?

Shiller: Yes, indeed, a lot of people are saying everyone wants to be short the market these days because we are all worried that the prices are going to go down. But all that means is that the futures market is likely to go into backwardation (future prices lower than spot prices).

I believe the futures market for housing will be one of those markets (like the oil futures market) that is frequently seen in backwardation. With backwardation in place, the longs will see that they are buying cheaply and will have an incentive to come in. Even when the futures market is not actually in backwardation, it will be attractive to longs if the price increase "predicted" in the futures market is less than the actual expected price increase.

It is important to note that even though I have said home prices have not gone up much in the long run, taking long positions in the futures market is likely to be a good investment for longs. Note also that because of a low correlation between home prices and other investments, long futures is a good diversifying investment too.

Question: Could the tax deductibility of mortgage interest be a material factor in explaining trends in housing prices?

Shiller: The federal income tax came into force in 1913, which is exactly the beginning of our series. Then, it was a millionaire's tax, but it became important after World War II. I don't think that explains the phenomenon well because the boom in the housing market really occurred in many countries. I think it started first in London. It wasn't first in the United States. I haven't heard a good tax explanation for all of these events around the world.

Question: Do you expect Fannie Mae and other government-sponsored enterprises to be active participants in the futures markets?

Shiller: We would love to have Fannie and Freddie hedge their portfolios in our markets. We've been trying to tell them that. I'm hoping that they will because they have an exposure to real estate risk, and I think they are in a somewhat risky situation because home prices may start falling. If they do fall, it could cause mortgage defaults, so they should be hedged against this.

Question: What are the macroeconomic implications of a housing price boom followed by a crash?

Shiller: The real estate boom that we've been in is quite a dramatic event, and it has been driving the economy substantially. The personal savings rate is negative now, at least in part because people view themselves as "saving" through increased home prices. But if home prices start to fall, their "saving" could suddenly evaporate, which could affect confidence and then consumption expenditure, which, in turn, could cause a recession.

If history is a guide, we might have a recession as part of the unraveling of a housing boom, but recessions tend to be rather short lived, 6–18 months typically, and we would see declining prices in real estate for five years or more. Keep in mind that this home price boom is essentially unprecedented. The only one that's similar is the post–World War II boom, but the World War II boom was different because during the war, 25 percent of the men were in uniform, which shut down the construction industry. The government also didn't want people building houses and diverting materials from the war effort. When the soldiers came back, that was a fundamental shock that drove the housing market. Recently, we haven't had a fundamental shock. There has been no world war. We're in a really different set of circumstances. This is more of a speculative shock this time.

Question: Does your caution about residential housing apply equally to the commercial realty market?

Shiller: Yes, I think that the correlation between home prices over the recent sample period and especially commercial apartment buildings has been fairly substantial; they are substitutes for each other. So, if we see a drop in home prices, we might see a drop in commercial real estate prices as well.

Investing in Commodities

RONALD G. LAYARD-LIESCHING

Investing in commodities remains controversial. But a long-only allocation to commodities brings risk reduction and inflation protection to a traditional portfolio asset
mix. As more public and private pension funds are searching for higher-returning
and liability-matching assets, interest in commodity investment is rising rapidly.
Currently, the majority of institutional investment in commodities is index based,
and trading to maintain index exposure makes this an active strategy. And although
institutional commodity investment is in its infancy, newer strategies, such as index
plus and active long-only, are increasing in popularity.

Commodities are now capturing the interest of institutional investors because, to put it simply, the math works. The average U.S. public pension fund has a return target of 8 percent, but the prospect over the next few years for the basic 60 percent/40 percent equity/fixed-income mix is dim. With the estimated return for bonds around 5 percent, a gross equity return of nearly 11 percent a year is needed to make up the difference. Few investors believe this type of return is achievable. Thus, plan sponsors are seeking new uncorrelated sources of return, such as commodities, to introduce into the traditional portfolio mix.

> Commodity index strategies, unlike U.S. equity index strategies, are active strategies because of the high turnover.

Funds are also increasingly concerned with managing liability-relative risks and are turning to liability-driven investment strategies. The United States has a huge problem with underfunded retirement benefits, but in many other countries, the situation is even worse. Hence, around the globe, pension fund chief investment officers are trying to find the asset class with an expected risk–return profile that improves upon that of more traditional investments and more closely matches their funds' growing liabilities. This quest is driving managers to alternative investments, in general, and to commodities, in particular.

This presentation will begin with a basic introduction to commodities before proceeding to a discussion of the controversies surrounding the commodity

Ronald G. Layard-Liesching is chief investment officer at Pareto Partners, New York City.

markets. Then, I will explain how commodities fit into a portfolio and will suggest a lens other than mean–variance analysis with which to view their contribution. Through that lens, commodity investment appears rather attractive. The existence of a commodity return premium is currently actively debated mainly because the asset class does not produce cash flow. So, I will outline the sources of commodity returns. Finally, I will explain the alternatives for institutions seeking to implement commodity investment programs.

Commodity Basics

Commodity strategies require investing cash collateral to support derivatives exposure. The principal derivatives are forwards and futures contracts. Note that a relationship exists between the spot (current) price of the commodity and the expected spot price of the commodity at the maturity date of the derivative contract. If the future price is above the spot price, this is referred to as "contango." If the future price is below the spot price, this is referred to as "backwardation."

Contango

When a commodity market is in contango, as illustrated in **Figure 1**, futures prices are higher than the spot price because market participants believe the spot price will be higher in the future. Contango often occurs when a commodity's price is high and volatile, as is the case currently with oil. For example, the oil consumer, such as an airline, drives the price of the futures higher than the spot price as it attempts to hedge against the risk of higher spot prices, which could ultimately cause it to go out of business.

Figure 1   Contango Illustration

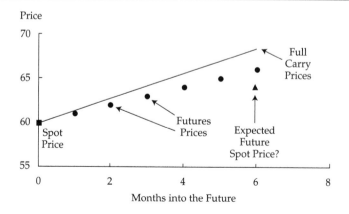

The amount by which the relative price of the futures can rise is limited, however, by a classic arbitrage trade. If the futures price goes too high, an investor can buy the commodity at the spot price, store it, insure it, and sell it forward. This "carry trade" is a pure financing activity and theoretically limits the futures price to a level called "full carry." A commodity like gold can be easily borrowed in large size, and the borrowing cost of gold is usually below dollar cash interest rates. Hence, this arbitrage means that gold will often be at full carry in the forward market. But different commodities have unique features that affect this relationship.

For example, there may be limitations on storing commodities for future delivery. Hogs, for instance, cannot be stored indefinitely because they have finite lives. There also may be physical limits on available storage for delivery. In these cases, the classic carry trade does not apply. So, forward prices can rise far above the spot price, reflecting a future supply shortage.

For most commodities, the investor buys a futures contract with a set maturity date. When the futures contract is purchased, the investor deposits cash as collateral for the contract with the exchange. This cash generates an additional return called the "collateral yield." But the investor wishes to maintain long-only commodity exposure. So, when the contract matures, it is closed out and another one is bought with a longer maturity. This trade is called "rolling the contract." This contract rolling creates a small profit or loss that is unrelated to the spot price movement. In this way, the investor maintains long exposure to the commodity. For most commodities, exceptions being precious metals, such as silver and gold, it would not be practical to actually hold the physical commodity.

Backwardation

The opposite of contango is when the forward price or futures price of a commodity is below its spot price. This situation is referred to as "backwardation" and is illustrated in **Figure 2**. Backwardation used to be common in the oil market. When the price of oil was low, producers wanted to hedge their risk of further price declines. Lower prices threatened their ability to stay in business. Backwardation actually used to be the norm in most commodities because a potential price fall had a proportionally bigger impact on the few large producers than on the many small consumers. This feature was analyzed by John Maynard Keynes, who referred to it as "natural backwardation." Commodity producers were willing to sell their commodity below the price they expected it to be in the future to protect against business risk. There was substantial dis-utility to this large group of producers if the price fell. So, long-only speculators gained by taking over this price risk from the producers. This natural backwardation may be changing, however, because derivatives trading and institutional investing

Figure 2   Backwardation Illustration

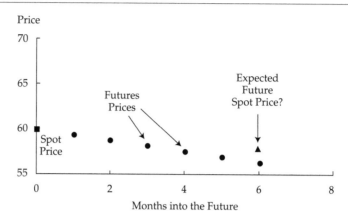

make for greater symmetry. When prices are low and volatile, producers hedge and the market enters backwardation. When prices are high and volatile, consumers hedge. At the same time, investors are attempting to hedge inflation risk. The combination of these two actions creates contango.

Sources of Return

Long-only investment in commodities is usually obtained via collateralized long positions in commodity futures, forwards, or swaps. The institutional investor receives three distinct sources of return: collateral yield, roll or convenience yield, and the spot price return. **Figure 3** plots the three yield components of a commodity index investment. The collateral yield is the return on cash used as margin to take long derivatives exposure. Generally, this is a T-bill return. Active collateral management can enhance this return.

The roll yield (also known as "convenience yield") is the return from rolling forward the maturity of the derivatives position. During the period shown in Figure 3, the roll yield was both positive and negative. The return to the long investor is positive when the market is in backwardation; the long investor can buy the commodity below the current spot level from a hedger. On maturity, the hedger pays the long investor the convergence in price between the forward and spot rates. Currently, the roll yield on commodity indices is negative because, on average, commodity markets are in contango. This negative roll yield is particularly the case for oil, which has a large weight in the major commodity indices. Because of future expected oil supply shortages, speculators have driven the futures price of oil above the spot price. For the majority of commodities, long investors are buying futures at a price higher than the spot price. Hence, if the spot price moves sideways, the long position will be closed out at a loss. That difference in price is lost, and as a result, the roll yield is negative.

Figure 3   Yield Components of Commodities, January 1986–December 2004

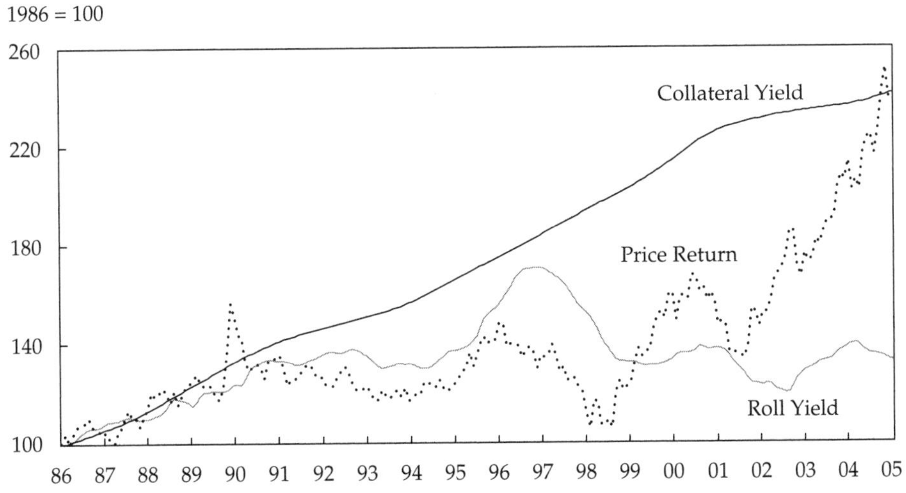

1986 = 100

Source: Based on monthly data from the Gresham TAP Index.

The price return can obviously be positive or negative based on fluctuations in its spot price caused by supply and demand. Over the past 25 years, price returns, although volatile, have been strong.

Commodity Controversies

Much controversy exists about whether commodities are an asset class. Fueling the debate over the classification of commodities as an asset class are the arguments that commodity prices decline in the very long run, roll yield may disappear, rolling costs may reduce returns, and the return premium may result from rebalancing. Of course, the argument that commodities cannot be an asset class because they do not generate cash flow is frequently heard, but I will address that later in the presentation.

Commodity Prices

Some argue that commodity prices decline in the long run (and hence are not an asset class). Over the last century, spot commodity prices have fallen by some 1.5 percent a year. The time horizons of most portfolios, however, are much shorter than 100 years. Figure 3 shows that from 1989 to 2000, the spot price basically moved sideways, generating minimal price return, but took off like a rocket in early 2001. Investors who bought the argument against holding commodities missed out on this spectacular run-up in price.

326 Alternative Investments

Commodity prices decline because of the introduction of new supplies and new production technology (such as the Alaska oil sands and coal gasification), substitution of one commodity for another when prices rise (such as aluminum for copper in power lines), and reduction in the use of certain commodities in technological processes (such as optical fibers for copper).

Offsetting these effects are the facts that global supplies are finite for many commodities, demand for storable commodities is rising, and the engagement in the global economy of the postemergent economies of China and India fundamentally alters global demand and supply.

Most of the fluctuation in commodity prices comes from the demand side of the equation. The supply-side shifts are usually smaller and slower to respond than are demand fluctuations (note that this is not true of electricity, for example, where supply disruptions can cause dramatic price moves). So, as demand rises for a finite supply of a commodity, the price of the commodity is bound to rise.

The demand for storable commodities, which can be held as hard assets, is also increasing. The lack of cash flow from these commodities is irrelevant: Investors hold U.S. dollar balances because of their usefulness as a store of value. The same dynamic is affecting the demand for commodities. Commodities are perceived as a good store of value in an increasingly risky and unstable world.

The prices of commodities will also rise because they are denominated in units of paper currency. As the value of a currency falls, prices of commodities denominated in that currency rise. In other words, the price of commodities operates as an exchange rate. It is the exchange rate between the commodity and the value of a paper currency—the U.S. dollar. So, if the dollar depreciates or loses its purchasing power, the value of commodities will appreciate. The existence of truly massive unfunded U.S. dollar deficits explains one component of the long-term return premium to long commodity investing.

Roll Yield

The roll yield is the yield that has historically existed in situations when the forward price is below the spot price. Producers sell commodities at prices lower than the expected future price to hedge their business risk, which benefits long investors and speculators. But the rapid growth in institutional long-only investors and growing worldwide demand for commodities may have created permanent structural change in the marketplace. It is raising fears that the roll yield may disappear. At the moment, it is indeed negative, but this has been seen before.

When Keynes formulated his theory of natural backwardation, developed futures markets did not exist and the preponderance of market participants were hedgers. The bottom line was that long investors won and hedgers lost. Today's market is no longer dominated by participants with a single motive, so the market can move both ways. Opportunities to add value have thus increased because of the disassociation between the price of the futures and the expected future price.

Rolling Costs

Investing in indices requires that the investor roll his or her exposure. In other words, at the maturity date of the futures contract, the investor can either take physical delivery of the commodity or roll the futures contract, which means buying another contract with a new maturity date. The rolling cost is the cost to sell the maturing contract and buy a new one.

The indices, such as the Goldman Sachs Commodity Index (GSCI) and the Dow Jones-AIG Commodity Index (DJ-AIG), roll on specified dates over five business days.[1] During this period, a very high volume of contracts trades because of the tremendous size of the indices' long holdings. The market makers know which contracts are involved, so the roll, not surprisingly, becomes more expensive. Thus, the dynamics of the roll inflict a hidden, but significant, cost on long-only investors that definitely reduces returns. Roll costs, however, can be reduced or avoided through active roll maturity and timing management.

Return Premium

An academic debate is stirring about the commodity return premium. The debate basically revolves around the fact that over the same time period, the long-term geometric return of the average commodity was close to zero but the geometric return of the commodity index was strong. How can the commodity basket have a higher geometric return than the components? The answer is that index volatility is lower than the average volatility of its constituents (29 percent). Rebalancing occurs when the weights of holdings in different commodities need to be adjusted back to the index weights after large price moves. So, if the oil price rises sharply, oil must be sold and the other commodities, purchased. Rebalancing can thus add value. Therefore, the geometric return of a rebalanced portfolio is higher than the average return of its constituents. The approximate relationship, according to Booth and Fama (1992), is

$$G = M - \frac{\sigma^2}{2},$$

where G is the geometric return, M is the arithmetic return, and σ is the volatility. Erb and Harvey (2006) argued that this rebalancing return provides essentially all the return to commodity investing. Gorton and Rouwenhorst

---

[1] Editor's note: The author is on the board of the DJ-AIG.

(2006) countered this argument, showing that rebalancing interacts with return seriality. The crucial point is that the primary driver of return in commodities is not simply the rebalancing process.

Commodities in a Portfolio

Long-term commodity investment offers several positives to a portfolio. The risk–return profile of commodities over the past 25 years is similar to that of U.S. equities. Commodities also provide a reduction in portfolio risk, which is the primary argument for adding commodities to traditional portfolios. Return-timing diversification as well as inflation shock and liability matching are other reasons for adding commodities to a portfolio.

Long-Term Return

Figure 4 shows long-term bond, stock, and commodity futures returns. All three returns were positive over the period. From January 1991 to April 2006, the volatilities of the two major commodity indices—the DJ-AIG (12.1 percent) and the GSCI (18.6 percent)—and the volatility of equities as measured by the S&P 500 Index (14.2 percent) were quite similar, as shown in **Table 1.** As one would assume, the volatility of bonds as measured by the Lehman Brothers U.S.

Figure 4   Inflation-Adjusted Performance of Stocks, Bonds, and Commodity Futures, July 1959–December 2004

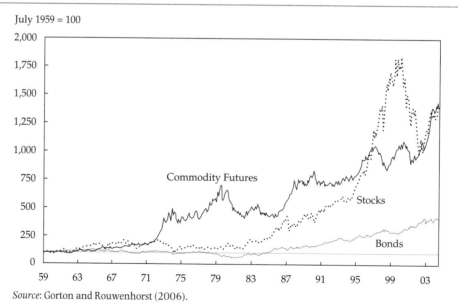

Source: Gorton and Rouwenhorst (2006).

Table 1   Return and Volatility, January 1991–April 2006

Index	Return	Volatility
S&P 500	11.2%	14.2%
DJ-AIG	4.2	12.1
GSCI	7.8	18.6
Lehman Brothers U.S. Aggregate	7.0	3.8

Note: Data are monthly.
Sources: Based on data from Standards & Poor's, Lehman Brothers, and Goldman, Sachs & Co.

Aggregate Index (3.8 percent) was much lower than that for either equities or commodities. Note that the volatility of the DJ-AIG was lower than that of the GSCI because it is a much more evenly weighted basket of commodities; the GSCI is currently 73 percent energy weighted versus 33 percent for the DJ-AIG. A mean–variance optimizer loves commodities because of their negative correlation with other markets and their interesting risk–return characteristics. As a result, it will allocate a higher percentage of the portfolio to commodities than prudence dictates is wise. There is a better way to analyze the commodity allocation.

Portfolio Risk

A.D. Roy, who published a paper in 1952 at about the same time Harry M. Markowitz was writing his Nobel Prize–winning paper on modern portfolio theory, said that investors do not want to know the long-run average expected rate of return on their portfolios. They want to know what will happen next year. Roy's point was that to be a long-term investor, you have to be able to survive the short run. As an alternative to mean–variance portfolio selection, Roy developed "safety-first" investing—choosing the highest-returning portfolio subject to the worst-case short-run outcome being acceptable.

Table 2 illustrates the portfolio impact of commodities during the period from January 1991 to April 2006. The first row shows the return, volatility, and worst-case return for a portfolio of 60 percent U.S. equities and 40 percent U.S. bonds. Hedge funds, alternatives, and international investing could also be included without changing the results. The annualized return was 11.3 percent, which easily exceeds the current 8.0–8.5 percent target return of most U.S. funds. Annualized volatility for this 60/40 portfolio was 8.6 percent. The return for the 60/40 portfolio over the worst 12 months of the period was −12.3 percent.

Note one caveat to this analysis: It assesses only the asset side of the fund, not the fund surplus over liabilities. A typical U.S. corporate pension plan has a liability duration of 14 years, which is equivalent to being short a 14-year-duration bond. Analyzing the surplus for this period would mean the worst-case

Table 2   Portfolio Impact of Commodities, January 1991–April 2006

Portfolio	Equities	Bonds	GSCI	DJ-AIG	Return	Volatility	Worst 12 Months
1	60%	40%	—	—	11.3%	8.6%	−12.3%
2	55	40	5%	—	11.3	8.0	−11.7
3	50	40	10	—	11.2	7.5	−11.2
4	55	40	—	5%	11.0	8.0	−11.2
5	50	40	—	10	10.6	7.4	−10.1

Note: Data are monthly.

Sources: Based on data from Standard & Poor's, Lehman Brothers, AIG, and Goldman, Sachs & Co.

12-month return would be −24 percent because liabilities rose at the same time asset prices fell in the perfect storm of 2000 through 2002. The proper analysis should thus always consider assets in relationship to liabilities. If the analysis outlined in Table 2 included the liability side of the equation, then the outcome—that adding commodities to a portfolio improves the worst-case return scenario—would be even more strikingly positive.

When 5 percent of the equity allocation is moved to the GSCI, the worst-case return is reduced by 60 bps, and with a 10 percent allocation to the GSCI, the reduction is more than 1 percentage point. The improvement is a result of the fact that when paper assets fall in value, the value of commodities tends to rise.

In the case of a 10.0 percent allocation to the DJ-AIG, the worst-case return is reduced to −10.1 percent, an improvement of more than 100 bps versus the 10.0 percent allocation to the GSCI. The GSCI does not produce as large an improvement as the DJ-AIG because of the dominant presence of oil in the GSCI. The price of oil is highly volatile and pushes the total index value up and down as the price of oil fluctuates; the DJ-AIG, in contrast, is influenced by the broader trend in commodities and demonstrates greater persistence. The bottom line is that in terms of risk reduction, the more diversified DJ-AIG historically has provided a more potent impact than the GSCI.

Return-Timing Diversification

Long-term returns of any asset class are concentrated in brief periods of time. If the past 20 years of equity returns were sorted from the highest-returning months to the lowest-returning months and then 7 percent of the highest-returning months were removed, the result would be a return equal to bonds. If 10 percent of the highest-returning months were removed, equities would have zero return. If daily returns are used, the return pattern is even more concentrated. Additionally, these periods of high excess return performance vary for different asset classes. So, not only are asset returns concentrated over time, but the periods of outperformance also vary for different asset classes.

Financial assets tend to perform weakly in the late stages of economic recovery, when there are inflation shocks and also when monetary policy becomes restrictive. These are the times when commodities tend to have strong returns because investors perceive that global capacity utilization is high, a shortage of raw commodities is at hand, and inflation is lurking around the corner. Ultimately, rising commodity prices will trigger further monetary tightening, which is not good news for bonds or equities. Clearly, the commodity markets are a natural complement to traditional markets and provide the element of time diversification of returns that is so beneficial in controlling portfolio risk.

The prices of commodities react much more to current supply–demand conditions than do the prices of equities and bonds, which respond more closely to the longer-term outlook. This deviation between time horizons of the two markets provides another interesting aspect of time diversification. Commodity investment also provides diversification across economic environments, which is an excellent corollary to time diversification. Some argue that energy cost is a core source of inflation and thus favor concentrated investment in, for example, the GSCI, which has a high energy weight. As good a solution as that might appear to be as a counterbalance to inflationary pressures, an equally important consideration is the diversification of risk, which argues for investment in a more equally weighted basket of commodities.

Inflation-Liability Matching

Long-term liabilities, whether they are pension payments from pension funds or grants from foundations and endowments, are exposed to erosion from inflation. In order to match the long-term inflation exposure in liabilities, long-only commodity investing provides a natural hedge. Of course, commodities do not match the U.S. Consumer Price Index definition of inflation, but they do match components of the index. Thus, not only does adding commodities to a portfolio reduce risk in the short run, but it also reduces the risk of longer-term inflation exposure.

Implementation of Commodity Strategies

Commodity index strategies, unlike U.S. equity index strategies, are active strategies because of the high turnover. For example, the constituent weights change, which is driven by changes in the weighting formula of the respective benchmark index. Second, a rolling methodology is implied by the index and largely determines the roll frequency of the portfolio. And last, the cash collateral position is continually reinvested as short-term cash equivalents mature and are replaced. Thus, my view is that all commodity investment is active.

Unlike in conventional investment indices, the return correlations between the commodity index constituents in different subcategories are close to zero. Obviously, heating oil correlates with West Texas Intermediate—a type of crude oil used as a benchmark—which correlates with unleaded gasoline. But the average correlation between pork belly futures and gasoline is zero. Within some of the clusters, such as the energy complex and base metals, correlations are high, but between the blocks, correlations are, in essence, zero, which maximizes the rebalance yield.

Commodity indices differ dramatically in their investability, their exposures, and their risk and return characteristics. Although new indices are created all the time, I will focus on just two of them: the GSCI and DJ-AIG. Started in December 1992, the GSCI includes 24 commodities, is production weighted, and gives oil a direct weight of 73.5 percent. The DJ-AIG began in July 1998, includes 19 commodities, and is weighted one-third to production and two-thirds to trading. Individual commodities are limited to 15 percent of the index, and concentration constraints limit energy to a 33 percent weight.

The current estimate of institutional investment in long-only commodity strategies is $120 billion. Of this amount, about $50 billion is invested in the GSCI. Another $30 billion is invested in the DJ-AIG and is expected to increase with the introduction of a new exchange-traded fund (ETF).

Note that a separate, but also growing, activity is institutional investment in active commodity trading. This trading includes the activities of managers of global macro strategies as well as those of long–short commodity trading advisers (CTAs). These long–short strategies, however, are an entirely different beast from long only and have absolute return targets.

The commodity trading industry has a notoriously poor information ratio. Furiously trading long and short commodity positions will not hedge the risk in a pension portfolio. Diversification provided by CTA strategies is beneficial, but allocations are too small for this to be relevant: A 0.5 percent CTA allocation having a correlation with the S&P 500 of −0.1 has minimal impact on portfolio return if the market drops 20 percent. For a CTA strategy to affirmatively impact portfolio-level risk, an allocation of at least 5 percent is required. That allocation would be very hard to sell to investment committees. So, although a CTA strategy is definitely an interesting component in a portfolio and earns its place in the alternative investments pool, that is where it belongs.

Core Commodity Investment Approaches

Commodity investment approaches range from pure index exposure to a CTA long–short strategy. To play a core role in a portfolio, commodity investment can be made by using one of three structures: an index fund, an index-plus strategy, or an active long-only strategy.

Index fund
An index fund strategy can be implemented simply by purchasing an ETF as well as an index swap or note directly from a dealer.

Index plus
The goal of an index-plus strategy is to provide an incremental return over the index. About a dozen firms currently offer this type of strategy. Four common ways to enhance the return of the index are through high-collateral return, roll management, rebalancing, and maturity management. In a high-collateral-return strategy, the cash held as margin collateral is worked as hard as possible to pick up any available return and often means moving into short-dated notes and weaker credits. Roll management involves a tactical approach to the timing of the roll on commodity futures contracts. The $80 billion invested in the GSCI and DJ-AIG indices roll on the prespecified five days in each contract settlement month. Deviating from this pattern and rolling earlier than the rest of the market or managing the maturities on forward contracts can result in a positive incremental return over the index. Rebalancing to the index can also be done more or less frequently to add value.

Active long-only
Active long-only strategies are a new and developing market. At present, they stand roughly equivalent in development to the currency strategies of the early 1990s. These strategies are usually built around several unique characteristics of commodities markets. These characteristics include the short-run seriality of commodity returns and the long-run reversion of commodity prices driven by market fundamentals. Another active strategy is broader diversification, which, as with any portfolio, improves risk-adjusted performance. For example, the quest for new reserves or alternative energy sources is being diligently pursued by many, and sooner or later, the price of energy will drop because someone will be successful. Portfolio diversification among commodities will protect against this eventuality.

   The structural dynamics of commodities argue for active investing. The following quote is from a recent article by Kat and Oomen (2006):

> We have shown that commodity futures returns and volatility may vary considerably over different phases of the business cycle, under different monetary conditions as well as with the shape of the futures curve. This suggests that a purely passive investment in commodities may not be optimal and, given the differences in behavior of different commodities,

that some commodities will be better at diversifying equity and bond portfolios than others. (p. 18)

Basically, Kat and Oomen argue that there are real reasons to believe the commodity markets are less than entirely efficient.

Impact of Institutional Investment

The commodity markets are being profoundly changed by the influx of institutional money. Backwardation, when the forward price is below the spot price, has become less stable. Because larger numbers of investors are putting on the same trades, rolls are becoming more expensive and dynamic, which is similar to what has happened to the cost of swapping between small-cap and large-cap U.S. equities.

Because of the influx of institutional money into the market, value is diverging from fundamentals. Copper is an excellent example; its price has risen 300 percent in two years. The situation is similar to what occurred in the currency market as institutional investors became involved. Thirty years ago, currency was primarily used to finance international exports and imports. There was minimal international portfolio investment by institutions in the 1970s, and so, there were minimal currency transactions by institutional investors. Today, institutional investor flows totally dominate currency markets; only some 1.6 percent of daily currency market activity is related to exports and imports. As institutional investor participation builds in commodities, prices will detach from fundamentals. But a commodity's price cannot detach indefinitely from fundamentals because supply will adjust to meet demand. A massive supply response in both the energy and copper markets is in progress and will reverse the dramatic price appreciation of the past few years for these commodities.

More extreme price moves will occur in commodity markets as demand and supply become more frequently misaligned, thus creating forced sales or purchases. In most commodities, a spectacular squeeze occurs as a result of a large market participant's exploitation of structural supply–demand imbalances in a certain commodity. More position squeezes are on the horizon as this market changes.

Conclusion

Commodity investment improves portfolios. The improvement comes not just from return but from reducing the risk of losing money when stressful market environments occur. An equally important point is that all commodity invest-ment is active; even a so-called passive program involves very high turnover and management of cash. But the real source of added value from active management is utility arbitrage, which is based on the premise that different investors have different objectives and thus accept a cost for transferring risk. Note, however, that institutional investing is altering, and will continue to alter at an escalating pace, the dynamics of the commodity markets. Institutional commodity investment is truly in its infancy.

This presentation comes from the 2006 Financial Analysts Seminar held in Evanston, Illinois, on 16–21 July 2006.

References

Booth, David G., and Eugene F. Fama. 1992. "Diversification Returns and Asset Contributions." *Financial Analysts Journal*, vol. 48, no. 3 (May/June):26–32.

Erb, Claude B., and Campbell R. Harvey. 2006. "The Strategic and Tactical Value of Commodity Futures." *Financial Analysts Journal*, vol. 62, no. 2 (March/April):69–97.

Gorton, Gary, and K. Geert Rouwenhorst. 2006. "Facts and Fantasies about Commodity Futures." *Financial Analysts Journal*, vol. 62, no. 2 (March/April):47–68.

Kat, Harry, and Roel Oomen. 2006. "What Every Investor Should Know about Commodities, Part 1: Univariate Return Analysis." Alternative Investment Research Centre Working Paper No. 29 (January).

Roy, A.D. 1952. "Safety First and Holding of Assets." *Econometrica*, vol. 20, no. 3 (July):431–449.

More from Ronald G. Layard-Liesching

This section presents the speaker's lively question and answer session with the conference audience.

Question: How would you characterize the commodity markets today?

Layard-Liesching: Some commodities are experiencing a price bubble—copper, for example. When a commodity trades at a multiple of its marginal extraction cost, it is without a doubt in the midst of a bubble. In my view, this does not preclude a strategic portfolio exposure to commodities.

The driver of the rise in commodity prices is the growth of the global middle class, not growth in China and India per se. Take sugar, for example. Poor people cannot afford it, but when formerly poor people migrate into the middle class and can afford it, they want it. The Chinese government estimates that the size of its middle class is now equal to the population of the United Kingdom, Germany, and France combined. And India, which is expected to overtake China in population, is experiencing a similar dynamic in its rapidly expanding middle class. This is why as an investor you want to be long commodities from a purely strategic point of view.

Individual commodities have always experienced price bubbles, and now, these bubbles will be even bigger as demographic change creates demand spikes.

Question: Can commodities offer protection against inflationary pressures in the cost of services, such as medical care?

Layard-Liesching: No. Obviously, service inflation is a big risk at the moment, but I don't think any investment can really hedge such steeply rising costs.

Question: Could you expand on your comment that commodity prices react more to current supply and demand conditions whereas financial asset prices respond to a longer-term outlook?

Layard-Liesching: The classic formula for the P/E multiple, which is commonly used in equity valuation, incorporates discounted future earnings. In today's stock market, if you eliminated the next three years' estimated earnings, 90 percent of the share-price valuation would still remain. So clearly, the price of shares is determined by long-term expectations of earnings. Commodities, however, have price dynamics that are related to a short-run storage component that in situations of excess causes the price to plummet, and vice versa.

A good example is the electricity market in the United States. When the market has excess electricity, the price plummets because electricity cannot be stored, and when electricity is in short supply, the price goes through the roof because stored capacity does not exist to relieve the demand. In contrast, an equity investment in a utility operates with a much longer time horizon so that the shares of the commodity producer and the commodity itself represent two extremes in time horizon with corresponding implications for the pricing of each.

Question: Can investors get exposure to commodities through commodity producers and extractors?

Layard-Liesching: When you invest in a commodity-producing or extracting company, you are also buying exposure to labor costs and political risk. Because of this, the bottom line is that commodities do better than commodity companies, and in the long run, commodities are also a better inflation hedge than the commodity companies.

Some very interesting opportunities present themselves, however, when commodity companies are severely underpriced in the market. In these instances, the companies will outperform commodities, and when the companies become overpriced, the opposite will be true. So in a portfolio, the two strategies would complement each other nicely.

CFA INSTITUTE BOARD OF GOVERNORS
2006–2007

Chair
Vincent Duhamel, CFA
Goldman Sachs (Asia) LLC

Vice Chair
Emilio Gonzalez, CFA
Perpetual Investments

CFA Institute President and CEO
Jeffrey J. Diermeier, CFA
CFA Institute

Alida Carcano, CFA
Credit Suisse Private Banking

George W. Noyes, CFA
Standish Mellon Asset Management

Pierre Cardon, CFA
Bank for International Settlements

Nicola Ralston, FSIP
London

Margaret E. Franklin, CFA
KJ Harrison & Partners

Brian D. Singer, CFA
UBS Global Asset Management

Monique E.M. Gravel, CFA
CIBC World Markets Inc.

John C. Stannard, CFA, FSIP
Russell Investment Group

James E. Hollis, CFA
Cutter Associates, Inc.

José Luis Velasco, CFA
RBC Dexia Investor Services Bank S.A.

Samuel B. Jones, Jr., CFA
Trillium Asset Management Corp.

Ashvin P. Vibhakar, CFA
University of Arkansas at Little Rock

Stanley G. Lee, CFA
David J. Greene and Company

Thomas B. Welch, CFA
Wells Capital Management

Daniel S. Meader, CFA
Trinity Advisors, LP

Teong Keat (T.K.) Yap, CFA
OCBC Securities